New World Poetics

Nature and the Adamic Imagination
of Whitman, Neruda, and Walcott

New World Poetics

George B. Handley

THE UNIVERSITY OF GEORGIA PRESS   ATHENS AND LONDON

© 2007 by the University of Georgia Press

Athens, Georgia 30602

All rights reserved

Set in Monotype Garamond by Bookcomp, Inc.

Printed and bound by Thomson-Shore

The paper in this book meets the guidelines for

permanence and durability of the Committee on

Production Guidelines for Book Longevity of the

Council on Library Resources.

Printed in the United States of America

11 10 09 08 07 C 5 4 3 2 1

Library of Congress Cataloging-in-Publication Data

Handley, George B., 1964–

    New world poetics : nature and the adamic imagination

of Whitman, Neruda, and Walcott / George B. Handley.

        p. cm.

    Includes bibliographical references (p.) and index.

    ISBN-13: 978-0-8203-2864-5 (hardcover : alk. paper)

    ISBN-10: 0-8203-2864-2 (hardcover : alk. paper)

1. Whitman, Walt, 1819–1892—Criticism and interpretation.

2. American poetry—19th century—History and criticism.

3. Neruda, Pablo, 1904–1973—Criticism and interpretation.

4. Chilean poetry—20th century—History and criticism.

5. Walcott, Derek—Criticism and interpretation.   6. English

poetry—20th century—History and criticism.   7. Ecocriticism.

8. Philosophy of nature in literature.   9. Ecology in literature.

10. Nature in literature.   I. Title.

    PS3242.N2H36 2007

    811.009'36—dc22   2006039625

British Library Cataloging-in-Publication Data available

For Amy

CONTENTS

ACKNOWLEDGMENTS

Although I cannot pass on responsibility for the weaknesses of this manuscript, I can lay claim to having received the help of generous friends and institutions. My home university, Brigham Young University, has been extraordinarily generous. I received financial support for research assistants, travel, book funds, and flexible teaching arrangements and a formal leave in the fall of 2004. This help was made possible by the deans of Humanities, Van Gessel and John Rosenberg; the dean of General Education and Honors, George Tate, and his associate, John Lamb, for the Alcuin Fellowship; the director of the Kennedy Center for International Studies, Jeffrey Ringer; and my chairs, Roger Macfarlane and Stan Benfell. I was especially supported by the Kennedy Center for International Studies and the College of Humanities with vital subventions funds that made this publication possible. I also received the Albert J. Colton Research Fellowship from the Utah Humanities Council, which enabled me to go on the road and share these ideas with an interested public; special thanks to Cynthia Buckingham. I had the assistance of brilliant graduate research assistants and students who helped me gain insight into these poets. They include Rex Nielson, Bethany Beyer, Rachelle Woodbury, Rebecca Miner, Andy Ross, James Krause, and Tomás Hidalgo Nava.

I have also benefited from the advice, support, and expertise of numerous colleagues across the wide geography of this study. In Chile I was warmly received and helped by the poet, scholar, and gentleman Jaime Quezada, who arranged on two occasions for me to lecture to the young poets of the Fundación Neruda's poetry workshop on Walcott and Neruda; the wonderful translator and lover of all things Chilean, Jack Schmitt; my dear friend Bernardo Reyes; the talented Walcott translator Veronika Zondek; the late Eugenia Neves, who recounted her personal memories of Neruda at her house and with whom I spoke late into the night along with Hernán Soto about the fate of Chilean poetry; the staff at Fundación Neruda; my guide, the talented painter José Riveros; and Tomás Harris at the National Library in Santiago. One contact who initially opened this world to me was the Chilean poet Rodrigo Rojas, whom I had the good fortune to meet at dinner after an NYU class Derek Walcott was teaching. No one helped me see Chile more clearly than my dear friends Leonardo Sanhueza, an extraordinary poet, and Nadine DeJong, who did everything from drawing me maps of Lago Budi to teaching me Cueca and taking me to the best bookstores.

In Trinidad I was greatly aided by Margaret Rouse-Jones and Glenroy Taitt at Walcott's archives on the campus of the University of West Indies, St. Augustine; my taxi driver and friend Tony Fernandez; and Albert Laveau and his colleagues at the Carib Theater. I could not have completed this project to my satisfaction had it not been for the generosity of Derek Walcott and Sigrid Nama, who graciously invited me to St. Lucia and who opened my eyes to St. Lucia's bounty. Walcott allowed me to interview him on four separate occasions, once in Salt Lake City, twice in St. Lucia, and once again in New York City, and he provided encouragement despite his understandable impatience with literary critics. I can only hope this book pays his poetry due honor and reflects my sincere gratitude for his interest and friendship.

Portions of this book have been presented at various conferences, including the inaugural meeting of the International American Studies Association, which provides a vital forum for the kind of conversation this book tries to have across the Americas; the American Comparative Literature Association, which has always provided exciting exchange for comparatists; and the Association for the Study of Literature and the Environment, with its ever vital conversations about the fate of the environment. I have many personal friends and colleagues in the profession who have been of particular service either as readers of drafts, as commentators on papers, or as general supporters in moments of self-doubt. They are Stan Benfell, Paul Breslin, Matt Cohen, Deborah Cohn, Edward Cutler, J. Michael Dash, John Elder, John Felstiner, Mark Grover, Robert Hamner, Jimmie Killingsworth, David Laraway, Jorge Marcone, Jack Matthews, Anita Patterson, Jaime Quezada, Peter Schmidt, William Slaymaker, Scott Slovic, Jon Smith, Kerry Soper, and my exceptional coeditors of *Caribbean Literature and the Environment*, Elizabeth DeLoughrey and Renée Gosson.

Portions of this book were published previously. Duke University Press has granted me permission to publish a revised version of "A New World Poetics of Oblivion" in my current chapter 2. The essay originally appeared in *Look Away!: The U.S. South in New World Studies*, edited by the able hands of Jon Smith and Deborah Cohn. Chapter 3 is a revised version of an essay published in *Mississippi Quarterly*; and chapters 8 and 9 represent cannibalized versions of two articles that appeared in *Callaloo*. I also wish to recognize that a previously published essay in *ISLE* on Derek Walcott represents the beginnings of this project, and even though the content of the essay is no longer recognizable in the present form of this book, I am indebted to Scott Slovic for publishing it. Special thanks to Nancy Grayson for believing in this project.

Finally, I have many personal debts. To Sergio and Dávila Ordoñez, wherever they may be, who shared their national pride with pictures of Chile and a gift of *Canto general* in 1985 as a token of their love when we all found ourselves strangely living in Venezuela. To Helen Houghton for giving me my first book of Derek Walcott's poetry and for passing on her love of poetry. To my brother Bill because he always stands by my efforts and is my most trusted critic. To my parents, whose insatiable love of beauty got me into this business. To my wife, Amy, for her utter reliability. And to my four wonderful children for their ability to transport me to vistas of unexpected joy. May their world always be capable of stunning renewal.

A note about language. All citations from Spanish language texts are my translations unless otherwise indicated. This includes secondary critical essays and the primary materials by Pablo Neruda. I have not exhaustively searched for all available translations of his poetry and prose into English but have borrowed from those I know best whenever possible. Otherwise, I have relied on my own translations, which have aimed for clarity more than for poetic integrity. In order to respect the differences between the original Spanish and the English translations, I have cited my primary sources for Neruda's work in both languages throughout. There simply wasn't space to do so with all of the secondary materials, however.

New World Poetics

Introduction

It is fair to wonder if terms such as "New World" and "adamic" haven't long since lost their utility, but this study is an exercise in revisiting the assumptions that inform these suspicions. Instead of an argument for a new terminology, this is an effort to extract more value from old and familiar resources, a kind of literary recycling project. My environmental metaphors are not mere coincidence, of course, since my objective is to argue for the relevance of poetry in building sustainable visions of human beings in the world.

Derek Walcott's essay from 1974, "The Muse of History," provided me the initial illumination that led to this particular comparative formulation of a New World poetics. Critics have loosely associated the essay with postcolonialism more generally, but, guided by questions posed by ecocriticism in my reading, I couldn't help noticing the centrality of nature in his argument. Walcott insists that colonialism is the "common experience of the New World" and that American letters can roughly be divided between those who in response to this history produce a "literature of recrimination and despair" and those "great poets of the New World, from Whitman to Neruda," whose "vision of man . . . is Adamic[,] . . . where praise of the earth is ancestral" (*What the Twilight* 36–38). This is a postlapsarian Adam, "a second Adam" whose New World is not the Edenic space of innocence: "[T]he apples of [this] second Eden have the tartness of experience. In such poetry there is a bitter memory and it is the bitterness that dries last on the tongue" (40–41). This adamic poetry is an expression of "awe" before the wonders of a New World whose beauty has survived or has even, paradoxically, been nurtured by the wreckage of colonialism.

It is this delicate but necessary balance of acknowledging the force of New World history but also embracing the newness of the American environment that informs my conception of a New World poetics and what I call a lowercase "adamic" imagination, Walcott's spelling notwithstanding. When nature writing has received poststructuralist criticism, particularly in the United States, where it is a more pronounced and recognized literary genre than elsewhere in the Americas, critics have typically pointed to its problematic tendency to dismiss or simplify the colonial history of American lands or to downplay the neocolonial gestures implicit in its urge to name the world for the first time. We can consider this latter impulse *A*damic, which, unlike the lowercase model, *a*damic, yearns for purity and innocence and facilely dismisses the claims of history. One implication of this study is that a New World poetics that draws from untapped insights in Caribbean and Latin American literature can transform the very logic of this important criticism to suggest an equally dangerous risk of assuming that expressions of New World elation in the natural world are categorical reinventions of colonial will. Since colonialism in the American hemisphere has left social *and* environmental depredations in its wake, postcolonialism must attend to both the human and natural domains of history. This involves a recognition not only of the human impact on nature but also of nature's regenerative capacity to heal from its human wounds as well as to persist, at times, independently of human choices. Failure to recognize nature's otherness leads to a rejection of the New World as a potential home for the displaced citizen of modernity, explaining why the Americas have seen their share of writers who, in the face of the New World's atrocities, find themselves "wailing by strange waters for a lost home" instead of recognizing the opportunities afforded by an "awe of the numinous" in nature (Walcott, *What the Twilight* 44, 40). As Walcott further notes, "it is not the pressure of the past which torments great poets but the weight of the present" (40).

The adamic imagination of this study attends to this weight without turning away from history, as if to dismiss the relevance of the Middle Passage, centuries of enslavement, indigenous genocide, and colonialism. History must be acknowledged, but, as Walcott insists, it must not determine a writer's choices. New World history tends to reduce those choices to "an oceanic nostalgia for the older culture and a melancholy at the new, and this can go as deep as a rejection of the untamed landscape" (Walcott, *What the Twilight* 42). A sober reckoning of the past must be tempered by an appraisal of nature so as to taste in the fruits of its sweetness "traces of melancholy [that] are the chemical survivals of the blood which remain after the slave's and the indentured worker's convalescence" (54). This adamic sensibility "will survive the malaria of nostalgia and the delirium of revenge" that beset the writers whose imagination is not yet attuned to the more-than-human world. A return to the elemental task of the poet to name the world in elation is to begin again the process of building a culture of possibility, even if the poet must pretend that it happens *as if* for the first time. Without this *as if* qualification the poet will become blind to history and only see the broad spread of the world's innocent newness; poetry will function as a neocolonial *A*damic possession of land. Alternatively, however, if the poet only sees the facts of history and ignores nature's promise of renewal, the past becomes an inevitable prophecy of perpetual New World victimization, both human and natural.

What is particularly striking about Walcott's argument is how nature's cause for cautious optimism and renewal also becomes a cross-cultural poetics of the American hemisphere, of a transnational "New World" of poetic opportunity. In addition to Walt Whitman and Pablo Neruda, Walcott invokes New World allies such as Aimé Césaire, Saint-John Perse, Jorge Luis Borges, Denis Williams, and Wilson Harris and even Old World cousins such as Ted Hughes, James Joyce, and Samuel Beckett. In other contexts he has invoked Octavio Paz, Alejo Carpentier, Gabriel García Márquez, Cesar Vallejo, and Carlos Fuentes. The only logic to his literary history is the poets' attempt to describe an ancient human existential task of making the world, which is to say that this is not a literary history but a poetics.

This is not to suggest that there are no biographical limitations to Walcott's definition of a New World community, since it disappointingly lacks women, most notably, the likes of Emily Dickinson, Gabriela Mistral, and Elizabeth Bishop. It is understandable to suspect a conspiracy afoot to define the true New World writer as not only postcolonial *in the right way* but also male.[1] This would be a fruitful line of inquiry, especially if it resulted in mounting evidence of systems of metaphor in which the colonial "Adamic" logic of appropriation, exploitation, and self-proclaimed innocence facilitates perpetual human transformation if not outright destruction of the environment. In the case of Whitman, Neruda, and Walcott, however, the evidence is not as compelling as the more consistent pattern in which they discover and exploit the ideological flexibility of inherited human cultural patterns brought to bear in our relationship to nature, specifically, the Judeo-Christian myth of Adam in the Garden and its historic use to enable and justify environmental exploitation. Their weakness of overreach becomes their strength as they enable the myth of Adam to be a sign of seeing anew things that under the pressures of metropolitan norms have been misnamed or are unknown or essentially unnamable. This flexibility is not the result of technological enhancements that remake nature to suit their metaphorical minds, such as the paradigm of the "still New World" offered by Philip Fisher. Instead, this is a study of the ways in which human culture's attempts to understand its relationship to nature can be seen to deconstruct in the face of nature's indifferent difference.

This study does not focus on those moments in the poetry of Whitman, Neruda, and Walcott when gender is markedly pronounced, for example, or explore compelling comparisons with female poets. (One might consider the love poetry of Neruda in which the female body is consistently naturalized.) A reckoning with the "awe of the numinous" in the natural world brings us instead to those moments when their own gendered metaphors start to lose coherence as a system, when their Adamic impulses give way to an adamic imagination. Walcott, in fact, self-consciously portrays this very destabilization in the breakdown of his sexualized metaphor of Helen as St. Lucia.[2] Elizabeth Bishop's own version of the Crusoe figure in "Crusoe in England," a figure also important to Walcott as the adamic, postlapsarian creator of a New World, similarly fails to live up to his male colonizer billing because of his openness to raw, regenerative nature. Reading about the geological phenomenon of a new volcano and "an island being born," Bishop's Crusoe recalls that "my poor island's still / un-rediscovered, un-renamable. / None of the books has ever got it right" (162). As her Crusoe's ruminations on the qualities of the island demonstrate, it is nature's own procreational force to remake itself that forces the hand of language to admit its failure to get nature "right." The New World, then, is the world in which nature fuels poetic energy by undoing and reorganizing the systematic tendencies of human language in surprising and unpredictable ways. This slippage is what creates the adamic moment, not some human or particularly male desire to subsume nature's meanings. Biographical limitations are evident in the poetry of this study, to be sure, but environmental degradation urges a more cautiously optimistic approach in order to discover the enabling limits of their poetics. This is because poetry's meaning exceeds the history of the poet in the same way nature exceeds metaphor.

While it is insightful to understand biographical limitations, identifying the ways in which poetry reaches deeper than the poet's historical conditioning might predict helps to develop an awareness that extends beyond the same predictable and inevitable human center to which criticism always seems to return to the point of redundancy. The anthropocentric impulse of most criticism makes it necessary to restate the obvious: an environmental imagination needs to extend into a more-than-human world. This isn't the old argument that poetry transcends experience but rather that it descends into cross-cultural, submarine, and subterranean zones where the poet seeks the dark, unilluminated spaces of human belonging in the larger scope of natural history. As we will see, these poets repeatedly fail in this endeavor, but in failure they succeed in highlighting the need for forging imagined communities that do not overreach their social bounds or underestimate the force and centrality of the natural world. Their willingness to begin again, "adamlike," with praise tempered by experience instead of with a learned despair produces metaphors that bespeak what Whitman once called this "strange chemistry" of natural regeneration; they open the possibility of new futures where the fates of human beings and of the environment are no longer separate concerns.

The New World of this study, then, is also the specific historical phenomenon of the broad cross-cultural space of the American hemisphere and its relationship to European colonial histories of European settlement, slavery, colonial subjugation of native peoples, environmental transformation and degradation, and the other diasporas that have shaped its social and racial history. We find again and again in their poetry the impulse to reconstruct histories lost under the impact of colonialism's violent erasure of countermemory. In their attempts to pursue the traces of the New World's shared history of trauma, violence, and injustice, however, they discover that nature appears to have conspired against them by rendering the past as a series of untranslatable hieroglyphics in its own renewed vegetal body. This is what Wordsworth once described as nature's "oblivious tendencies" whereby it dooms human memory to amnesia and becomes the coterminous point of contact between nature and culture. In the modern sensibilities of these poets history's liminality in the natural world tempers nature's promise of facile innocence, but it also does not foreclose the possibility of renewal, as is the case with Walcott's second Adam. Their nature is neither a sign of the Eternal Garden nor the inevitable victim of human destruction. It becomes a sign of an always dying present that paradoxically makes poetic language potentially new and new futures possible. This is not the Adam who is complicit with the devastation of the era of discovery or who insists on the myth of "original innocence and unity," looking backward with "nostalgia for a better-than-present world" (Legler 72). It is not a trifling coincidence, then, that the apparent crux of each poet's poetics turns on the question of the relationship between a more-than-an-island New World community and its more-than-human New World. A poetics emerges in which natural history and human history are mutually metonymic of each other, thus suggesting that nature/culture is neither a sharp binary nor a facile equation.

Whether we examine Whitman's meditations on leaves of grass, Neruda's exploration of the natural history of Machu Picchu's ruins, or Walcott's interrogation of a former plantation, we find in the adamic imagination that nature's opaque and deep history serves as an untellable repository for the transnational history of the New World and its shared colonial violence. A New World poetics implies that aesthetic appreciation and ethical care for the health of the immediate physical environment need not be at odds with the search for social justice and broad forms of solidarity in the Americas. Indeed, these poets suggest these aims should not be divided; bioregionalism must be the foundation of just human communities, since the roots of human fate are literally in the soil.

I bring these poets together not only because of their significance to the literary histories of their regions but, more importantly, for their shared and pronounced preoccupations with defining in an epic, even biblical, vein a "New World" literature that would attend to the cross-cultural and environmental facets of the hemisphere's shared legacies. Walt Whitman's articulations of a New World Bible stand as perhaps the earliest expression of this ambition, which was to have a significant influence on Pablo Neruda, who in his monumental stature in Latin American political and literary life strove to speak for the continent. Derek Walcott does not share this vatic ambition, but he nevertheless has hoped for a New World poetics that does not shrink from the epic task before the writer who wishes to contemplate honestly and sincerely the human place in the Americas. This hemispheric ambition of their poetry has not received due comparative attention. Moreover, little ecocritical attention has been paid to their poetry, despite each poet's considerable preoccupation with natural history, ecological process, and nature as his primary subjects. These aims are not just coincidental, as I argue, but are instead coextensive. Comparative studies of American literatures serve to disrupt naive assumptions about literature's exceptionality, as I have elsewhere argued more extensively.[3] But this study additionally joins the work of other ecocritics and suggests that, given the broad geography of New World environmental history that has shaped national histories throughout the Americas, ecocriticism also stands to benefit from aggressive comparative work.

Both Jonathan Bate and John Elder have explored poetry's unique relationship with imagining our human place on the earth, and many others, including Lawrence Buell, have argued similarly on behalf of all genres of literature. My purpose here is to place such a poetics more specifically within the cross-cultural geography of the New World. My aim is to test its viability as the basis for a sense of place within a transnational and cross-cultural space characterized by a history of extraordinary, even exceptional, human and more-than-human transplantation and adaptation since the onset of modernity in 1492. The New World context yields crucial insights into the specific ways poetry can respond to modernity's ironies of loss, global and local change, and the emergence of the new. This in turn reveals ways to strike the delicate but necessary balance between human and natural histories in a modern world where facile Arcadian returns to the land are no longer plausible.

The Mexican Nobel Prize winner Octavio Paz in an essay about modern poetry once argued quite simply: "[T]he immense, stupid, and suicidal waste of natural resources must come to an immediate end if the human species wishes to survive on this earth" (*Other* 156). Paz's point is instructive because it demonstrates that we have come to identify the end of human time as synonymous with the destruction of our natural environment. That is, natural history and its long march through deep time, its expansion and complexification over the course of millions, even billions, of years is subsumed entirely under the rubric of humanity's tiny moment in time. The result is the false assumption that human history *is* nature's story and that what happens to us happens to the earth in undifferentiated parallel lines. The telos of inevitability that such apocalyptic thinking tends to inspire has led some to insist on a categorical distinction between natural and human histories. Untouched nature, uncontaminated by human hands, signifies something eternal that defies the inexorable march of human history toward an apocalyptic end. This is one justification for wilderness preservation, since wilderness expresses hope against the telos of environmental degradation. Environmental change, global warming, depletion of species, the rising level of the ocean, all become signs of nature outside the Garden, subject to historical contingency and ultimately to death, and of nature's apparent mortality. Hence, in our day natural degradation so easily lends itself as evidence of the inevitable death of nature and the end of human history, especially within an imaginary influenced by Christian apocalypticism. The problem is how to avoid the unfruitful dichotomy that apocalyptic thinking produces, that is, the notion that nature must be either outside history and therefore eternal or within history and therefore doomed. In either case it would seem that human history is defined by its inevitable end, thus rendering us impotent to imagine and act in the interest of other futures.

What is perhaps remarkable about Paz's argument is his suggestion that poetry might have the power to hold off the end of history and reverse the trend toward "universal destruction and contamination of lakes, rivers, seas, valleys, forests, and mountains" (*Other* 157). For Paz, the direction of history is toward an apocalyptic end of history only because society has been handed over to a market that simply "does not know how to choose. Its censorship is not ideological; it has no ideas" (144). Consequently, we live in a state of "aesthetic impoverishment," able to discern only what technology can transform or what the market can value. Our strange human kinship with and yet difference from the natural world collapses into a simple sameness in which nature is merely an extension of or backdrop to all human activity.

To prevent the end of history Paz insists that poetry must help us exercise our imaginative freedom, judge values, and establish relationships between the physical world and humanity without collapsing their differences. He explains that "the operative mode of poetic thought is imagining, and imagination consists, essentially, of the ability to place contrary or divergent realities in relationship. All poetic forms and all linguistic figures have one thing in common: they seek and often find, hidden relationships. In the most extreme cases, they unite opposites" (Paz, *Other* 158). He calls these relationships "buried realities" that are "restor[ed] to life" through the poetic imagination. While this is a pretension that poetry mnemonically recovers lost truths from the past, the glance of this poetics is essentially to the future. Paz argues for a poetry that is not archaeological but rather a creative process of forging bonds of commonality in the present despite the lack of historical evidence that would have necessitated such relationships. That is, he hopes for a freedom from and defiance against historical or biological causation; his earth-saving poetry would take up the vestiges or detritus of the past *as if* to create evidence of the past in what might otherwise appear to be a "virgin" landscape in order to keep time moving forward beyond the possibility of its end.

Gary Snyder shares this hope that poetry can serve to recycle an ancient human memory of our belonging in the natural world, but he is also aware of poetry's failings in this regard. Significantly for my purposes here, Whitman's democratic vistas are his emblem of poetry's as yet incomplete realization of its ecological relevance. According to Snyder, Whitman's New World was an incomplete and unfulfilled vision of variety and freedom, Whitman's two great characteristics of what he called New World poetry. As Snyder remarks, "The actual place of this New World is not new but is an ancient continent, hundreds of millions of years old. Any human hope looking to the future can no longer treat the land, the indigenous people, and nature as a backdrop, but must henceforth totally incorporate them, or be ultimately irrelevant" (452). For this reason bioregionalism calls for "an ecological/poetical exercise that starts with the analysis of how the political boundaries of the American States, or those between Canada and

Mexico, can occult the biological and cultural realities that often make up our real life" (454). The result would be a New World poetics that not only perceives the newness of a transnational "New World" but also discovers "the possibility of membership in the Ancient World of Turtle Island. If Walt Whitman were with us today, he might well give his heart to the new native and bioregionalist movement with as much hope (and perhaps hopelessness) as he gave to his own uniquely enlightened version of the nineteenth century dream of progress" (454). Snyder's conception of the New World as "Turtle Island" is based on indigenous myths that describe the world sustained on the back of a turtle. With this cross-cultural and ancient mythology Snyder portrays an image of the continent as a biosphere in which human beings act as participants in an ecological community of life.

It is a paradox but no accident that Snyder appeals to Whitman's New World vision of "democratic vistas" that extend across the Americas (the same vistas to which Walcott refers admiringly in his essay "The Muse of History") as the very means of criticizing Whitman's own limited understanding of the Americas, bioregionalism, and deep time. With greater historical and natural insights at hand, Snyder suggests that we would do well to revisit Whitman's vision. But it is Whitman's energy, perhaps more than the specific outlines of his vision, that is the vital tool for beginning again to rise to the challenge of understanding our place in an ancient community of others, both human and natural.

It is the aim of this study to perform similarly generous rereadings of these poets to uncover each poet's potential for leading us into this membership in an Ancient New World. These poets' intimations of an ancient earth are paradoxically fed by the newness of the world, a newness that is sustained neither by historical youth nor by willed amnesia or ignorance but rather by an awareness of temporal renewal; the world appears new at each instant, and the language used to describe it, although also presumably old, rediscovers its freedom as imagination. The adamic imagination gives reason to the hope that we can understand the determinacies of our own natural and human histories without forsaking the freedom of the imagination by which we can act in the interest of better, more sustainable futures.

All the poems in this study are triangulations between the living world and the poet who responds to this dynamic life with metaphors directed at a third party, the reader. In order to aid my own perception of the living world that inspired their poetry it seemed necessary to me that in addition to expending the critic's obligatory efforts in archives and libraries I needed to acquaint myself with the lands, seas, and rivers of these poets. I believe, with Whitman, that *where* you read matters as much as *what* you read. Of the three environments I have only had the luxury of having personal and family history on the Long Island Sound, so I can't claim a native's intimate knowledge of the other environments. But that was not my ambition. I suspected that if I could breathe the sulfur fire of a Chilean volcano, feel the motion of the Caribbean Sea underneath me along the St. Lucian coast, or recall my own childhood contacts with the sound I might find my readings vivified. In landscape design triangulation is a vital means of determining the particular shape and outline of the world by means of triple differentiation. To understand the relationship between two points a third provides additional perspectives and relationships that bring land into more clear and interdependent perspective. In other words, in order to gain clarity regarding each poet's relationship to land I felt it necessary to establish my own relationship as well. My readings have triangulated their relationship to nature by placing me in front of the same sites of inspiration for, say, Walcott's *Omeros* and Neruda's autobiographical accounts of Temuco. To be clear, I have never made efforts to argue for a kind of "I was there" authenticity in these readings. As Bishop thematized so well in "Questions of Travel," it is fair to ask if travel is really more necessary than the imagination, but, as Walcott explores in *Tiepolo's Hound*, the presence of natural light can stir our imagination to picture the present moment of the artist. Reading along Whitman's proverbial "open road" makes interpretation as much a rendering of the natural world as art is, and this helps to alleviate the anxieties of authenticity that obsess literary and art historical studies.

What is more, I have triangulated my readings of these poets' New Worlds by reading them together in a comparative New World context. My aim has not been to construct a literary history of influence from Whitman's *Democratic Vistas* and his call for a New World poetry to these engendered "poets to come." Triangulation takes them out of the constraints of chronology and the tracings of literary influence and allows us to see the three poets rising to a similar challenge of exploring the meaning of human community within the context of an emergent conception of a biocentric cosmos. In other words, this is a simultaneous assessment of each poet's attempt to establish ties between his community and his physical environment in order to point the way toward a more environmentally healthy and cross-cultural sense of place in the Americas. Any choice of points of comparison runs the risk of rigidifying the very thing a critic hopes to loosen, but my triangulated readings aim to highlight the value of a third possibility that destabilizes the binaries that inform many of our assumptions about the boundaries of human communities, be they political, social, or environmental. The aim is to vivify our awareness of human and natural others operative within the communities poetry imagines. If poetry is to gain the force Paz ascribes to it, this seems a necessary beginning.

Part 1 of this book tackles the broad hemispheric questions of ecology and its relationship to literature in the Americas. Chapter 1 traces the significance of nature in formulations of the "New World" and the emergence out of natural history of a poetics of nature that escaped the trappings of colonial epistemological control over the hemisphere. I also examine why, strangely, ecocritical concerns have been largely neglected in the early formulations and continued practices of American and Latin American studies, something this study aims to reverse.

Chapter 2 attempts a definition of a New World poetics that I hope might serve to ameliorate these limitations of area studies in the Americas. The net effect of my argument is to highlight the ecological and cross-cultural implications of a view of New World history that does not overspend its accounts in anguish over irrevocable loss of ancestral memory but instead embraces the ironies of a regenerating and regenerative natural world.

Chapter 3 concludes part 1 with an exploration of the implications of the ecology of New World literature in the story of Whitman's influence in the hemisphere, including an overview of his specific impact on José Martí and on Neruda and Walcott. The upshot of the chapter is to suggest that what links the various manifestations of an adamic imagination is not necessarily an indebtedness to Whitman or even a common preoccupation with the hemispheric reach Whitman's *Democratic Vistas* exhibited but central attention given to the dynamics of a changing, evolving natural world and the refractions and fragmentations that nature reveals of a transcultural New World story.

Part 2 begins my ecocritical readings of the poets. The comparative aim of these chapters is to establish an implicit and sometimes explicit dialogue among the poets that provides a picture of different strategies for negotiating with nature's alternations between radical otherness and strange kinship with the human viewer. In chapter 4 I begin with Whitman, who presents a particular challenge to an ecocritical appraisal due to his bipolarity as a poet, which led, on the one hand, to a Hegelian poetics of imperial expansion and sweeping generalizations and, on the other, to the liberating potential of a democratic poetics of the local and the particular. In the former case I examine poems such as "Song of the Broad-Axe," "Song of the Exposition," and "Song of the Redwood-Tree." In the latter among the works I examine are "Song of the Open Road," "Passage to India," "Prayer of Columbus," the *Calamus* poems, *Specimen Days*, portions of "Song of Myself," "This Compost," and, most especially, "Out of the Cradle Endlessly Rocking." By highlighting how Whitman himself was able to negotiate an opening that led him away from the neocolonial impulses of an Adamic poetry, I suggest reasons for cautious and circumspect hope regarding poetry's potential for liberating the imagination from the limitations of an anthropocentric and Eurocentric definition of the New World. With the exception of some very recent scholarship on Whitman, critics have largely bypassed his contribution to an American environmental literary canon. Fewer still have addressed his relevance, as I seek to do, to the broader poetic traditions of the hemisphere.

Chapter 5 continues to explore the effect of a New World poetics that learns to respect nature's otherness in the work of Pablo Neruda. I begin with his autobiographical themes in *Canto general*, *Memorial de Isla Negra*, various prose writings, and the significant works of *Tercer libro de odas* [Third Book of Odes], *Estravagario*, and *Piedras de Chile* [Stones of Chile]. The significance of Neruda's autobiographical meditations on the natural world is not widely recognized, although he has been widely read and translated arguably as much as any poet of the past century. Overshadowed by his love poems and his strident and controversial political themes, his nature poetry is among the most significant, sustained, and profound in his time. My readings in this chapter suggest a growing and unresolved tension in Neruda's self-conception between the political demands of social injustice and of nature's slow and patient regeneration. I attempt an ecocritical revision of the assumptions that have driven analyses of Neruda's nature poetry and argue that the irony of his later poetry is not postmodern but rather an articulation of a biocentric view of human being.

Chapter 6 attempts to identify the seeds of this vision in *Canto general*, the epic poem that presumably functions as Neruda's epic recovery of a hemispheric past buried by the violence of conquest and colonialism. From his recognition of the eroding effects of natural water cycles in "Alturas de Machu Picchu" [Heights of Machu Picchu] to the sea's forceful cannibalization of human traces in "El gran océano" [The Great Ocean], my reading suggests that Neruda's epic ambition is not to recover history per se but to recognize the need for the poet to ally himself with natural regeneration and to found New World culture on nature, not history.

I turn in part 3, the final three chapters, to Derek Walcott and begin in chapter 7 with an exploration of the poetic expressions of the ideas he articulates in his 1974 essay, "The Muse of History." Walcott's critics furnish our understanding of Walcott in his unique Caribbean and postcolonial condition, but there is similarly little discussion in the critical literature of the relevance of his poetry to the environment or of the meaning of his frequent invocation of the "New World." In chapter 7 I identify his "American phase" as a stage of his career when he began to speak and write more frequently of his implicit alliances with New World authors, north and south of the Caribbean, who shared a similar natural and historical sensibility. By looking at his poetry leading up to and including his autobiographical poem, *Another Life* (including "Air," "The Sea Is History," "The Schooner *Flight*," "Origins," "Ruins of a Great House," "Verandah," and his Crusoe poems), I trace a growing obsession with the New World's experience of amnesia that informed Whitman's and Neruda's understanding of natural process.

Tiepolo's Hound, which I discuss in chapter 8, employs triangulation to establish a simultaneity instead of hierarchy and priority between Old and New Worlds and serves as a model for this study's comparative thinking in the Americas. In an effort to protect what Walcott calls the "insulted landscape" of marginalized cultures he seizes upon the aesthetics of impressionism as a way of prioritizing the present physical space of the Caribbean subject for the foundation of a New World culture and the adamic task of laying claim to place as home. Walcott continues the intense interest in visual art he first expressed in *Another Life*, and my analysis focuses on the effect of ekphrasis and of the inclusion of his own paintings in the book.

In chapter 9 I argue that Walcott's refusal to declare the end of meaning after his mother's and his father's deaths in *The Bounty* and *Omeros*, respectively, allows Walcott a self-consciously ironic exploration of the possibility of nature's promise of the perpetuation of human historical value. Walcott's agnostic balancing act becomes especially crucial in the conclusion to *Omeros*, where Walcott confronts the possibility of irrevocable global climatic change and its effects on nature's capacity to provide renewal. The poem's agnosticism becomes an expression of his ultimate faith that art is perhaps our best hope to save the world.

The premise of this study is that until we have learned to tap poetry for its highest potential to transfigure our environmental imagination, we ought not to prematurely despair of our degraded plot of New World soil. If poetry can remake nature without diminishing its resources, it would seem to be at least as important as the latest hybrid technologies. Its hybridity lies in its strange fusions of natural and human histories, allowing us to catch glimpses of our natural belonging as well as of our unique human opportunities to choose to act on behalf of the greater whole of what we can only hope remains a new world.

Part One

What you see is what you get.

ANNIE DILLARD

CHAPTER I

Ecology, the New World, and the "American" Adam

The *New* World? Of course it wasn't new, least of all to the estimated 54 million native inhabitants in the hemisphere, nor did it prove to be younger than the Old World, as some naturalists would theorize in the wake of 1492.[1] These anachronisms have resulted in understandable un-easiness or downright displeasure with this term. Edmundo O'Gorman, for example, insists that the term "New World" merely invites European settlement: "The concept of a 'new world' . . . refers to an entity which is a world only in so far as it is capable of transforming itself into a replica of the 'old' world" (*Invention* 140). Newness is a ruse, temporarily holding forth as a difference so as to facilitate the remaking of the world into an image of the old and familiar. Such facile dismissals of this term—and there have been many—may justifiably detect its taste of Eurocentrism, but no mention is ever made of the patent anthropocentrism inherent in naming such a massive geography "new." In the early twenty-first century we are unique in our understanding of ecosystems and of our capacity to destroy them entire, so it seems that we can no longer afford to ignore the underlying biogeographical story of the New World encounter. The Western Hemisphere is not alone on the globe in containing an ancient and deep history, both natural and human, but what we now know of this story is largely due to the modern work of anthropologists, archaeologists, geographers, geologists, historians, and botanists. Although the specifics of this collective story remain incomplete and conjectural, an awareness of an underlying biogeographical reality in the hemisphere is enough to challenge our assumptions about the smooth catenation of the human narrative in the Americas. Ecological understanding suggests that a profound rupture lies at the heart of the hemisphere's natural history, a rupture that has divorced its modern human inhabitants from an awareness of their place in the physical world.

The natural sciences have taken their stripes from literary critics and historians for their complicity in the history of colonialism and for the constructed nature of many of their "objective" findings, but it would be recklessly simpleminded to dismiss the lessons of natural science as mere constructions in the face of global environmental degradation. And given the profound distrust of science that is now emerging out of religious fundamentalism, it would seem even more important for literary criticism to take science more seriously. This is for many reasons, not the least of which is the paucity of memory of such deep time in modern life. Deep time is inconvenient to modern society, as many of the best environmental thinkers have amply demonstrated, but it is also quite simply overwhelming for the limited human imagination. While we fish for analogies to help us understand the length of something like a hundred million years, our under-standing of deep geological and ecological processes has been made even more difficult; we live in a hemisphere whose modern historical memory is rarely more than five hundred years old due to the violent transplantation of its peoples, plants, and animals and the intensive expansion of European settlement.

The capacity to imagine deep time was hard to come by for early settlers whose historical memory was a mere few thousand years old. And until

Amerigo Vespucci named the continent for what it was (i.e., a previously unknown world, *new* to the European mind, at least), this brief history was believed to have transpired entirely on the other half of the globe. That is to say, while the name "New World" indicates European ignorance of the Western Hemisphere, it more importantly *acknowledges* that ignorance. Vespucci's declaration was a confession of limited knowledge and of a certain regard or awe in the face of what had not been anticipated. Although an insufficient account of a new reality, this was at least preferable to collapsing the New World into already familiar Old World models of, say, Columbus's Asia.

The hemisphere's various differences in climate, flora, fauna, and human racial complexions challenged the authority of the Bible and its Adamic story of singular human origins from the same parents. "Adam" was a symbol, in this sense, of Europe's attempt to lay claim to a genealogy of a racially restricted definition of human unity in shallow time. Yet the American continent and its islands played a crucial role in developing an entirely new, universalizing history of natural processes that challenged Adam's significance as a sign of human exceptionality. Although the authority to tell this story of new lands and peoples initially lay in the hands of explorers, missionaries, and settlers, by the eighteenth century at least the new European measures of validity and believability regarding this extraordinary geographical reality were reason and natural science. In the hands of thinkers such as Georges-Louis Leclerc de Buffon, Abbé Raynal, Cornelius de Pauw, and Alexander von Humboldt the New World's reputation as a younger continental region was established, believed to be subject only recently to the natural and historical forces that had already shaped and matured the Old World. De Pauw and Buffon went so far as to argue that the New World had been subject to a separate and belated deluge, akin to Noah's flood, that had left in its wake "universal organic degeneration" (Cañizares-Esguerra 47). The implications of this global anachronism are plainly obvious: the New World's lands and peoples were denied their place in historical time, as it was then understood by the European mind, thus justifying the hand of colonial violence on both the peoples and the land itself. European colonialism wiped the American slate clean, or at least pretended to do so, so as to plow its own story anew—to affirm its Adamic innocence in the face of New World atrocities—in Edenic virgin soils.

Peter Hulme points out that the common image of "America" as woman reflects an anxiety about the novelty of the New World that can be traced in "the relationship between European, native, and land," in which case the latter two are handily conflated in a naked and visually accessible woman's body (xii). As Carolyn Merchant has also argued, this prelapsarian Adam's Eve would eventually fall once Europeans discovered the unruly wildness of the New World, since the rawness of the hemisphere would only further inspire the attempt to tame nature into a recovered Eden, brought back into the catenation of Western history. Consequently, the colonial machine would produce a refurbished "Mother Eve," or nature as an "improved garden, a nurturing earth bearing fruit" (Merchant 137). For Merchant, Eden, like female virginity, attracts the masculine impulse to ravage and possess, and thus a perpetual cycle of sin and redemption is created that requires endless frontiers of new lands. According to Annette Kolodny, land-as-woman became a useful image for nation building, but the image was flawed by an internal tension "between the initial urge to return to, and join passively with, a maternal landscape and the consequent impulse to master and act upon that same femininity" (27).

These efforts to master the unruly gardens of the New World involved settlement, agriculture, animal husbandry, monocultural plantations, mining, and other deleterious economies that wrought profound ecological changes, such as massive soil erosion, deforestation, and crop diseases. If one writes of New World environments today, one inevitably encounters evidence—even if it is not always admitted into the court of literature— of this deep colonial and even precolonial history of human-instigated environmental change. Any modest attempt to learn the flora and fauna of, say, the Caribbean, the American West, or the Chilean coastline becomes anachronistic, since a great number of trees, wildflowers, and weeds have European, Asian, or other foreign origins. Cultural assessments of the impact of Europe on the development of American civilizations have all but ignored the "biogeographical realities that underlay" and facilitated European successes and made of the entire hemisphere a blossoming, although often consequently degraded, desert (Crosby 196). Smallpox, the single greatest killer of indigenous populations in the hemisphere, was a product of Europe's long history of animal husbandry and agriculture and is surely as significant a historical fact as any military struggle or colonial violence. Widespread biotic colonialisms throughout the Americas inspired historian Alfred Crosby to call the Old World pioneer "a sort of botanical Midas changing the flora with his touch" (160).

Despite the fact that biotic knowledge helped to nurture the growing awareness of national consciousness and yearnings for political autonomy, the environmental history of the Americas clearly demonstrates that the environmental histories within specific geopolitical borders were much more widely shared than the various mythologies of national exceptionalism allowed (see Dunlap 48). Such historical parallels and shared colonial legacies have paradoxically meant that the closer one observes any peculiar quality of the local landscape, whether it be the breadfruit, the peach, or the eucalyptus tree, the more one is drawn outward beyond the bounds of the nation or region and into an intricate web of human and natural historical parallels. As a result, the very dichotomy between natural and human histories begins to break down as a useful distinction.

Even as European contact with the Americas was changing the face of the earth, the emerging natural sciences sought to bring order to the chaos in the eighteenth and nineteenth centuries. The naming of American biota developed by Linnaeus tended to tame the unknown and restore it, as it were, within Western chronology and was largely developed in the academy apart from the "folkbiology" of local agricultural peoples (Dunlap 23–24). This practice was not the ancient impulse of what Jonathan Bate has called the "pre-scientific magic of naming" reserved for poets but the disenchantment of an unknown and particular world into a known and generalized narrative (175). The result was what was known as the "second conquest" of Latin America, as the monocrop industries in the late eighteenth and nineteenth centuries resulted in the "largest environmental transformation of Latin America since the conquest" (McCook 5). The search for precious metals gave way to an engineered exportation of plants: tobacco, sugar, coffee, and others.

Local and intimate botanical knowledge came in fits and starts; the so-called rediscovery of nature was "largely rhetorical," since the main objective was to "rationalize nature" and maximize yields (McCook 25, 12). It is for these reasons that many environmental thinkers tie our contemporary environmental problems to the restless and aggressive economic drive of European settlements in the New World. Wendell Berry, for example, writes: "[A]t the same time that they 'discovered' America, these men invented the modern condition of being away from home. . . . [T]hey arrived contemptuous of whatever existed before their own coming, disdainful beyond contempt of native creatures or values or orders" (54–55).

But the news is not all bad, and perhaps this is most to the point. Natural history was linked to the colonial machine, to be sure, but it also showed increasing awareness of nature's elusiveness and interest in local, indigenous folkbiology. Jorge Cañizares-Esguerra demonstrates that the creole epistemology of nature did not mirror the ideals of the European Enlightenment exactly because it more successfully rooted itself in close alliance to the dynamism of native lands and biota. The only problem, of course, is that this knowledge often comes belatedly, and therefore what is known is not what the land is per se but perhaps what it had been before human action provoked changes. But at least, as Thomas Dunlap argues was the case in the English diaspora, some individuals managed to change from wanting to remake nature to wanting to "become settlers and to value the land for what it was, or had been" (17). The environmental degradation of colonies in the New World (the most devastated were the Caribbean islands) was a high price to pay for a growing awareness of human beings as agents of global and perhaps irrevocably deleterious environmental change. We have what Derek Walcott might call a "strange thanks" to give for this colonial history because, as Richard Grove argues, "the seeds of modern conservationism developed as an integral part of the European encounter with the tropics and with the local classifications and interpretations of the natural world and its symbolism" (3).

Grove insists that the limited geographical space of island ecologies in the Pacific and in the Caribbean particularly hastened European scientific understanding of evolution as well as of the environmental limits of human economic behavior. Islands did not allow the perpetual westward movement beyond the consequences of previous actions that so characterizes the experience of the U.S. West or interior regions of South America, for example. As European colonial experience widened to include greater diversities of peoples and climates, seventeenth-century Calvinism, for example, adopted a revised version of the Adam myth in which the fall of humankind and the fall of nature were no longer conceived of as purely parallel events. God was seen as the Creator of a world that, rather than offering itself intact and imminently knowable, was full of surprising beauty and wonder, creating what Grove calls an "empirical aesthetic" that made it possible "to recognize nature's qualities rather than its 'defeat'" (47). The growing awareness of impending environmental ruin caused by human-introduced changes to the natural world inspired colonial scientists to reimagine the fate of the Garden's fall as still yet to be determined. If deforestation, soil erosion, and extinction continued, "the human race appeared to face expulsion from the garden altogether"; thus, awareness of environmental risk became a "veritable tree of knowledge" (15).

The end of humankind was not a new idea in the centuries following the conquest, of course, but never before had it been suggested that human environmental behavior might hasten it, perhaps even prematurely. This new uncertainty about human fate "deprived [Europe] of the security of biblical chronology" and opened up the possibility that the "natural world [was] a path to a knowledge of God or . . . a means to recreate a (social) paradise on earth" (Grove 14–15). That is, the Adamic story retained its usefulness in a new empirical world by placing more responsibility on human shoulders for gaining knowledge and taking care of the "fallen" world of nature. Adam might find out who he is by finding out *where* he is. Whereas biblical myth had been threatened by the new sciences, a revised Adamic myth stimulated such learning about the physical world. At least by the late eighteenth century, the observer of nature had become a reader of a new sacred text—the sanctified body of the earth—and that reading had the potential to provide a blueprint of human escape from environmental ruin. The colonial experience in the New World tropics, in other words, gave rise to a new sense of "caution about the impact or desirability of the works of man upon the 'New World'" (47).

What is particularly important about this history is the warning it provides against overly structural or ideological critiques of the myth of Eden as it was imposed upon the American hemisphere. Merchant, Margarita Zamora, and others have argued for a coherent Edenic discourse that predictably structured European settlers' environmental devastation in the New World. A search for Eden might very well lead to ruin, but it might also lead to a preservationist ethic, and history seems to suggest that it did both. It might be more accurate to say that there was no single, coherent Eden "discourse" per se but that the Adamic idea assumed a variety of ideological impulses, often contradictory, and that the outcome of such discursive practices depended, among other important factors, on the ways in which individuals opened themselves up to the particulars of their local ecologies. There is no doubt that discursive practices die hard, that they are virtually never fully conscious to us, and that they therefore deserve our most circumspect critiques. But, as Kolodny points out, we must not assume that "symbol systems, by their very universality, are thereby totally fixed and unavailable to conscious attempts at alteration" (151). She insists: "The choice is ours: whether to allow our responses to this continent to continue in the service of outmoded and demonstrably dangerous image patterns, or whether to place our biologically—*and* psychologically—based 'yearnings for paradise' at the disposal of potentially healthier (that is, survival-oriented) and alternate symbolizing or image systems" (159).

This freedom to reimagine language rather than to seek a new one merely is precisely the advantage the poets in this study assume. While they gesture toward a native history and language that might offer some resistance to the Adamic yearnings of European culture, they also do not hesitate to absorb and change the legacies of European names, literatures, and myths. And what stimulates their imagination is the fact that their language, no matter how well constructed, will inevitably fail to subsume the temporally and spatially dynamic natural world around them. This elusiveness of natures helps to liberate language, despite its penchant for mythologizing things, from fixity or even predictability. The work of weeding out neocolonialisms in culture, arguably the raison d'être of much contemporary critical discourse, has not yet successfully addressed the question of how we can understand our human place in the physical world. The (good) problem ecocriticism has created is to present another category of ethical inquiry, that of our relationship to the natural world, that at least temporarily contextualizes our social ethics within a broader range of choices. American societies have not learned how to balance social and environmental ethics satisfactorily, but the best of ecocriticism helps us to see the artificiality of separating one form of ethics from the other and challenges us to identify and critique neocolonialisms as well as how these discourses might still offer salutary relationships to the environment.

A characteristic example of this unanswered question in poststructuralist criticism can be found in the work of Roland Barthes, who once argued that nothing is more "natural," that is, more easily mythologized, than nature itself. "What is more *natural* than the sea?" he queries (144). As I will discuss in subsequent chapters, the sea figures prominently in the environmental imagination of these poets as a sign of the contact zone between human history and natural oblivion. Barthes insists that representations of the sea invariably betray the political power that has enabled them. Given the pervasiveness of colonial discourses, it is irresponsible for critics to ignore these traces, but it is an equal risk to assume that representations of nature can only be understood in political terms. It is both solipsistic and tautological to argue that a poet, Whitman listening to the sea whispering to him, for example, is *merely* constructing nature. The difficult but necessary challenge is to move beyond the rather facile and dead-end conclusion that human beings construct their world and to ask what those constructions mean in relationship to a prenamed physical world to which they refer, especially if it appears that our actions are threatening that world and our place in it.

The constructionists will say that our world has become so constructed by human engineering and technology that the thirst for something beyond an overbuilt world may be nothing more than escapist fantasy. But perhaps precisely because of an overengineered reality we need environmentally oriented literature more than ever, especially if it can remind us, as Jonathan Bate suggests, that "although we make sense of things by way of words, we do not live apart from the world" (23). Otherwise we only see a world of our own making and ignore nature's capacity to change through time independent of human labor or perception.[2] Despite extensive human modification of the environment in modernity, Lawrence Buell argues that we should not simply conclude that the result is a "comprehensive, irreversible transformation of 'nature' into artifact" (*Writing* 5). To do so would categorically ignore evidence, so prevalent in the poetry of this study, of the "physical environment as destabilizing force" (17).

We might still hope that the natural sciences will be relevant enough to us to provide a picture of this destabilization. However, they have not successfully penetrated society's imagination and deepened our sense of time, taught us appropriate humility and awe, or strengthened our resolve to live sustainably. Indeed, New World history teaches us just how slow we are to drop quixotic habits of seeing as a self-fulfilling prophecy; that is, we see what we expect and want to see. Since "what you see is what you get," as Annie Dillard reminds us, the quest should be to see as unscrupulously and as unexpectedly as possible (17). It is the difference between seeing with a camera and "letting go" so that our "own shutter opens" (33). "The secret of seeing," she continues, "is, then, the pearl of great price. . . . Although the pearl may be found, it may not be sought. . . . [I]t is always a gift and a total surprise" (35). We are no better off if we read literature as if with a camera, willing only to read what we expected when we framed it.

Max Weber felt that science resulted in an *Entzauberung*, or disenchantment, with the world, by which the mysteries of nature were rationalized for human ends, thus leaving the imaginative work regarding the environment to poets and artists. It is for this reason, perhaps, that Derek Walcott emphatically insists on a willed ignorance of science in front of the natural world so as to retain the power of the metaphorical imagination to make poetic meaning of what the senses communicate to us. The reverse is the case for Walt Whitman and Pablo Neruda, however; the more deeply they studied the science of their day, the greater their experience of awe. For Bruce Foltz, disenchantment is perhaps the fruit of applied sciences, but the natural sciences stimulate awe in the initial discovery of new knowledge similar to the reinhabitory commitment Buell underlines in environmental writing. Foltz writes: "The questions of reconnaissance—questions of orientation in the interest of inhabitation—are the basic questions that animate all of our knowledge of the physical world" (32). In the writings of the foundational thinkers in the sciences Foltz finds no evidence of disenchantment "but instead an astonishment at finding oneself inhabiting a new kind of place, at finding out that one is not residing in quite the same kind of universe that it had seemed to be, in discovering that one is living in a new world. Is it, after all, an accident that Europeans were discovering and exploring what to them were new worlds of territory at the same time that scientists began to discover that nature itself had become a new kind of world to them?" (30).

Despite advances in scientific knowledge, the sciences continue to run into a world of tremendous complexity, and this has in turn required what Daniel Sarewitz has called a strategy of "adaptive management" that understands "policies as experiments," acknowledges the diversity of knowledge that science produces, and recognizes the fact that "there is no ultimate source of knowledge that can dictate the 'correct' action under conditions of natural and societal complexity" (95). Politics has shown little patience with scientists who want to insist on the contingency of their findings because such admissions place a much heavier moral burden on human choice, and they tend to slow the economic drive for short-term gain (92). From Europe's initial contact with the New World, Western society has wanted the sciences to provide certainty regarding the outcomes of human actions, but the reality is that scientific knowledge more often offers "insight into the importance of context and the limits of foreknowledge" (92).

The upshot is this: the defense of a poetic relation to nature does not have to become a diatribe against science or even a categorical rejection of the legacies of Western colonialism. Instead, the task is to reimagine those legacies and rescue from them that which pertains to and can help ameliorate our contemporary social and environmental crises. One aid in kicking the colonial habit, as history has suggested, is an empirical aesthetic and an awareness of biodiversity and deep time. An understanding of the workings of nature on culture would be better suited to address the otherness of nature, but only if it avoids the environmental determinism of nineteenth-century naturalism or the determinism of some forms of modern scientific thought. That is, a "mutual constructionist understanding of placeness," as Buell argues, allows us to see pitfalls of the nature-culture binary that continues to characterize much contemporary criticism. We are left, then, with imaginative acts that are "oneiric and mimetic, self-referencing and referential, . . . at the same time" (*Writing* 27).

The correspondence between human-constructed knowledge and empirical experience is by no means a guarantee of an escape from the solipsism of cognition, but not all constructions are created equal, and not all readers are Don Quixote. There is in this exchange between empirical aesthetic experience in nature and the natural sciences the potential, however tenuous, for a process of revision and readjustment according to the story nature tells. Dillard's findings at Tinker Creek are in fact marked more by surprise and awe than by confirmation, despite her own extensive reading (or perhaps because of it); what she calls the "glorious extravagance" of death, violence, and diversity in nature most draws her attention and feeds her voice. The more she knows of the natural world, the less rational it seems to her and the less cognitive or social control she has over it; a poetic mode of knowing comes to the fore as a means of communicating this irrationality. On its own, regeneration is nature's eventual outcome, and extravagant abundance is its rule.

Dillard insists that the only way to obtain this kind of sight in front of the physical world is to learn to see within time rather than seeing self-consciously. That is, the human observer learns to discard, ever so briefly, the illusions of atemporality that human self-consciousness fosters and instead experiences the changing and surrounding world as if within it. We cannot escape ourselves as individual, conscious beings, but opening our own shutters results in a profound questioning of the reality of self-consciousness, since we discover ourselves, despite our selves, within the world and within the flow of time marked by nature's changes. John Elder describes this turn from self-consciousness to environmental awareness as an act of imagination that "creates man's self-conscious isolation [and simultaneously] also allows him to comprehend processes integrating his human lot in the turning of the world" (*Imagining* 20). As the poetry in this study demonstrates, this willingness to suspend disbelief in the ambiguous borders between natural and human history yields postlapsarian fruit worth tasting.

The American Adam and American Studies

This manner of seeing is a vital component to the adamic imagination that I explore in Whitman, Neruda, and Walcott, and it offers an alternative to the historically naive and exceptionalist paradigm of the American Adam. Whitman's Adam figures prominently as a cornerstone in the twentieth-century conceptions of "American" literature, but early and more recent criticism has largely ignored the inter-American impulse of Whitman's own views, the inter-American story of his extensive influence in the hemisphere, the many different and simultaneous adamic expressions in Latin American literature, and the relevance of the adamic ideal to ecology.

American studies was initially a reaction against the overt formalism in the first half of the past century. The first generation of critics of the new field emerged in the 1950s and were intent on bringing into critical discourse a consideration of the material reality and context in which formal practices took place. This allowed the new criticism to be more attentive to the distinctions within American experience that a strict formalism seemed to ignore. U.S. critics, particularly Henry Nash Smith, Leo Marx, and R. W. B. Lewis, pointed to the tendency of U.S. authors to imagine themselves as Adam in order to establish separation from Europe and to found an American personality. This was most often accomplished, according to Lewis, by imagining a "radically new personality, the hero of a new adventure: an individual emancipated from history, happily bereft of ancestry, untouched and undefiled by the usual inheritances of family and race; an individual standing alone, self-reliant and self-propelling" (5). It is not surprising, argues Lewis, that the new hero "was most easily identified with Adam before the Fall. . . . [Adam's] moral position was prior to experience, and in his very newness he was fundamentally innocent. The world and history lay all before him. And he was the type of creator, the poet par excellence, creating language itself by naming the elements of the scene about him" (5).

Lewis and others criticized this mythical tendency of American letters because it tended to whitewash the past and exempt American experience from the responsibilities of its history. But in the eyes of more recent generations of Americanists the earlier generation's criticism of the American Adam only seemed to perpetuate this exceptionalist myth because these supposedly shared traits upheld a notion of the unique character of American experience. Gene Wise, for example, criticizes the assumption that there is such a thing as a homogeneous "American Mind" located in the "New" world because cultural expressions, including those by many women, that did not confirm this view were marginalized as objects of study. The new interdisciplinary approach of American studies did not diversify but rather consolidated "*the fundamental meaning of America*" (179–80) and served to undergird the exceptional mission the country had assigned itself as global policeman against Communism.

This newfound mission deepened U.S. influence throughout the American hemisphere across frontiers of colonial history, language, and racial difference, all in theoretical defense of democracy. Latin America became the neocolonial backyard to U.S. imperialism, which managed its profound ambivalence about itself as such by means of political sleights of hand. The force of U.S. political and economic imperialism was as keenly felt in Latin America as it was denied or ignored within U.S. national borders. Although patently obvious, it is still necessary to point out that in virtually all of the criticism of American exceptionalism launched by U.S. scholars during and shortly after World War II they never seemed to think it relevant that the "New World" of "America" was multinational, multilingual, and multiracial. This limitation has become a point of focused attention among the so-called New Americanists in recent years, but even these recent criticisms of the idea of the New World as Eden or the American writer as Adam generally remain situated in the transatlantic discourse between the Old World of northern Europe and the New World of the United States.

The New Americanists have rightly focused on the dangers of American exceptionalism, but sometimes it seems their criticism has fetishized exceptionalism to the point of ineffectiveness. The unflagging and sometimes self-congratulatory strategy of identifying exceptionalism wherever it rears its ugly head can be likened to military intelligence: while at times useful in weeding out hidden enemies, it is not clear at what point such an epistemology becomes self-fulfillingly prophetic or incapacitated by its own rampant paranoia to form alliances with parties of distinct interests. A hemispheric snapshot of the life of the adamic idea brings into clearer relief not only the specific dangers of its implicit exceptionalism but also, just as importantly, its emancipatory potential. As Buell suggests, we must learn to "conceive of American myth [beyond the] . . . terms of its ideological character" ("Commentary" 14). Given the adamic idea's diverse hemispheric history, it is not even clear that we can speak of a coherent transhistorical or transnational idea at all. Of course, if the use of adamic rhetoric in other American literatures is only coincidence, we would need to limit strictly our criticism within national borders. Exceptionalism's hemispheric career notwithstanding, national borders are rarely impermeable. This is particularly important when we consider the wide audience Walt Whitman's idea of the adamic poet has enjoyed throughout the Americas, as I explore in chapter 3.

Literary criticism in the Americas desperately needs comparative studies of how ideas have moved across borders, how they have appeared with a kind of inexplicable transnational simultaneity, or how their diverse locations in the Americas have perpetually transformed their ideological function. Moreover, ideas can serve ideological as well as ethical or aesthetic functions, particularly when we shift from a merely social or political analysis to an ecocritical consideration of the impact of an idea on the natural world within a particular context. The adamic idea for the American writer, from whatever nation, has always run the risk of promoting national exceptionalism, but it has also enjoyed a fruitful history throughout the Americas as a cross-cultural and environmental stimulus. Its fullest poetic expression places democratic and egalitarian ideals within the context of a broad, transnational, and deep natural history. This New World Adam is Adam and Eve after the Fall, seeking renewal from the wreckage of history in both senses of the preposition "from": seeking to move beyond patterns of history that have demeaned the New World and its citizens but also using the very material of that history to construct a new poetic vision of the future. This adamic imagination has the potential, then, to escape the worst consequences of exceptionalism: that of chauvinistic claims of Americanness, of male claims to the logocentric privilege, and of devastation to the environment in the name of redeeming the wilderness. Let me be clear: this is not a historical argument about how the idea of the American Adam has played itself out in practice but rather a suggestion that the problems that have attended the idea of an American Adam have more to do with our deficiencies as readers than with the idea itself. To critique an idea for its mistaken uses is to perpetuate the same bad habits of reading that led to the problems in the first place.

Latin Americanism

It is a symptom itself of exceptionalism to ignore the parallel history exceptionalism has enjoyed in Latin America. The emergence of U.S. political clout in Latin America, in conjunction with the legacies of European positivism in the late nineteenth century, sent Latin American modernists searching for a transnational cultural solidarity that could rescue what Francisco García Godoy called in 1917 "an artistic creed, of noteable flexibility [de visible elasticidad], that would reflect with characteristic intensity all that is entailed by and conjoins our American soul" (17). This creed, he insists, must reflect all of Latin American culture, an entity he trusts is "coherent and progressive . . . very distinctive and autonomous" (24). What was at stake in the development of this Latin Americanism was, in the words of George Yúdice, a contradictory struggle to " 'integrate,' that is, to dominate the world on the part of several competing imperial and industrialized powers and, also, to resist these attempts locally" (54). The Latin American avant-garde's relationship with Europe and the United States bifurcated the cultural field into cosmopolites who accommodated foreign metropolitan norms and, in the case of García Godoy, creoles who emphasized local autochthony as resistance to and cannibalization of European modernism. In both cases, tolerance for immigrants, the poor, and racial complexity within individual nations was low.

Two of García Godoy's intellectual models of this new continental soul were José Enrique Rodó and José Martí, both of whom were inspired by Whitman and called for a transnational solidarity that would oppose the crass materialism and hegemonic tendencies of U.S. economic aggression in Latin America. García Godoy writes that "Siren songs of countless appearances of alarming adornment [*innúmeras exterioridades de deslumbrante atavío*] have seduced us. The superficiality of what has been presented to us in a more or less brilliant way has always arrested and dominated us" (14). The North had already been characterized in 1900 by Rodó as mechanized and materialistic, and this myth was coupled with a similarly oversimplified notion of the South as a place of spontaneity and idealism (Franco 53). What will counter the seduction of imperial artificiality, for García Godoy, is local realism, an adamic assessment of the particulars of people and land. In other words, like Whitman's problematic argument in *Democratic Vistas*, which I explore in chapter 3, García Godoy believed that if Latin America didn't yet have its exceptional character, it could be cultivated by the right kind of literature: "Americanism . . . represents a kind of approach that can provide a necessary intellectual and artistic unity to the cultural life of Hispanic America" (22).

This *mundonovismo* of Latin American modernism, as the term came to be known, was instrumental in shifting the focus away from the metropolitan centers of Europe and in establishing at least a rhetorical cultural autonomy that would be repeatedly invoked to defend Latin America against the advances of the United States. The Spanish American War of 1898, the coup de grâce of Spanish imperialism in the New World, allowed long-held anti-Spanish sentiments in Latin America to shift toward the North and thus helped to forge a growing sense of Hispanic solidarity and anti-U.S. sentiments among Latin American continentalists. Modernists became less interested in the abstractions of symbolism and yearned for a more telluric and genuinely American form of expression. One of the leading proponents of *mundonovismo* in the early years of the new century was José Santos Chocano, a Peruvian creole who in 1908 wrote *Alma América*, a poem of continental reach, and was hailed as the Poet of America by many critics. He once famously declared: "Walt Whitman has the North, but I have the South" (qtd. in Rodríguez-Peralta 110).

His stature as such was not long upheld due to what became an increasingly obvious limitation to *mundonovismo*: although aimed at rescuing the American soul and soil from oblivion, its practitioners were only rhetorically interested in indigenous cultures and native landscapes. Their literature was unable to fully transcend the fact that they remained, on the whole, a class of white creole elites. This was especially obvious to the subsequent generation of *indigenistas* and regionalists, who, despite their own similar failings, were at least arguably more deeply involved in the autochthonous tasks the modernists had first assigned themselves.

But despite its early history as a transnational phenomenon of suspect coherence, García Godoy's coherent and autonomous Hispanic America held sway as the foundational idea of Latin American studies when it emerged as an academic field after World War II. Curiously, however, this same conception of Latin America now served to "reinforce and underpin the U.S. hegemonic position in the Americas" at least until the 1970s (Berger 2). Up to that point Latin American studies as a field was well enmeshed within the politics of U.S. hegemony in the Americas due to advances of government-funded area studies programs within U.S. universities. A homogeneous conception of Latin America, especially under the Good Neighbor policy of the 1930s and the subsequent rise of the Communist threat, helped to consolidate a portrait of the region as "in need of protection, guidance and leadership from the U.S." (15). For this reason the comparison between the North and this homogeneous South became especially useful after World War II and at the beginning of the cold war.

In his 1949 treatise, *New World Literature: Tradition and Revolt in Latin America*, Arturo Torres-Rioseco writes, for example, that the Spanish American mind is characterized by romantic inspiration, artistic creation, and subjective and emotional appeal, and it lacks the "organized method" and the objectivity of the North American mind (7). He was indebted to Whitman's argument about the New World even though his description of the North American mind excluded Whitman, along with many other U.S. authors. (Curiously, it was the Chilean Torres-Rioseco's translations of Whitman that found their way to the fifteen-year-old Pablo Neruda on Chile's southern frontier.) As Whitman was tempted to do, Torres-Rioseco insists that these distinctions are geographically determined. "Everything," Torres-Rioseco exclaims, "is transformed in America under the influence of the climate and atmosphere. . . . Although its external forms may be those of Europe, Spanish American literature has gradually acquired a personality of its own, until it has become the revelation of a new type of man and of a different world" (10). It is not clear why the climate and geography of, say, the southern or southwestern United States would not form part of this new entity; ultimately, what proves to be the most important unifying factor is the common stock of the Iberian peninsula, the root of what Torres-Rioseco calls the "spiritual values of America" (19).

Torres-Rioseco nevertheless works within the American grain, that is, within the context of U.S. academia, a problem in the field that continues to concern Latin Americanists. His book, published by the press of the University of California, where he taught, was originally written in English (it was later translated into Spanish) because Torres-Rioseco intended to introduce Latin American culture into the U.S. academy. It is not clear, however, that such efforts served to do anything but reinforce the idea that "American" literature and "New World" literature were separate entities, with separate and unitary legacies and sensibilities.

The notion of a Latin American unity was not solely reproduced within the U.S. academy, however, even if its international manifestations were nevertheless responsive to the cold war context. From 1966 to 1968 Emir Rodríguez Monegal directed the journal *Mundo Nuevo* from Paris. The journal was clearly situated within a cosmopolitan literary discourse, and its aim was to promote an emerging literature, what later became known as the "boom," that was "international and local at the same time; it ought to establish a dialogue that transcends the known limitations of nationalisms and political parties . . . in order to forge a culture without frontiers, free of dogmas and fanatical servitude" (Rodríguez-Carranza 906). The journal espoused the idea that Latin American creativity would be preserved under the rubric of the continent's unity (Cortínez 299). It is not true, then, that the concept of Latin American cultural unity was new in the context of the cold war world order, but it certainly was accentuated by the circumstances and the promotion of a new generation of novelists—García Márquez, Fuentes, Vargas Llosa, and others—who were eager to meet these new criteria.

While *mundonovismo* in Latin America offers a parallel instantiation of the author as Adam, American and Latin American studies were nevertheless in agreement that the Rio Grande marked a distinct border of contrast between these visions of "America." It is this reluctance to think comparatively across the geopolitical borders of the United States that has debilitated both fields in their recent attempts to move away from their respective exceptionalist tendencies. Latin American studies has only recently begun to take advantage of its deep-seated heterogeneity. The field stood to make more broad and quick advances in the study and interrogation of "America" because it was always transnational, its coherence as a discipline with an identifiable and widely shared methodology was always questionable, and its institutional formulation was truly hemispheric because it was explicitly linked to the politics of the Good Neighbor policy, the cold war, and U.S. economic interests in the region. But instead of using these circumstances as an opportunity for profound interrogation of Hispanic exceptionalism, scholars in the immediate postwar period relied heavily on the U.S. academy at the same time that they perpetuated the North American–South American polarities once portrayed by José Martí, José Enrique Rodó, and others. Consequently, no Latin American exploration of New World literature ever managed to explore commonalities between and among nations that included the United States. The most significant comparative thinking has emerged in recent decades from the experience of the borderlands and the increased levels of emigration from Latin America into the United States. The significance of this interrogation of the border should not be underestimated, but a focus on borderlands will not suffice to assess the transnational and diasporic histories of European immigration, African slavery, Native American genocide, and disfranchisement that preexisted said borders, to say nothing of the oft-neglected ways in which the New World's nonhuman biotic communities link regions of the hemisphere.

There is an important exception to this reluctance to consider the Americas hemispherically during the first half of the twentieth century. Herbert Eugene Bolton, a renowned professor of history at UC Berkeley and the "effective founder" of Latin American studies within the United States, taught several generations of students at Berkeley an introduction to "America" that was aggressively hemispheric in its approach (Berger 53). His claim was that "the study of the thirteen English colonies and the United States in isolation has obscured many of the larger factors in their development, and helped to raise up a nation of chauvinists. Similar distortion has resulted from the teaching and writing of national history in other American countries" (Bolton 68). Bolton was writing for a generation who had inherited extreme forms of Anglo-Saxonism, a deep-seated prejudice against Hispanic history and culture, and a willed ignorance of all things hemispheric. This bias, bolstered by a highly developed conception of social Darwinism in the latter decades of the nineteenth century, held that the United States represented a natural selection of superior political institutions and cultural pedigree (Hanke 12). This was a prejudice long in the making, and it has its roots in English-Spanish conflicts in the Old and New Worlds. In 1821, for example, one U.S. historian claimed that Spanish American history was not worthy of U.S. attention because "[w]e hold it to be a maxim clearly established in the history of the world, that none but the temperate climates, and the climates which produce and retain European complexion of skin in its various shades, admit of the highest degrees of national character" (qtd. in Hanke 5). Ignorance, indeed, is bliss, even for some historians.

Because his comparative approach was largely intended to lay claim to somewhat facile and simplified commonalities, Bolton's inter-American approach was not widely adopted. A clearly demarcated set of differences between North and South proved too important to U.S. political interests that needed Latin America as a discreet object of study (Berger 53). The discourse of *mundonovismo* had prepared the ground for a Latin American rebuttal, one provided by the important Mexican historian Edmundo O'Gorman. O'Gorman insisted, and rightly so, that Bolton was simply passing over important distinctions between, for example, Protestant and Catholic influence in the hemisphere and that what unites the Americas, in Bolton's Hegelian sleight of hand, are not the important "spiritual manifestations" of cultural character that are determined by historical choices but rather "the great geographical unity for which no man is responsible" and that transcend history ("Americas" 106).

O'Gorman's critique, however, is guilty of his own kind of Hegelianism. O'Gorman's *The Invention of America*, stressed that the New World was not discovered but rather invented, named, and brought into historical meaning by virtue of a series of European projections of its own philosophical and cosmological debates. Western civilization took two distinct paths in the course of this invention, paths delineated again by the southern geopolitical border of the United States. The New World's objective in thus being named was to become "another Europe," but this process was bifurcated and became a choice between "imitating Europe . . . [or] accepting European values but realizing them in . . . [its] own way" (141). The English settlers, runs his logic, razed the environment and indigenous life according to their objective of transplanting Europe onto American soil, whereas the Spanish accommodated themselves to the contours of American environments and peoples. O'Gorman does nothing to explain why, given this supposed disregard for place in English culture, bioregionalism and conservation have enjoyed a strong commencement in the United States or why the environments most devastated in all of the Americas lay on the islands in the Caribbean Sea where Dutch, English, French, and Spanish settlers shared equal responsibility. It is a contradiction to insist that Spanish settlers conformed to the land if he denies nature any ontological status, as if all New World encounters were an ex nihilo christening.

And so we return to the question of Vespucci's "New World." Cristián Roa-de-la-Carrera argues that Amerigo Vespucci, for whom the Americas, of course, are named, provided an example of a European encounter with this hemisphere that was not simply a transferal of European language and science onto the American map. When Vespucci declared in 1503 that he had encountered a "mundus novus," he opened a new epistemology that produced "knowledge of the territory on the basis of direct experiences . . . opening an intellectual discourse that would make debate and dissension possible" (Roa-de-la-Carrera 558). Similar to Grove, she sees in the era of encounter the emergence of a healthy and intense debate regarding the definitive contours of the earth that led to increasing value placed on empirical experience and an openness to correction and emendation. The New World, in other words, was not simply invented by European language and science, but its environmental particulars—the flora and fauna and geography—also destabilized the knowledge of nature that culture sought to perpetuate.

Despite the intensity of this quest for the local and authentic truths of Latin America by artists, intellectuals, scientists, and novelists in the twentieth century, this identitarian obsession has waned significantly in the field of Latin American studies. The obsession has remained transnational in its adoption by critics of Latino experience within the United States, since the political pressures of minority experience make it more viable to stress the commonality of all stripes of Latin Americans north of the border. However, pan-Latino identity has bypassed the challenges Latin Americanism presented since its inception. It remains to be seen how we can insist that commonalities between, say, a gaucho from the pampas of Argentina, a Maya from the highlands of Guatemala, or a cane worker in Haiti are more significant than those between any one of those three and a white rancher from Oklahoma. The point is that foregrounding the environment and our aesthetic relationship to it in area studies destabilizes the exceptionalist assumptions upon which the declared borders of those areas are based. A tentatively comparative model emerges in which area or, more specifically, land is triangulated by conceptions of community, North *and* South.

In a recent issue of *Radical History Review* exploring the contemporary dilemma of "Our Americas," critics agree that it is no longer possible to return to the dream of a coherent Latin Americanism unified in its resistance to Old World and U.S. globalization. Martín Hopenhayn argues that Latin American political failures, the missteps of development, the overwhelming diversity of social reality throughout the region, increasing specialization and professionalization of academic practice have all contributed to the impossibility of such a return to Latin Americanism (28–29). However, this questioning of Latin America nevertheless still relies on the relatively unquestioned coherent difference of the United States and Canada, which are not viable "other Americas." Nestor García Canclini notes the need to continue to consider the coherence of a "Latin America" but seeks a middle ground that avoids, on the one hand, the nostalgia for art that expresses the merely autochthonous and telluric and, on the other, the presentism of contemporary cultures of global capitalism; that is, he seeks a "way to narrate temporality" that does not create the illusion that "each event lacks history" but that also does not pretend to facile recovery of buried realities (23). My notion of a New World poetics that I explore more fully in the next chapter is an example of this kind of middle ground. As I explain, the adamic imagination sees nature as what García Canclini calls "an imminence in absence" (21). This impels us to a broad hemispheric and comparative context for the consideration of the unique particulars, both historical and natural, of either North or South.

There may be no foolproof way of talking of identity in the Americas without risking some residual exceptionalism, but we also cannot afford to neglect the particulars of where we live. It is probably safe to say that the New World encounter was indeed an exceptional moment in history, never to be repeated again, even if its legacies are repeated and diversified indefinitely. What is needed is a language of identity that imagines an absent but imminent harmony between American communities and between their various human and natural histories. Even with its attendant risks, we cannot afford to neglect the cultivation of a truly hemispheric imagination simply to preserve old identitarian polarities. This quest must begin, in the words of William Carlos Williams, by "making a start out of particulars" in the land. Such an "aesthetics of the earth," in Édouard Glissant's terms (*Poetics* 150), stimulates an identity that is not historical or genealogical, since, as I demonstrate in the next two chapters, such identities assume a continuity of historical memory that is inconsistent with New World experience. The fundamental facts of New World oblivion do not have to condemn New World subjects to a fruitless search either for autochthony or for ancestry in some Old World. When identity is founded instead on an aesthetic belonging in the land, it remains open to the surprises the environment might reveal, which is another way of imagining ourselves as natural and as other to ourselves. So yes, a *new* world.

If history could be that which annihilated all
memory of past things from our minds it would
be a useful tyranny.

WILLIAM CARLOS WILLIAMS, *In the American Grain*

CHAPTER 2

A New World Poetics

To write with an adamic imagination like Whitman, Neruda, and Walcott brings attendant risks, especially the prospect of denuding a place of its history, both human and natural, in order to facilitate the perception of newness. Longings for Eden tend to lay the ground for the decimation of peoples as well as of the landscape that appears to lie in wait for despoliation. However, it is important to be able to distinguish brazen acts of erasure from a more genuine and honest reckoning with the past and, of equal importance, with what has inevitably and irrevocably fallen into historical oblivion. This is particularly urgent in the context of New World experience. The historical patterns that pertain to many areas of the Americas are, among others, those of European colonization, Amerindian genocide and displacement, African slavery, deep civil conflict in the struggle for political autonomy and democracy, and concomitant dramatic environmental change. These historical parallels, though commonly shared in the hemisphere, do not produce homogeneity across nations because they are characterized by the transplantation of peoples and other biota and the systemic rupture of historical and environmental continuity. Their parallels, however, can illuminate the relation between the particulars of regional experience with the plight of neighboring communities. The problem is that they are experiences that defy facile representation. They have necessitated a variety of strategies for the re-creation of viable human memory and the recovery of a sense of place and belonging in the New World.

It would be accurate to characterize this thrust of New World literature as reinhabitory, asking the same fundamental questions of the natural sciences that Bruce Foltz describes, by seeking to understand one's place in a new world. It is not, however, the argument of this book that this is an epistemic discourse that shares common traits and ideological meanings wherever it has shown up in the hemisphere. My readings of Whitman, Neruda, and Walcott seek to identify the symptoms of this characteristic New World experience of transplantation and reorientation as eruptions on the surface of different New World cultures of, if you will, unseen common roots. Their imaginings of their place in the New World are responses to the particulars of the local landscape and to the challenges of historical amnesia in their social and political circumstances. I do not read their adamic imagination as cohering into a singular ideological discourse of a traceable genealogy but rather as relational manifestations of distinct and idiosyncratic responses to buried historical parallels. The uncertainty of historical memory and the dynamic particulars of their immediate environments render their language unstable, even unpredictable, but ultimately new. To the extent that they ignore the particulars of the landscape or will upon their readers a coherent historical memory of the continent (a desire no one of them is invulnerable to), their poetry manifests traces of Old World fantasies of Eden and Hegelian notions of inevitable progress.

While historical rupture and amnesia are certainly not unique to the New World, it is nevertheless important to attend to the particular challenges to American memory they pose. If not, one is left to imagine that the parallels that bring New World cultures together were never subject to original violence or historical trauma, which is to ignore and perpetuate the untraceable facts of New World oblivion. The very task of rendering human meaning to natural history wrestles with the fundamental limitations of human language to subsume nature's otherness. Nature's living force is ultimately beyond human language even if it is perhaps its most patent and potent inspiration. The dramatic environmental changes throughout the New World incurred in the wake of the conquest have made it impossible to recover full knowledge of the New World's pre-Columbian natural state. And of course a complete understanding of the human historical events that accompanied these environmental changes such as the murder and displacement of millions of Amerindians or the Middle Passage of African slavery and its plantation legacies of untold suffering for millions of Africans and their descendents is often beyond representation because aspects of their lived realities were either initially understated or erased in historical documentation in an attempt to conceal accountability. Dead victims cannot speak, notwithstanding the shamanistic yearnings of these poets, and those that did survive had little or no access to written expression, or their testimonies held feeble legal force. And this is to say nothing of the daunting challenge of simply finding the adequate forms of representation to be able to sum up such atrocities.

Sympathetic discourses that have tried to recollect the history of such violence in and on the land have done so most often as volunteer imagined witnesses to what never was firsthand. Such sympathy, however, often avoids careful consideration of the dizzying challenge of giving representative force to such cataclysms. It might not be reckless to suggest that very little New World literature and its critical reception have succeeded in awaking from a fundamental numbness toward these hemispheric primal scenes. New World writers interested in understanding the parallels among the Americas confront the conundrums of the hemisphere's environmental and human stories and overcome this numbness paradoxically by recognizing the fact of a saturated, collective amnesia about those stories. A confession ensues that the evidence that remains of historical parallels in the New World is, due to this violent and traumatic nature of its history, fragmented, partial, and, even though undeniable, ultimately unknowable. Consequently, when a New World writer endeavors to establish a sense of place in a particular New World clime, as is the case with these three poets, nature becomes the site of this oblivion, since the newness of nature appears to conceal history's traces. That is, the Edenic promise of the New World that first attracted those burdened with Old World guilt is haunted by a prior history that renders nature's capacity for regeneration and renewal an illusion of innocence. But the newness of the world is just as undeniable as the history that it hides, and thus, as the poet starts from the soil of home to rebuild in the wake of New World devastation, John Elder argues that the "chosen spot defines the interchange of past and present through that spot's own cycle of renewing, surrender, and inheritance" (*Imagining* 40). The poet is not burdened by perpetual guilt and nostalgia but rather turns to the pragmatic task of building a new culture. The poet acknowledges oblivion but is willing to praise and be moved by newness, and thus the devastations of New World history become what Elder calls a "fruitful oblivion" (51). He explains that poetry begins to resemble ecological process because "only with the detritus of the past can soil be made to sustain the cycle of life into a new present" (31).

Because New World history has blocked historiographic access to much of its evidence, memory is an act of reconstruction that acknowledges that whatever the contours of a total history might look like, the past can only be known in its remnant parts. To respond to this problem, Édouard Glissant argues for a "poetics of relation" that is cross-cultural. He writes: "[N]ot knowing this totality [of history] is not a weakness. Not wanting to know it certainly is. Consequently we imagine it through a poetics; this imaginary realm provides the full-sense of all these always decisive differentiations" (*Poetics* 154). The New World past is opaque, to be sure, but that does not excuse us from trying to *imagine* the totality of that history, *as if* we were capable of making it transparent to our perception (55). Glissant's representative figure of this kind of poetic knowing is the one who is errant, not the discoverer or the conqueror, but one who, like a postdisillusionment Quixote, "conceives of totality but willingly renounces any claims to sum it up or to possess it" (21).

The alternative to striving to imagine this totality would be a genealogical thrust into the past, seeking legitimacy, justification, and simplification of the past and of community. This comes at the expense of excluding otherness, either human or natural. For Glissant, looking cross-culturally throughout those regions affected by the historical patterns of the New World and commemorating that which was lost in our mutually shared histories opens cultures into relation with others and with the natural world. When writers dig deeper and more intimately into the particulars of a homeland, they are presented with the seductions of the Columbian gesture of staking a flag in the sand. The myth of this clean slate beginning is what

Glissant calls a "sacred root," tapping deep into a soil appropriated as territory and pushing out other genealogies and other communities. But to the degree that a poet imagines the untraceable facts of history, nature and history both prove more opaque and resistant to the singular diachronic claims of borders and of memory. The poet finds recourse to metaphors, figural language, and an imagined belonging in the land that is at once loyal to place and imaginatively open, synchronically and relationally, to other cultures and regions in the hemisphere.

Poetic Language and Oblivion

To speak of oblivion, of course, is risky business. Categorically refusing to believe nature's communicability renders us indifferent to what it might seem to say to us. We turn a deaf ear to a living system that contextualizes all of our human endeavors and imaginings. Similarly, assessing the devastation suffered by indigenous populations risks failing to recognize the ways in which native cultures have survived, adapted, and transformed themselves in the wake of Columbus's arrival. A poetics of oblivion potentially becomes a kind of negative sublime that expresses a neocolonial wish to erase a still thriving and vital indigenous presence in the Americas.[1] To invoke oblivion in relation to the Middle Passage similarly risks a dismissal of the lifeways and rhythms of African culture that have found new roots in American soil. It can be argued, in fact, that the Middle Passage has signified a new transformation and flourishing of African memory in the Americas, as evidenced by an increased interest in the history of slave experience in much fiction from the United States and the Caribbean.[2] In either case, to speak of oblivion might overstate the power of European colonization of the New World to control or obliterate contestatory cultural and political memories.

Failing to recognize the fact of oblivion (that something has been lost and is no longer accessible) runs parallel risks, however, chief among which is the risk of believing in the pathetic fallacy and failing to recognize the fictional rhetoric of anthropomorphisms. Nature becomes our puppet and stage scenery. Without recognition of oblivion we risk perceiving existing memories of conquest, enslavement, and colonization as naturally born from history itself, not as selected recollections that have emerged in the context of a struggle among competing powers of representation. Even when our sympathies are with the victims of such historical events, we risk identifying traces and transformations of ancestral cultures as significations of their original form. To do so is to render the historical agency behind colonialism and slavery invisible and to imagine anachronistically that contemporary expressions of devotion to Africa or to Native America or imaginative acts of historical recovery today signify a pre-Columbian primordiality. This is an Oedipal risk, since we elide our own imaginative desire by mythologizing origins and presenting them to ourselves not as manifestations of our desire but as objectively given historical realities.

Literature can only suggest, point to, or imagine a larger context in which our own story takes place. Toni Morrison, in her Nobel Prize speech of 1993, insists: "[L]anguage can never live up to life once and for all. Nor should it. Language can never 'pin down' slavery, genocide, war. Nor should it yearn for the arrogance to be able to do so. Its force, its felicity, is in its reach toward the ineffable" ("Nobel" 321). As this study seeks to demonstrate, such a poetic impulse feeds the richest poetry of Whitman, Neruda, and Walcott. As Walcott stated in his own 1992 Nobel Prize speech, "Break a vase, and the love that reassembles the fragments is stronger than the love which took its symmetry for granted when it was whole" (*What the Twilight* 69). Poetic language is an expression of this love; it is an expression of a self-conscious desire for wholeness, not a pretension to mimeticism or historical recuperation.

Similar to the way language responds to and seeks to represent an elusive and dynamic physical world, Morrison and Walcott imply that the limits of representation are both a symptom of historical events that have rendered language weak *and* a limitation inherent in language itself. It seems that if we don't at least admit both possibilities, the specific historical quality of New World experience becomes insignificant and easily transferable to any other context, *or* history becomes almost enshrined in its ubiquitous power to limit language and is granted a permanent primordial position always in demand of linguistic obeisance. That is to say, a poetics of oblivion might certainly become necessary in other historical contexts both because the historical events themselves create similar crises of language *and* because all languages presumably suffer similar limitations. However, we must be careful not to assume that all problems of oblivion are equal; to do so means that either all languages transcend history altogether or that we don't really need to pay attention to the particulars of any one region's history. The poetics articulated by these poets sees language as symptomatic representation of a primary historical oblivion but also as autonomous performative mourning for what has been forgotten.

We see this pendular swing when these poets insist that the limitations of poetic language, although presumably an ontological problem, signify something grounded and specific that lies beyond words. Their poetic language reconstructs a conscious fiction of historical rootedness, and in its self-consciousness it betrays its own failure. This is because, ultimately, what is more important than language is what it cannot say, especially in regard to place. As Walcott stated in 1974, "We may not even need literature, not that we are beyond it, but in the archipelago particularly, nature, the elements if you want, are so new, so overpowering in their presence that awe is deeper than articulation of awe" ("Caribbean" 57). A poetics of oblivion declares that what is said, what is remembered, is always less than that which it reaches for; language always defers to what it tries to express, but not because the past, or nature, is a sublime muse but because ultimately what matters more than language is what it tries to represent. Or, as Walcott phrases it in *The Bounty*, "memory is less than the place which it cherishes" (27).

Oblivion creates difficulties for cultures seeking to understand their place in the land. It is not hard to imagine that the extraordinary history of transplantation in the New World has led to a disregard for the environment. Wallace Stegner suggests the role literature can play: "[A] place is not a place until people have been born in it, have grown up in it, lived in it, known it, died in it—have both experienced and shaped it as individuals, families, . . . communities . . . until things that have happened in it are remembered in history, ballads, yarns, legends, or monuments" (201–2). Indeed, "no place is a place until it has had a poet" (205). Stegner responds to the American West's particular form of restlessness that has allowed modern U.S. culture to ravage the land without facing long-term consequences and explains:

> [W]e have no business, any longer, in being impatient with history. We
> need to know our history in much greater depth, even back into the
> geology. . . . History was part of the baggage we threw overboard when
> we launched ourselves into the New World. . . . Plunging into the future
> through a landscape that had no history, we did both the country and
> ourselves some harm along with some good. . . . "The land was ours
> before we were the land's" says Robert Frost's poem. Only in the act of

submission is the sense of place realized and a sustainable relationship between people and earth established. (206)

Closer attention to history is indeed necessary if we are to become more rooted in our landscapes, but, as Elliott West has responded, Stegner's own conception of history isn't historical enough, since he seems to imply that "history doesn't really get going until Europeans show up and start changing things" (89). Akin to Glissant's notion of the sacred root, Stegner dreams of a story that "moves unbroken" so that "westerners feel properly grounded in a continuous past that is theirs alone" (86). However, West emphasizes the need to rely on archaeology and anthropology in order to fill in the missing pieces of Native American history that will save us from a more shallow and ethnocentric sense of history in the American West. Curiously, however, he neglects an account of deep time, of the environmental history and ecology of the places we inhabit, something Stegner himself called for. Neither West nor Stegner fully grasp, however, what is apparent to the poets in this study: deeper historical knowledge, in most New World contexts, leads us to many dead ends, violent eruptions of historical change, and a tremendously discontinuous series of historical narratives, obstacles that archaeologists or even the most attuned biologists may never overcome. Because identity in the New World—and the language we use to define it—is always "fragmentary, based on a gleam of racial memory," Walcott insists that "history is irrelevant, not because it is not being created, or because it was sordid; but because it has never mattered, what has mattered is the loss of history, the amnesia of the races, what has become necessary is imagination, imagination as necessity, as invention" ("Caribbean" 53). Walcott concludes that "amnesia is the true history of the New World." Acknowledging historical erasure in the New World avoids the "malaria of nostalgia and the delirium of revenge" (*What the Twilight* 39, 54). The allure of an unbroken history has led to many neocolonial and rather facile attempts to smooth over the inherent discontinuities of the New World story. The dream of historical continuity in the land may have some dangerous and dark corners, and thus greater historical knowledge, though valuable, may lead to a deeper and more false sense of place unless we can also recognize our hermeneutical limitations.

Like O'Gorman's invented America, Stegner's historicized sense of place paradoxically relies on an ahistorical conception of nature as an original, prelinguistic space void of human stories and outside of human history until it is named and thereby brought *into* history *as* place. In other words, prior to a landscape's conversion into a place it must be prehistorical and Edenic, without a name and in need of its Adam, the poet, who will perform the historicization of nature through language, tales, legends, and so on. Place is a category that needs a poet because it is defined as a space where human and natural history merge; it is where human beings understand themselves and their history in relationship to natural, physical space. West effectively describes the dangers of this paradigm: "What a bleak joke it would be if European Americans come to believe that they can find their 'sense of place' only by denying to their neighbors what *they* must have for their own legitimate sense of belonging" (94).

Frost's poem invoked by Stegner, "The Gift Outright," once recited by Frost himself (at John F. Kennedy's inauguration), demonstrates this risk of founding a poetics *from* historical erasure instead of a poetics *of* oblivion. Frost's poem echoes many of Whitman's complaints in *Democratic Vistas* and García Godoy's call for appraisals of local realities in Latin America; Frost describes a lack of a sense of place in the United States that is a function of continued colonial dependency on British culture. A sense of place will presumably achieve this independence, but his logic implies that we would therefore need an original relationship to the land around us, one that is pure and untainted by a displaced cultural imagination. He explains that this postcolonial possession *by* the land became possible once we surrendered ourselves "To the land vaguely realizing westward, / But *still unstoried, artless, unenhanced*" (Frost 348, emphasis added).

Frost's rhetoric relies on the very same structures of power and of thought with which he set out to argue. In an ironic twist Frost needs to depopulate the lands to the west, rid them of Native American or Mexican poets and storytellers prior to the arrival of Anglo-Americans in order to imagine the possibility of this post-Anglo "fresh" start. On this point Walcott once wrote in complaint about the poem: "This was the calm reassurance of American destiny that provoked Tonto's response to the Lone Ranger. No slavery, no colonization of Native Americas, a process of dispossession and then possession, but nothing about the dispossession of others that this destiny demanded. . . . [T]he 'ours' and the 'we' of Frost were not as ample and multihued as Whitman's tapestry" (*What the Twilight* 193–94).

This is the Adamic sense of place that voids the landscape of its already very human story in order to pretend a first time beginning. The danger is that this becomes a simple replication of colonialism across new frontiers rather than a fundamental epistemic break from it. Elder argues against this false dichotomy between nature and human civilization, propagated by many writers of the American West, and insists that the "green impression" of nature potentially becomes "a scouring away of historical details" or "an undifferentiating pastoral blur" (*Reading* 19).[3] This in turn implies a kind of human "self-loathing" where humanity is "viewed as taboo with relation to wilderness—not only people but, in the emphasis upon roadless and 'untrammeled' areas, our human history" (117).

Unlike this masculine Anglo-American insistence that alienation from nature is caused by excessive mobility and transience, there are various causes for alienation from nature that differ according to the historical conditions of peoples in the wake of the violence of western expansion. If the neglect of nature in the Americas has its roots in the very beginnings of New World colonial history, colonialism has created divergent relationships to physical space. Recent work in environmental justice demonstrates the need for a close examination of shifting particulars for different people and places, an approach more akin to postcolonial criticism.[4] Postcolonial literature has given more attention to this problem than U.S. nature writing; placelessness in the former tends to be seen more as a particular political problem rather than as a universalized moral one, as in the latter. Wendell Berry believes, for example, that for the modern American citizen "geography is artificial; he could be anywhere, and he usually is" (53). While this may be true of many white male Americans, it is certainly a harder argument to make for immigrants, women, or, as Melvin Dixon has argued, people of color.

Recognizing the contributions of Western culture to current environmental degradation, many environmental thinkers have concluded that they must situate themselves rhetorically against the legacies of colonialism by symbolically (if not genealogically) placing themselves in a line of descent from the early native inhabitants of the New World down to the present. The problem is that this risks denying complicity in the very legacies they ostensibly wish to overturn. The "simplification of choosing to play Indian instead of cowboy," to quote Walcott, "is the hallucination of imperial romance" (*What the Twilight* 58). Mere self-loathing, as Elder calls it, has never proven an effective means to meaningful and lasting change in individual or societal behavior. Western self-loathing has become a highly developed skill in the West matched only by its ineffectiveness in promoting fundamental and salutary change. Learning from the lessons of non-Western cultures can no doubt help in this matter, and there is evidence in Whitman, Neruda, and Walcott that Asian, Native American, and, for Walcott, African cultures as well have exerted significant influence on their visions of the human place in the natural world. But Western civilization has shown no signs of fading from the future of the modern world, and so it would seem equally important to avoid the temptation of thinking of New World cultures as categorically in need of a Western whitewashing. A New World poetics is cross-cultural, but precisely for that reason it does not shy away from resuscitating or cannibalizing Old World values still worth preserving.

Because of increasing environmental degradation and the erosion of community a sense of place remains a vital need for many New World cultures, whether they are excessively mobile or because of their history of containment. The question is how to establish that sense of place in the context of genocide, degradation, and transplantation. A vital strategy for moving beyond the reach of such colonial legacies is to insist on a specific sense of place in representations of the marginalized. Local nature, then, is key to a dismissal of colonial discourse because it involves a radical resituation of the marginalized, a speaking from and to those circumstances that have been passed over. Glissant explains that "any group that is limited by the stubborn inability to take control of its surroundings is a threatened group" (*Caribbean* 160). What Stegner and Berry describe as a moral crisis of placelessness can be understood as a political crisis as well if we consider the displacement and murder of Native Americans, the violent transplantation of Africans, and the chaotic scattering of many Europeans, Asians, and others in New World history. By so doing we come to see the cross-cultural implications of a sense of place. Establishing it is inherently an intercultural, intergenerational struggle as well as a natural-cultural struggle for the autonomy to name a place and identify a human history in it.

The danger is when the political struggle is only resolved in a partisan fashion and all competing historical claims on the land are erased. For Glissant, a crucial strategy to avoid this is a metaphorical archaeological dig for the "subterranean convergence of *our histories*" (*Caribbean* 66). We must not be seduced by the temptation to seek a singular, diachronic history of one people that stretches back through time and into the landscape but rather develop what he calls a cross-cultural poetics whereby we discover that landscape is rife with sites of oblivion. Any claim to it, to our history in it, must be partial, tentative, and imaginative rather than historical or genealogical. This is because the land "is not saturated with a single History but effervescent with intermingled histories, spread around, rushing to fuse without destroying or reducing each other" (154). For the survivors of New World diasporas who have experienced traumatic and sometimes violent transplantation and outright dispossession, "ambiguity was the first necessity of survival" (Glissant, "Creolization" 272).

Glissant's point is that New World cultures are rarely anything but amalgamations of traces or fragments of prior cultures. The construction of New World identities occurs "by proceeding not from preserved folklores . . . but from these *traces*, and by combining them with countless other elements, from China or India or the Middle East, and so on" (Glissant, "Creolization" 273). A genealogical approach only leads to disillusionment and disappointment and perhaps renewed violence aimed again at dispossessing others. A sense of place and belonging in this New World is conditioned by an always incomplete knowledge of natural and human histories and therefore necessitates re-creating our sense of place always in the present. As Glissant explains, the New World subject faces the rather paradoxical "obligation to remake oneself every time on the basis of a series of forgettings," since every step forward in forging a new identity and sense of place from the fragments created by New World experience means leaving behind a forgotten whole. All cultural and natural signs that are intended to communicate our sense of belonging to a place must be read backward, metonymically reaching back to a wholeness of which the sign is simply a part. In other words, a sense of place is perhaps just a hint or hope that we belong.

So perhaps more important than Stegner's call for deeper historical knowledge, we need deeper historical imagination. While recognizing that "the broader our perspective, the more immediately present do our ancestors in the land become," Elder also insists that a poet's re-creation of this ancestral belonging in the land is an illusion, even if it remains a truthful one (*Reading* 110). The illusion avoids the status of myth as long as there is a recognition of the poet's role in the expression of this *desire* for belonging. Elder's defense of wilderness as an integration of natural and human history is akin to the adamic imagination. He explains that this faithful desire for wholeness and ancestral belonging in the land is a function of one's love and desire for reconciliation: "We don't remember, and love, the past because it was painless and perfect. We don't cherish our parents because they had it all right. Love grows with the growing recognition of perpetual brokenness" (177). We become aware, then, not so much of the concrete historical density embedded in nature but of our own participation in the making of a sense of place. That is why that wholeness often appears in *imaginative* literature; in representing the historical past of our landscapes imaginative literature also performs our loving desire to construct our home in the land.

This New World poetics implicitly argues with Hegel's dialectic that determined that the future belonged to "America," by which Hegel meant those areas of the United States that would reject racial amalgamation and thus further the development of Western civilization (81). Hegel declared: "America is . . . the land of the future, where, in the ages that lie before us, the burden of the World's History shall reveal itself—perhaps in a contest between North and South America" (86). I will explore this claim more fully in chapter 3, specifically as it relates to tracing literary influence transnationally in the Americas, but here I wish to suggest how the problem of oblivion undermines Hegel's claim. The Hegelian dialectic doesn't account for historical events for which there is no record or for the inevitability that in many cases there will never be a sufficient account; therefore, it ignores the possibility that some events will inevitably fall outside the bounds of the dialectic, which is supposed to perpetually produce historical meaning. Historical meaning, of course, will not always be recoverable by a poetics of oblivion. Amnesia cannot simply overturn the Hegelian dialectic or be essentialized because it signifies what is essentially unknowable. To be ethical a New World poetics would always have to retrace its steps to acknowledge its failures, even if that means forsaking a thirst for unearthing forgotten histories.

Thus a New World poetics suggests that Hegel's mapping of world history is perhaps upside down, since it will be the spaces of oblivion that will inevitably resist and fundamentally change the direction of and perhaps render unpredictable the historical outcomes of the dialectic. Those spaces include many New World sites where exploitation, environmental degradation, cultural and racial mixing, and historical neglect have rendered their stories ironic, fragmented, and cross-cultural in imaginative scope. If the United States has become the bearer of the burdens of Western history, as Hegel prophesied, it is time to acknowledge that those burdens stem from historical amnesia about the "other" America Hegel dismissed, not by the extent to which the United States has continued Western legacies. This poetics involves unreading representations of the past in order to invoke what lies underneath what has been said and remembered. It recognizes the fact of amnesia in New World history and that therefore, as the Martinican *créolité* manifesto declares, "our chronicle is behind the dates, behind the known facts: *we are words behind writing*." For this reason, "only poetic knowledge, fictional knowledge, literary knowledge . . . can discover us, understand us and bring us, evanescent, back to the resuscitation of consciousness" (Bernabé et al. 896). The recourse to poetic language is crucial to this transformation of oblivion in filling in the "space between memory and history, . . . the space left by historical omission," because instead of trying to compensate, it redresses an absent history (Pedersen 51).

William Carlos Williams, in his remarkable *In the American Grain* from 1925, articulates a conception of New World history that recognizes the facts of the hemisphere's atrocities. "History," he writes, "begins for us with murder and enslavement, not with discovery" (39). While recognizing modernity's inauguration in the contact between Europe and the New World, Williams imagines modernity's origins from the perspective of the continent's native inhabitants. Whitman and Neruda, as we will see, appeal to a Native American voice for this reason, plying at times the art of poetry for its shamanistic potential to resurrect the wisdom of nature, the dead, and native peoples. Walcott makes a similar appeal, but, perhaps due to the notable absence of a native population in many areas of the Caribbean, he is more inclined to see the ironies of this appeal. For Williams, the poet does not have to play Indian to Columbus's cowboy; it means for a poet to be like Daniel Boone, "to be *himself* in the new world, *Indianlike*" (137, emphasis added). "No, we are not Indians but we are men of their world," he explains. "The blood means nothing; the spirit, the ghost of the land moves in the blood, moves the blood. It is we who ran to the shore naked, we who cried, 'Heavenly Man!'" (39).

Racial essentialism, historical distance, respect for otherness, and a paltry imagination are among the reasons authors might shrink from the task of imagining the indigenous experience of those early encounters. But if they don't at least explore the ironies of the historical imagination, the past remains dead, puppetlike. Williams asks: "Do these things die? Men who do not know what lives, are themselves dead. In the heart there are living Indians once slaughtered and defrauded" (42). What Williams stresses here is that the facts of New World history are essentially unknowable and that the concept of "blood" fails to function genealogically and to shore up identity. We are what we can imagine, what we can call forth from the ghosts of the past through our own empathetic historical imagination. This is not to say that a poetics of historical memory facilely makes us all people and thus frees us from individual accountability. These are no doubt attendant dangers of such a poetics, but it also enables us to look underneath the record of the past for "the strange phosphorous of life, nameless under an old misappellation" (v). Rather than reifying the present into a position of perpetual nostalgia or regret about the past, the facts of violence and amnesia create the circumstances for a history that is dynamic, elusive, and never fixed. This enables the poet to imagine the New World past beyond simple binaries and to integrate into a present sense of identity and place what has not been told and what cannot be summed up.

While historians work to shape events according to patterns, it is precisely against the grain of this monumentalization of the past that the adamic imagination must strive. The goal is not to be free from the restraints of history or to ignore it but rather to free the imagination to move among its ghosts, to keep dead things alive and elusive. Williams explains:

> History follows governments and never men. It portrays us in generic patterns, like effigies or the carvings on sarcophagi, which say nothing save, of such and such a man, that he is dead. That's history. It is concerned only with one thing: to say everything is dead. . . . Not at all. History must stay open, it is all humanity. Are lives to be twisted forcibly about events, the mere accidents of geography and climate? . . . If history could be that which annihilated all memory of past things from our minds it would be a useful tyranny. (189)

It is important to stress that this adamic rhetoric must be distinguished from the obliviousness of a New World innocent, intent on ignoring the land as a palimpsest of previous signatures of human and natural events and instead willing only to see it as a blank slate upon which the Adamic writer begins history and founds a sense of place. The adamic imagination is instead a kind of exorcism, a revisiting of the past so as to liberate it from the cold grasp of both impotent imagination and historical determinism. It is to make the past present, to render it usable as material for poetic, empathetic cross-cultural imaginings, to free the imagination from the restraints of the present—namely, national, racial, and other communal claims on fixed boundaries. And what is key to this adamic imagination is a view of nature beyond the binary of being either totally outside of this history or completely circumscribed by its claims, a view consistent in Williams's own poetry (see Buell, *Writing* 116). As Elder explains, the contemporary environmentalist view of "[n]ature, with science's vivid apprehension, offers a vision of creativity and memory both analogous to human experience and distinct from it. A revitalized perception of nature counters the entropic drift of culture toward a rigid formulation of the past—through making available a dynamic present beyond the reach of *merely* human continuity" (*Imagining* 35).

Many New World writers of course have preferred to pretend to Adamic innocence and have staked their flags of legitimacy in New World soil. Nature, then, becomes merely instrumental as a purely ahistorical space upon which they write a radical new beginning. But the greatest New World writers, a group that includes these poets, understand the irony of such gestures even though they share the desire to found a new home. They have not failed to see the tragedy of fading imprints of human suffering on the land, but neither have they refused the elation at the newness provided by nature's indifferent self-regeneration. Nature for them is alive because it represents both the continuity and rupture of poetic meaning.

Regionalism, with its accompanying celebration of a fixed notion of place as background, has generally avoided the challenges of this balancing act and has instead functioned essentially as a narrative of national progress. Even literature by African Americans, beginning with slave narratives in the United States and the Caribbean primarily and the introduction of poetry, novels, and essays, has typically been valued for its apparent contributions to national ends. The reaction against the containments of nationalism since the 1960s inspired the study of ethnicity apart from national literary histories. However, this increase in literary specialization has, perhaps unintentionally, helped to rigidify a separate discussion about "race" outside of the national dialogue, thus abdicating any national responsibility for an accounting of race and racial difference. Toni Morrison and others have helped to argue why black and white literatures in the United States, at least, need to be brought back into the scope of a rigorous comparative scholarly eye, but as long as such comparative work remains trapped within national and regional boundaries and focuses on a thematics and not a poetics of identity, the binary oppositions that have infected our reading of race will remain largely intact.

Comparative American studies help to expose the various ways nationalisms have relied on establishing cultural and historical roots in a local place. This has typically involved representing racial and environmental differences that rhetorically respond to the nation's colonial challengers and yet signify its secure, fixed, and almost sacred rootedness in a particular place. Such rhetoric, as Glissant's critique of the idea of the root suggests, is anything but historical, since it displaces historical rootedness with an ahistorical conception of racial identities and of land despite the historical reality of diaspora, environmental transformation, and various forms of transculturation that lie at the very foundation of New World nationalities (see *Poetics* 11–22). Typically, a search for national rootedness often neglects to consider its own "forgettings" and sinks into the realm of a kind of touristic regionalism, or what Glissant calls the "folkloric" (*Caribbean* 101). This is usually because the nationalistic impulse too hastily jumps from the particular to the general because of a thirst for transcendence, and thus the specific qualities of oral language and of the historical qualities of the landscape are glossed over. As a result, literary nationalism, rather than emphasizing the plasticity and historical nature of its own expression, becomes teleological in its search for fixed origins. It disguises its performance of desire for rootedness as rootedness per se.

Whether race or place stands in for absent history, the tendency in much regionalist literature and in its readership has been to celebrate a new point of origin, divorced from that chaotic and cataclysmic past declared no longer relevant to the concerns of a national legitimacy. The paradox here lies in the fact that recourse to place or to race is typically an attempt to *recover* history. Regional qualities are typically read diachronically and, for that matter, anachronistically as representing a past that nurtures our present identity as a nation. But the literature that most honestly confronts the challenges of historical oblivion in Plantation America is paradoxically the most true to history, since it acknowledges the insufficiency of regionalisms and the memories they provide.

The Return of an Untraceable History

Regionalism is a literary manifestation of what the Guianese writer Wilson Harris contends are the Oedipal risks of nationalism. He writes: "[T]he reaction to dread" often leads to "the withdrawal into cells of ideological or racial or cultural purity," or what he calls "political incest" ("Oedipus" 10). Regionalism, in its retreat from the historical dread of colonialism and imperialism, often resorts to these dehistoricized racial and cultural ideologies and thus disguises its own imitation of the father culture in the very name of a nationalist rebellion against him. The trap of regionalism is that it cannot cure the degradation it depicts because it *needs* a disease or colonial trauma in order to establish its anti-imperialist authority.[5] Carlos Alonso has noted that Latin American regional novels "reenact that crisis in their own rhetorical structure" (7). Such writing is, then, a kind of paternalism itself, since it relies on the eccentric and ahistorical position of the writer who, by virtue of his own disguised position outside history, can offer cures with no account of his own historical genesis. The paternalism of literary regionalism has the potential to be perpetually recycled by an eternal recourse to a diseased past for which it continually offers itself as a cure.

What contributes to this erasure of human historical accountability in the land, in the fiction of writers such as William Faulkner, is turning nature into property. Ownership inherently contradicts the facts of New World history because it is fundamentally tied to the anxiety about genealogical legitimacy, an anxiety initiated by the violence of New World history. Ownership serves to invent identity because it will always keep history at bay, at least any history that is inclusive of a heterogeneous past. The arrogance of ownership is that it parcels off, sets apart, and delimits ecological process and our human belonging within it. It also fails to recognize kinship with what lies beyond the boundaries ownership creates; it is a pretension to purity and inviolable difference regarding that which lies within those boundaries, and it defers a confrontation with the differences and similarities expelled in order to expedite that purity. And this, of course, is also the inherent thrust of nationalistic views of regionalism wherein the local color of place is appropriated as a pure expression of national origins and identity. Nationalism, in this sense, simply serves as a centralized form of cultural and geographical ownership whereby regions are kept within boundaries and apart from any "foreign" claims.

Faulkner's works imply that a New World sense of place is established by a cross-cultural awareness of the historical presence of various peoples in the landscape, and the only way to assure that a sense of place does not simultaneously displace others is to abdicate ownership and accept mutual responsibility for that history through action and labor. In "The Bear" Faulkner describes New World history as "that dark corrupt and bloody time while three separate people had tried to adjust not only to one another but to the new land which they had created and inherited too and must live in for the reason that those who had lost it were no less free to quit it than those who had gained it were" (283). Faulkner argues for an open-ended relationship toward the land that recognizes the folly of a belief in genealogical inviolability and embraces the ironies as well as the possibilities of a *collective* history. As Lois Parkinson Zamora contends, this historical imagination of New World writers involves "the countenancing of multiple, coexisting, conflictual, *unfinished* histories" (196, emphasis added). In order to countenance this multiplicity and inconclusion, Faulkner's sense of place concerns itself with synchronic, cross-cultural relationships that extend beyond and beneath the local landscape. This is a kind of regionalism that expresses a yearning for belonging simultaneously with a fear of a possible "irrevocable demarcation," to borrow from *Absalom, Absalom!*, from others, and from the past.

A sense of place that neither ignores an absent history nor pretends to replace it demonstrates that identities and landscapes alike are haunted by the appearance of metonymical fragments of a larger range of possibilities. The remedy for the arrogance of possession or a sacred root identity is not simply *including* multiple histories in some kind of facile multiculturalism but also somehow acknowledging those histories that cannot be included precisely because New World history has made them unavailable. In *The Bounty* Walcott provides an example:

> your devotion
> to pursue those bleached tracks that disappear into bush, in the rain—
> something of weight in the long indigo afternoon,

the yam vines trying to hide the sugar wheel's ruin;
of something unconnected, oblique as if, after the motion
of history, every object we named was not the correct noun. (48)

Nature's prodigious and disinterested growth renders language always displaced, or at least always "as if" displaced, since to be sure of the precise displacement is to believe in the capacity to define history's motions exactly. Language, in its recovery of the past or perhaps in its recovery *from* the loss of the past, resorts to "as if" constructions, to similes, metaphors. History's traces arise in an adamic imagination as not entirely traceable because they are mere metonyms that language cannot dominate. In fact, we will always have to suspect that language will have misnamed. All we can do then is turn to the land and seek to praise it anew so as to move forward from a backward spiraling thirst for nostalgia or revenge. Historical reconstruction through a poetic language means doing the impossible: imagining a history that only nature has witnessed, which is another way of reversing Stegner's paradigm. To be true to *history*, one must be devoted to *nature*.

New World poetics involves commemoration but with little or no recourse to monumentalization or institutionalization of the past. It represents a past that is not outside of time but ever subject to its reformation in the natural present. Even as the past is remembered, our attention is drawn to the environment that gives representative shape to that past. Michel de Certeau argues that when representations of the past are "historicized" in this manner, we discover that "time is precisely the impossibility of an identity fixed by a place" (147). Conceptions of rootedness in a place that disguise time are merely "dogmatic" (151). A temporally unstable place makes history alive precisely because its destiny is natural and it cannot be reified, embodied, or immured. The past must be perpetually recalled through the imagination, but because it is only recovered as an untraceable ruin, it signifies the insufficiency of our sense of place and belonging.

Lawrence Buell has insisted that a New World "aesthetics of the not-there" has aided authors to make the transition from a neocolonial pastoral language of environmental appropriation to one that delineates the contours of a genuinely new sense of place (*Environmental* 73). "Place-consciousness in literature," he writes, is "an incompletion undertaken in awareness that place is something we are always in the process of finding, and always perforce creating in some degree as we find it" (260). Our historicity emerges as the chief symptom of historical oblivion, since the absence of a recoverable past is always haunting our places of habitation, like Toni Morrison's 124 Bluestone Road in *Beloved*. A poetics of oblivion perpetually re-creates a sense of place, generates the need for more stories, and will always highlight, self-consciously, our own desire for rootedness and our own reading practices. It leads to the paradox of having to declare perpetually, as does Morrison, that "this is not a story to pass on" (*Beloved* 275).

Recognizing that incompletion stimulates cultural expressions that seek rootedness ensures perpetual renewal. This is because, in the words of Joseph Kronick, "to be original is to expose the past that lies before one, and to do so, the poet must cross the border to reappropriate the past and thus meet his own death" ("On the Border" 58–59). The writer crosses over into the space of oblivion, which is also the space of nature. My next chapter explores further the implications of this for the act of reading. Suffice it to say here that a New World poetics leaves the reader with the task of bringing new life, which begins with reading the dead, those who have passed on, and thus "passing on" their story. Kronick explains that "reading personifies . . . the poet; that is, reading gives a face to the dead" (*American* 116). Thus "to renew the visions and aesthetics of relating to the earth," as Glissant puts it, means to forsake the search for a myth of origins, for the Adam of Genesis, and to imagine "adamlike," to rephrase Williams, how our interpretive choices as readers reveal us to ourselves and enable a vision of ourselves as agents of rhetorical resurrections (*Poetics* 148).

Cross-Cultural Implications

New World poetry begins with a passionate search for history, but ultimately, according to Glissant, poetry "renounc[es] the notion, the beginning of history. These kinds of failure matter. Failure leaves a trail that permits others to go forward. The literary work, so transcending myth, today initiates a cross-cultural poetics. . . . In its impenetrable nature history feeds our desire" (*Caribbean* 82). His point is that if history is a muse, it is because it fails to be recovered and hence produces a desire to return to the land and to those synchronic parallels of historical experience that lie across a multinational and multicultural landscape. Diachronic history fails to inspire because, within one nation's borders, what it reveals is merely a metonymic part of a greater range of possibilities, the contours of which we can only imagine cross-culturally.

A powerful example of how this failure to root oneself in the past becomes meaningful is found in an essay by Wilson Harris from 1973 entitled "A Talk on the Subjective Imagination." I cite this example because it provides a framework for understanding similar adamic moments in the poetry of Whitman, Neruda, and Walcott. In this essay Harris argues: "[C]learly there is a signal lack of imaginative daring to probe the nature of roots of community beyond fixed or static boundaries. Also there is a signal lack of imaginative daring to probe the function of roots as a criterion of creativity and capacity to digest and liberate contrasting spaces" ("Talk" 37). As an example of the kind of imaginative daring he refers to he describes an episode on the Potaro River, a tributary of the Essequibo that runs out of Guyana into the Atlantic. He was working on a project to gauge the river for its potential hydroelectric power. The men placed two anchors, stern and aft, to fix their boat while they did their work. The boat began to take water, and the men had to cut the rope attached to one of the anchors. Three years later they returned to continue this work, and the identical problem occurred. This time they failed to cut the rope; instead, they yanked on it until the anchor moved and the boat righted itself. As they pulled the anchor into the boat they discovered that it had hooked into the very same anchor they had lost three years before. The appearance of these two anchors provided Harris an epiphany:

> It is almost impossible to describe the kind of energy that rushed out of that constellation of images. I felt as if a canvas around my head was crowded with phantoms and figures. I had forgotten some of my own antecedents—the Amerindian/Arawak ones—but now their faces were on the canvas. One could see them in the long march into the twentieth century out of the pre-Columbian mists of time. One could see the lost expeditions, the people who had gone down in these South American rivers. One could sense a whole range of things, all sorts of faces—angelic, terrifying, daemonic—all sorts of contrasting faces, all sorts of figures. (40–41)

Harris's own subjective imagination allows him to situate his experience in the context of a heterogeneous community's experience with the same place. The anchor represents a relic, a ruin from a previous attempt to root oneself in a place that, as is nature's wont, is ever shifting in a flowing current of time. The repetition of his attempt to gain a tenuous hold on place is uncanny and against the odds created by a violently changing place. Like an attempt to name his place, his anchor only repeats its objective by uncanny means, leading him to conclude that our repeated attempts to name our place reveal hints and phantoms of multiple and now faded human histories that haunt his own attempt at anchoring himself there. To feel at home is itself uncanny and repeated throughout history by many others before us. He contends that "the mystery of the subjective imagination lies, I believe, in an intuitive, indeed revolutionary, grasp of a play of values as the flux of authentic change through and beyond what is given to us and what we accept, without further thought, as objective appearances. It is not a question of rootlessness but of the miracle of roots, the miracle of a dialogue with eclipsed selves which appearances may deny us or into which they may lead us" ("Talk" 47).

Harris describes an imagination that adapts itself to nature's currents and refuses to accept one's place as given, as beyond the contingencies of human history. Harris's poetic imagination works through and past objective appearances to arrive at the violent and changing flux of human history and values embedded in the physical environment. To be rooted is not to own territory, to lay claim to a homeland or nation, but to discover oneself eclipsing, as words in a palimpsest, the lives and races that went before. And it shows us that the miracle of roots does not lie in the possibility of finding ourselves uniquely belonging to physical space but in recognizing nature's capacity to renounce our feeble efforts. Rather than lamenting this as a kind of doomed rootlessness, however, Harris insists that precisely because of this failure we are in a greater position to realize the potentials of a "heterogenous community beyond static cultural imperatives" ("Talk" 45).

The irony is that the New World's history of exploitation is precisely that which makes this kind of community possible, since it brought together seemingly incompatible peoples within the same landscapes. According to Harris, those discourses that would subject the "fantastic density of place" to the mere "poetry of science" and reduce it to "banalities" can only be overcome by linguistic humility ("Talk" 38, 41). Harris explains his own awareness of limitation: "[O]ne was aware of one's incapacity to describe it, as though the tools of language one possessed were inadequate. It was pointless describing the river as running dark, the trees as green, or the rocks as grey. All this seemed less to do with the medium of place and more to do with the immediate tool of the word as representing or signifying 'place'" (38–39). Only by discovering the "relative faces of the dynamic mystery of language" does he feel he has made "a groping but authentic step into the reality of place" (39). By failing to see our lives interwoven into the very life of the earth and by insisting on "absolute ethnicities and racial compartments . . . [w]e have *blocked* the flow of *measureless* cross-culturalities. We tend to claim fixed boundaries and to gain support for such absoluteness from animal habitats" (Harris, "Theater" 261). One careful look at animal habitats, however, is enough to teach us of "the incredible evolutionary detail" in all animals and that, like human societies, an "animal habitat, though apparently grounded, at a particular moment, in absolute space, is itself partial *in the life of the earth*" (261).

A simple process of digging into the history of a people in a local place leads to the inevitable discovery, like that of a deep map, that one people alone do not possess a place or have a solitary history in it; only comparative New World readings expose what Glissant calls the "concealed parallels in history" that haunt New World places (*Caribbean* 60). He calls for "an aesthetics of the earth" in which "land henceforth has no limits. That is the reason it is worth defending against any form of alienation" (Glissant, *Poetics* 150–51). This implies a critical approach to literature in the Americas that is simultaneously ecocritical and comparative, so that the work of ideology in its erasure of competing histories within a place is thereby more effectively exposed. The bodies of those thrown overboard in the Middle Passage, as Glissant expresses, for example, "*sowed in the depths the seeds of an invisible presence.* And so transversality, and not the universal transcendence of the sublime, has come to light. It took us a long time to learn this. We are the roots of a cross-cultural relationship. Submarine roots: that is floating free, not fixed in one position in some primordial spot, but extending in all · directions in our world through its network of branches" (*Caribbean* 67).

If underneath New World land and seascapes lie concealed parallels, we return to the question of how such parallels will find their way into representation so as to be recognizable. Harris suggests that those parallels can only be hinted at through repeated attempts to name them. J. Hillis

Miller contends that only through this process of trying to say again what failed the first time to sum up do we begin to understand that there is some "thing" to which multiple texts respond. Through comparative readings of, say, encounters with the rawness of nature or the experience of slavery we don't recover history in its entirety, but we begin to catch a glimpse of that "thing," that ethical obligation necessitated by historical omission, that has motivated the written text and to which it repeatedly responds. And the fact that we have different stories responding to the same ethical obligation liberates "the real thing latent in both" (Miller 123). Miller explains: "[O]nly if there is difference and deviation is it possible to distinguish between a knowledge simply of what the text says, which is relatively without value, and a knowledge of what the text represents or allegorizes" (117). Only by comparison can we understand the dimensions of our own uniqueness in the land.

We are then faced with the dilemma of choosing to believe that the gaps and violence of history and place shape language or that language is ontologically limited by its inherent brokenness. Faced with this dichotomy, we must either choose a hierarchical cultural model that imposes one region's experience onto all others or a cross-cultural model that imposes the shape of one New World language onto all regions. In other words, either O'Gorman was correct to insist that the New World was an invention, or it was a discovery. But as I have insisted, a New World poetics rejects this dichotomy as false, since it insists that the simultaneous gaps in New World history and in language itself make it unlikely that we will ever know which obstructs our access to the past and to our places of occupation more. It is in accepting this uncertainty that we can begin to appreciate the truth that oblivion lies at the root of both our New World language practices and our experiences in the land. New World authors suffer historical hunger in their search for roots, but, in failing to recover a whole and coherent past that gives reason to their presence in the New World, some turn to the cross-cultural space of landscape. Nature teaches that the reasons for our amnesia are as much due to rupturing violence and overlapping histories of transplanted peoples as they are due to natural process itself. The hope for building a different future depends on our capacity to balance our strange imaginative freedom from the life of the earth with our equally strange biological dependence on it. We need comparative ecocritical understanding of the Americas not because we anticipate facile parallels with other American experiences but because we recognize that parallels cannot be ignored any more than they can be definitively identified. Without recognition of what we don't and can't know about our relation to places and peoples, it will little matter what we do pretend to know, since we will have fantasized a community and a land that were always immune to violence, trauma, or loss.

If the pages of this book contain some well-crafted verse, may the reader forgive my daring in having composed it before him. We are all one; our trifles are of little import, and circumstances influence our souls to such a degree that it is almost a chance occurrence that you are the reader and I the writer—the diffident and zealous writer—of my verses.

JORGE LUIS BORGES, *Fervor de Buenos Aires*

CHAPTER 3

Reading Whitman in the New World

Between his 1605 publication of part 1 of *Don Quixote* and the 1615 publication of his promised part 2, Cervantes was beaten to the punch. An unknown author, Avellaneda by pen name, published a faux part 2 of the *Quixote* just one year before Cervantes. Instead of being stifled, Cervantes took full advantage of this crisis of authenticity. Knowing full well that his book questions the very notion of authenticity and thus leaves him vulnerable to imitation, he pleads in his prologue to part 2 for readerly patience and generosity. Finding the author's hand is a matter of forsaking the search for authenticity, suspending disbelief, and discovering what Cervantes calls virtue: "[T]he poor man may attain to honor, but not the wicked. Poverty can cloud nobility, but not obscure it altogether. Let virtue but show some light of her own even though it be through the straits and chinks of penury, and it will come to be valued by lofty and noble spirits, and so win favour" (469–70).

Poetry's capacity to enrich and teach depends on the reader's similar willingness to approach its most epiphanic moments as revelatory of deeper dreams and visions that do indeed transcend the limitations of particular personalities and nationalities. I say this neither lightly nor naively. We may only be able to intuit these dreams, but at least we will become generous rather than penurious readers, eager to be more creative of potentiality in our impulses than much literary criticism today teaches. Cervantes teaches here that it is a mistake to read literature as psychology or ideology writ large; we should instead read it as vision writ small. While it is important to recognize an author's hand, we must remain open to the work's poetics. If not, we render literature impotent in the face of our hemisphere's most pressing social and environmental problems.

Paradoxically, the poets with the greatest ambitions—and each of these three had legendary poetic ambition—have equally enormous personalities that would seem to always be integral to and thus also obstruct their most transcendent verse. The challenge for the reader is also to develop an adamic imagination that can return to the awe without naïveté but also without cynicism. Such a poetics of reading guided these poets in their own assessments of literary precursors, which would suggest that to place these poets together is not a study of literary history that traces lines and anxieties of influence or an "area studies" version of traditional notions of national literature. There are undeniable lines of influence extending from Whitman to Neruda to Walcott. Whitman exercised an important influence on both poets when they were only in their teens (the most emphatically on Neruda), and Walcott in the 1960s would discover and make use of Neruda's revision of Whitmanian New World possibility. But it is also equally true that all three poets drew idiosyncratic inspiration from their native lands and that Neruda and Walcott remained extraordinarily voracious readers of poetry from Europe and elsewhere in the Americas throughout their careers.

This chapter will explore first the way in which both Neruda and Walcott have read Whitman, specifically, his articulation of New World poetry. Rather than relying on a strict portrait of the "authentic" Whitman in order to expose their misreadings or intentional appropriations of the Good Gray

Poet, I will describe a model of reading as a poetics, as the epigraph suggests, that seeks to liberate the potential of New World poetry from the reductive claims of literary history or area studies. My hope is to lay the ground, to prepare the soil, as it were, for a reading of their work that reveals the dynamics of a sustainable and cross-cultural New World sense of place.

Neruda's Whitman

When one visits the houses of Pablo Neruda in Chile, one cannot escape the face of Walt Whitman. Neruda liked to place the portraits of his most important literary influences—Whitman, Baudelaire, and Rimbaud—on the desks and in the rooms where he did his writing. On one occasion a carpenter who was helping in the construction of Neruda's home in Isla Negra asked if the picture of the bearded bard wasn't Neruda's grandfather. "Yes, of course, my grandfather," Neruda reportedly said (Rodríguez Monegal, "Pablo" 204). More importantly, the intertextual evidence strongly suggests that Neruda felt a sustained admiration for Whitman throughout his prolific career. Neruda's Whitman is consistently the voice of the common workingman, the prophetic voice of democratic potential beyond the limitations of national chauvinism, and the great lover of the New World's lands and seas.

As Neruda became increasingly convinced that international socialism would alone provide the force necessary to combat the divisive and dehumanizing effects of First World capitalism, his determination grew to perform a poetic reach that extended North and South in the Americas. The very title of Neruda's famous *Canto general* alludes to Whitman's "Song of Myself," some of which Neruda translated and published. And the poem, as I explore more fully in chapter 5, invokes Whitman as Neruda's "hermano profundo" [deep brother], inhabiting the forest in his "barba de hierba" [beard of grass] (*OC* 1:689). He wrote two poems specifically in praise of Whitman, one in 1955 and another in 1973 shortly before his death. In the former he wrote that "me enseñaste / a ser americano" [you taught me / to be an American] and that

> entre los pueblos con tu amor camina
> acariciando

el desarrollo puro
de la fraternidad sobre la tierra (*OC* 2:433)

—

among the people, with the help of your love
caressing
the pure unveiling of fraternity
moves across the earth.

In the latter Neruda invokes Whitman as his "hermano necesario" [essential brother] in the battle to recover the soul of U.S. goodness from the evils of the Nixon administration:

Pidiendo al viejo Bardo que me invista,
asumo mis deberes de poeta
armado del soneto terrorista (*OC* 3:709)

—

Asking the old Bard to endow me,
I assume my duties as a poet
armed with the terrorist sonnet.

Neruda's Whitman is not only a prototype of the militant political poet but a model of the postcolonial struggle for new independence. Such was the message he gave to an audience of U.S. authors in his famous speech in 1972 to the PEN Club in New York City. Neruda sees himself as continuing Whitman's postcolonial adamic labor of bringing forth new civilizations from the wreckage of imperial history, portraying "la ascensión y la aparición de nuevos hombres y nuevas sociedades . . . a pesar de los dolores del parto" [the rise and appearance of new men and new societies . . . despite their birth pangs] (*OC* 5:359). Now an inspiration to aspiring nations in Asia and Africa, Whitman was in his time "el protagonista de una personalidad realmente geográfica que se levantaba por primera vez en la historia con un nombre continentalmente americano" [the protagonist of a truly geographical personality and the first in history recognized as a continental American to arise] (*OC* 5:359). Whitman offered Neruda and his Latin American contemporaries a voice of American possibility, of raw individualism and compassionate democratic impulses, that was never able to emerge, according to Neruda, during "tres siglos de dominación española en toda América" [three centuries of Spanish domination throughout the Americas] (*OC* 5:359). And it didn't hurt, either, that Whitman was an imagined ally "in the belly of the beast," in the words of José Martí, one who could be invoked as a conscience against the actions of the United States. That he was a dead ally was helpful too, since, given Neruda's prodigious ego, Whitman offered no direct competition; he could be Neruda's Virgil in his deep search for the soul of the continent.

What is especially significant for my purposes here is that Neruda read Whitman's adamic poetics as a vital postcolonial strategy rather than as the foundation of an American imperialism, as some critics have suggested. Arturo Torres-Rioseco, it will be remembered, was a Chilean academic at Berkeley who was instrumental in the 1940s and 1950s in promulgating not only Latin American literature within the United States but also the work of Whitman to new generations throughout Latin America. His influence reached Neruda directly as early as 1922, when Neruda reviewed Rioseco's translations of Whitman (Santí, "Accidental" 166). In a fragment entitled "Walt Whitman según Arturo Torres Rioseco," written in the 1920s, Neruda seizes upon Whitman's Adam as a figure that empowers the dispossessed. He writes: "[C]ada poeta cantará lo que quiera, sin hacer caso de preceptos higiénicos. Porque cada uno para cantar debe situarse como Adán: creerse el primer descubridor de las cosas y su primer dueño al entregarles nombre" [Every poet will sing what he will without paying attention to hygienic precepts. Because every poet in order to sing must put himself in the place of Adam: believe himself to be, in the act of giving things names, their first discoverer and first owner] (*OC* 4:310).

Growing up as he did in a country whose geography is often compared to an island because of its narrow land strip surrounded by the ocean and the Andes and its southern regions relatively untouched by Euro-Americans until the late nineteenth century, Neruda felt his isolation keenly. That Whitman's adamic expansiveness helped him to see himself in a context of broad solidarity diminished the anxiety of influence as well as the political distance between North and South:

> Si mi poesía tiene algún significado, es esa tendencia espacial, ilimitada, que no se satisface en una habitación. Mi frontera tenía que sobrepasarla yo mismo; no me lo había trazado en el bastidor de una cultura distante. Yo tenía que ser yo mismo, esforzándome por extenderme como las propias

tierras en donde me tocó nacer. Otro poeta de este mismo continente
me ayudó en este camino. Me refiero a Walt Whitman, mi compañero de
Manhattan. (*OC* 5:688)

——

If my poetry has any meaning at all, it is this tendency to stretch out in
space, without restrictions, and not to be happy to stay in a room. I had to
break out of my limited world by myself, not having traced it within the
framework of a distant culture. I had to be myself, striving to branch out
like the very land where I was born. Another poet of this same hemisphere
helped me along this road, Walt Whitman, my comrade from Manhattan.
(Neruda, *Memoirs* 262)

This adamic apprehension of a new world appealed to Neruda because
it implied a political solidarity that begins with careful attention to the local
environment. His own contact with the Edenic, historyless wilds of La
Araucanía first inspired him to write, as I explore in chapter 5, but it did
not take Neruda long to learn that he did not live in Eden because his New
World had a long and tragic story. If an adamic poetics was still desirable,
he had to emphasize more emphatically than Whitman did the political
implications of an Adam who builds and names a new society after political
apocalypse. Such was his intention in his startling and unusual poem *La
espada encendida* [The Flaming Sword] from 1970. Here the newness of the
world is "creada por la muerte" [created by death] (*OC* 3:560), but history's
victims are freed from the determinism of past events; by means of human
love "fue procreado . . . un mundo nuevo interno" [an inner new world . . .
was engendered] (*OC* 3:553). Rhodo is the "hombre enlutado / cubierto
de raíces y recuerdos . . . Adán / de las desdichadas guerras del hombre"
[a man in mourning / covered with roots and remembrances . . . Adam
/ of the wretched wars of man] (*OC* 3:592). Human love between the
postapocalyptic couple Rhodo and Rosa creates the inner new world, which
is a reflection of the innocence of nature that they remember; each lover's
presence causes a surge of "una fragancia de bosque verde" [a fragrance of
green forest] (*OC* 3:579).

This was Neruda's only book-length exploration of a postlapsarian
adamic poetics, but, as I have suggested and as my readings in chapters
5 and 6 demonstrate, it was an idea long germinating in his mind. A key
example is his prologue to the first issue of *Caballo verde para la poesía* [Green

Horse for Poetry], a journal of surrealist poetry that sought to publish the best young poets of Spain in 1935. Neruda had been criticized by the Spanish poet (and later Nobelist) Juan Ramón Jiménez, who advocated a notion of "pure poetry," for being a "great, bad poet." Neruda's response has strong Whitmanian echoes. He sought

> una poesía sin pureza . . . gastada como por un ácido por los deberes de la mano, penetrada por el sudor y el humo, oliente a orina y a azucena, salpicada por las diversas profesiones que se ejercen dentro y fuera de la ley. (*OC* 4:381)
>
> —
>
> an impure poetry . . . worn down as if by acid by the duties of the hand, penetrated by sweat and smoke, smelling of urine and lilies, sprinkled by the diverse professions performed within and outside the law.

This poetics attended to the spaces of contact between the human and the natural; it sought used and even wasted things because

> de ellos se desprende el contacto del hombre y de la tierra como una lección para el torturado poeta lírico. Las superficies usadas, el gasto que las manos han infligido a la cosas, la atmósfera a menudo trágica y siempre patética de estos objetos, infunde una especie de atracción no despreciable hacia la realidad del mundo. (*OC* 4:381)
>
> —
>
> from them the contact between man and earth is released as a lesson for the tortured lyrical poet. Used surfaces, the waste our hands inflict on things, the often tragic and always pathetic atmosphere of these objects, infuses the poet with a kind of attraction, not to be taken lightly, to the reality of the world.

Although this manifesto does not yet mention poetry's political engagement, which Neruda would advocate after 1936 and the Spanish Civil War, it is nevertheless a poetry of intent focus on the environmental and material life of man, one that would often lead Neruda into labyrinthine anaphoric enumeration that evoked Whitman (Stone 10). Such a poetics is what Peter Earle refers to when he notes that "Whitman's and Neruda's creativity were based on a standard of experience rather than theory" (190). This conclusion leads Earle further to observe that Whitman's romance with Manifest Destiny had more to do with a value system "based primarily on our potentialities" that provided Neruda an opening for recovering a New World poetics (190).

The New World poetics Whitman helped Neruda to forge required that Neruda overlook the possibility that Whitman's expansionism shared any affinities with, say, Nixon's imposition of democracy through violent means that Neruda so vehemently opposed. To admit this would have meant losing an important ally that allowed him recourse to the conscience of citizens of the United States as well as to his fellow Latin Americans whose vision of New World revolutionary potential was too geographically and culturally narrow. He either ignored or was unaware of Whitman's racial ambivalence in his poetry (e.g., Whitman's "The Sleepers" has been debated extensively by critics in this regard), his support for the U.S. cause in the Mexican-American War, and the unabashed embrace of U.S. expansionism he expresses in poems such as "Song of the Redwood-Tree" and "Song of the Exposition," which I explore in chapter 4. Perhaps more important, Neruda seemed unaware of the historical use in U.S. culture of Whitman as a voice of Manifest Destiny. The Mexican critic Mauricio González de la Garza vehemently argued just two years before Neruda's death that Whitman had been whitewashed by "mythomania" and that "no one has dared to look at him directly as the poet, par excellence, of Manifest Destiny" (13).

But Neruda sees something more transcendent, something "del eco subterraneo" [from a subterranean echo] (*OC* 2:428), about Whitman's democratic vistas. It is no accident that he argued in front of U.S. Marxists and sympathizers in the PEN speech that "su nacionalismo evidente es parte de un organismo universal" [his undeniable nationalism is part of an organic universal vision] (*OC* 5:359). Again asserting Whitman's affinity with the Latin American condition, Neruda turns away from stressing the differences of the Hispanic heritage of Latin America by insisting that "Whitman me enseña más que Cervantes" [Whitman teaches me more than Cervantes] (*OC* 5:359). By means of this kind of comparative triangulation between Chile, Spain, and New York Neruda appeals to a politically liberal, geographically broad, and postcolonial vision latent in Whitman. This terrain of Whitman's poetics had already been prepared by Martí, Torres-Rioseco, and others, as I explore below, so it isn't exactly idiosyncratic that Neruda saw him this way. What is more surprising is that Walcott would draw inspiration from both Whitman and Neruda and yet remain, by contrast, as consistently ambivalent as Neruda was celebratory about Whitman's importance to a New World poetics. A triangulation of the three poets exposes the ironies of their misreadings as well as what Earle calls the New World's "potentialities."

Walcott's Whitman

Walcott was similarly inspired by Whitman at an early age, perhaps even younger than Neruda's fifteen years, when a friend of his dead father, Grace Augustin, introduced him to Whitman's verse. Although she warned him against Whitman, presumably because of his sexuality, it appears that this was a time when Walcott's vision of his poetic potential germinated. Most specifically, this was the moment of his epiphany on the hillside he describes in *Another Life* (which I explore in more detail in chapter 7) when he fell to the ground, overwhelmed by reverence for life (Baugh 34). According to his biographer, Bruce King, under Augustin's tutelage, at the young age of eleven he "took an oath to live longer and be a better poet than his father," who died an amateur painter, poet, and playwright when Walcott was only one year old (24). Most evidence suggests, however, that Walcott never seriously undertook an attempt to write like Whitman (his attack on free verse throughout his career is legendary, and he often complained about William Carlos Williams, Allen Ginsberg, and others who expanded free verse under a Whitmanian banner). But, as I explore later in chapter 7, it is apparent that Whitman's elemental formula of instinctive praise for the immediate world was a vital tool, as it had been for Neruda, for Walcott to begin naming his island world with an epic ambition and to establish dialogue with fellow Americans in the hemisphere who suffered and yet took advantage of similar degradations under colonial conditions.

As he became more well known, particularly in the United States, he frequently invoked Whitman in admiration of several of his qualities. Patricia Ismond submits that Walcott's "political outlook retains the widest spirit of [Whitman's] ideal" of "democratic vistas" that outlined a "New World republican order—anti-imperialist, antihierarchical and antipaternalistic" (119). Like Neruda, he appreciated Whitman's capacity to dignify the common man but insisted on a distinctly nonpolitical view: "Pity the society that needs heroes. The people I honor and glorify from simplicity, not from a Marxist or political point of view, rather say from a whitmanesque one, are my heroes. Fishermen. Working men, isolated artists" (Walcott, "Interview" [Sjöberg] 80). He likewise recognized the Caribbean's need for poetry of Whitman's epic reach. Walcott complained in 1987 that Caribbean literature lacks the "epic of the Indian or the epic . . . of crossing the country. I don't just mean the Western; I mean something with a scale and width to it like Whitman's poetry. And it doesn't have any *tribal* power. It's all hermetic and private and individualistic and diaristic" ("Interview" [Montenegro] 141).

Walcott's Whitman, then, is not a prototype of the political militant, even though Walcott shares Neruda's appreciation for Whitman's poetics of local landscapes. From the perspective of his own context of rather marked racial and colonial suffering, Whitman's elations in the natural world strike Walcott in his youth as an opportunity to build a society anew. He is adamant, however, that society is built on art and nature, not on politics. It is Whitman the elated naturalist who is not embarrassed to embrace the New World that most appealed to Walcott. Drawn as he was to the most elemental aspects of the Caribbean environment as the basis for forging culture, he noted that many U.S. poets spend too much time indoors, whereas "the pages of a lot of great American poets like Frost and Whitman are ventilated by wind and weather" (Walcott, "Interview" [Montenegro] 141). While Neruda had access to ancient ruins in Mexico and Peru to inspire his historical vision of a New World alterity to European colonialism, Walcott preferred a vision that was more emphatically natural. As he argued in "The Muse of History," awe and praise for the natural world was more forceful in a postcolonial condition because it avoided the New World temptation to see history "as a creative or culpable force." Invoking poets such as Saint-John Perse, Aimé Césaire, and others, he explains that "the great poets of the New World, from Whitman to Neruda, reject this sense of history. Their vision of man in the New World is Adamic. . . . [T]hey seek spaces where praise of the earth is ancestral" (Walcott, *What the Twilight* 37–38). He adopts Neruda's notion that Adam is postlapsarian but insists on nature's superiority to politics. He acknowledges that Whitman's "leaves of grass" signified the "vernacular republic, the phenomenon (and the contradiction) of a daylight moon, powerful in its persistence, elate in its indifferences to digital time" (184).

In a recent interview Walcott elaborated on his vision of New World poetry:

If you were traveling in St. Lucia now, and you come across a ridge, and you look across the mountains, and you see mountains that are very forested, and you say, "Nobody has been over there"—it's still virgin in that sense. So to have that given to you, offered to you, it's something you couldn't do anything else but accept and consider yourself blessed to have. . . . I think even Borges feels that. I think that that sense of access is given and open because of history. It's not just an open gift, a lot of pain has gone into that, that is true of Neruda, and it's true of Octavio Paz. It's the idea of the New World, but not as an idea of exploration, of discovering something, because all that stuff was there. Nothing is discovered in the New World, because people lived in the New World. When the first ships come across, Western society teaches that these people are the pioneers, the people who are going to found cultures, and to teach, and to adapt the natives to their cultures. One has to consider the proportion of pain on the other side of the New World, that the New World is also very old. The balance that has to be found between the two is in believing that a possibility can happen, a new possibility of something really happening that is not political and is not racial and offers the possibility of sharing in the exhilaration of trying to make a new civilization. That's what's there in Whitman, though he doesn't say too much about the Indians, and I'd say in Paz and Neruda. ("Sharing" 142)

His allusions to the New World's ancient history recalls William Carlos Williams's argument that we must start with the facts of murder and conquest, but this last comment about Whitman's Indians illuminates Walcott's persistent ambivalence. It highlights a concern that Walcott expressed some twenty-five years earlier in a poem. Walcott began to explore Whitman's limitations at the same time he was exploring the redeeming aspects of that vision in the 1970s. Just two years after publishing "The Muse of History" Walcott wrote "Over Colorado," a short poem that invokes Whitman directly in the only such case in his oeuvre. The poem depicts Walcott flying over the Rocky Mountains on his way to Los Angeles, and as he contemplates the scenery below he thinks he sees

a frozen brave, his fossil
a fern-print on the spine of rock,
his snow-soft whisper . . .

the snow his praise, the snow

his obliterator. (Walcott, " 'Over' " 301)

Walcott introduces the devastation of the American Indian during the era when Whitman "prophes[ied] the great waggons." (This introduction comes at the cost of overstating it; Native Americans in the U.S. West are hardly fossils.) His aim is at least to qualify Whitman's democratic ideals with the presence of tragedy:

I see only this

through those democratic vistas

parting your leaves of grass. (301)

Walcott likewise has reiterated on several occasions that something in Whitman's broad embrace is not convincing, perhaps because he doesn't dig enough into the particulars of place: "Whitman's vigorous and hearty exhortations can tire, like a camp counselor urging all us tired boys to come down to the old Indian lake, when we'd rather sit here considering Miss Dickinson's worms or sparrows" (*What the Twilight* 186). Walcott's point is to suggest that although the New World's history of tragedy and suffering should not mire the New World poet in the trenches of revenge or nostalgia or morose modern individual angst, suffering should not be dismissed flippantly or handily, as he suspects Whitman sometimes does.

What is significant about this revision of Whitman is that we still see Walcott seeking to avoid a categorical rejection of Whitman on the basis of these limitations. Again from a recent interview:

All these large poets, poets with great vision, whether they are Neruda or St. John Perse or Whitman, the width of their vision is immense, it can be immense, but I don't necessarily think it's a racial thing, and it's not necessarily something you can attribute to a particular poet of a particular society either. And if that's the case then it's a limited vision of a thing. If you talk of vision, ultimately, you talk of vision that comes through experience, and so there's a radiance that comes out of experience. The inevitability of a Whitman comes out of history. It's an idea, it's a vision of things growing, and so on, but it is also a vision of something that is really confined strictly to perhaps one race, or perhaps one kind of American. Here's a Negro carpenter, a black carpenter, maybe an Indian doing something, and that catalogue of democracy that is there is fine, and Whitman is saying I am infusing all these people with a breadth, and a love, and a width, and a direction that is democratic, that is a vision of the future. But still, as pure as that may be, and as lovely as that may be in terms of the faith, the belief of what can happen, it doesn't go down deeper in terms of "Why is the carpenter not a General?" He says that there is a social order, and each person has the function in that society, that broad vision of a great America in which everybody has a job to do. But the jobs are the same jobs. They are hierarchical. It's not like saying, "I have a vision in which tomorrow the black man will be president." That would be polemical and a little dumb in a sense. On the other hand it would be closer to a radical possibility than the generic bliss that was there in Whitman, which can offend people who feel they are not particularly a part of that reality. (Walcott, "Interview" [Handley] 98)

Walcott's suggestion here is that Whitman's vision of democracy was of course limited by the age and by his personality, but Walcott's overall ambivalence suggests that he finds something in that vision worth revisiting and salvaging. And we must ask, Why? Aside from perhaps some advantage he won whenever, as a poet from a marginalized culture, he could prove himself widely read in the canonical tradition, Walcott was genuinely and deeply moved by Whitman's island poetics. Specifically, Whitman impressed him with his ability to start with the specificities of his own locale and extend outward to others in comparable New World circumstances. Walcott's own life experiences in the Caribbean were enough to stimulate this generous response to Whitman's vistas. Like Neruda, Walcott's emergence from geographical isolation brought into relief the potential of Whitman's grand vision over and against his limitations.

And perhaps there is another matter at work here, and that is the ambivalence apparent in Whitman himself, as I explore in the next chapter. This is an ambivalence, a New World dialectic of modernity, if you will, that stems from the complex nature of New World experience itself and that we find in all three poets. I am speaking of their visions that to varying degrees of success simultaneously strive to encompass an understanding of New World tragedy *and* potentiality. This struggle sometimes leads them into simplifications of New World experience, as evident in Whitman's overstatements of New World innocence, Neruda's ideological readings of New World history, or Walcott's backhanded erasure of Native America.

However, this struggle also bears good fruit, as they discover a sobering procreative power of language and an open-eyed apprehension of the human relation to ecology.

In his discussion of Whitman's and Darío's distinct visions of Columbus Ilan Stavans has described a seemingly irrevocable duality in New World experience that I believe is evident in their poetry. He notes a difference between "two civilizations, two psychologies, two Weltanschauungs: that of the South, timid and introspective, wounded by abuses, usurpation, and violence, with its eyes fixed on the past, and that of the North, victorious, confident, with its view to the future. In the year 1492 the twelfth of October is the hour zero, the ultimate date, the inauguration of tragedy for some and victory for others" (Stavans, "Whitman" 107). He concludes that the result is "two visions of the world: one individualistic and one collective, triumphant and fatalistic, democratic and politically corrupt, one futuristic and the other unjust" (111). Such dichotomies predominate in descriptions of the differences between the United States and Latin America, as we saw in chapter 1, and while the differences are not illusory, my readings of these poets intend to show the inherency of this dichotomy and its resultant ambivalence in all three poets. While their geographical and cultural locations inform their poetry, such specificities do not determine their poetics; a comparative New World poetics demonstrates how their ambivalence yields surprising and often unexpected results, especially in relation to the natural world, and that no longitude strictly marks their differences.

Reading Hegel

In light of this brief outline of how Neruda and Walcott have read Whitman we must ask, What kind of literary history accounts for these readings? How do we explain their similarities and differences? Can they be explained geographically or biographically? Historically or idiosyncratically? How can we justify any particular comparative choice without granting to the relations between the chosen writers some kind of historical fixity or causation? In other words, how can we avoid reinventing American exceptionalism on a larger hemispheric scale? To avoid this we must be content with knowing that the similarities and differences can't be satisfactorily explained, but once they are at least identified by the process of comparative readings, as the rest of this book will do, we can begin to imagine a context within which the comparisons obtain meanings. We begin to understand how a poetics in the Americas can plumb the more deeply seated questions of how to orient ourselves in the neighboring worlds we inhabit; our readings help us to see the strategies and ellipses whereby an adamic imagination surfaces and resurfaces in the complex texture of New World literatures and establishes a sense of place in a new world. It is perhaps easier to take one of two routes so as to avoid the complexity of this phenomenon. Either we assume that poets of the South read and admire Whitman because they are colonized by his seductive democratic embrace, or, in an effort to insist on a paradigm that doesn't privilege Whitman, we conclude that they consciously rewrite him in their own contexts and thus excise Whitman's imperialism from the concept of New World literature. That is, they cannibalize his democratic embrace for their own ends. I wish to demonstrate that these two choices are falsely dichotomized, but in order to demonstrate my point we must next turn to Hegel.

According to a Hegelian point of view, standing outside the determinacies of the Old World is nothing but a delusion, and while this Hegelian overreach is certainly frustrating, it is at least naive not to be wary of the illusions of postcolonial exceptionalism and the persistence of historical determinism. What makes Hegel prophetic, I wish to argue, is not that he was correct about the lands and peoples who were supposedly without History, of course, but that he sensed that the concept of Western civilization's telos would face its greatest challenge in the interaction of and relationship between competing outcomes—North and South—of Western civilization's advance in the Western Hemisphere. The United States and its southern neighbors, as Octavio Paz once argued, are at least "two distinct versions of Western civilization," and in reconciling or at least in coming to a historical understanding of their differences we can obtain a measure of freedom from the illusions of exceptionalism that have driven so much of postcolonial thinking in the Americas ("Mexico" 357).

It is perhaps in reaction to the determinism of such Hegelian logic that New World creoles of the nineteenth century so frequently insisted, as did Walt Whitman and then the Cuban poet and liberator José Martí, that the natural environment and historical experience of the New World were new and that they would inevitably create an exceptional political culture of freedom from the tyrannies of Europe. This creole belief in the abruption of Western civilization's longitudinal continuity in the Western Hemisphere opens the possibility of articulating a New World commonality that stretches along a north-south latitudinal axis. It may be obvious to us nowadays that nationalism in its various forms in the New World has replicated many of the Old World's colonial evils. Of course, José Martí, who endured a fifteen-year exile in the United States beginning in 1880 before his death in Cuba at the onset of the War of Independence, witnessed how the growing imperial aims of the United States were carefully couched in the rhetoric of democracy and postcolonial nationalism. His rather prophetic warning that "the colony lives on in the republic" has had strong currency of late (Martí 145). That currency, however, does not elide the fact that expressions of hemispheric solidarity run similar risks, evidenced by then–secretary of state James Blaine's Pan-American Congress in 1889. In the early modernist era of the late nineteenth century the idea of a hemispheric New World exceptionalism was particularly appealing to Whitman and Martí because it offered a north-south axis that promised liberation from Old World tyranny.

While this hemispheric strategy runs similar risks, the alternative to this creole vision of a transnational north-south exceptionalism may be even less desirable. To stress the inevitable continuity of the West in the New World typically results in emphatic denials or at least subtle occlusions of commonalities in the Americas. A key example of this would be Frederick Jackson Turner, whose frontier thesis stresses the western motion of empire. Although this movement presumably creates an exceptional U.S. culture in Turner's view, the frontier creates a democratic space that only moves west, not south to other American spaces, and ignores Hispanics, Native Americans, African Americans, those who are apparently without history and therefore without legitimate claim in Turner's polity. In his important comparison of the two thinkers Brook Thomas argues that Martí redirects Turner's famous frontier thesis along a north-south axis. Turner argued that the frontier facilitated the consolidation of the United States in the wake of the Civil War by turning our focus from the war's North-South conflict and arguing that "the slavery question is an incident," but it was not formative of American character, as was the western frontier (qtd. in B. Thomas 277). Thomas insists that "Turner's frontier creates a community of inclusiveness only through a subtle process of repression" of Native American and borderland peoples (282). Martí, he argues, picks up where

Turner left off and attempts to be more inclusive of those very subjects—
the exiles, the displaced, the transplanted—who have been affected by
the westward movement of empire. In so doing he brings our focus back
to a north-south axis by reminding his readers of the threat the United
States poses to Cuban and other Latin American chances for democracy.
"America," argues Martí, is not necessarily an increasingly democratic space
but rather a fissured entity in which the gap between democratic rhetoric
and the reality of social and racial divisions potentially widens as long as
colonialism persists. I agree, however, with Thomas that Martí is seduced
by his own version of American exceptionalism and that the success of
contemporary reconfigurations of American studies will depend on our
ability to confront the blind spots incurred by his exceptionalism.

What I wish to suggest is that the two possibilities of understanding
the New World's relationship to the Old are vulnerable, on the one hand,
to hemispheric neocolonialism and, on the other, to national chauvinism.
These two choices in turn produce the symptomatic reading of Whitman
south of the border as the categorical result of either Whitman's neoim-
perialist aggression or Latin America's savvy cannibalization. And perhaps
the impossibility of avoiding either of these two rather Hegelian choices
constitutes precisely the structure of the conflict that Hegel imagined between the North and the South. We can choose either to be inclusive of a
greater diversity of American peoples in our view of American possibility
(but at the risk of producing a vision that is hierarchical) or to be exclusive
of differences in an unmanageable heterogeneity so as to facilitate a more
narrowly delimited equality. That is, we can simplify the Americas and thus
risk a kind of cultural NAFTA that crushes fragile but vital differences or
we can simply ignore other competing Americas for the sake of managing
a less chaotic national identity. This is the very choice that Octavio Paz
argued exists in Mexico and the United States, respectively, a choice that
has led to a "history of a mutual and stubborn deceit" ("Mexico" 358) about
our north-south kinship; such deceit, he suggests, leads to two different
versions of national exceptionalism, both of which fail to reconcile equality
with diversity.

But perhaps these choices or these axes are false, since they lead to the
same redundant conclusions. Hegel believed that the true bearer of Western
civilization in the hemisphere would be the United States because of its
rejection of racial amalgamation. Perhaps he foresaw how slavery would

challenge the course of empire because of the violent transplantation and juxtaposition of races, and for this reason in his view only those American spaces that rejected the Latin American notion of a mestizo nationality (what the late-nineteenth-century Louisiana writer and civil rights advocate George Washington Cable once called "the maxim of barbarous times and peoples") would become the avatars of Western history (Cable 130). Exceptionalism was presumably the assertion of a break from the West, but Hegel and recent critics strangely agree that exceptionalism was an exceptionally Western impulse. It was the West at its most pure, renewed by its relocation into this hemisphere. Since the United States failed to reject and expel the amalgamating effects of slavery, we must consider the very real possibility that exceptionalism is not unique to the United States and that its symptoms appear in a variety of national contexts. This implies something quite simple really: exceptionalism is not so, well, exceptional, and perhaps if it is an "it" that occurs transculturally, at least it doesn't necessarily have the same function or results wherever it crops up.

What my readings of Whitman, Neruda, and Walcott reveal is not a family tree of American Adams, then, linked by historical causation and its anxieties of influence. Rather, we see poets who all wrestled with varying degrees of success with the persistent temptation to blame New World history on the Old World or on other foreign exploiters. Succumbing to this temptation allows the creation of a New World garden innocent of any history. But another equally strong temptation is to see in nature nothing but a denial of the shared legacies of the New World past, something each poet cannot easily accept. By "legacies" I mean the symptoms of colonialism that survived independence, such as racial segregation and other forms of racial discrimination and division; the contradiction of democracy's rise within such racially divided societies; and the complexity of cultures that emerged from fincas, plantations, and other local consequences of global economics that defied facile racial or geopolitical categorization. Those legacies are the material witnesses of what Glissant calls the "concealed parallel of histories" in the Americas, and yet they are also witnesses to the creolization of colonialism itself; that is, they bear witness to this hemisphere's responsibility for its own fears of racial contamination, racial injustice, and other onetime Europe's colonial sins (*Caribbean* 60). What facilitates Whitman's exceptionalism is his tendency to attribute these legacies exclusively to the colonialism of the Old World and to ignore those intra- and extranational spaces that challenged the autonomy, coherence, and particularity of the United States. In their own way Latin American poets who adopted Whitman's influence, starting first with José Martí and of course Pablo Neruda, similarly fell victim to their own versions of Latin American exceptionalism in their effort to cast off the burdens of foreign colonialisms. It is fair to wonder, then, where the seeds of this exceptionalism lie. An examination of Whitman's conception of New World literature will lead us to an answer.

Whitman's *Democratic Vistas*

Only six years after the completion of the Civil War, a war that many critics have argued was U.S. imperialism's first victory in its hemispheric reach toward Latin America, Walt Whitman wrote *Democratic Vistas*, an essay steeped in Hegelianism and intent on defining the parameters of a New World democratic community that would stretch from Canada to at least Cuba and Mexico if not farther to the south. The essay, written in several stages over four years, was a response to Thomas Carlyle's vitriolic attack on democracy's tendency to eclipse traditional cultural values in the interests of the mob (Reynolds 476–77).[1] While acknowledging the limitations of democratic society, Whitman's essay is an attempt to suggest ways in which that tendency can be kept in check by the powers of literature. Opposed to the Fifteenth Amendment on the grounds that insufficient literacy among voters would degrade democracy, "his postwar plan was primarily literacy" (Loving 303). Literature that inspires and guides democratic fervor is what Whitman denominates "New World literature," "athletic" and original works of hemispheric reach that would facilitate a consolidation of a "stock" personality emanating from the United States.

His impatient desire for unification in the Americas was understandable, given his close observation of the violence and social strife of civil conflict. Literature was a peaceful means of healing the nation, and the larger hemisphere offered a broader context in which a democratic push could work successfully against the colonial pull of racial slavery, inequality, and cultural dependence. It was apparent after the Civil War and the Mexican-American War that preceded it that the direction of American democracy was ultimately, in Whitman's words, to "dominate the world" by moving first southward into the rest of the New World. He did not say much, however, about slavery in other American nations or the existence of any other similar conditions, but to the extent that expansion meant contact with increasing racial diversity, his belief was that with a vibrant literary U.S. culture at the core, U.S. imperial influence would benignly eradicate colonial conditions on both sides of the border. The result would be a global solidarity with "all nations communing . . . one heart to the globe" (*PW* 246). As I show in my analysis of his poetry in chapter 4, Whitman's naive imperialism remained strangely and deeply blended with his considerable postcolonial ambition to the end of his life.

Democratic Vistas responds to the great postslavery debate of his time between the radical aims of political liberalism and the notion of a collective rule. Whitman writes of his concern about the "appalling dangers of universal suffrage in the United States" and concludes that unless we can muster a cultural force equal to the task of shaping a national personality, "[t]he United States are destined either to surmount the gorgeous history of feudalism, or else prove the most tremendous failure of time" (*PW* 318). While some offered the "rule of law" as the way to manage the potential chaos of mob rule, Whitman offered instead a democratically oriented poetic imagination infused by nature as the means by which those tensions could be reconciled. As Ed Folsom has cogently argued, however, Whitman's democratic vistas are plagued by a "paralyzing ambivalence" regarding universal suffrage and racial amalgamation, the issues that were most heatedly debated during Reconstruction (65). Consequently, although he frequently expressed more direct antipathy toward the notion of a democracy that included free blacks in much of his unedited prose, he consistently excised these comments from his work. The result of this "working against himself" was that he was able to "keep his books—and the Walt Whitman that lived in them—more open to diversity than the old Walt Whitman who lived in Camden, New Jersey was" (Folsom 82).

When Whitman speaks of feudalism in this essay he means to refer us back to the European origins of American culture: "European chivalry, the feudal, ecclesiastical, dynastic world over there" (*PW* 321). He does not appear to acknowledge the presence of a feudal system in the South that was still kicking after the Civil War and that was to play a major role in shaping the racial politics of segregation in the United States for the next eighty years at least. His democracy opposes this dynastic world but evades the tough question of universal suffrage in its presentation of a rhetorically free but racially unmarked (but therefore white) society. As Folsom explains, "while he says that he will not 'gloss over' the issue of universal suffrage, in the final version of *Democratic Vistas* that is exactly what he does" (79). Instead, what he celebrates is the rhetorically democratic openness and busyness of urban New York. Whitman of course was aware that hierarchical traditions lingered in the United States, and it was for this reason he hoped his poetry and that of "poets to come" would provide a curative for a nation that was expanding "with little or no soul" (*PW* 326). But it is clear that he did not wish to demean the word "American" by using it to denote any of the U.S. South's atrocities or their continuance on New World soil; he offered no admission of New World responsibility for such traditions.

So even though Whitman admits that what "continually haunts [him]" are "conflicting and irreconcilable interiors, and the lack of a common skeleton knitting all close" (*PW* 324), those internal conflicts are only evidence that Americans have not yet realized their separation from the Old World and that the lessons of American nature have not yet been able to take root. That is to say, he draws a demarcation between the Old and New Worlds but leaves an open door of possibility between the North and South of the United States and between the North and South Americas. The door, it might be more accurate to say, was only ajar, since his knowledge and understanding of the diversity of cultures in the two Souths was limited to only a few Spanish words, including *viva, libertad, americanos*, and the somewhat bastardized *camerado*. Notwithstanding the tremendous life his poetic influence has enjoyed throughout Latin America, Whitman's Latin America was vague and undefined, even though it was a crucial ally in his deposition of European hierarchy.

Whitman's "New World literature" holds this simultaneously liberating and consolidating promise by its adamic attentiveness to nature rather than by a colonial submission to tradition. It is a literature, as Whitman puts it in his famous opening to "Song of Myself," that puts "creeds and schools in abeyance" and that responds to "Nature without check with original energy" (*LG* 25). Valuing the geographical source of foreign literature more than one's own geography can be a significant colonial mistake. Old World "songs, ballads, and poems . . . permeat[ed] to the very marrow" its culture and taught the values of exclusion, hierarchy, and monarchy (*PW* 321). At least until the advent of his New World democracy, "literature, strictly considered, has never recognized the People"; for this reason Whitman believes that a New World poetry has the unique opportunity to manage America's increasing heterogeneity as it becomes a hemispheric community.

It is important to recognize that while Whitman's view of literature was, by his own definition, simultaneously liberating and consolidating, taken to their extremes these two poles create a polarity between revolution and despotism. Whitman's pen certainly trumps the sword: literature has more power to "cause changes, growths, removals, greater than the longest and bloodiest war, or the most stupendous merely political, dynastic, or commercial overturn" (*PW* 322). His reasoning about literature's power sounds anything but democratic: "The great literature penetrates all, gives hue to all, shapes aggregates and individuals, and, after subtle ways, with irresistible power, constructs, sustains, demolishes at will" (*PW* 321). However, literature's despotic power can be tamed if the reader is well situated on native soil. In "A Song for Occupations" he notes: "If you were not breathing and walking here where would [all histories] be? / The most renowned poems would be ashes" (*PW* 102).

Reflecting Emerson's philosophy of the primacy of revelation over tradition, Whitman's hope is placed in the writerly capacity of the reader to transform old texts with new understandings. As Robert Olsen explains, "Whitman values the activity and the enterprise that unearths new poetic wealth over the 'old spots and lights' of a heritage that deadens life because it does not give any place for living creativity, the ongoing activity of poetic production" (309). In his own poetry of course he expressed an unprecedented and explicit openness to the transformations of his meaning that would be wrought by future generations of readers. This openness requires, as Olsen further argues, that America "remain an unstable construct which resists the structure of a patriarchal tradition implicit in other parts of ["Song of Myself"]. The poem therefore has to turn on itself" (318). Literature elicits the individual response, and yet it is supposed to shape a community. These moments of contradiction in Whitman's thought are symptoms of the "ambiguities of liberalism, which wants to make individual liberty into the basis for a stable community" (319).

Consequently, literature's most important trait that serves to temper its own despotic tendencies is what Whitman calls in *Democratic Vistas* its "curious removes, indirections" (*PW* 375). While he insists on the dangers of reading the wrong (i.e., European) books, he more emphatically stresses the creative space such indirections open for the reader. Joseph Kronick notes that this is because literature's indirect speech, especially in the hands of a writer of such intent interest in facilitating the reading process as Whitman, removes itself from a diachronic model that subordinates the reader to literary tradition. Kronick states: "[T]he poet's pathway to the present . . . must be through language, and this pathway, says Whitman, proceeds originally by indirection, or diacritically, and not dialectically, no matter his identification with 'Hegelian formulas'" ("On the Border" 63). Cyclical time, not genealogical and linear history, characterizes the interaction between author and reader. This is because, as Kronick explains further, indirection means that "truth is always derivative; it is inextricably bound to history in a process whereby the signified is only knowable in its reconstitution in the trace, hence his emphasis on the need of every reader to reconstruct the book" (75).

The need to eschew penury in our readings of New World literatures is because truth derives from the passage of time and is only knowable indirectly through literature's metaphors, since, as Whitman wrote in "Passage to India," the past is "the dark unfathom'd retrospect." While this might sound like a repetition of Emerson's formula that the inevitable failure of memory leads the poet to appraise the present, Whitman's adamic imagination does not see such a dichotomy between the past and the present. Whitman's presentism, his adamic pose, escapes the arrogant claims of being beyond history because Whitman understood that "we know the present only in retrospect," and therefore its apprehension is as historicized as is the past (Kronick, *American* 95).

This understanding was not Hegel's influence but that of Whitman's growing knowledge of the natural sciences and evolutionary theory, which taught him that "we are all of us—every old man and baby, every rock and breeze and spear of grass—the same age, since we have all been around since the dawn of creation" (Kepner 193). Chapter 5 explores in more detail how Whitman's poetics of nature were influenced by the sciences, but it is at least helpful to point out here that although these sciences embodied the teleological spirit of Hegelian thought, it was nevertheless more apparent with each passing decade of the middle nineteenth century that the only access to this history was through focused reading and translation of the hieroglyphic signs in nature deposited in the present. History is realized as truth only in the act of reading, and thus Whitman "redefines history as a poetic interplay between texts" (Kronick, "On the Border" 61). He is not so much looking for new virgin ground to break but for poems and soils "containing history" (Kronick, *American* 5). Poetry here becomes a "troping . . . of the tropes that constitute history" and exploits the "rhetorical interplay that poses history as a problematic of reading, wherein temporal relations are generated by a linguistic process of exchange. A poetics of history will therefore be a poetics of reading" (6).

Reading others reading Whitman becomes one strategy for delineating his New World adamic imagination, but of course this too is a reading, and as such I am obliged to relinquish the pretense of "discovering" a History and instead recognize that I compose a new New World literary story. The intertextuality of Whitman in the Americas is a temporal relationship, as Kronick implies, and comparative literature, informed by the ever present moment of reading, I hope to show has the potential to temper if not deflate the hierarchies and priorities implied in the questions of generational influence, geographical centers and peripheries, and other genealogies of literature.

Latin America's Whitman

Despite his deep racial and democratic ambivalence and the despotic implications of an expansion of the United States' stock personality into the New World, most readers of Whitman from elsewhere in the New World welcomed his call for a natural poetry. Indeed, it was precisely the specter of this expansion that inspired José Martí to write his now famous invective against U.S. imperialism, "Our America," an essay that many critics today celebrate for having opened the study of "America" from the point of view of the Latin Americans who wage their own struggles for autonomy and freedom against the grain of U.S. imperialism into the hemisphere. However, what is rarely acknowledged is Martí's romance with American exceptionalism and his incapacity to accommodate racial difference in his own political vision, both of which are strongly apparent in his famous essay on Whitman, first published in Buenos Aires in 1887. Historically, it is undeniable that Martí's writings on Whitman and on Emerson and Poe as well had an enormous influence for years to come on Latin American thought; this was the moment that eventually brought Whitman into contact with Spanish America's "poets to come," including Rubén Darío, Pablo Neruda, and Jorge Luis Borges, among many others, and during the modernist movement in Brazil, where Whitman arrived via France (Bonetti Paro 59). Even within Chile Whitman's influence was extensive and went far beyond Neruda and included many of his rivals, including Pablo de Rokha, Vicente Huidobro, and, more recently, Gonzalo Rojas and Raúl Zurrita (Morales). Critics of Martí's relationship to Whitman's poetry celebrate the "symbiosis that existed between the two poets" (Doumont 207) and the idea that theirs was a kinship as "new American men who, although different in their ethnicities of origin, were yoked together in their vision of America and of the world" (García 83). As Fernando Alegría astutely observed, "no one dared doubt [Martí's] word, and Whitman continued to be accepted by the various literary schools as the unquestioned Apostle and the greatest poet of American democratic genius" (*Walt Whitman* 16–17).

Perhaps some doubt was called for, since, as I mentioned earlier, Mauricio González de la Garza somewhat polemically demonstrates that Latin America's Whitman was more a myth than a reality and that his political views were not always in harmony with Latin American interests.[2] Early-twentieth-century Brazilian critic and poet Tasso da Silveira expressed the desire for a Brazilian Whitman in part because of what Whitman inspired but also because of what he neglected. Whitman, for Silveira, was the " 'wonderful incomplete' because, although he exalted the whole world, when he sang America he referred to only one half of the continent" (qtd. in Bonetti Paro 60). It was up to southern poets to fill in the picture. The phenomenon of Whitman's popularity throughout the Americas raises the question as to whether Whitman succeeded in his own despotic aims to shape the hemisphere or whether we can consider his popularity as a kind of writerly revision and expansion of Whitman's democratic impulses. Was he misread or was he prophetic? What sense might we make, for example, of Pablo Neruda's puzzling claim that Whitman "es el primer poeta totalitario y es su intención no sólo cantar sino imponer su extensa visión de las relaciones de los hombres y de las naciones" [was the first totalitarian poet: his intention was not just to sing but to impose on others his own total and wide-ranging vision of the relationships of men and nations] (*OC* 5:359; "We Live" 232).

The separation of fact from myth in assessing Whitman's hemispheric career is challenging, not the least because of Whitman's own rhetorical stance as the prophet of "poets to come" who would provide greater syntheses of his vision of New World possibility. Alegría, in his 1954 classic,

Walt Whitman en Hispanoamérica, insists that Whitman's myth of himself became historical by virtue of his influence on numerous Latin American poets; thus, questioning the validity of the Whitmanian myth would itself seem to be undemocratic. Alegría documents the fact that Latin America, more consistently than the United States, has perpetuated this myth: "[I]n English the reader is accustomed to reading all kinds of opinions about Whitman, from the most inflammatory attacks and perfidious insinuations to the most inspired and fervent praise. In Spanish, as is well known, the tone of Whitmanian criticism has always been strictly that of veneration, if not of exalted tribute" (*Walt Whitman* 49). Despite the many ironies of Whitman's use among a variety of Latin American poets and critics that he observes, Alegría himself cannot help defending the myth against the latest findings in Whitman's biography. (What exactly he means by "perfidious insinuations" is not stated, but it would at least suggest the possibility of Alegría's refusal to acknowledge the possibility of Whitman's homosexuality.)[3] Too much, it would appear, was at stake to be critical of Whitman. Besides, Alegría reminds us that we are dealing with a "man who remade his own mundane image into that of the protagonist of *Leaves of Grass,* who made use of his new appearance in his dealings with his contemporaries, and who ends up believing so firmly and blindly in it that, in the end, he died in it, so that now we can no longer identify the simple man of letters who gave birth to the idea" ("¿Cuál Whitman?" 12).

Alegría implies that Whitman is a Don Quixote who died in an enchanted state, seduced by the word (his own), leaving us unable to insist on distinctions between author and protagonist, between his word and the world, or between his America and the Americas. While such a dilemma might not be such an unhappy circumstance, as Cervantes himself playfully explores, we are left with no choice but to be seduced by Whitman's powerful rhetoric, to assume what he assumes, and to make his prophecies realities. Olsen similarly argues that Whitman's vision of New World potentiality is so deeply infused by his performance of masculine "mating with his natural mothering force" that his "procreative powers are exhibited by the enormity of his poetic productivity, an exhibition by which he charges his readers to rival his potency in the creativity of the reading act. We become Americans in so far as we reproduce the act of poetic conception, gain entry into the male community Whitman calls the American poetic 'class'" (310–11). We have no choice but to join his club.

Olsen recognizes, however, as cited earlier, that Whitman must turn on himself, contradict himself, and thus prevent the reproduction of Whitman clones and the demise of democratic strength. But does this have to mean that all post-Whitman visions of New World democracy are his progeny? Is he the procreator of all of his readers, the Adam progenitor of the adamic imagination? If this is the case, then Whitman's openness is merely rhetoric and only serves to obliterate the difference made by any reader's imagination and particular circumstances. If this is not acceptable, and it is hard to imagine how it could be, then our only recourse as literary critics is to historical biography in order to make our documented case for the discrepancies between the myth and the man of Walt Whitman. Comparative literary critics in the Americas can say good-bye to textual exegesis because their task is now restricted to historical research.

Jorge Luis Borges offers a way out of this dilemma. A firm believer in the world-making powers of fiction, he nevertheless insisted on the need for at least a rhetorical acceptance of the reality against which poetry gains its metaphorical power. "Almost everything," he writes, "that has been written about Whitman is falsified by two persistent errors. One is the summary identification of Whitman, the man of letters, with Whitman, the semidivine hero of *Leaves of Grass*, as Don Quixote is the hero of the *Quixote*. The other is the senseless adoption of the style and vocabulary of his poems by those who write about him, that is to say, the adoption of the same surprising phenomenon one wishes to explain" (Borges, "Note" 236). He concludes quite simply that "the mere happy vagabond proposed by the verse of *Leaves of Grass* would have been incapable of writing them" (236–37). In other words, it is precisely the discrepancy that makes the literary achievement possible and valuable, just as in the case of Cervantes's Quixote it makes little sense to celebrate the pleasure of illusion without also understanding the necessity of the suspension of disbelief, a notion apparently lost on Neruda in his claim that Whitman was a more important teacher than Cervantes; even if we can never adequately name and represent the world that lies beyond representation, the idea of such a world nevertheless must not be abandoned.

Even though this tension is vital to the power of poetry and fiction, it is elided in Martí's assessment of the Good, Gray Poet. He argues that *Leaves of Grass* is a "natural work," not a book, that provides the New World with an example of a "fresh and robust philosophy" (Martí 239,

243). Martí wanted distance from Domingo Sarmiento, who appealed to literature as a means to civilize the indigenous barbarism of Latin America. The Cuban instead diagnosed Latin America's struggle as "not between barbarity and civilization, but between false erudition and nature" (141).[4] To share Whitman's belief in the spiritually dead work of European writers, the inherent potential of organic American letters, and the possibility of an inter-American democratic community, as did Martí, means believing that literature exercises an almost tyrannical power over the souls of readers and that, therefore, *what* one reads becomes more important than *how* one reads. Like Whitman, he wishes to harness literature's despotic power over the imagination in order to do the seemingly impossible: create a literary world without schools or creeds or even a pedagogy; this New World literature will be innocent of all ideology, since it is merely a space whereby American possibility might see and realize itself in its purity. This was, according to Julio Ramos, a significant move toward granting "an enormous degree of social authority to areas of Latin American literature, even within the state" (257). Martí writes: "[A]s a pudding conforms itself to its mold, so men take their shape from the book, or the enthusiastic teacher who first introduced them to the fad or fashion of the moment. The philosophical, religious, and literary schools straiten men with their liveried confinement of the lackey; men allow themselves to be put to the iron like horses . . . so that in the presence of the naked, original, loving, sincere, potent man . . . of a Walt Whitman, they flee" (239–40). Martí's *Leaves of Grass* is so natural that it is not a book but a naked man. This is as Whitman seemed to wish: "Camerado, this is no book," he wrote. "Who touches this touches a man" (*LG* 419).

The point here is that Martí sees literature as *mimetically* transparent. Even if he was distrustful of the implications, Hegel was right to insist on the inevitable discrepancies between form and content in literary representation. For Martí, literature will foster democracy when it transmits its content—impossibly—without mediation or rhetoric.[5] This seemingly advocates for literature as reproduction of the world.[6] The implication is disturbingly simple: just as he "defends the necessity of an unmediated, transparent form of knowledge" in literature, New World democracy will similarly render invisible, or at least benign, whatever rhetoric, institutions, and ideologies are necessary to forge it (Ramos 262). As Ramos explains, the danger is that "this defense of 'being,' articulated from within the emergent sphere of literature, implied a new frame—hierarchical and subordinative—of the heterogeneous American experience" (264). This exceptionalism, or what Ramos calls "the 'truth' of being[,] . . . is the effect of a formidable will to power" (264).

Martí agrees with Whitman that organic poetry, born of the soil and local reality of the Americas, can do more to shape democratic vistas in the Americas than anything else. In one rapturous moment in his praise of Whitman he exclaims: "Every form of society brings its own expression to literature in such a way that a truer account of the history of nations can be drawn from the stages of literature than from the parchments and chronicles of history" (Martí 245). Like Whitman's own avowed Hegelianism, which I explore further in chapter 4, for Martí this is because "there can be no contradiction in Nature" (245). A government inspired by nature and by local conditions will experience no racism because ultimately "there are no races" (150). Literature drawn from nature brings contradictions into synthesis and proclaims a vision of "the oneness in a higher peace of the dogmas and rival passions that divide and bloody nations in their primitive states" (150). He goes so far as to claim that poetry's vision should replace religion and the "hollowness and insufficiency of its ancient creeds" (150). Ramos explains that "[l]iterature, in the face of change, attends to the transformations and necessities of a modern life that invalidates all dogmas. . . . As we see in Martí, an avid reader of Whitman, literature reclaimed for itself the empty place in the secularized world left by the gods" (228). Influenced by Whitman and Thomas Carlyle alike, Martí calls forth like a prophet in the wilderness: "Arise, for you are the priests. Liberty is the definitive religion, and the poetry of liberty is the new cult" (246).[7]

The first of many New World myths of Whitman, Martí's appraisal of Whitman "does not necessarily give us a new Whitman, [but] it does give us, provided we read it carefully, a new Martí" (Molloy 379). Martí's (self-) portrait of Whitman influenced subsequent generations of poets in the Americas whose divergent assumptions of what Whitman had assumed have created various sects from the same sacred book. So perhaps Whitman is not such a demagogue after all, since whatever limitations he might have as a poet or as a visionary of democratic possibility in the Americas have been revised and synthesized in the Americas; his limitations have thus been rendered innocuous.

Doris Sommer argues that this is because of the paradox once expressed by Jorge Luis Borges in his short story "Pierre Menard, Author of the *Quixote*" that because all readings of the written word come from different geographies and chronologies they will inevitably mistranslate the word's meaning and thus escape monotonous repetition. Literature, in this sense, could be arguably perpetually Adamic, since it always signifies anew with every reading. "[Whitman's] seduction depends in fact," writes Sommer, *"on our initiative*, especially from our distance in time and from the spatial distance of readers, say, in Latin America. And this initiating willfulness on the part of his fans was an invitation to seduction that the idol had to accept; Whitman could not have dared to conquer that readerly will without losing all hope of his ultimate conquest" (78–79, emphasis added).

Maybe he isn't an imperialist, despite himself, since literature manages but can never control heterogeneity in the contact between the written word and millions of unpredictable readers who through the writerly imagination participate in a variety of imagined communities. Whitman understands the reading moment as the relationship between the "singleness of man" and "the mass," which, he writes, "for imperative reasons, is to be ever carefully weighed, borne in mind, and provided for. Only from it, and from its proper regulation and potency, comes the other, comes the chance of individualism. The two are contradictory, but our task is to reconcile them" (*PW* 13). Poetry is better equipped for this task than ideologies, schools, and creeds. Unlike a political ideology of, say, the United States as the world's promoter and defender of democracy, literature uses "indirection" and willingly submits itself as the agency of readers who will in a variety of unpredictable ways amend, even cannibalize, the text. Whitman's naive imperialism, while important to recognize, does not rob readers of their agency. Although poetry might engage in the rhetoric of prophecy and aspire to be beyond metaphor, it will nevertheless always rely on a suspension but never an abdication of disbelief in the act of reading.

But the pendulum mustn't swing too far in the other direction. Sommer insists, for example, that Martí is "winking" at us, knowing that he must praise the American bard if only to wrest from Whitman's grasp a workable vision of a hemispheric Hispanic solidarity and democracy. This only implies that all writing is innocent since all reading is autonomous. Such a view renders irrelevant any consideration of context. For example, we would have to ignore, as Sommer does, Martí's own ambivalence about Latin America itself and the philosophy of Latinamericanism, so shrewdly documented by Enrico Mario Santí ("Our America"). What of his intolerance for racial difference within his conception of a Cuban democratic polity and its role in founding a political philosophy that resulted in Cuba's race war of 1912?[8] Were these not factors that also shaped his view of Whitman, or must we assume the liberating misreading is automatic and inevitable? Must we disregard any relevance to the fact that Martí, although thirty-four years younger than Whitman, spent much of his time in the same part of the United States? Must we assume Martí is winking, or would it be arguable that Whitman's naive imperialism seduced Martí?

Or perhaps even more to the point, since literature's form is never irrelevant to its reproduction of the world, it is possible that Whitman's limited understanding of democracy was not always apparent in his words because of literature's inherent limitations. It is likewise possible that Martí's productive misreadings of Whitman were not always self-conscious or automated by virtue of his different origin but were perhaps the result of Martí's own idiosyncrasies. Did Martí apprehend Whitman's potential (and fail to see Whitman's failings) because of his own New World contradictions developed in parallel New World contexts in his native Cuba and in exile within the United States? All books are not equally despotic, and it seems no less simplistic to equate all acts of reading as acts of cannibalization and subversion. If we view literature, as does Whitman, as always earthbound and more conditioned by historical and geographical context than by the ethical choices of readers and writers, we imagine writers anywhere else in the Americas as categorically incapable of or invulnerable to their own troubling ambivalence about significant social problems.

Literature's adamic qualities arise neither from an insistence on New World exceptionalism nor from the reader's autonomy but from a dual openness in the exchange between writer and reader. As critics of "Pierre Menard" have pointed out and as my epigraph to this chapter humorously captures, "the creative process is essentially a reading," and therefore "only through an act of interpretation can that which is postulated take on meaning" (Matthews 63). This happens both at the moment of literary creation as well as in the moment of reading, according to Borges. Hence, "meaning develops from the twofold relation of the interpreter: to a literary dream world *and* to historical context" (Matthews 66, emphasis added). If comparative literary studies are to escape the dead-end choices of historical inquiry, reading must deny neither historical process nor the agency of the creative imagination.

The New World dialectic of modernity I referred to earlier must learn to find this balance if authors are going to escape the extremes of New World vindictiveness or triumphalism. This has been essential to Latin American authors' attempt to forge a unique Latin American, or New World, cultural reality through literature. Their struggle has been to work against the notion of historical determinism without pretending to work against history. The result has been, as Enrique Pupo-Walker argues, a blurring of the distinction between history and literature. To invoke Edmundo O'Gorman's important New World thesis from chapter 1, Columbus first "invented" America by using its geography as evidence of ancient legends, and since then "the lasting material of history has its deepest roots not in facts and ideas but in the perpetual flux of belief" (Pupo-Walker 11). Consequently, Latin American authors offer a historical philosophy that "enriches and enables a creative reading of the American past: a reading that, far from involving contemplative activity, induces us instead to remake and amplify our own cultural tradition" (13). This is consistent with a Borgesian vision of the literary imagination, which, unlike Whitman's and Martí's, stipulates in the words of Juan Goytisolo that "there are no sacred works, no works that function as fetishes, because time and other works are forever modifying them" (qtd. in del Río 467). To fetishize or demonize literature because of its political, geographical, or historical origin is to miss altogether the playful power of fiction's rhetoric, as does Martí when he praises Whitman's fleshy words; it is to forget that we are reading fiction, not viewing a life.

We cannot assume that as long as one reads Whitman from the South Whitman's imperial influence is innocuous and perpetually fruitful of new and improved democratic vistas. What is missing in such a belief is any evidence of parallels between the colonial legacies of other Americas and Whitman's, and we end up with a new southward-leaning frontier thesis à la Turner. This would ignore, among other factors, the vital transatlantic triangulation with Europe that Santí has documented influenced Latin America's reading of Whitman. Whitman, he insists, was not so much imitated as invoked in the modernist struggle for cultural emancipation. "The production," argues Santí, "of a Whitman question in Latin America constitutes a revealing instance of an alienated colonial discourse" in which Whitman's name was invoked as a defense against imperial impositions coming from the North and from Europe ("Our America" 162). Discursive practices in a globalized modernity in the Americas have undergone complex dis-locations, meaning that multiple geographical locations of influence and anxiety characterize many forms of modernism in the New World, thus rendering the question of borders secondary to a poetics of relation, to invoke Glissant's term, among New World authors. As Charles Pollard argues, "Models of literary influence that isolate writers by geography or race or that oppose writers in Oedipal struggles are simply not multifaceted enough to describe the transcultural relationships between writers in the twentieth century" (22). Inspired by Walcott's postcolonial reading of T. S. Eliot's "Tradition and the Individual Talent," Pollard remarks that the "si-multaneity of tradition is a superior way to conceive of art and culture than the linearity of historical progress" (49). This was what Borges meant to suggest when he claimed in "Pierre Menard" that all reading is "deliberate anachronism and erroneous attribution" (*Labyrinths* 44).

Such a vision of simultaneity preserves awareness of the agency of reader and writer alike and helps to expose the ways in which New World liter-atures, considered in comparative context, express both convergence and divergence. As Santí argues is the case with Whitman's history in Latin America, New World literatures "show the heterogeneity of [their] origins and the denial of a synthetic product. What purports to be the result of simple, direct influence is actually a rhapsodic production of contradictory, often erratic effects. . . . To acknowledge the erratic, accidental nature of that history does not lessen the values that spurred it originally. . . . [I]t merely restates the question" ("Accidental" 174). The transnational phe-nomenon of the adamic imagination otherwise becomes nothing more than evidence of a hemispheric transfer of Lewis's American Adam I outlined in chapter 1, with identical ideological content. Such is the logic of the Hegelian dialectic; as the Western "text" is displaced, transplanted into the New World, it is inevitable that its new readings will simply be syntheses of former contradictions, and a deeper and fuller realization of the freedom of self-consciousness will result. And Hegel's imagined conflict between North and South America may very well be won by the North to the extent that Anglo-American writers bear intertextual fruit in the Americas to the south. If Martí winks, then Whitman (and Hegel) wink back and have the last laugh because we cannot seem to see Latin American cultures on their own terms, riddled by the contradictions of their own historical experience and, most importantly, their writers vulnerable to their own limitations and privileged by their own inspirations.

A New World Poetics of Reading

While literature may seek to suture divided communities through the collective imagination and thus offer a possibility of democratic integration, literature also exposes rifts in communities that it does not always recognize. While it may be tempting for the reader to reduce the significance of these rifts to political limitations on the part of the author, Glissant suggests that such approaches are unfruitful; it would be far more useful to see these rifts as witnesses of a collective, almost Jungian, possibility that one writer, however flawed, brought within range of our perception, however imperfectly. While a writer may try to imitate literary models provided by preceding generations or by dominant geographies or, for that matter, to try to eschew those models and imitate a local reality, literature fails. But as Anthony Cascardi observes, "on such occasions, the articulation of the significant difference that 'makes it new' comes about through what Adorno might call the process of a 'second reflection' on the place of mimesis . . . [and this] allows the work of art to reassert its claim to be something more or other than a mimesis of the world, in part by reflecting on the impossibility of its ever being a full and complete mimesis of the world" (116). Reading in this sense is not merely Menardian by virtue of the reader's shift in geographical or chronological context but because of the reader's generative capacity to identify *the gaps between* literature and its context. Such readings rewrite imagined worlds and become works of fiction in their own right without a single author; after all, readings are, as Borges claims about Menard's text, palimpsests of previous writings and readings.

As the Guyanese author Wilson Harris believes, if we can avoid the temptation to allow our understanding of literary imagination to be overdetermined by obsessions with nationalism, we can begin to "assess a kind of seismic quality in a changing culture [of transplanted peoples], an epicentre that releases a suddenly fissured crack" on the global surface of human culture (*Womb* 127). That is, a given work of cultural imagination within one nation becomes an expression, or a "fissured crack," in a larger landscape shaped by subterranean, submarine cross-cultural forces. Harris envisions that literature, sometimes more radical and cross-cultural than even its own authors envision, is constantly drawn in and "conscripted by collective 'imperatives'" that seek evidence of exceptionalism. Literature, however, is "subtly enriched within and against other apparently alien imaginations," and by reading cross-culturally "each work complexly and peculiarly revises another and is inwardly revised in turn in profound context" (127).

As I discussed in the previous chapter, this poetics of reading is facilitated by a recognition of history's ellipses in a New World context conditioned by events of traumatic and often undocumented force. Glissant's analysis of William Faulkner is a helpful case in point. He states that Faulkner "needed to see whether he had been right to keep the county apart from the rest of the world in order for it to represent the world in its entirety" (Glissant, *Faulkner* 53). That is, in the end Faulkner's regionalism tells the story, now retold by Glissant, of the divisibility of the place, not its insular exceptionality. This divisibility does not present Whitman's "appalling danger" to the aims of collective social good but quite the opposite. It opens a community to its submarine, subterranean parallels with the other Americas, parallels that are not visible but intuited. This community of synchronic relations, for Glissant, is the surrogate, composite creation story for the Americas. New World history, with all of its fragmentation and creolization of foreign elements, makes fruitless the search for origins *ex nihilo* or even *ex occidente* of a whole and legitimate community. Literature in the Americas teaches that "we can accept that the sacred 'results' not only from an ineffable experience of a creation story but also, from now on, *from the equally ineffable intuition of the relationship between cultures*" (115, emphasis added). If New World literature is adamic, it is not because it is procreative of a new reality but because its readers imagine cultural origins in the future by contemplating what is between and among the Americas. We stand a chance of hearing how New World literature expresses these possibilities if we refuse the temptations of atavism and embrace relationality and if we understand that old familiar texts do not force themselves upon us as stories of other sacred origins for which we feel eternal nostalgia or even envy. Rather, they are remade in the interrelational readings that become possible in the context of composite cultures. We begin to imagine, then, that literature's force cannot be "mapped" according to history or geography by focusing on its lands of origin and reference. This does not have to be an overstatement of its power to forge metageographical imagined communities; its power is that it can expose the fissures, the liminal spaces between communities. This means that we need not fear or exoticize the West or the competing Americas of the North and the South but rather that we should remain open and cautious about our perceptions of our own cultural singularity.

To expect literature to confirm the singularity and exceptionality of either "World" or of either "America" would be to succumb to Hegel's a priori conception of Western Civilization and to create further conflict and division in the Americas. This would, of course, mean that literature of European origin, despite Whitman's and Martí's warnings, is not so toxic; indeed, their own literary careers demonstrate their fascination with and admiration for a number of European figures, including, among others, Rimbaud and Carlyle for Martí and Coleridge and Hegel for Whitman. For this reason, Angel Rama goes so far as to argue that "the axis that links European aesthetic inventions with American contributions (from Poe and Whitman to Martí and Darío) does not prevent us from recognizing the existence of this other strictly American axis defined by poets from the United States and Latin America," thus opening a triangulated view of these literatures as participants in Atlantic cultures (115).

But if we no longer read with the anticipation that literature will reveal something new to us, transmitted from the world of the writer, why read at all? As Cascardi insists, "forsaking the ambition to fashion anything radically new affords the possibility of an affective relationship to reality . . . [and] suggests that the weight of 'novelty' . . . will fall most heavily on the adjectival moments of thought. . . . Such inflections establish differences and validate the artwork's claim to truth, marking it as being both *like* and *unlike* the world" (122). That is, it is instructive to imagine that poetry participates in a conversation with textual precursors as well as with what Walcott insists is its "collective memory." In this way novelty no longer is a source of anxiety but rather becomes a symptom of a poet's capacity to respond to the voices of the past and to the weight of the present, what Walcott calls the "silent language of trees, stars, crabs, . . . ancestors, stones, squirrels, and God" ("Caligula's Horse" 140). "This is an injunction to critics," continues Walcott, "that their subject is not literature but God, or the gods, that poets should be judged by their approach towards this subject, and the source of that subject is chaos, ignorance, and its emblem is (how sweet Latin sounds in such contexts) *Dominus illuminatio mea*, Lord, who art the light of my life" (139).

If we remain open to the dual possibility that poetry is both creation and revelation and we therefore seek what it says beyond the bounds of the individual poet's personality, we will not lock ourselves into polarizations that present false choices between Old and New Worlds or between North and South Americas. We will place more responsibility on our own writerly shoulders to imagine like and unlike relationships. While we become self-conscious in this schema, self-consciousness is not passively given to us by our knowledge of historicity. There are simply too many gaps, ellipses, or deferrals that have generated present identities for various American communities. Origins are not found chronologically in the past or geographically elsewhere but are remade in our contemplation of the relations and spaces between borders in the present; if we are *self*-conscious, we are also conscious of others and conscious of the fact that we face the chance to remake ourselves every time.

I am speaking of literary influence that is fraught neither with anxiety nor with reactionary insistence on originality. While the adamic imagination has enjoyed a transnational and transgenerational career, triangulating Whitman, Neruda, and Walcott does not have to imply the existence of a transhistorical and exceptional New World unity. Not only would this elide my own agency as a reader, but it would limit my readings of their conceptions of adamic potentiality in the New World as manifestations of a literary genealogy. The triangulation of these authors helps to expose that it is not so much that Neruda and Walcott revise or rewrite Whitman but that all three attempt in their own ways to write the New World. Their Adams are eruptions on the surface of New World cultures that seek to understand their particularity and relationality. In this sense they represent creolizations of the adamic imagination rather than syntheses. This comparison highlights simultaneously the tenuous possibility of a kind of subterranean continuity as well as evidence of disruption. Just as Martí opened Whitman's door of inter-American democratic possibility wider and in his own way also narrowed the opening, so too do these poets respond to the particularities of New World experience. In any case the door still remains ajar, and the adamic idea may yet serve as a gateway to broader democratic vistas in the hemisphere, if as readers of American literatures we can tolerate this ambiguity.

Part Two

Who speak the secret of impassive earth?

Who bind it to us? what is this separate Nature

so unnatural?

What is this earth to our affections?

WALT WHITMAN, "Passage to India"

CHAPTER 4
Nature's Last Chemistry

The figure of Adam appeals to a desire for innocence in apprehending and naming the world so as to ensure a New World originality and authenticity. Such yearning for a complete break from the Old World has paradoxically fostered a Hegelian belief in the inevitable and utterly reliable directive of Western history and a paradoxical lack of interest in social and environmental particulars. Of these three New World poets there is no doubt that Whitman is the most attracted to this kind of Hegelian thinking. He is, indeed, a troubling tale of two poets: the poet who captured the spirit of Manifest Destiny and modern globalization and the poet who seeks to celebrate and liberate the local. My purpose is not to make a biographical or historical argument about why Whitman seemed so contradictory in this regard, but I intend to rise to the challenge of understanding what ecocritical difference these two versions of an adamic imagination make in his work. Whitman's struggle to overcome this ambivalence in his relationship to nature, while strange and often disturbing, is by no means unique; indeed, it is arguably emblematic of many of our continuing challenges to live sustainably in the New World.

Nature as History

As a member of the first generation of Americans born and raised in the newly independent nation, Whitman stood on the cusp of U.S. possibility. Born on Long Island in 1819 in an agricultural community and later raised in Brooklyn on the frontier of new urban expansion, Whitman was well positioned to witness the interaction between rapid democratization, urban growth, and the fate of the land. He continued to visit the countryside and shoreline of Long Island as a boy, and this vacillation between busy human activity and natural peace became an important dialectic in his poetry (Folsom and Price). Jerome Loving, for example, believes that Whitman was "essentially an island poet" because his experience with the unique combination of circumstances on Long Island became "the foundation of his aesthetic appreciation of nature" (27). Whitman spent his early adulthood working in journalism, teaching, and absorbing the arts and life of urban life and became a highly skilled observer of political life. When news came that his brother had been injured in the Civil War, he went south to serve as a nurse and witnessed firsthand how the nation was directly challenged by the war's violence and social upheaval. These were dark days for Whitman that provided the impetus for his poetic imagination. Jimmie Killingsworth notes that the war appeared to challenge directly his "earthly mysticism and his faith in the redemptive cycles of nature" but that he seems to have found in Hegel's dialecticism a balm for this particular wound (14).

Although Whitman's direct contact with Hegel's writings may have been negligible, he was influenced by Joseph Gostwick's 1854 book, *German Literature*, and by Frederic Hedge's *Prose Writers of Germany*, both of which gave accounts of Hegel, Schelling, Kant, Fichte, and others.[1] As M. Wynn Thomas argues, "he was in constant danger of being overwhelmed and undermined by the arbitrariness of events. His emotional survival depended on maintaining a teleology of conflict, on being credibly able to make the bewildering story of the war, as it actually unfolded, conform to his majestic vision of History" (90). Hegel offered Whitman a dialectical process by which the sufferings and ruptures of history facilitate growth and forward progress. By 1882, when he published *Specimen Days*, Whitman was convinced Hegel had presaged his own poetics of synthesis:

> According to Hegel the whole earth . . . with its infinite variety, the
> past, the surroundings of to-day, or what may happen in the future, the
> contrarities of material with spiritual, and of natural with artificial, are
> all . . . but necessary sides and unfoldings . . . in the endless process
> of Creative thought, which amid numberless apparent failures and
> contradictions, is held together by central and never-ending unity—not
> contradictions and failures at all, but radiations of one consistent and
> eternal purpose. (*PW* 608)

Whitman's belief in synthesis, of course, emerged long before whatever contact he had with Hegel's writing. Whitman expressed his sense of democratic optimism regarding the New World when he first wrote about Thomas Carlyle's conservatism in the *Brooklyn Daily Eagle* (Altman 104). In the 1840s and 1850s he was finding his voice in journalism as an impassioned defender of democracy, of political union, and of the laboring man. He was hesitant to advocate violent positions, as evidenced in his criticism of the more radical platforms of the abolitionists, but once armed conflict became a reality, even in the case of the Mexican-American War, he typically saw such eruptions of violence as imbued with a kind of inevitability (Allen 164). What he read about the German philosopher only seemed to confirm his own proto-Hegelianism. This was especially true as a result of winds of political change that made his own "free soil" views increasingly unpopular (ultimately costing him his job as a journalist), followed by the outbreak of the war, which placed democracy in full crisis (Allen 166).

Stephen Mack suggests that the first two editions of *Leaves of Grass* in 1855 and 1856 portrayed human events as manifestations of natural will. Agency and moral accountability are hard to fit within a philosophy that sees all things, all events, as so deeply interconnected and cooperative for the generally beneficent outcome of the future as to render individual agency nonexistent or at the very least irrelevant. Mack insists that this was consistent with the laissez-faire and Panglossian notions of Jacksonian America (60). We can see his synthesizing poetics in some of his more famous dicta from the 1855 edition, such as "I resist anything better than my own diversity" and "Do I contradict myself? / Very well then I contradict myself, / (I am large, I contain multitudes)" (*PW* 49, 96). He wrote in outrage of the failed revolutions of 1848 in Europe that "liars" now ruled the roost, but by 1860 he had concluded that "there are really no liars or lies after all" (*PW* 208).

While he did not exclude his incriminating attack on European liars in later editions, it seems that he was seeking a new way of thinking about human evil in which, as in Hegel's philosophy, difference, moral wrongs, and regrettable turns of history turn out to be less alarming than at first blush. In his 1855 preface he suggests that it is the task of the American poet to say to the past "Rise and walk before me that I may realize you. He learns the lesson. . . . [H]e places himself where the future becomes the present" (*PW* 13). The priority of the present and future over the past enables the poet to see the patterns of eternity emerge in individual moments and textures of the present. "Eternity," he writes, "gives similitude to all periods and locations and processes and animate and inanimate forms, and . . . is the bond of time, and rises up from its inconceivable vagueness and infiniteness in the swimming shape of today" (*PW* 24). Then, as if acting on his own directions, he adds these lines in the 1856 edition:

A vast similitude interlocks all,
All spheres,
. . . .
All souls, all living bodies though they be in different worlds . . .
All nations, colors, barbarisms, civilizations, languages,
. . . .
All lives and deaths, all of past, present, future,
This vast similitude spans them, and always has spanned
And shall forever span them. (*WWA* 251)

In his moments of dialectical optimism, which are by no means rare, there is no threat of apocalypse or of a return to the past. In lines composed in 1855 Whitman famously declared:

The smallest sprout shows there is really no death,
And if ever there was it led forward life, and does not wait at the end to
    arrest it,

And ceas'd the moment life appear'd.
All goes onward and outward . . . and nothing collapses,
And to die is different from what any one supposed, and luckier. (*PW* 37–38)

That he later connected this optimism regarding this eternal process of synthesizing opposition to Hegel is made evident in his brief 1882 poem, "Roaming in Thought (After Reading Hegel)": "Roaming in thought over the Universe, I saw the little that is Good steadily hastening towards immortality, / And the vast that is call'd Evil I saw hastening to merge itself and become lost and dead" (*LG* 231). In his 1860 poem written in order to introduce the book in place of his 1855 preface, "Starting from Paumanok," he claims: "I am myself just as much evil as good, and my nation is—and I say there is in fact no evil, / (Or if there is I say it is just as important to you, to the land or to me, as anything else)" (*PW* 16). (Paumanok is the indigenous name for Long Island, where Whitman was raised.) While this appears to suggest a kind of ecological wisdom regarding the danger of making distinctions between human and natural history, it seems to undo itself as an ethics simply by virtue of its dismissal of the possibility of irreparable harm or evil. His aesthetic capacity to experience wonder, to insist, as he does further in the same poem, that "all the things of the universe are perfect miracles, each as profound as any," appears to be irreconcilable with ethics (*PW* 19).

The ethical problem here is that when human and natural history are perfectly coincidental, human action becomes determined by cosmic forces far beyond the limits of human choice. Despite what Whitman believed was the intimacy of human and natural trajectories, he eventually discovered, in part due to the challenge posed by the Civil War and a democratic body in full crisis of collapse, that "social life is shaped by human events and decisions, not natural processes—that human history is not natural history" (Mack 100). Without this realization of what Mack calls a "failure of correspondence" between human imagination and will and whatever natural laws appear operative in the world we inhabit, poetry cannot teach us self-awareness or anything regarding our answerability to nature (108). "The terms 'human history' and 'natural history,'" he continues, "do not name quite the same things; as Whitman's poetry demonstrates, however impossible it may ultimately be to disentangle them, the great sin in failing to try is that it leaves solipsism insulated from critical scrutiny" (107–8).

Whitman's growing interest in the natural sciences and their seeming accordance with Hegelian teleology helped to sustain his confidence and optimism. Among the more significant influences on Whitman, a remarkably curious student of the sciences, are James Hutton's notion of deep geological time (Piasecki 35) and Charles Robert Youmans's confidence in the eternal nature of all matter in a "deathless universe" (Salska 40). Cecelia Tichi notes the impact of Arnold Guyot's 1849 book, *The Earth and Man*, which argued that the New World initiated the age of globalization. In Guyot's terms globalization offered a Hegelian synthesis of East and West, ancient and modern culture, and justified the rightful exploitation of the New World's natural resources (Tichi 221).[2] Gay Allen suggests that Whitman obtained his ideas about evolution from books on geology and astronomy and indirectly from the writings of Jean-Baptiste Lamarck (1744–1829), whose early evolutionary theories stressed the inevitable progress of all change and a guiding intelligence, or "cosmic teleology," that moved species forward according to an overall design (178). These developments shared a common understanding of nature as a "system of law-bound matter in motion" (Piasecki 35) and a common optimism that nature determined its own bounteous outcome. This suited well Whitman's notion of an open-ended democratic impulse he saw in both human and natural histories.

Mack suggests that the ongoing creative process implied in Whitman's cosmos helped to "undermine the myth of origins" by suggesting multiple and egalitarian roots of human beings (41). According to Glissant, multiple myths of origins create unpredictable results and are less likely to inspire a people's genealogical claim to territory. In this spirit Whitman argued that Spanish and Native American sources were of equal import to national identity: "[W]e tacitly abandon ourselves to the notion that our United States have been fashion'd from the British Islands only, and essentially form a second England only—which is a very great mistake" (*CPW* 388). A view of an amalgamated culture of multiple origins provides the challenge and opportunity for cultural self-creation. As Mack similarly asserts, "to believe that the cosmos is fluid and mutable is to doubt its capacity to ground stable and immutable moral principles. Or to put it somewhat differently, if we take seriously the idea that the universe we are a part of is still in the making, then we must consider it likely that we, too, are in the process of self-creation" (47–48).

No doubt this is the potential of Whitman's cosmological vision, but it is hard to argue that Whitman consistently accepts the existential burdens such a vision implies. The degree to which Whitman believes that the fluidity of the universe is nevertheless also always moving, according to Lamarckian design, its fluidity imbues human choice with little moral depth. We end up with the Whitman who saw his universe as "the cosmic analogue of American imperialism, Manifest Destiny gone stellar" (Mack 46). The difference has to do with Whitman's shifting degrees of confidence in the human capacity to read the signs of nature's seemingly inscrutable ways. In Whitman's poetry nature as a solved riddle or as an inscrutable mystery was the difference between a prelapsarian and a postlapsarian adamic imagination.

As I discussed in chapter 1, early natural science did not have evidence of human-instigated global environmental ruin, but by the late eighteenth century it began to shift to an epistemology that would eventually detect the signs of this ruin. With regard to Darwin, Joseph Kronick observes: "[I]n preserving a teleological understanding of the ends of man, evolutionary theory transformed the book of nature into a variable system of signs that could only be deciphered if read in historical terms" (*American* 90). This opposed the traditional Christian conception of the creation as eternal and embodying "a fixed and unitary meaning" (90). The epistemology of science to which Whitman appealed for a new, more democratic sense of New World possibility relied increasingly on empirical observation, a fact that strained his Hegelian confidence in inevitable synthesis. Instead of relying on revelation for a knowledge of our destiny, human society was impelled to place greater emphasis on its own capacity to gain knowledge. Although teleological, this emergent view of natural history implied that nature's outcome would depend on human understanding and behavior.

Songs of Synthesis

Whitman, however, wavered in his willingness to forsake his confidence in an "invisible hand" teleology, and this has to do with his growing anxieties about the direction America was taking after the Civil War. With the postbellum rise of corporate capitalism, increasing bureaucratization and centralization of the federal government, and growing American imperial ambition, Whitman felt increasing pressure to shape the "stock personality" of the modern America. His New World is rich with democratic possibility precisely because, like its natural environment, it is rife with variety and difference but holds forth an eternal promise of perpetual synthesis. When the war did not prove to have given birth to a new national spirit, Whitman gave himself the task to forge it. In his overt expressions of this national potential he appears to be the Hegelian poet par excellence. Among the poems that perhaps most embody this cosmic teleology are "Song of the Broad-Axe," "Song of the Redwood-Tree," and "Song of the Exposition." As Betsy Erkkila astutely notes, the latter poems' "strident, overbearing rhetoric is itself a sign of the psychic wound left by the war and the vigorous effort Whitman had to make in the postwar period to overcome the war's disruptive" force (*Whitman* 276).

"Song of the Broad-Axe," first published in the 1856 edition of *Leaves of Grass*, demonstrates, however, that the seeds of the Hegelian Whitman were sown even before the war. The poem announces itself as praise of human labor in the natural world. Reynolds explains: "The axe's connection to nature, to the past, to artisan labor, and to the construction of an ideal nation made it seem to him a superb symbol of unity," one that Whitman hoped would rival the eagle (359). Whitman's praise of labor was instrumental in his desire to instill greater appreciation for the diversity and range of American people, and for Whitman as well "American" is broadly defined as including the "shapes of a hundred Free States, begetting another hundred north and south" (*WWA* [1856] 160). That is, labor implies for Whitman both a foundational and cross-cultural moment.

Whitman's view of labor as a sign of the newness of the world and of future solidarity exercised a powerful influence on Neruda and on other left-leaning sympathizers with the working class. Similar to Neruda's advocacy of an "impure poetry" that would later serve his socialist views, Whitman developed a protosocialist aesthetic philosophy embedded within a democratic, geographical, and materialist focus (Erkkila, *Whitman* 73). He was reluctant to go as far as Hegel did to advocate the strength of the state to restrain individual interests and instead believed, like many socialists, in the importance of solidarity and freedom found "within a political community," something he hoped poetry could forge (255). He once admitted that despite his reservations about political extremism his poetry was socialist "intrinsically, in my meanings" (qtd. in Reynolds 142, see also 496). That the latter poems, "Song of the Exposition" and "Song of the Redwood-Tree," would appear to be extensions of the logic of the "Broad-Axe" poem only demonstrates the ease with which Whitman's protosocialism could furnish the expansionist spirit of U.S. capitalism. Whitman was, after all, admired by fans such as Andrew Carnegie.

Section 2 of the poem is a litany of praise for the diversity of climes, soils, landscapes, and natural resources available in his country, but there are evocative hints of a much broader hemispheric economic history. Whitman suggests, for example, that the white and sweet potatoes, lands of sugar and rice, as well as lands of wheat and maize should be equally celebrated. He then links the hemisphere with a celebration of those who labor on the frontiers of westward expansion and have discovered the "beauty of independence, departure, actions that rely on themselves, / The American contempt for statutes and ceremonies, the boundless impatience of restraint" (*PW* 137).

Whitman adamantly insisted that working the environment will do more to shape America's democratic personality than the material consequences of that work. The essence of the struggle for life is the human personality that emerges from the fray ("nothing endures but personal qualities," born of raw contact with the earth). He uses this anthropocentrism to New World advantage: European civilizations, with their monuments, heroes, and martyrs, will "fill their hour, the dancers dance, the musicians play for them, / The show passes" (*PW* 140). The typical indicators of achievements of civilizations, "the tallest and costliest buildings or shops selling goods from the rest of the earth, / Nor the place of the best libraries and schools," will not tell the true story of what endures. Presaging Neruda and Walcott in their disavowal of monumental history, what endures for Whitman is an intangible reality of democracy "where no monuments exist to heroes but in the common words and deeds" (*PW* 141).

The song of the broad axe is the song of democracy, the song of an emergent New World that uses tools not for warfare and rebellion but for constructive labor: "O see the scaffold untrodden and mouldy, I see no longer any axe upon it, / I see the mighty and friendly emblem of the power of my own race, the newest, largest race" (*PW* 144). Instead of queens' heads rolling, "The solid forest gives fluid utterances, / They tumble forth, they rise and form" into the many shapes that make a new society possible (*PW* 144). Social violence in a hierarchical society has been replaced on the altar by natural violence within a democracy. And, more to the point, both forms of violence, because of their supposed democratic consequences, are categorically innocent.

Nature in such a scheme is relegated to mere backdrop, at the service of human civilization. It is true, as Gary Snyder alleges, that Whitman seems hard-pressed to accord to nature the same democratic respect he does to his fellow human beings (453). In "Song of the Broad-Axe" nature has "always served and always serves" the foundations of human civilization. In Whitman's poetic history nature's service is hidden by its "sterile" and "forbidding appearance," but since the time of the Greeks, the early American "mound-raisers," and "those whose relics remain in Central America," human beings have learned how to extract its goods for their own benefit with technologies such as the axe (*PW* 144).

One important development of Whitman's time that also fed this Hegelian optimism was the notion of environmental reform. Tichi has traced the origins of environmental reform to the Puritans and argues that the idea reaches its apotheosis in Whitman's poetry. Environmental reform is based on the premise that nature in its postlapsarian state is in need of improvement and that humankind can redeem itself to the degree that we reform and improve the natural world. Although this is a flawed environmental ethic because of its overt anthropocentrism and reluctance to understand nature on independent terms, Tichi insists that the idea clearly denounced "promiscuous exploitation of the earth" (2). As she explains, "man evinces his dominion (and correlatively his stewardship over God's created world) by making a visible impress upon the natural world. He legitimates his claim to America by manifestly improving it" (10). While stewardship can temper the most egregious offenses of exploitation, it is clear, both on historical and ethical grounds, that this philosophy has often motivated manipulation and degradation of nature just for the sake of exercising this privilege.

Environmental reform relied on two contradictory positions, both of which are implicit in Whitman's vision. The first is the notion of "an intrinsically regenerative American geography" and the idea that "the New World itself was somehow exalted by the very presence of these chosen people, the Americans" (Tichi 246). The contradiction lies in this simple question: does New World nature redeem human society, or do New World Adams redeem nature? One's answer to this question will largely depend on what kind of intrinsic qualities can be ascribed to human intention or, for that matter, to nature. One way out of this dilemma philosophically is to forsake the idea of any intrinsic value ascribed to either and to measure the worth of all interactions with nature on the basis of their outcome for the larger biotic community, as Aldo Leopold argued in 1949.

For Leopold, the axe is valuable because of the natural history it lays bare. Although some form of "necessary violence" is required to sustain human life, an eye to the well-being of the entire biotic community opens us to a broader ecological ethic that does not displace but rather contextualizes human social ethics. What the axe yields is both human benefit and a history of the violence that provides it. Leopold's journal is a poetic record of the violence his presence in nature reveals. Writing about one's violence potentially serves the same function as the axe, since it confesses the hand of violence that enables the telling. Like Walcott's appraisal of Crusoe's adze and Neruda's belief in poetry as a form of carpentry, Whitman similarly sees the "poet as forger, maker, welder, temperer" and implies that poetry itself is a kind of "creation, renewal and transformation" of the world (Tichi 230). Unlike the rather pronounced violence Walcott's poetry exposes in *Omeros*, for example, we have no reckoning in "Song of the Broad-Axe" of the violence that the axe's constructions have left upon the earth. The poem consistently points forward to a time when all acts of violence will be synthesized and rendered necessary by the telos of history. The future becomes the space whereby Whitman's merely materialist view of America is spiritualized. As Tichi explains, his view of a "carpentered America" is a poetics of the future, beyond the end point of "the airless fixity of a materialistic New Earth" (234, 231).

Whitman's 1856 optimism was transformed by the Civil War and its aftermath into a more emphatic future-oriented poetics of national unification. Even his 1867 edition of *Leaves of Grass* showed the efforts of a poet anxious to "bind up the nation's wounds" (Erkkila, *Whitman* 260).[3] His perpetual obsession with revising the book—including new poems, deleting others, and revising some of the staples of *Leaves*—parallels an era in which the nation was seeking to reconstruct itself. He still felt the same urgency to shape and speak for America but with a growing awareness that the more radical views of his poetry needed tempering according to the age (261). He had always exhibited conservative caution even before the war in the face of more extreme demands for change, such as those proffered by the abolitionists, but his poetry became increasingly expressive of a future-oriented progressive optimism further and further removed from reality.

One result of this shift is a more focused interest in the transformative effects of human technology and labor on the environment that he describes in "Song of the Broad-Axe." Like many in his time, Whitman "looked upon advances in science, technology, and industry as part of the march of humanity out of the feudal past and toward the democratic future" (Erkkila, *Whitman* 266). Democratic benefits notwithstanding, this approbation of technology leads to a dangerous tendency to read nature's significance only in terms of how human events register changes on the pages of the landscape; that is, it leads to a "substitution of nature for history" in which nature is "emptied of its earthly contents and filled with human politics and history," which, as Killingsworth argues, is precisely the case in Whitman's "globalized" poems such as "Song of the Redwood-Tree" (70, 75).

As it became more apparent that U.S. society was rapidly developing the capacity to transform the entire continent, Whitman tried to find in that spirit of expansion and inventiveness traits that would rescue America from soulless materialism. His resolution is, in effect, a marriage of human and natural histories, resulting in a vision of a "man-managed" utopia, "directed by the willful desires of humankind" (Piasecki 40). This was Whitman's New World revision of naturalism, replacing the god of transcendence with a god of immanence who "resides in the workings of man in nature, not above them" (40). The advantage of this philosophy is that it stresses the agency of human beings to determine environmental outcomes.[4]

Whitman's most explicit approbation of New World Manifest Destiny, "Song of the Redwood-Tree" from 1873, exonerates social violence as well as violence inflicted upon the natural environment. Providence, as in Hegel's view, is naturalized, and man becomes the agent of earth's and his own becoming and of history's telos. While Whitman places ethical trust in human agency and not in biblical promises of divine design, he creates difficulties in apprehending nature on autonomous terms. He is less inclined to yearn for a pre-Columbian natural paradise or for wilderness and instead marvels at the effects on the natural world of the remarkable expansion and development of postbellum society. "American settlement and expansionism" for Whitman, argues Robert Olsen, "are the poetic outcomes both of natural processes and the progressive consequence of willful human activity" (307).

Despite the poem's refusal to confront the era's economic and social anxieties head-on, Whitman makes at least one important claim about the natural world that would not have surprised the Native Americans dispossessed by American expansionism: the tree has a soul and speaks. Whitman's animism arose in the period prior to the Civil War as a result of the convergence of several philosophies of the time. Influenced by William Paley's view of the sacredness of all physical things and more especially by the spiritualist Emanuel Swedenborg's doctrine of correspondence, which stipulated that all physical matter had a spiritual counterpart, Whitman's animism was a self-made patchwork philosophy (Reynolds 242, 265). As we will see in later analyses, this view pulls him back from some of the extremes of his Hegelianism, especially when it emerges independent of human economic interests and appears to represent an autonomous and intrinsic subjectivity. Such forms of imagined animism, although clearly products of human imagination, manage to temper his teleology and provide what William Major calls a "more benign instrumentalism" (91). As Major argues, "such slippage between the instrumental and animistic philosophies, their confluences as well as their incongruities, essentially defines the culture's inability to recognize in nature a living presence not wholly in the service of human interests" (92).

This struggle between instrumental and animistic worldviews informs the dynamics of this poem. Whitman's redwood announces: "*For know I bear the soul befitting me, I too have consciousness, identity, / And all the rocks and mountains have, and all the earth*" (*LG* 175). Rather than providing a consciousness that counters the progressive logic of the Manifest Destiny of the frontier, however, the trees submit:

> *We who have grandly fill'd our time;*
> *With Nature's calm content, with tacit huge delight,*
> *We welcome what we wrought for through the past,*
> *And leave the field for them.*
> *For them predicted long,*
> *For a superber race, they too to grandly fill their time,*
>
> . . . .
>
> *In them these skies and airs, these mountain peaks, . . .*
> *To be in them absorb'd, assimilated.* (*LG* 175)

Despite Whitman's insistence elsewhere that nature feeds itself on human loss, in this case the opposite occurs. These trees bear no vestiges of any prior human history; Native American history among these trees has vanished, and the result is that the trees are both wholly other and wholly subordinate to the evolving human story of western man, which they welcome with "*tacit huge delight.*" The forests

> But come from Nature's long and harmless throes, peacefully builded thence,
>
> These virgin lands, lands of the Western shore,
>
> To the new culminating man, to you, the empire new,
>
> You promis'd long, we pledge, we dedicate. (LG 175)

Society on the eastern seaboard continued to disappoint Whitman or at least forced a postponement of his elation in the present; no doubt influenced by William Gilpin's exalted view of America's westward expansion and by his own earlier "free soil" views, Whitman's West offered the possibility of renewal and synthesis (Loving 382; see also Klammer 31). Whitman is clear that the invisible supernatural realities of the New World have a very particular aim. These realities are the "*unseen moral essence of all the vast materials of America*"; they constitute the Zeitgeist of forces that "*really shape and mould the New World, adjusting it to Time and Space, / You hidden national will lying in your abysms, conceal'd but ever alert*" (*LG* 176). Instead of seeing the microbial laws of degeneration and transformation of life that constitute the indifference of nature, Whitman here sees beneath the soil "*vital, deathless germs*" that move the hemisphere's environmental history forward in ways that are beyond our comprehension but well within our human interests. This prelapsarian adamic view sees evidence of the newness of the New World in the germinations of the past, which have been totally transformed so as to enable the *arrivants* to be "assuming, taking possession" in order to establish "a grander future" (*LG* 177).

The point here is that because Whitman declares the New World's indigenous past irrelevant, its natural history is subordinated to and assimilated by a human future. This amounts to a simultaneous extermination of Native Americans and nature in order to achieve a New World nativity in the land and forecloses the possibility of an admission of nature's open-ended and unguessed outcomes; the New World is new but only because it offers no competing historical claims, human or natural, and was simply "long prepared" for its destiny in the hands of "broad humanity, the true America" (*LG* 177). To know nature on its own terms and to understand its particulars are not necessary, since the promise of a "grander future" renders all of our environmental behavior categorically innocuous.

Whitman articulates this postbellum embrace of the possibility of historical synthesis in the "Song of the Exposition." The poem was written on the occasion of the Fortieth National Industrial Exposition, to which Whitman had been invited to deliver a poem in 1871. The context explains the poem's overt celebrations of American technology and industry. Despite his adamant distrust of all things European expressed in his contemporaneous essay, *Democratic Vistas*, the poem betrays a deep-seated confidence that Western civilization will find its highest expression on American soil. In this sense the New World is new by means of a pure creation of a synthetic transformation and appropriation of European values on American soil:

After all not to create only, or found only,
But to bring perhaps from afar what is already founded,
To give it our own identity, average, limitless, free,
To fill the gross the torpid bulk with vital religious fire,
Not to repel or destroy so much as accept, fuse, rehabilitate,
To obey as well as command, to follow more than to lead,
These also are the lessons of our New World. (*PW* 262)

This is an invitation to the Muse of History to "migrate" to "a better, fresher, busier sphere, a wide, untried domain" (*PW* 262–63). This Muse responds to the summons but is perhaps moved by a kind of Hegelian "long-nurs'd inclination" and "natural gravitation" toward the West. Her presence on this side of the Atlantic will not threaten the New World with obeisance to foreign metropolitan norms because she departs a dead world, a

once so mighty world,
now void, inanimate, phantom world
. . . .
Pass'd to its charnel vault. (*PW* 264)

Whitman's sleight of hand here allows the Muse to arrive on New World shores orphaned, no longer at home in the halls of ruined castles but "here, install'd amid the kitchen ware!" (*PW* 264). Instead of an architecture of monumentality to match the Old World,

We plan even now to raise, beyond them all,
Thy great cathedral sacred industry, no tomb,
A keep for life for practical invention. (*PW* 265)

When faced with the paucity of material witnesses to the events of Caribbean history, Derek Walcott embraces the ironies of the empty landscapes of the New World as the starting point for the construction of a new culture. Whitman, on the other hand, cannot resist the lure of the Muse of History and celebrates American inventiveness, practicality, and material manifestations of civilized modernity. This is not a disavowal of metropolitan norms emanating from Europe but rather a declaration that the New World will do the Old World better with superior accomplishments in photography, natural science, mining, printing, agricultural advances. The poem is, in other words, an exercise, without irony, in naturalizing the signs of modern industrial and technological development. Whitman insists that these signs of labor along with the workmen themselves "shall be your pyramids and obelisks" (*PW* 267). His growing awareness, evidenced here, of the problem of alienation caused by modern labor becomes a proto-Marxian poetics that praises "the present and the real, / To teach the average man the glory of his daily walk and trade," that of "manual work" (*PW* 268).

The common man and common labor provide the foundation of a New World unity, a vision that would prove irresistible to the more fully Marxist visions of the Mexican muralist Diego Rivera and of Pablo Neruda by the mid-twentieth century:

And thou America,
. . . .
Thou Union holding all, fusing, absorbing, tolerating all,
Thee, ever thee, I sing.

Thou, also thou, a World,
With all thy wide geographies, manifold, different, distant,
Rounded by thee in one—one common orbic language,
One common indivisible destiny for All. (*PW* 269)

What inspires this neoreligious vision of a unified hemisphere is the industry of American capitalism, the axe men, the steamers, the blacksmiths, the foundries, and the farms of the United States. Only the violence of the Civil War appears to have slowed the advance of the Muse and her economic and social progeny, but with the conclusion of the war Whitman portrays a nation that stands not only to unify under a single flag but to unify the hemisphere under this "universal Muse" (271).

Illegible Nature

There is, however, one significant difference between Hegel and Whitman that at times dates his adamic imagination after the fall and liberates his poetry from the seductions of Manifest Destiny. Whitman once prepared a never-delivered lecture on the German philosophers based primarily on his reading of Gostwick's book. In these notes, later included in *Specimen Days*, he concludes that ultimately Hegel's rationalism is unsatisfying: "[C]ompared with the lightning flashes of the old prophets . . . [Hegel exhibits] something cold, a failure to satisfy the deeper emotions of the soul—a want of living glow" (*PW* 610). He concludes that the theories of philosophers and of Darwinian evolution "neither comprise nor explain everything." Although he believes in the same end result as Hegel of synthesis of all contradiction and in the similitude of all matter and men, the synthesis can only be expressed through metaphor and is thus only intuited. Mack explains that "metaphor reminds us that the objects of experience do not tightly control our words. The failure of correspondence [between words and their objects] may have forced the poet to confront the inevitability of metaphoric language, but in so doing, it liberated him to exploit its rich potential" (8). It is vital to remember that "Whitman's poetry [unlike the rhetoric of philosophy, history, or science] implicitly seems to demonstrate an awareness of the arbitrary nature of linguistic communication" (5). Whitman's self, in other words, in the final analysis is not determined by history, environment, or context; it is "irreducible to any conception of external reason" and is thus free to imagine and act in the interest of myths and metaphors that might produce a worthwhile future (5). For this reason, although agnostic on a great many religious questions, Whitman's antinomianism resembles a kind of religious faith, because we arrive at understanding by means of intuitive trust and not through deduction, logic, or phenomenological study. Note, for example, these lines from "Song of the Open Road":

> Wisdom is not finally tested in schools,
> Wisdom cannot be pass'd from one having it to another not having it,
> Wisdom is of the soul, is not susceptible of proof, is its own proof,
> Applies to all stages and objects and qualities and is content,
> Is the certainty of the reality and immortality of things, and the excellence of
>   things;

Something there is in the float of the sight of things that provokes it out of the
soul.

Now I re-examine philosophies and religions,
They may prove well in lecture-rooms, yet not prove at all under the spacious
clouds and along the landscape and flowing currents. (*LG* 126)

Despite his claim in the above lines that a "certainty of the reality and
immortality of things" is within reach, he also acknowledges that this certainty is only paradoxically realized in the uncertain experimentation of the
poetic imagination in relation to nature. Poetry paradoxically is the memory of unofficial histories, all that "eludes discussion and print," including
those of "the interminable hordes of the ignorant and wicked," the poor
and unknown, as well as the spiritual and natural realities that escape the
grasp of human historical imagination (*PW* 100, 113). He creates poems
so as to provide "a psychological tool to help the ego gain leverage over
the internal and external conditions that would deprive the self of any
power of autonomous action (however relative that autonomy might be)"
(Mack 78). Poetry is the language that attempts to give shape to what is
otherwise unseen and unknown and in so doing signifies the poetic freedom of the soul to interact with the world. This is why poetry proceeds,
according to Whitman in "On a Beach at Night," by means of "indirection."
Killingsworth explains how this works ecocritically:

> What we have then is a metaphor in which the figurative element (the
> word) is named but the literal referent (something the earth has or does)
> is left unclear, in the form of a riddle or a mystery. The earth has or does
> something that corresponds to what people do when they communicate
> with words, but this something cannot be communicated directly in
> language. . . . The soul shares with the earth a system of language and
> meaning distinct from what we normally understand to be human
> language and logic. The one may "echo" or resonate with the other
> without containing or fully comprehending it. (26, 28)

While Whitman clearly declares his interest in "Song of Myself" in society's
forms, its banks, schools, churches, schools, he also confesses that his
poetry fails to capture nature and the lived reality of human society: "My
words are words of a questioning," he admits, "and to indicate reality; /
This printed and bound book . . . but the printer and the printing-office

boy?/ The marriage estate and settlement . . . but the body and mind of the bridegroom?" (*PW* 84).

Completed in 1870 at the same time he wrote *Democratic Vistas*, "Passage to India" is one of the more Hegelian poems he would write, mostly because it imagines the present as fully embedded in and fruitfully born from the past.[5] It was an expression of the evolution of New World history, "the unfolding of cosmic purposes," as Whitman later explained (qtd. in Reynolds 500). There are no ruptures in this evolutionary process: "For what is the present after all but a growth out of the past? / . . . / So the present, utterly form'd, impell'd by the past" (*PW* 275). This past is not clearly discernable (it is "the dark unfathom'd retrospect!" [*PW* 275]), but, given Whitman's enthusiastic response to the recent completion of the transcontinental railroad, the opening of the Suez Canal, and the start of a new chapter of trade with the East, he cannot escape the conclusion that the outcome is certain (Mason 508). The poet tells us that the meaning of Columbus's voyage was to globalize the world, to cross oceans and bring racial and geographical distances near, "The races, neighbors, to marry and be given in marriage, / The oceans to be cross'd, the distant brought near, / The lands to be welded together" (*PW* 276).[6]

Walcott's assessment of the meaning of the Columbian exchange, almost a century after Whitman, brings to the fore Whitman's simplification of the New World's historical ironies. On its face, Whitman's theory is correct in suggesting that ultimately Columbus's voyage has brought us into the modern world of global contact and its resultant racial and cultural mixtures. Even though Walcott feels compelled to express gratitude for the Americas Columbus has left in his wake, his is a gratitude forged in a dark reckoning with the evils of New World history. The past is neither forgiven nor condemned by the present, since no causal or intentional links can be made. The bounties of the New World are the fruits of accident, whereas for Whitman they are expressions of a deep and hidden purpose. Hence, in contrast to Whitman's triumphalism, for Walcott his thanks are "strange and bitter and yet ennobling" (*What the Twilight* 64).

Walcott insists on the value of Whitman's conclusion, however, that the New World is cause for grateful praise. Whitman's poetics leave enough room for this reckoning of New World evils because his vision of the past's unbroken continuity into the present, the Zeitgeist, is measured poetically, not historically. History's continuous and consistently expanding meaning is like some subterranean movement, "As a rivulet running, sinking now, and now again to the surface rising, / A ceaseless thought, a varied train— lo, soul, to thee, thy sight, they rise" (*PW* 277). History's shape is perceived by the soul of the poet who is not deceived by what appears to be a fragmentation and interruption of the linearity of Western culture. He sees instead, for example, that Columbus's Asian error was in fulfillment of a much deeper purpose. Whitman tells Columbus: "Centuries after thou art laid in thy grave / The shore thou foundest verifies thy dream" because America was born (*PW* 277).

His search for continuity of purpose in history leads him to the first parents, which signals his intent to displace history with myth and thus announce his poetics. He describes Adam and Eve's state as one of bewildered, almost troubled, wonder full of "yearning" and "restless exploration" as they seek to find a sense of place and belonging. He then asks who will soothe them and explain the meaning of these unsettled feelings: "Who speak the secret of impassive earth? / Who bind it to us? what is this separate Nature so unnatural? / What is this earth to our affections?" (*PW* 278). The poet alone rises to this task so as to "justify" and explain that the commotions of human history are at their root an elemental response to the oddity of particular environments in which we find ourselves. The irregularity and "stubborn particulars" of the earth around us, which are so much more prevalent in Whitman's earlier poetry, resist any attempt to transcend moment and place in the interest of synthesis (Erkkila, *Whitman* 273). In this poem to "justify" these particulars is to link them to the development and motion of the modern New World and its global age. The poet will be the one who imagines what starts to look like Glissant's totality, which can only be imagined:

> All these separations and gaps shall be taken up and hook'd and link'd together,
> The whole earth, this cold, impassive, voiceless earth, shall be completely
>   justified,
> . . . .
> The whole earth, this cold, impassive, voiceless earth, shall be completely
> Nature and Man shall be disjoin'd and diffused no more,
> The true son of God [the poet] shall absolutely fuse them. (*PW* 279)

The paradox of this assertion reveals itself when we consider that poetry's force relies on the silence and opacity of the garden in which Adam and

Eve find themselves. If the gaps are stopped and the voiceless earth finally speaks its meaning, poetry ceases to be metaphor and becomes revelation. For poetry to realize this dream it would require bringing an end to bewilderment before nature and calming the restlessness it inspires. The reader of the poetry of the "true Son of God" will not need imagination, even though it is the poet's task, as Whitman argues repeatedly, to train the reader's mind to imagine more than is apparent on the page. Whitman assigns himself a task, the impossibility of which he does not seem entirely ignorant. Mack explains that Whitman is the pragmatic, rhetorical prophet, one who does not worry himself so much about his poetry's "correspondence to known fact or its ability to explain the present but on its capacity to produce a worthwhile future" (5). The poem becomes a means of testing the efficacy of ideas. Whitman's poetry has the high ambition of knitting together the seeming disparate directions taken by natural and human history presumably under the rubric of some "ceaseless thought" that would unite them, but this can only be accomplished by means of metaphors, metonyms, and *as if* constructions that point to but cannot embody the "ceaseless thought."

This postlapsarian Adamic imagination is forever foretelling but holding at bay the summation of experience, pointing to a future possibility of fulfillment and justification of adamic awe and wonder. As Kronick puts it, "Eden, says Whitman, is what lies before us" ("On the Border" 79). His adamic impulse here is not nostalgic but procreative, seeking to forge a world in which nature and human beings are no longer "disjoin'd." To the extent that Whitman gives in to the temptation of believing in poetry's constative rather than merely performative function, he seems to lose his own sense of wonder and bewilderment before nature; mystery is reined in under the yolk of ideology. Fortunately, he was not always guilty of this impatience.

At the poem's conclusion the poet cannot escape his own adamic restlessness in the face of nature. His are Tennysonian journeys of the soul and mind, not of the body through the physical particulars of the earth, that take him back "To reason's early paradise, / Back, back to wisdom's birth, to innocent intuitions, / Again with fair creation" (*PW* 281). He suspects that he will gain the perspective from which to stitch together the gaps of human experience from these intuitions that are born in the raw encounter with Nature. And yet as he nears this supernatural realm of reality the boundless and fearless soul of the poet nevertheless "shrivel[s] at the thought of God, / At Nature and its wonders" (*PW* 282). The soul, the "actual Me" of the poet, does not share this fear and will draw the poet nearer to the "orbs" and the "vastnesses of Space" precisely because it is not bound by the body or by language, but that does not mean the poet can escape his bounded, earthly condition (*PW* 282). Complete transcendence of the "stubborn particulars" of the earth is neither desirable nor possible. His adamic imagination moves into the very mystery of "waters of the sea," "winding creeks and rivers," "woods and fields" at the same time that the soul calls him to "farther, farther, farther sail!" (*PW* 283, 284). This unresolved polarity exemplifies the dialectic of New World modernity to which I referred in the previous chapter and helps to explain why Whitman's adamic poetics move between the extremes of hegemonic globalization and cross-cultural and ecological solidarity.

Only four years later Whitman expands further the adamic ideal, only this time in direct reference to Columbus himself. For Neruda and Walcott Columbus is too deeply tied to the machinery of colonialism to vie for this role. They will choose more ambiguous figures from the colonial experience such as the poet/soldier Alonso de Ercilla y Zúñiga and Dafoe's Robinson Crusoe in order to make a similar claim that adamic potentiality lies at the root of New World experience. Whitman's choice of Columbus is symptomatic of his political naïveté, perhaps, but it nevertheless allows him to insist on the power of the physical world of the Americas in dispelling Old World myths, an idea that proves useful to the later poets. Whitman's "Prayer of Columbus" portrays a man both surprised and bewildered about where he finds himself. Instead of offering a celebration of the evolutions Columbus's actions have made possible, as he does in "Passage to India," Whitman chooses to portray Columbus at his moment of greatest challenge and self-doubt, nearing seventy years of age, shipwrecked on Jamaica, without the support of his crew and of the nation that sponsored him. An unmistakable emblem of Whitman's own age and situation, his Columbus prays:

> Is it the prophet's thought I speak, or am I raving?
> What do I know of life? what of myself?
> I know not even my own work past or present,
> Dim ever-shifting guesses of it spread before me,

Of newer better worlds, their mighty parturition,
Mocking, perplexing me. (*PW* 290)[7]

Columbus is an emblem of the poet not because he represents the quintessential conqueror of new space but because of his error and confusion. Whitman suggests that the world's newness and seemingly perpetual births mock Columbus's and the poet's attempts to name the world and to assign it fixed meanings. The particulars of the earth, always resistant to facile transcendent ways of knowing, come through the senses and challenge the autonomy of the mind. Mack provides relevant insight here: "But what is truly miraculous about the visual, auditory, and tactile sense is not simply that they are inexplicable organic marvels that enable the body to operate; it is more that, as contact points with the environment, they provide the machinery for the self's reorganization" (29). Physical contact with the world provides an opportunity for exploration of the self's predetermined boundaries, but in so doing it also lays the grounds for the discovery of the imagination's freedom. The self does not transcend the physical world but is creatively invented by the senses that open a relation to particular places. The unexpected and yet undeniable moment when human choice meets the inhabited world constitutes the adamic moment for Whitman, a moment in which human language and comprehension seek to bridge the gap between "disjoin'd" human beings and the "impassive earth" they inhabit, but Columbus's anguish communicates that certain knowledge of the natural history of human beings is elusive.

Whitman did not intend this adamic encounter with nature to remain irrelevant to or apart from the concerns of human social good, as is evident in an ecocritical reading of *Calamus*. The poems under this title are today most famous for their coded celebration of homoerotic love, and while I would not deny that Whitman may have intended to give covert expression to such love, it is equally important to recognize how Whitman intends to combine the possibility of homoerotic love with the politics of fraternal democracy and the poetics of New World nature.[8] Whitman himself explained: "[T]he special meaning of the *Calamus* cluster . . . mainly resides in its Political significance" (*CPW* 751). For Whitman, "affection of man for man" was a crucial means by which "the United States of the future . . . are to be effectually welded together, intercalated, anneal'd into a Living Union" (*CPW* 751). Critics note, however, that the poems remain "Janus-faced" by virtue of their simultaneous expression of homosexual love and political "democratic brotherhood" (Erkkila, *Whitman* 179). An ecocritical reading of the poems demonstrates perhaps a different basis for their apparent duality, one that pits homosocial themes against those of natural history. We find ourselves, in other words, once again exploring that attenuated link between human society and the "impassive earth." Whitman's experience of his own attenuated link between homosexual desire and democratic unity perhaps allows him in these poems to give powerful expression to the similarly anguished task of linking human and natural history for a society that has not fully embraced its natural roots.

The first lines of "In Paths Untrodden" announce Whitman's intention to take us away from society temporarily to remote places in nature where we can explore the world that lies beyond appearances. If his poems are leaves, they are also roots, tapping into an unseen world. We enter into "paths untrodden, / In the growth by margins of pond-waters, / Escaped from the life that exhibits itself" (*PW* 188). Nature, it turns out, is itself an appearance of life, and we must learn to see "behind the mask of materials" (*PW* 190). The subterranean, almost microbial life of the soil and roots is the "real reality" he seeks, as the title "Calamus" implies. That is, we are metaphorically in an unseen social world that hides behind the physical phenomena accessed by the senses where nature does its unrecorded work. Here he can listen and respond to nature without the mediation of culture, and thus these poems emerge: "Tallying and talk'd to here by tongues aromatic, / No longer abash'd (for in this secluded spot I can respond as I would not dare elsewhere)" (*PW* 188). So we enter a subterranean world of germination and change but not in order to escape the "life that exhibits itself" in human society but rather to unlock the secrets of our own being. For this reason Whitman declares that the root, like his poems, functions as "the token of comrades" (*PW* 194). His poems are now digging deeper beneath the surface of appearances that exhibit nature's indifference to human death in order to understand more directly the chemistry by which love and death "are folded inseparably together" (*PW* 190).

Such chemistry is vital to human social bonds because death is the "real reality" that "will perhaps dissipate this entire show of appearance." Social bonds formed in denial or in ignorance of nature's strange laws of death and regeneration are superficial, as Keats once thematized, since "unnatural" love of this sort clings to "the life that exhibits itself" in a false hope for stasis. Since the material of nature appears, disappears, and transforms itself in a perpetual play of fort/da, it offers itself as an enigma not only of the reality of the environment but, as Whitman's title "Scented Herbage of My Breast" implies, of the kinship his own "conceal'd heart" shares with nature's roots (*PW* 189). Leaves, like poems, are tangible samples of the "life that exhibits itself," but a New World poetics suggests that they hide a deeper story, one that he cannot access. Speaking dually to his poems and to roots, he admits: "I do not know what you mean there underneath yourselves, you are not happiness, / You are often more bitter than I can bear" (*PW* 189).

Because nature's perpetual changes offer only a troubling and uncertain meaning, he acknowledges that "you make me think of death" (*PW* 189). But rather than thinking of death as an antithesis to life, as a bitterness to be shunned, he notes simply: "And yet you are beautiful to me you faint tinged roots. . . . Death is beautiful from you" (*PW* 189). The poet perhaps had anticipated that happiness would be found in the apprehension of nature's meaning, but its persistent elusiveness inspires first bitterness and ultimately an appreciation for the fact that this strangeness of nature makes it beautiful. The ubiquity of death means that if we find anything beautiful and living in our mundane world, it must be because death itself is beautiful. In "Of Him I Love Day and Night" the poet's relationship to all of "the life that exhibits itself" is changed by death. He wanders looking for the true resting place of a comrade, since he was not to be found at his gravesite. The poet concludes that "every place was a burial-place; / the houses full of life were equally full of death" and that we should all be "distributed to the winds" upon death.

In "Of the Terrible Doubt of Appearances" Whitman develops this idea further by exploring the anxiety inspired by nature's uncertain meaning. He writes:

May-be the things I perceive, the animals, plants, men, hills, shining and flowing
    waters,
The skies of day and night, colors, densities, forms, may-be these are (as
    doubtless they are) only apparitions, and the real something has yet to
    be known,
(How often they dart out of themselves as if to confound me and mock
    me! . . .) (*PW* 195)

He finds himself in a perpetually unfamiliar world, and the ephemerality of things raises the troubling question that "we may be deluded, / That may-be reliance and hope are but speculations after all" (*PW* 194–95). His anxiety is relieved only by "my lovers, my dear friends" because in social bonds the meaning of things coheres beyond language:

> When the subtle air, the impalpable, the sense that words and reason hold not, surround us and pervade us,
> Then I am charged with untold and untellable wisdom, I am silent, I require nothing further,
> I cannot answer the question of appearances or that of identity beyond the grave,
> But I walk or sit indifferent, I am satisfied. (*PW* 195)

The love of social bonds calms the anxieties that nature's ephemerality inspires with a wisdom beyond language. Nature's changeability—its apparent conformity with the law of death—provides the foundation of social bonds made all the more strong because of the power of aesthetic experiences that link us, mysteriously and inexplicably, to the physical world.

Whitman's vision of social progress here depends upon a recognition of nature's otherness and mystery because by offering resistance to facile interpretations of the world nature teaches humility and gratitude for social bonds. As I detailed in previous chapters, Glissant critiques the ways in which Western societies have typically established their relationship to land by means of what he calls a "sacred root," but, unlike Whitman's calamus, this root is sacred by virtue of being knowable; it tells the genealogical reasons for belonging in the land, which for Glissant merely serves to exclude others by rendering the land as "territory" and background to a human drama. Whitman's notion of the root here resembles Glissant's call for rhizomic relations to place that allow for a poetics of relation with others that is inclusive, relational, tentative but vital. For Whitman, without the wisdom silence and the opacity of things can inspire we cannot expect our perceptions of and interactions with the world to contribute to the construction of meaningful communities. The test is provided by poetry, since its words attempt to express that which is beyond expression. If words live perpetually in the realm of failed correspondence, we face the same potential for dismay and bitterness Whitman described as he contemplated the vegetation before him: it may be that we are deluded and that the worlds we build on paper and inside our minds have no correspondence to the real world.

As I argued about a New World poetics in chapter 2, Whitman's poetry gains its power from its nod to what it cannot know. Whitman's poems, he insists, are "useless without that which you may guess at many times and not hit, that which I hinted at" (*PW* 192). The force of living in a surrounding and inner reality that must be intimated is that it calls forth imagination and helps to spur on an inner life that, for Whitman, is the fundamental ingredient to human relations. In a dual metaphor Whitman asserts in "Roots and Leaves Themselves Alone": "If you bring the warmth of the sun to them [these roots, these poems] they will open and bring form, color, perfume, to you, / If you become the aliment and the wet they will become flowers, fruits, tall branches and trees" (*PW* 198). Whitman describes the contours of inner powers of perception that allow nature as well as poems to exhibit the life that lies beyond appearances and thus provide the basis for social relations of genuine depth and creativity. As we will see in chapter 8, Walcott will call this poetry's capacity to make the desert blossom as a rose through the powers of perception alone. This notion is consistent with sustainable treatment of the environment because it will give us pause in assuming the world needs our technological enhancements. This is what Aldo Leopold meant when he criticized the "qualitative bankruptcy" of our skills of perception. He insisted that the way to help Americans appreciate nature more profoundly had less to do with building more "roads into lovely country but of building receptivity into the still unlovely human mind" (176).

Whitman's intense interest in the cosmic implications of evolutionary theory, of animism, and of the findings of natural science tended to draw him away from the romantic language of epiphany and of personal ecstasy inspired by isolated places, the so-called genius loci, that inspired romantic poets in Europe. As Bruce Piasecki argues, Whitman's poetic subject was "the entire globe uniformly receptive to the comprehension and material transformations of humankind" (36). But when he became semiparalyzed following his stroke in 1873 he sought personal healing at Laurel Springs, New Jersey, along the banks of Timber Creek. The result was his notebook *Specimen Days*, a book of uncharacteristically ruminative, inconclusive, and personal interactions with the particulars of a place, what Erkkila calls "autobiography written in grand cipher" (*Whitman* 294). Daniel

Philippon states that *Specimen Days* as a result provides "the most thorough consideration of the relationship between humans and their nonhuman environment" in Whitman's work (188). We find a repeated admission of Whitman's "inability to perceive all of nature at once, and the inability to perceive nature directly" (Philippon 187). It seems Whitman preferred not to know nature too precisely for fear that this would diminish his imaginative freedom; to this end he maintained a certain deferential distance, what he called "a certain free margin" (qtd. in Outka 42). Consequently, nature does not serve as mere metaphor, nor is it appraised for its instrumental value; what emerges in the "Nature Notes" is an image of "something more than mere model in the natural world: he finds a type of subjectivity that allows him to move past his own brand of humanism" (Major 84).

Whitman states, for example, in "The Lesson of the Tree":

> [P]erhaps the greatest moral lesson anyhow from earth, rocks, animals, is that same lesson of inherency, of *what is*, without the least regard to what the looker on (the critic) supposes or says, or whether he likes or dislikes. What worse—what more general malady pervades each and all of us, our literature, education, attitude toward each other, (even toward ourselves,) than a morbid trouble about what *seems*, (generally temporarily seems too,) and no trouble at all . . . about . . . humanity's invisible foundations and hold-together? (*PW* 495)

Nature's opacity, its rudeness and silence, begs questions from the poet about the interior life of things, including himself, and helps him to access that which is invisibly brought forward through time by history. As the poet engages in the adamic task of naming he inevitably renames, rediscovers that which has been buried and concealed from view. The retrospective aspect of apprehensions of a natural present is explained by Emerson, whose influence on Whitman has been well documented. In his introduction to *Nature* Emerson notes: "We must trust the perfection of the creation so far as to believe that whatever curiosity the order of things has awakened in our minds, the order of things can satisfy. Every man's condition is a solution in hieroglyphic to those inquiries he would put. He acts it as life, before he apprehends it as truth" (27). Whitman would later characterize Emerson's conception of nature's perfection as an ideal that ignored nature's rugged irregularities caused by its "unconscious *growth*" and thus failed to "be Columbus-like, sailing out for New Worlds" (qtd. in Loving

395). Nevertheless, he concurred that the poetic encounter with nature, although an awakening, is also a re-cognition, a remembering of what has already been lived and experienced. Kronick explains that the questions we put to nature are "themselves the belated interpretations of actions, and consequently, not without their presuppositions. . . . In the interpretation that renders past action as 'truth,' we discover our past as that which lies before us" (*American* 100).

This paradox of an old newness is exemplified by Whitman's extensive descriptions of light on October 20 when he moves from observations of "the transparent shadows, shafts, sparkle, and vivid colors" to an interrogation of the meaning of transient human happiness. Very much akin to Walcott's reappraisal of impressionism in *Tiepolo's Hound,* which I explore in chapter 8, the frame of temporality light provides equalizes all things into a state of mutual "isolation and permanence" (Tedeschi Lalli 29). In this way light on the environment leads the poet away from the illusions of human society toward society's hidden and underlying laws of equality and balance. He finds nature to be both escape from and return to the cultural and historical environment of his New World. He asks, "How one dwells on [nature's] simplicity, even vacuity! What is it in us, arous'd by those indirections and directions? That spread of waves and gray-white beach, salt, monotonous, senseless—such an entire absence of art, books, talk, elegance—so indescribably comforting" (*PW* 501–2). After asserting that this reality of what *is* proves superior to what *seems* in literature and art, he confesses: "Yet let me be fair, perhaps it is because I have read those poems and heard that music" that he is able to have such enjoyments (*PW* 502).

Aesthetic experience in nature is "the spirit's hour—religion's hour—the visible suggestion of God in space and time—now once definitely indicated, if never again" (*PW* 533). This isn't exactly pantheism—God in nature—but something more akin to "God's revealing His power and Beauty *through* matter" (Allen 196). Nature is the proximate Christ, the embodiment of God in a moment, but it just as soon flees, leaving the observer alone with words to try and praise what is already no longer new. The physical world leads the thoughts of the poet into metaphysical realms, so that ultimately what the poet discovers is not provided directly by nature. The poet's imagination must invent something in response to nature's "uselessness growing wild" and its "stolid and deaf repugnance to answering questions" (*PW* 597).

This is Whitman at his most adamic and interesting, when he is not as concerned with making these experiences conform to philosophy but when he is aware that his philosophy is invention—meaningful to be sure, but invention all the same—and specifically invented to respond to nature's rude and mute beauty. He must confront the possibility of his own fiction making, "the uncertainty after all, that we may be deluded," as he says in *Calamus*, in order for him to begin to discover the contours of the world that *is* (*PW* 194–95). Nature's body appears to threaten the clear delineations of the physical self, but as it does so it stimulates the process by which self-consciousness becomes more clearly defined. With characteristic clarity Mack describes this process thusly: "[W]hat the poet imports into consciousness is not a set of objects that he, in some simplistic sense, becomes but a set of latent acts regarding those objects, which, through the reconstructive work of the imagination, becomes a kind of architecture of relations defining the self. What he becomes is the totality of those relations—manifested to the self objectively as the things that induce the self to act" (27).

We see the seeds of such an adamic poetics in the 1856 poem "Song of the Open Road." The poem opens with a dual declaration: he both seeks the freedom of the future and confesses the historical burdens he carries. He insists that the freedom he seeks is not a freedom from earth stains but rather a freedom to be earthly: "The earth, that is sufficient, / I do not want the constellations any nearer" (*PW* 123). Although the thought of eternity and earthly release that the stars inspire offers attractions, Whitman insists: "Still here I carry my delicious burdens, / I carry them, men and women, I carry them with me wherever I go" (*PW* 123). These are the burdens of human history, the stories of human joys and sorrows that are his assigned task to express collectively. Whitman seeks not freedom from history but freedom within history, freedom to reimagine the past poetically. These stories do not merely fill and weigh upon him because he can project his own poetic imagination into the past: "I will fill them in return," he says (*PW* 123).

Similarly, he is not determined by his physical environment. Whitman announces that all that surrounds him is unbounded by something much grander and unseen: "I believe you are not all that is here, / I believe that much unseen is also here" (*PW* 123). His earliest version of the poem of 1856 states with notably less vatic ambition "something unseen" (*WWA*

224). This simple declaration heightens the rhetorical dimension to his prophetic role, since he does not "see" the unseen but merely wants us to imagine its presence, with him. In this poem the unseen world is the very substance of human experience and history that surrounds and infuses all physical matter visible to the poet's eye. In accordance with the spiritualism of his time, Whitman believes that the physical environment allows him entrance into poetic imagination of human history, since all things are "latent with unseen existences" (*PW* 157). In later editions he seems to have grown more confident in his vatic powers, since the 1856 poem insists merely on latent "curious existences" (*WWA* 225). "You objects," he declares, "that call from diffusion my meanings and give them shape! / You light that wraps me and all things in delicate equable showers!" (*WWA* 157). All the objects he names, like the remnant ruins at Machu Picchu for Neruda, hold secret stories: "From all that has touch'd you I believe you have imparted to yourselves, and now I would impart the same secretly to me, / From the living and the dead you have peopled your impassive surfaces, and the spirits thereof would be evident and amicable with me" (*WWA* 158). The freedom to imagine and move within this unseen world of historical experience will never fully yield itself to the poet precisely because of Whitman's poetics of oblivion. This space of freedom is invisible and can only be accessed through physical things, which hold imperfect and cryptic imprimaturs of human stories. Whitman declares that great poetry and great nations are forged by individuals who "grow in the open air and . . . eat and sleep with the earth" (*WWA* 125). Although often tempted by the ahistoricism and innocence such natural spaces imply, Whitman here articulates a poetic vision of the physical world that is both dependent on but not limited to what is tangible, inherited, or predetermined. He aims for a kind of Rilkean invisible space of the dead and the future that ultimately remains beyond his reach.

His version of naturalism here helps to explain his ambivalence regarding Old World literature discussed in the previous chapter. Whitman argues in "Backward Glance" that what helps to safeguard the New World reader against anxieties of influence that reading Old World texts might inspire is the physical environment "*where* you read" (*PW* 305). We are reminded of his claim that "[w]isdom is not finally tested in schools" and that "philosophies and religions" can best be tested "under the spacious clouds and along the landscape and flowing currents" (*PW* 126). Direct contact with the natural world teaches wisdom because by handling the world that we can touch and smell and see we begin to imagine an invisible world of meaning that envelops objects and, by means of the oblivion of language nature intimates, delimits our sensual experience of them: "Why are there trees I never walk under but large and melodious thoughts descend upon me?" (*PW* 126).

Whitman recoils from the more radical implications of his thinking here because he is so singularly focused on the outcome that his readers will discover themselves as "larger, better than [they] thought" (*PW* 159). There is little room for self-questioning in such an assignment. Whitman, of course, also proved not to be as interested in direct contact with diverse peoples and environments as his poetry implies. This perhaps facilitated the ease with which he was able to conclude that Nature, although presenting itself as a mute difference to the human observer, will ultimately yield:

> The earth never tires,
> The earth is rude, silent, incomprehensible at first, Nature is rude and
>   incomprehensible at first,
> Be not discouraged, keep on, there are divine things well envelop'd,
> I swear to you there are divine things more beautiful than words can tell.
>   (*PW* 161)

Nature's impenetrability is an illusion because ultimately "the kernel of every object nourishes" (*PW* 160). The Hegelianism here is apparent, since the process of synthesis will be ongoing, always moving toward a higher progression of human spiritual being. Whitman writes: "[F]rom any fruition of success, no matter what, shall come forth something to make a greater struggle necessary" (*PW* 166). Although we can never be sure that we have succeeded in achieving a particular set of aims or that such aims are the desired end, it is nevertheless inevitable that we are moving "toward something great" (*PW* 165).

What is fascinating in Whitman's poetry is to see how his own Hegelian belief in the poet's ability to fill the gaps of history, to span the divide between the human and the natural or the earthly and the heavenly, ultimately does not deliver on its promise. This collapse does not signify a failure but results in a transformation of the culture-nature relationship, one in which the poet discovers himself surrounded by mystery. He may not have always expected those failures, especially when we consider that in his time the idea of the poet as prophet was perhaps more literal than literary. Séances were not an uncommon practice in the 1840s and 1850s, even for prominent and well-educated Americans. Swedenborg's ideas held an enormous influence over Whitman's generation, and Whitman was clearly convinced that in a world inhabited by the spiritual, invisible to the naked eye, the poet should act as a medium. "The poets are divine mediums," he wrote in his notebook. "[T]hrough them come spirits and materials to all the people, men and women" (qtd. in Reynolds 263). Acting as a mouthpiece for the mute dead in his poetry clearly allows him to affect a recuperation of the past and to synthesize the New World's troubling past into the seemingly innocent natural present. As evidence of what Lawrence Buell calls nature's destabilizing force on literature, nature's opacity muffles Whitman's clarion call with uncertainty. In one of the more famous passages of the 1855 "Song of Myself" Whitman asserts:

Through me many long dumb voices,
Voices of interminable generations of slaves,
Voices of prostitutes and of deformed persons,
Voices of the diseased and despairing, . . .
. . . .
Of the trivial and flat and foolish and despised,
Of fog in the air and beetles rolling balls of dung

Through me forbidden voices. (*PW* 57)

The New World's elusive past of unrecorded lives includes and confuses natural and human histories and thus situates the poet at the crossroads of mourning and elation. Neruda also attempts to speak for the dead at the ruins of Machu Picchu, but, as we see in chapter 6, his failure to do so becomes the necessary justification for the "American love" he invokes among his readers. As in the *Calamus* poems, solidarity is made possible by one who poetically fails to speak for nature's law of death and must find recourse to fraternal mourning as a balm. What emerges is "the unlikely image of a people unified by their mutual participation in a . . . rite of perpetually mourning their own death" (Mack 127).

In the 1855 edition of "Song of Myself" Whitman answers the child's question "*What is the grass?*" with a litany of prophetic but uncertain wishes. His guesses simultaneously suggest his desire to be history's mouthpiece and to respect nature's opacity; they suggest, in other words, a New World poetics of oblivion:

> I guess it must be the flag of my disposition, out of hopeful green stuff woven.
>
> Or I guess it is the handkerchief of the Lord,
> . . . .
>
> Or I guess the grass is itself a child . . . the produced babe of the vegetation.
>
> Or I guess it is a uniform hieroglyphic,
> And it means, Sprouting alike in broad zones and narrow zones,
> Growing among black folks as among white. (*LG* 36–37)

He begins to play with his own ideas, as the unreadable hieroglyphic sign of natural growth seems to change like a kaleidoscope before him: "And now it seems to me the beautiful uncut hair of graves" (*LG* 37). With this thought he explores a subset of other possibilities: "*It may be* you transpire from the breasts of young men, / *It may be* if I had known them I would have loved them" (*LG* 37, emphasis added). He finally seizes upon this idea that grass signifies an untold democratic story of the dead, black and white, men and women, old and young, Canadians, Indians, and congressmen, and that he is the self-assigned mouthpiece for their tales. Even though he boldly declares, "O I perceive after all so many uttering tongues," the meaning of these utterances is never finally intelligible: "*I wish I could translate* the hints about the dead young men and women" (*LG* 37, emphasis added). He concludes with his Hegelian belief that "All goes onward and outward, nothing collapses" (*LG* 37), but he has already revealed how his figurative language gives metonymical expression to history's gaps and irretrievable losses. The hieroglyph metaphor suggests a meaning "on the border between abstract language and the world, between nature as linguistic construction and nature as unspeakable, unconstructed material" (Outka 46). It is akin to Glissant's poetics of relation, in which poetry must acknowledge such loss but not forsake the obligation to imagine totality. Kronick appropriately notes that Whitman's answers to the child's question demonstrate that "the book does not lead beyond its signs to spirit or nature but is no different from either one. . . . Speech, therefore, does not represent the self, for Whitman uses 'tongues' not as a metonymy for speech but as a synecdoche for the body and, ultimately, as a metaphor for writing" (*American* 106). Edward Cutler likewise argues that the grass's metonymical "significance ultimately derives from the total *process* of organic and figurative transformation, wherein people, grass, elements, even human utterance are thoroughly integrated. There is no identifiable moment where the buried dead 'end' and the grass 'begins' " (151). This adamic poetry is not a translation of nature's meaning or of history's truths but a rhetoric that acknowledges the appropriateness of both remaining opaque to human understanding. The advantage of such an admission is that it enables aesthetic experience of beauty in a New World without leading to the impulse to denude it of its prior history. Nature's otherness is both explored and respected as the poet intimates the kinship of human beings and the natural world without falling prey to the pathetic fallacy.

Nature's Last Chemistry

Whitman had been an early devotee of the novel *A Few Days in Athens* by Frances Wright (1822), which articulated the view that all matter was made up of eternal substances that were simply rearranged in different physical phenomena, based on the philosophical ideas of deistic materialism (Reynolds 42). He also became aware in the 1840s of the work of Justus von Liebig, the founder of agricultural chemistry who provided a conception of natural regeneration that resonated with his belief in nature's healing power. Through a primitive conception of organic chemistry Liebig argued that all natural matter transformed itself from dead and decaying flesh to new life through the rearrangement and exchange of atoms, what to Whitman suggested "an ongoing and a democratic exchange of substances inherent in nature" (Reynolds 240). In accordance with Liebig's theory Whitman wrote in his 1845 story "Shirval: A Tale of Jerusalem" that the earth is a "huge tomb-yard of humanity" and implied that soil itself was the stuff of history (qtd. in Loving 91). This exchange, although occurring in the material realm and involving a merging of atoms to create the seen world, is invisible and inspires the same mysticism the poet expresses before an immaterial God.[9]

This procreative energy found in the finest material substance further suggested to Whitman that nature itself could transform depravity, violence, and tragedy into sustenance, beauty, and peace. Initially, at least, he doesn't seem certain how much trust he can place in the process. The metaphor of poetry as a kind of composting of the past and regeneration of meaning had been suggested to him as early as 1849 in a Scottish journal, a passage of which he marked that read: "In this way minute portions of the past are constantly entering by new combinations into fresh forms of life, and out of these old materials, continually decomposed by continually recombined, scope is afforded for an everlasting succession of imaginative literature" (qtd. in Klammer 73). Compos(t)ing offered a means by which the New World could wrest itself from the grips of the Old World, and when Whitman became aware of the process by which soils composted he saw an ecoliterary opportunity that was needed in the years of crisis prior to the Civil War.

Despite the reasons for confidence Whitman wrestled with the promise of these regenerative powers in an 1856 poem, "This Compost," which was initially entitled "Poem of Wonder at the Resurrection of the Wheat." In lines that are hard to believe were written before the Civil War the poet is frightened by nature's seeming innocent indifference to history's violence. He struggles to let go of his own pathetic fallacy:

> How can the ground not sicken of men?
> . . . .
> How can you furnish health you blood of herbs, roots, orchards, grain?
> Are they not continually putting distempered corpses in the earth?
> Is not every continent worked over and over with sour dead? (*WWA* 202)

He is confident that even the innocence of plowing a new field will "expose some of the foul meat" of the dead (*WWA* 203). All growing things, then, signify some "part of a sick person" (*WWA* 203). The irony is that "the summer growth is innocent and disdainful above all those strata of sour dead! / What chemistry!" (*WWA* 204). Nature's chemistry that conflates human and natural histories is worthy of our cautious respect, as he notes: "I am terrified at the Earth. . . . It grows such sweet things out of such corruptions" (*WWA* 204–5). The sweetness, however, is not a lie; nature's bounty is safe to enjoy, it is "harmless and stainless," but to gain access to this enjoyment one has to first process what nature itself has ingested in order to appreciate how "it gives such divine materials to men, and accepts such leavings from them at last" (*WWA* 205). As he notes in "Song of Myself," one must learn to see life itself as "the leavings of many deaths" (*PW* 94).

It does not appear that Whitman or the scientists of his generation could yet conceive of leavings that would toxically poison the air, water, soil, or body. Despite these limitations of contemporary science in Whitman's day, his expression of simultaneous admiration and horror at earth's regenerations allows his poetry to respect nature's mystery; this makes "everything strange and new" (Killingsworth 29). This aesthetic of the earth depends on the poet's willingness to recognize the earth's untranslatability. His own impending death means his tongue will join the inarticulate language of dirt: "I bequeath myself to the dirt to grow from the grass I love / If you want me again look for me under your boot-soles" (*PW* 76). His poems are, after all, "leaves of grass," like so many mute witnesses to a meaning that he hints at and hopes for and even wishes at times to embody but that remains beyond his grasp. This provides a new ecological dimension to his famous claim: "I too am untranslatable / I sound my barbaric yawp over the roofs of the world" (*PW* 96).

Liebig's law of regeneration is an early manifestation of ecological thinking that questions the utility of the nature-culture binary. Whitman's poetics of oblivion here means he encounters in nature not a metaphor of human history but the very material of eclipsed human lives from the past. This in turn causes him to question both his individuality and the determinism of environment and history. Self-consciousness becomes a kind of tentative and inevitable cross-cultural solidarity precisely because the poet can never be sure whether nature or history presents a continuity of the self. The self is drawn to them but cannot entirely hold them or contain them. Nature then becomes alive with eclipsed histories always having just ended and always beginning again to find new life.

Whitman walks the fine line between mourning and celebration of regeneration this awareness requires in his 1859 poem "Out of the Cradle Endlessly Rocking." The title of the poem in the 1860 *Leaves of Grass* was "A Word out of the Sea," and the first line, before it became the same as the later title, simply announced "Out of the rocked cradle" (*WWA* 269). Erkkila notes that "in seeking to improve his poems artistically, Whitman frequently eliminated or toned down passages of crisis, anxiety, and doubt, giving a smoother line to the arc of his own and the nation's development than had in fact been the case" (*Whitman* 170). In this case she sees in the earliest version of the poem a closer approximation to the "experience of discord, fracture, and separation" Whitman sought to express in the context of a nation on the verge of civil war (170). We see the poet, accustomed since childhood to "blending [him]self with the shadows" and listening "long and long" to the "echoes, the sounds and sights after their sorts," now in adulthood "throwing [him]self on the sand, confronting the waves" (*PW* 173–74, 172). His attentiveness to the "white arms out in the breakers tirelessly tossing" and other communications along the shoreline distinguishes him from those who cannot translate the meaning of ocean- or birdsong (*PW* 173). The poet's environmental sensibilities ("peering, absorbing, translating") allow him to imagine the discourse of a male bird who has lost his mate and whose song is one of lament (*PW* 172).

Significantly, the poet interprets the bird as aware of nature's attempt to soothe the pain of loss: "*Soothe, soothe! soothe!* / *Close on its waves soothes the wave behind*" (*PW* 174). Despite nature's reassurance of regeneration, the bird is unconsoled. Instead, his refusal to be soothed becomes the very substance of his beautiful music of lament. "*Shake out carols!*" the bird declares. "*Solitary here, the night's carols!* / *Carols of lonesome love! death's carols!*" (*PW* 175). Indeed, the bird's song is carried further by the baseless hope that he will see his lover's form against the white of the moon or hovering over the waters or that his voice will draw her out from the dark woods: "*With this just-sustain'd note, I announce myself to you* / *This gentle call is for you my love*" (*PW* 175). The bird pleads with his lover not to confuse the sounds of the ocean spray and the wind with his voice; "*decoy'd*" is the word Whitman uses to describe the murderous intentions of nature's indifference to the individual story of suffering. In light of the poem's conclusion, that death itself is the substance of the ocean's song, it would appear that the birdsong, as poetry, stands in direct competition and perhaps dialectical relation to death's erasure of linguistic meaning.

The boy-poet begins to hear something, "some drown'd secret hissing" still untranslated and murmured by the sea, "the savage old mother incessantly crying" (*PW* 176). In almost prophetic anticipation of how the loneliness of the sea will inspire Neruda to write poetry, Whitman discovers his poetic task as he realizes that the song, although intended for the bird's mate, was also intended for him: "Now in a moment I know what I am for, I awake, / And already a thousand singers, . . . a thousand warbling echoes have started to life within me, never to die" (*PW* 176–77). His poetry will forever be an expression, then, of "the cries of unsatisfied love . . . the unknown want" not only of human beings but of all of nature (*PW*

176). The "trio" is complete once the sea's murmured message becomes clear to the boy: "[D]eath . . . the word up from the waves . . . that strong and delicious word which, creeping to my feet . . . the sea whisper'd me" (*PW* 178).

Death, of course, is a universal law of the natural world, but the oblivion that it here implies also signifies nature's defiant resistance to the human longing both for the immediacy of the physical world and for complete recovery of our past. The two longings, one for a purely more-than-human being and the other for a distinctly and fully realized humanness, are exposed as symptomatic of one another and symptomatically impossible. The tone of lamentation of the poem implicitly argues that even though nature presumably refashions "leavings" into new life, there is still a remainder that is not so transformed; poetry's task is to recover or to lament what it cannot recover from nature's space of death. Just as the birdsong relies on the absence of the lover, so too the poet's voice depends upon the absence of his subject. The sea provides the repository of stories of unrequited yearnings for union that result from the passing of every living thing. The sea lies below the conscious world of human social interaction, and just as it separates us from the dead, so too, Whitman writes in *Calamus*, it implies a world above "of beings who walk other spheres," as different in character as the "World below the Brine" from ours (*PW* 202).

This conception of the sea was not simply a philosophical or scientific view; as a child in Brooklyn Whitman had found some of the bones of the twelve thousand American prisoners who had been held captive and eventually buried in shallow seaside graves by the British in nearby Wallabout Bay (Reynolds 14). Presaging Walcott's notion that "The Sea Is History," in "Song of Myself" Whitman declares the sea the space of the dead:

> Vivas to those who have fail'd!
> And to those whose war-vessels sank in the sea!
> And to those themselves who sank in the sea!
> And to all generals that lost engagements, and all overcome heroes!
> And the numberless unknown heroes equal to the greatest heroes known!
>   (*PW* 50)

The bird's lover is a metonym of a much deeper loss. The sea holds "the half-burned brig [that] is riding on unknown currents, / Where shells grow to her slimy deck, and the dead are corrupting below" (*PW* 67). Although

Whitman's Atlantic does not entail the tragedies of the Middle Passage, Native American genocide, and disease-related deaths in New World history as it does for Walcott, Whitman plants a seed of suspicion that will be developed further by Neruda and Walcott that the known story of the New World casts a shadow on what has been forgotten and that the sea's engulfing relationship to national landforms represents the space of this oblivion. Whitman's sea is democratic and universal in its indiscriminate erasure of the "life that exhibits itself"; it is full of "unshovelled and always ready graves," "[p]artaker of influx and efflux" and "[e]xtoler of hate and conciliation" (*PW* 54).

The sea's crepitations in "Out of the Cradle Endlessly Rocking" offer themselves as comfort for the bird, but the bird's song continues as a lament and refusal to be consoled. The poem, in other words, "raises the prospect of annihilation and concludes that there is nothing to do about it but sing it" (Bauerlein 495). However, the sea's unheeded whisperings and the bird's relentless mourning are expressed as poetry, and thus Whitman translates both the suffering and pathos of all life and the reasons, however unconventional, for joy. The joy comes from the creation of song, which can be nothing more, as he says to the sea, than a "guess at what you mean" (*PW* 54). As a "chanter of pains and joys" Whitman stresses several important aspects of his adamic imagination: quiet and careful observation of nature, profound capacity for sympathy, and acceptance of the terrible fact of nature's indifference to suffering. Balancing these emotions allows the poet both to hear the thousand songs of sorrow as well as to transform them, just as nature transforms death, into songs of beauty. While they are adamic songs of praise for the newness nature creates, his poems are also, by indirection at least, lamentations for what is lost. As Erkkila observes, "beneath and beyond the poem's artistic resolution we still hear the fumbling of a darker sea that floats up the sediment and debris of 'As I Ebb'd'" (*Whitman* 176). That is, poetry perpetually attempts to remember what it cannot translate and thus brings us closer to the paradox of our own natural being. "The human will to power," writes Killingsworth, "understood as the struggle against death can only countenance a parallel struggle against the earth. The great Mother becomes the great Other, and reconciliation becomes the chief task of the poet as a sort of mystical ecologist" (111).

The intensity of Whitman's wanderings on the gray coast of Long Island, what amounted to a "sacred space" for Whitman, according to

Killingsworth, substantiates the idea of Whitman as an emerging ecologist. His "island poetics," characterized by metonymy and observation, provides a template that resurfaces in the work of Neruda and Walcott (Killingsworth 98). Wandering the shoreline becomes a fundamental poetic task, since it allows the poet to contemplate the enormity of natural space, the abyss of death as well as its remnants that lie on the borders of solidity all around the globe, wherever ocean and land meet, or "the rim, the sediment, that stands for all the water and all the land of the globe," as he states in "As I Ebb'd with the Ocean of Life" (*WWA* 195). The poem, written in 1860, was originally entitled "Bardic Symbols." In it Whitman portrays the sea as an architectural space of death where the voices of the dead echo in the song of the waves: "As I listen to the dirge, the voices of men and women wrecked, / As I inhale the impalpable breezes that set in upon me" (*WWA* 196). In the liminal space between land and sea— between life and memory, on the one hand, and death and oblivion, on the other—the poet "[g]ather[s], and merge[s] [him]self as part of the sands and drift" (*WWA* 196). Presaging Neruda's obsession with shells and other debris, these are the very materials of Whitman's poeticizing: "Chaff, straw, splinters of wood, weeds, and the sea-gluten" (*WWA* 196). The debris of the sea signifies, then, the brokenness of things, the surviving vestiges of human existence. They have survived contradiction "[f]rom the storm, the long calm, the darkness, the swell" and chaos "drifted at random" and make ideal candidates for truly natural metaphors (*WWA* 199).

These fragments have been shaped, conceived as it were, equally by what he will later call "Mother sea" and "Father land," and they are, as he tells us, "types" or symbols of what we are: "I too am but a trail of drift and debris, / I too leave little wrecks upon you, you fish-shaped island" (*WWA* 198). His poems would seem to be fashioned out of the debris and then left again as drift, as if to suggest the failure of his poetry to transcend these fragmentations of humanity's own natural history. They are instead only able to participate in the dichotomies, since he himself remains divided between his attempts to realize himself in his poems and the "real Me" that "stands yet untouch'd, untold, altogether unreached" (*WWA* 197). This real Whitman of the soul would seem to be coming from beyond the realm of the knowable, the articulated, and the poetically represented, and although this real Whitman is not knowable, his presence creates doubt in the poet regarding what meaning he attempts to make of the shoreline. Since the sea is the space of death and oblivion, it also represents that which always contextualizes and questions his efforts to assert lasting meaning:

> O I perceive I have not understood anything—not a single object—and that no man ever can.

> I perceive nature here, in sight of the sea; is taking advantage of me, to dart upon me, and sting me,
> Because I was assuming so much.
> Because I have dared to open my mouth to sing at all. (*WWA* 197)

Critics have noted a distinct tone of pessimism in this poem, as if to suggest Whitman's waning confidence in the great "I" of his earliest poems, the poetic subject through which all contradiction will be expressed and synthesized. Agnieszka Salska, for example, notes that Whitman's encounters with the sea demonstrate that "the self . . . seems dwarfed because the organizing cycles of experience are provided by the natural power of the sea with which the self struggles to commune and integrate" (43). A similar shift, as we will see, appears to occur to Neruda, as his own belief in the poet's capacity to speak for all the liminal dead and buried voices of the New World declines just as his obsession with stones, shells, and other oceanic debris increases in his later years. In both cases, the poet is not making a dramatic turnaround in his poetic objectives but rather discovering the logical and ecological conclusions of his adamic poetics. As Outka explains, "Whitman both wants to break out of language into the 'real world,' and to 'translate' that world—the landscape, people, animals, himself—back into language" (50). That he fails equally in both tasks suggests that his poetry seeks a balance between nature and culture.

The poet begins with the quest to understand the natural world and to give voice to its secrets, and although he discovers the impossibility of this task, he cannot stop asking himself, What if my metaphors could become transparent and were capable of overcoming the "failure of correspondence" and birds, the sea, and all of life could speak through me? The rhetorical question is asked repeatedly by Whitman, and the answer here, as elsewhere, appears to be this: "If this is your ambition, then you must accept that your poems will follow the same fate as the natural world. They too will fragment into the great currents of flotsam and jetsam of the world, pass through death and regeneration, and become fragments, that is, metaphors, of themselves. You can speak nature's history only if you are willing to accept your natural metaphors as metaphors of yourself. In other words, you will have to renounce your separateness from the world. Your readers will be left approaching your poems with the same muddled confusion with which you contemplate the shorelines of the world." For this reason, Whitman imagines his poetry dissipating like so many shoreline fragments tossed by the sea's deathly movements, despite his longing for a permanence of meaning. This poetic failure enables the poet to comprehend his own natural history. He imagines his own dying, sea foam oozing from his lips, while above him an Other walks: "[W]e too lie in drifts at your feet" (*WWA* 199). And rather than representing an abrupt change, this view echoes his previous claim, cited earlier, at the conclusion of "Song of Myself" that the poet's destiny is a natural one.

This more biocentric conclusion is necessarily unsettled and perhaps unsettling, since it means that his poems will fall back into the world as something to be interpreted, something natural. If the adamic imagination is productive of new understandings of the nature-culture dichotomy, it seems to suggest that the closer we come to understanding our own citizenship in the natural world, the more opaque and impenetrable our metaphors will become. There is no mode of representation that will adequately sum up our nature, as it were, and poetry is hardly natural. If the environment is prior to interpretation, poetry that attends to its particulars must become as opaque as nature itself. Since it is not clear what distinguishes the environment from our interpretations of it, however, and since some interpretations are dangerous to its health, poetry must respect nature's otherness by becoming beholden to mystery and death. In so doing it will dissipate and transform itself along with the rest of the natural world into something new and unrecognizable, which is the essence of the New World poetics of reading I described in chapter 3. So either the poet can choose to remain aloof and outside of nature and render his poems self-consciously banished from the muteness of the physical world, or, if he strives to join the unsung realities, he must himself become mute and untranslatable.

Nature's Indifference to War

This was a hard fate to accept when Whitman had witnessed so much human suffering during the Civil War and had come to hope that his poetry of the war would somehow help to heal the nation's wounds. However, he turned to poetry precisely to help assuage the disappointments of his earlier activism in politics and journalism, which perhaps explains why his poetry was more interested in suturing wounds than balancing justice (Klammer 88). Unlike Neruda's self-assigned role as judge at the tribunal of poetic justice for New World sins in *Canto general,* Whitman's *Drum Taps* sees history's pains as almost inevitable and yet inevitably healed by natural processes of reconciliation and reunion. Indeed, little mention is made of the issue of slavery or even of the North-South divide, largely because he believes only universal compassion can become the mechanism of synthesis that will balance the scales of justice; in "Song of Myself" he had earlier written of the many varieties of human experience and decided on the centrality of compassion to his poetics. Presaging Neruda's and Walcott's discovery of sympathy for ancient civilizations, he writes: "I am the man, I suffer'd, I was there. / . . . All these I feel or am" (*PW* 71–72).

In "The Wound-Dresser" poetry serves to stop the bleeding and dress the wounds of any man, even though Whitman's service as a nurse in the military hospitals rarely involved dressing wounds. He learned instead to use words as wound dressings as a letter writer, listener, and comforter. The purpose of the many images Whitman provides, often without commentary, is to train the reader to understand democratic compassion and synthesis: the moon softly shining down, for example, on unidentified "faces ghastly, swollen, purple, / On the dead on their backs with arms toss'd wide" (*PW* 233). The image of these faces, here illuminated by an undiscriminating moonbeam, stresses the common humanity of the dead.

And yet if nature is a witness to the countless horrors of the war, it remains mute. In *Specimen Days* Whitman describes in agonizing details the physical suffering of the soldiers with simple focus on their mangled bodies. He asks: "What history . . . can ever give—for who can know—the mad, determin'd tussle of the armies, in all their separate large and little squads?" (*PW* 424). The only other witness to as much as he has seen appears again to be the moonlight, but it cannot provide the history any more than he can: "[S]till again the moonlight pouring silvery soft its radiant patches over all. Who paint the scene?" (*PW* 424). So it is to a mute natural world that the poet must find recourse in order to capture the saga of extensive division and suffering. Nature becomes the potential unifier, the ally, although it remains aloof in the poet's effort to appeal to a cohesive story. As he states simply, "the real war will never get in the books" (*PW* 483). Just as the sea's song of death urged the birdsong and his poem on, the prospect of the war's "interior history" vanishing and "being totally forgotten" inspires his poetry even as he confesses its limitations. He had concluded that perhaps it was best that this totalized history would be forgotten because that incompletion helps to inspire readers to have compassionate imaginations. He hoped that "the few scraps and distortions that are ever told or written" should give the reader pause to imagine "how much, and of importance, will be . . . buried in the grave, in eternal darkness" (*PW* 484).

The inevitability of memory's failure makes poetry both necessary and insufficient. It also renders nature the paradoxically central historical preoccupation of poetry. As Whitman wrestles to sum up the "million dead," nature is the only repository large enough to contain their memory. Neruda and Walcott will extend their geographical and cross-cultural reach and extend this million to millions more, including Native Americans, Africans, and others whose stories have been buried in nature's silent indifference. But again Whitman's emergent New World poetics in its reach for "the infinite dead" seems to have provided an impetus for this hemispheric acknowledgment of what has been lost. Whitman explains this infinitude as having natural dimensions: "the land entire saturated, perfumed with their impalpable ashes' exhalation in Nature's chemistry distill'd, and shall be so forever, in every future grain of wheat and ear of corn, and every flower that grows and every breath we draw" (*PW* 482). In 1876 he concluded that the essential components of human life lay in "the affinities of a man or woman with the open air, the trees, fields, the changes of seasons—the sun by day and the stars of heaven by night. We will begin from these convictions" (*PW* 485).

This is not an escape from the ravages of history but rather a means of understanding natural regeneration of death so as to find newness in the wake of a traumatic past and open new prospects for the future. In Whitman's elegy for Lincoln, "When Lilacs Last in the Dooryard Bloom'd," as in "Out of the Cradle Endlessly Rocking," we listen to a translation of the bird's song, which is a song of praise for death. Death's universality causes the poet to remember all of the dead of the war:

I saw battle-corpses, myriads of them,
And the white skeletons of young men, I saw them,
I saw the debris and debris of all the slain soldiers of the war,
But I saw they were not as was thought,
They themselves were fully at rest, they suffer'd not,
The living remain'd and suffer'd, the mother suffer'd,
And the wife and the child and the musing comrade suffer'd,
And the armies that remain'd suffer'd. (*PW* 242)

Memory of such extensive suffering potentially expands without bounds, perhaps like the starry sky above, and threatens to undo the constitution of the soul. Instead, this suffering collapses or condenses into metaphorical density, a poetic expression of the suffering of the living, which for Whitman is the substance of his verse: "their memory ever to keep, for the dead I loved so well" (*PW* 243). Nature's expansiveness and the universality of death would seem to render poetry unnecessary or meaningless, but precisely because of the enormity of the task poetry is able to focus on the pains of living and the particular, to mourn those known dead, and rhetorically to commemorate the unknown.

This theme is continued in "Ashes of Soldiers," in which again we see Whitman rhetorically functioning as the mouthpiece of the dead. Rather than being a kind of séance, however, his poetry offers a gesture to the living. What emerges is, like Neruda's communion with the Inca dead, an expression of love that binds the wounds that would keep the past separate from the present. Despite the sounds of Whitman's words, the dead are "noiseless as mists and vapors" that "silently gather round" the poet (*PW* 247). In the presence of his poem, although mute, "the slain [are] elate and alive again, the dust and debris alive" (*PW* 247). Recalling his poems about the detritus on the shores of the sea, we see here that poetry is the living song of the fragmented dead, that which has decomposed in the violence of history as well as of nature and that according to those same laws of nature has now found new life in regeneration. Whitman will ask them to "speak not" because although heard voices are "sweet," so too are "the dead with their silent eyes" (*PW* 248). Whitman reminds us of the inevitability of oblivion even though he resists the accompanying impulse to turn away from the forgotten. This ability to walk such a fine line defines his particular version of "American" love, a theme of no small influence on Neruda; his adamic poetics stimulates a love that heals and binds New World peoples and nations because it follows and mimics natural process:

> Dearest comrades, all is over and long gone,
> But love is not over—and what love, O comrades!
> Perfume from battle-fields rising, up from the foetor arising.
>
> . . . .
>
> Perfume all—make all wholesome,
> Make these ashes to nourish and blossom,
> O love, solve all, fructify all with the last chemistry. (*PW* 248)

Nature itself, in all of its seemingly independent glory, reminds us of this love whenever we feel inclined to praise its bounty. Nature's innocent appearance as that which lies beyond the bounds of human history is deceptive. Its bounty is always a reminder of unknown suffering as well as of the promise of its fruitful transformation. Because we are natural ourselves it is only appropriate that the poet concludes by pleading: "Give me exhaustless, make me a fountain, / That I exhale love from me wherever I go like a moist perennial dew" (*PW* 248). This is the prayer too of "Pensive on Her Dead Gazing," in which the poet pleads in the voice of "the Mother of All" that the earth will "lose not an atom" of the young dead, that the air, the waters, the mountains, and the trees will all "absorb" them and give them back again "in unseen essence and odor of surface and grass, centuries hence" (*PW* 249). In sum, to be true to New World history, to human memory and suffering, the poet must be a nature poet.

The implications of this paradox are not only that Whitman does not fully escape the temptation to substitute nature for history but that he also develops a poetics of nature that is fed by an imagination capable of recognizing and wrestling with the problems of historical amnesia. We see this tension at the beginning of "Song of Myself" when he expresses his own paradoxically adamic naturalism:

> My tongue, every atom of my blood, form'd from this soil, this air,
> Born here of parents born here from parents the same, and their parents the
>   same,
> I, now thirty-seven years old in perfect health begin,
> Hoping to cease not till death.

Creeds and schools in abeyance,
Retiring back a while sufficed at what they are, but never forgotten,
I harbor for good or bad, I permit to speak at every hazard,
Nature without check with original energy. (*LG* 25)

Originality is made possible not because nature lies like a blank slate before Adam but because the determinacies of history and environment, although undeniable, are not entirely knowable. Whitman insists that poetry, and culture more generally, must return again and again to nature for the adamic privilege of learning a new American language and possibility. The aim of culture, as John Burroughs would correctly intuit in his own close readings of Whitman's verse after his death, is not to deny nature but to liberate its "inherent values" (qtd. in Warren 95).

This remains one of the great unexplored territories of Whitman's thought and his contribution to U.S. culture and American cultures in the hemisphere. As Betsy Erkkila and Jay Grossman's edited volume, *Breaking Bounds: Whitman and American Cultural Studies,* recognizes, Whitman has long been recognized as a pivotal figure because of his politics, sexuality, urbanity, and views of democracy, but he has yet to be exploited for his insights into the nature-culture divide in the New World. As the aforementioned volume asserts, one of the deeper fears that Whitman brought to the surface is that "in its purest form democracy would lead to a blurring of sexual bounds and thus the breakdown of a social and bourgeois economy based on the management of the body and the polarization of male and female spheres" (Erkkila, "Introduction" 7–8). No mention is made, however, of how Whitman's democratic vision for the Americas included a productive nature-culture dialectic that would prove equally destabilizing to traditionally polarized concepts of humanity's place in the physical world.

As this examination of Whitman has sought to demonstrate, however, the remedy is not simply a facile call for humanity to lend greater attention to nature. As we have seen, Whitman's repeated return to nature is always fraught with the risk of denying the poet's own historicism. And there is another risk: if he always assumes that the vestiges of the past continue on through a dialectical process that synthesizes in the future, then he will be forever blind to the possibility of original ideas, language, or experience in the world around him. Since he was never satisfied by either outcome, again and again he reimagined the earth through poetry and tried to maintain the balance between the ontology of the earth and the agency of imagination. That Whitman is today simultaneously celebrated as a model poet of American, even New World originality and as the quintessentially self-deluded voice of American imperialism is perhaps indicative of his only partially convincing success in striking this difficult balance. But perhaps the fault lies with us as his readers. As William Major argues, "we might say that by dramatizing the incongruities in a democratic practice whose foundation is the natural world, Whitman helped to question the human propensity toward values that were, and often are, entirely centered around capriciously temporal and political interests" (93). The fact that we have not learned a way out of these incongruities suggests that we are insufficient readers of nature and the New World story it still tells.

One way or another

we speak and fall silent

with the earth.

PABLO NERUDA, *Tercer libro de odas*

CHAPTER 5

Natural History as Autobiography

Pablo Neruda was born in Parral in the southern region of Chile, an area that Neruda insists in his *Memorias* was analogous to the American Wild West. The area, known as La Araucanía, is also called La Frontera and is named after the monkey puzzle tree used by the Mapuche Indians for its nutritious nut, *pehuen*. It is important not to understate the influence of the frontier experience on Neruda's poetic imagination. It is a land that, despite considerable modernization, still contains areas where Mapuche influence predominates, and it is a region of extraordinary natural beauty: intense rainfall, dense humidity and fluvial ranges where water and land commingle ambiguously, high mountain ranges, volcanoes, some remaining tracts of hardwood forests, glacial lakes, and dramatic and seemingly unending coastline. Even though the area is notable for this natural beauty and for relatively sparse evidence of extensive urbanization, its forests have been dramatically reduced over the last century, and some warn that the native hardwoods may disappear within a generation, such as one of the oldest living organisms on earth, the Chilean redwood, or *alerce*, which has been known to age up to four thousand years. The native hardwood forests of Neruda's youth have largely ceded to monocultural tree plantations used to export woodchips.

The area was controlled by the Mapuche Indians from their revolt against the Spanish in 1599 until their reconquest by the Chilean government in 1883. Neruda, who was born only twenty-one years later, would witness the early years of the arrival of the railroad, the development of the timber industry, and the phoenixlike rise out of the wilderness of a small, primitive, but stable Western society. Whitman drew his inspiration from distant frontiers that he knew only superficially and indirectly, but Neruda experienced the newness of circumstances directly from his infancy. This facilitated an awareness in Neruda of the adamic possibilities of language and appreciation for the regenerative powers of nature that nurture such language. Although Neruda was not directly influenced by indigenous culture, newness in the context of a previous and continuing history of indigenous oppression also established a tension in his poetry between the call of the natural world and that of the need for radical social and political change. These two strains in Neruda have moved in and out of his poetic work throughout his prolific career. It is not true, in other words, that he only became interested in writing nature poetry after his Marxist fires began to burn more dimly (Suárez Rivero). As I explore here and in the following chapter, these dual interests enjoyed a sinuous and interweaving pattern throughout his life. To be sure, his fierce demands for radical political change often overshadow or sidestep a land ethic in the more immediate interest of protecting the human community and sometimes in the same books of poetry where such an ethic seems laid out with passion and clarity. Although Neruda is widely known as one of the most strident political poets of his century, what is less known is his lifelong meditation on the natural world that lays claim to being one of the most important contributions of the century for its range of insights and remarkably prolific and sustained attention. This ambivalence in Neruda is a rich vein to explore, one that highlights a tension that fuels his adamic imagination, since it is characterized by the cycles of death and renewal, despair and resurrected hope and by the tenuous balance between human and natural histories.

Pablo Neruda, born Neftalí Ricardo Reyes Basoalto, changed his name and left La Araucanía in his teens to pursue the bohemian life of a poet in the city of Santiago, a pattern followed to this day by many Chilean poets born outside the capital. One can only imagine the sense of loss, nostalgia, and longing that such departures caused because of the abrupt break from overwhelming natural beauty to the grime of city life. Similar to Walcott's spiritual epiphany on a St. Lucian hillside at the age of fourteen and his early teenage declarations of devotion to nature, which I explore in chapter 7, Neruda wrote at the age of fifteen:

> "Ahora yo me entrego, Madre Naturaleza,
> a vivir la belleza sagrada que hay en tí,
>
> . . . .
>
> Y errando en los caminos he aprendido a adorarte
> como a una inmensa amada, plena toda de amor;
> (ahora sumo toda mi sed en contemplarte
> en el divino éxtasis de toda anunciación . . .)." (*OC* 4:80)
>
> —
>
> "Now I give myself over to you, Mother Nature,
> to live in the sacred beauty I find in you,
>
> . . . .
>
> And wandering in pathways I have learned to worship you
> like an immense beloved, all full of love;
> (now I reach the height of all my thirst in contemplating you
> in the divine ecstasy of every annunciation . . .)."

Walcott came to imbue his view of nature with this same kind of rhetorical language of sacred liturgy, even though in his case he did so with a greater sense of irony, since he never abandoned entirely the faith of his parents, as did Neruda.

Chile's southern frontier, then, became Neruda's Paumanok, his sacred space. Especially as he grew older he became more nostalgic for his family, for his stepmother, and for the rainy city of Temuco, its prodigious and haunting forests, and the Cerro Ñielol, a national monument that remains in Temuco as a reminder of the vegetation that once covered the region. It wasn't until Neruda was in his forties that he, like Walcott, began an overt project to reconstruct the birth of his poetic self in his early raw contact with nature, however. Also similarly, once he began, the process of reconstruction obsessed him to the end of his life. The opinion of the jury for the Premio Nacional de Literatura de Chile (National Prize for Literature of Chile), which he was awarded in 1959, specifically cited the notable influence of the region of Cautín and La Frontera in his poetry, "a fact beyond debate or doubt" (qtd. in Raviola Molina 161).

Autobiography for Neruda is an exploration of the ecological components of his own consciousness formed in the lands of his youth. This reconstruction deconstructs the anthropocentric conception of the self and explores the self as part of a living entity that extends well beyond the bounds of the body. This leads the poet into the realm of the unsayable and the unrecoverable experience of Wordsworthian youthful unity with the world that a more mature consciousness can only intimate and attempt to re-create in fragments. In the context of ecological process the self is undone, decomposed, "annihilated," as Alain Sicard argues (479). Sicard explains that Neruda's own exploration of a poetics of oblivion stems from the fact that "the feeling that there is a totality beyond individual consciousness is inseparable from the 'continual succession of an abyss' that the consciousness experiences. This retrospective experience of a fulfillment, by means of continual denial, has a name: oblivion" (341–42).

In Neruda's descriptions of his origins he is immersed in an Edenic natural world in Temuco and emerges with pen in hand. His consciousness cannot be separated, in other words, from his earliest awareness of the presence of forest (Carrasco Pirard 54). As Carrasco Pirard argues, for Neruda "the exercise of consciousness consists of the unity of subject and object, of the self and its circumstances" (57). This unity of self and world, he explains further, is forged in the act of poetic memory, a synthesizing force that unifies the present with the past, self with place. In this sense Neruda is never "a poet in some abstract sense, he is a poet of a particular [*determinado*] 'where'" (59).

While this is undeniably the primal urge of Neruda's poetry, it is also his poetry's paradoxical dilemma to find itself as a primal symptom of the subject's alienation from his environment. His poetry, in this sense, is a continual attempt to re-create the circumstances in which his poetic consciousness was born. In his *Confieso que he vivido*, written in 1970 and published posthumously, Neruda explains simply: "Tal vez el amor y la naturaleza fueron desde muy temprano los yacimientos de mi poesía [Perhaps love and nature were, very early on, the source of my poems]" (*OC* 5:407; *Memoirs* 12). He notes:

> Bajo los volcanes, junto a los ventisqueros, entre los grandes lagos, el fragante, el silencioso, el enmarañado bosque chileno . . . Se hunden los pies en el follaje muerto, crepitó una rama quebradiza, los gigantescos raulíes lavantan su encrespada estatura, un pájaro de la selva fría cruza, aletea, se detiene entres los sombríos ramajes. Y luego desde su escondite suena como un oboe. . . . Quien no conoce el bosque chileno, no conoce este planeta. (*OC* 5:399–400)

> ——

> Under the volcanoes, beside the snow-capped mountains, among the huge lakes, the fragrant, the silent, the tangled Chilean forest . . . My feet sink down into the dead leaves, a fragile twig crackles, the giant rauli trees rise in all their bristling height, a bird from the cold jungle passes over, flaps its wings, and stops in the sunless branches. And then, from its hideaway, it sings like an oboe. . . . Anyone who hasn't been in the Chilean forest doesn't know this planet. (*Memoirs* 5–6)

Neruda always depicts himself as alone in this natural world, and yet the sensuous experience of the wild continually teaches him the truths of his radical human separation from his environment.

Just as Whitman's fraternal bonds turn on his encounter with the otherness of nature, Neruda's explorations in the forest become a discovery of his solitude, something that paradoxically causes him to seek the embrace of human society in the city. The difference, however, is that Whitman rarely articulated his encounter with nature as an experience of solitude. This is partly due to the fact that Whitman was rarely as poignantly autobiographical as Neruda and was more intent on creating his poetic persona as a socially engaged, democratic lover. Neruda went much further than Whitman to become that persona in the flesh (including a successful campaign for a seat in the Chilean senate and an unsuccessful run for the presidency) and thus could rely more on his public persona to generate his poetry's influence; not a stranger to mythologizing his own life, he could afford to focus more intently on the particulars of his autobiography than could Whitman. Consequently, Neruda is less apt to exhibit Whitman's anxiety regarding the need to shape the "stock personality" of the Americas. Poetry's function is to serve as the bridge between radically individual experience and a collective whole that includes the natural world, something Neruda claims it did for him:

Se comenzó por infinitas playas o montes enmarañados una comunicación entre mi alma, es decir, entre mi poesía y la tierra más solitaria del mundo. De esto hace mucho años, pero esa comunicación, esa revelación, ese pacto con el espacio han continuado existiendo en mi vida. (*OC* 5:413)

—

Along endless beaches or thicketed hills, a communion was started between my spirit—that is my poetry—and the loneliest land in the world. This was many years ago, but that communion, that revelation, that pact with the wilderness, is still a part of my life. (*Memoirs* 18)

Hardie St. Martin's translation in *Memoirs* of *espacio* into "wilderness" and not simply "space" is a bit misleading. Neruda was consistently able to establish a poetic dialogue with many environments, whether they could be defined as wilderness or not. The point here is that Neruda's poetry is a dialectic that seeks to diminish and also to reflect upon his solitude within a more-than-human world. It is both what exacerbates and provides the soothing balm for his human condition.

A later visit to the stretch of coast near Puerto Saavedra—an area of undeveloped roads, small villages, and seemingly endless beach that remains largely influenced by Mapuche culture—that he first visited in his youth still yielded glimpses of the solitary condition he earlier described. About this stretch of coast Neruda wrote:

Cuando estuve por primera vez frente al océano quedé sobrecogido. Allí entre dos grandes cerros (el Huilque y el Maule) se desarrollaba la furia del gran mar. No sólo eran las inmensas olas nevadas que se levantaban a muchos metros sobre nuestras cabezas, sino un estruendo de corazón colosal, la palpitación del universo. (*OC* 5:411)

—

The first time I stood before the sea, I was overwhelmed. The great ocean unleashed its fury there between two big hills. . . . It wasn't just the immense snow-crested swells, rising many meters above our heads, but the loud pounding of a gigantic heart, the heartbeat of the universe. (*Memoirs* 16)

In *Memorial de Isla Negra* he remarks that this encounter taught him his connection not only to the more-than-human world but also to the broader societies around him. It created a curiosity that would eventually drive him from the frontier to the city. Following the Cautín river to the sea, the young poet is prelapsarian Adam:

> pequeño
> inhumano,
> perdido,
> aún sin razon ni canto,
> ni alegría (Neruda, "El primer mar," *OC* 2:1148)

> ——

> small
> inhuman,
> lost,
> still without thought or song,
> or any joy.

What gives birth to poetry is a fall not so much from innocence as from insularity of space and region bounded by land. The poet arrives at the sea for the first time and experiences a rupture of the boundaries of his world:

> salí de las raíces,
> se me agrandó la patria,
> se rompió la unidad de la madera:
> la cárcel de los bosques
> abrió una puerta verde
> por donde entró la ola con su trueno
> y se extendió mi vida
> con un golpe de mar, en el espacio. (Neruda, "La tierra austral," *OC* 2:1149)

> ——

> I departed from my roots,
> and my homeland was expanded,
> the unity of wood was broken:
> the prison of the forests
> opened a green gate
> through which entered a wave with its thunder
> and my life was extended
> with a slap of the sea, in space.

And yet Neruda also recognizes that it is literature, not the companionship of the wild, that soothes the pains of his solitude: "Que soledad la de un pequeño niño poeta, vestido de negro, en la frontera espaciosa y terrible. La vida y los libros poco a poco van dejando entrever misterios abrumadores [How lonely a small boy poet, dressed in black, feels on the vast and terrifying frontier wilderness! Little by little, life and books give me glimpses of overwhelming mysteries]" (*OC* 5:415; *Memoirs* 20).

When Neruda arrives in Santiago he realizes that poetry will now become the vehicle by which he transports himself back to the wild. He writes in his 1950 epic poem, *Canto general*:

> Luego llegué a la capital, vagamente impregnado
> de niebla y lluvia. Qué calles eran ésas?
> Los trajes de 1921 pululaban
> en un olor atroz de gas, café y ladrillos.
> Entre los estudiantes pasé sin comprender,
> reconcentrando en mí las paredes, buscando
> cada tarde en mi pobre poesía las ramas,
> las gotas y la luna que se habían perdido. (*OC* 1:810)
>
> ——
>
> Then I arrived in the capital, vaguely impregnated
> with mist and rain. What streets were those?
> The clothing of 1921 pullulated
> in an atrocious smell of gas, coffee and bricks.
> I circulated among the students bewildered,
> concentrating the walls within me, seeking
> every evening in my poor poetry the branches,
> the raindrops and moon that had become lost. (*Canto* 376)

The paradox here is that his poetic imagination comes alive as soon as the deep time of natural history becomes a memory, something to be longed for as a result of his entrance into the social world of human historical time. In *Memorial de Isla Negra* Neruda explains that this involves closing his eyes to the stimuli around him and drawing now upon memory as a means to transport him to natural time:

> La tierra surge como si viviera
> en mí, cierro los ojos, luego existo,
> cierro los ojos y se abre una nube,
> se abre una puerta al paso del perfume,

entra un río cantando con sus piedras,
me impregna la humedad del territorio. (*OC* 2:1202)
—

The earth surges as if it lived
within me, I close my eyes, later I exist,
I close my eyes and a cloud opens,
a door is opened to the wafting of perfume,
a river enters singing with its stones,
I am filled with the humidity of the territory.

Poetry's response to the fragments of memory embedded in the physical
senses is the only means by which the self-conscious adult can return to
natural time. Although nature is still available to the poet, his consciousness of loss has made it impossible to achieve stasis within deep time. In
1927, during his famous ambassadorial mission to Asia, Neruda recorded
the sensation that "entre yo y la naturaleza aún queda un velo, un tejido
sutil" [between nature and me there remains a veil, a subtle cloth] (qtd. in
Rodríguez Monegal, *El viajero* 58). He was referring literally to the mosquito
net that surrounded his bed but also to his discovery of a profound alienation he would spend his life seeking to overcome. Asian culture taught
him lessons about human belonging in the landscape that he felt he had
implicitly learned in La Araucanía (Teitelboim 142).

Wordsworth explored the dilemma of gaining self-consciousness and
sociality at the cost of losing youthful union with nature, but modernism
revised this paradigm, as is evident with Neruda. First, the unity with nature
he experiences is not imbued with a sense of spiritual belonging but is rather
conceived as a kind of material unity in deep time, and because the unity is
merely biological the self-consciousness of the poet presents the problem
of awareness of separation. Second, his preadolescent romps in the woods
are prelinguistic, and thus any attempt to represent the meaning of these
experiences betrays them. To the extent that Whitman is a romantic, for
example, he is aware of this challenge but does not fully embrace the
irony that language becomes a betrayal of the sought-after objective of
unity. Third, the experience of unity is for Neruda itself fraught with this
early, even if poorly articulated or understood, awareness of solitude and
separation. Indeed, the solitude he discovers in society would appear to be
an extension of the solitude he first discovered in nature. Ben Belitt com-

ments that Neruda rejects a visionary romanticism in favor of portraying "the enigmatic," which is "what is totally given us, what is totally *there*— inexhaustible, ordinary, inapprehensible" ("Pablo" 148–49). The question then must be raised, Why does he long for the raindrops and moon he has lost if they only filled him with the enigmatic realization of his separate human smallness? Neruda is plagued by an existential alienation that begins even in his early contacts with nature and extends into his social relationships. This alienation informs Neruda's major social and political poetry as he anguishes over his distance from his compatriots. His impatience with the intensity of this anguish helps to explain why he wrote so prolifically, why nature haunted him, and why he embraced socialism so passionately to the end of his life.[1]

He saw this isolation as a particularly Chilean problem due to both its social and its natural history. In 1962 he wrote that Chilean poets tended toward an expression of "soledad hemisférica" [hemispheric solitude] that is conditioned by "la dominante influencia de nuestra geología" [the dominant influence of our geology] (*OC* 4:1086). Indeed, many Chileans speak of their nation as an island, separated from the continent by the Andes and confronted by the sea. Neruda himself would give the name "Isla Negra" to his coastline town outside of Santiago to fulfill his desire to live on an island. Neruda explains:

Pero no hay duda que somos protagonistas semisolitarios, orientados o desorientados, de vastos terrenos apenas cultivados, de agrupaciones semicoloniales, ensordecidos por la tremenda vitalidad de nuestra naturaleza y por el antiguo aislamiento a que nos condena las metrópolis de ayer y de hoy. (*OC* 4:1086–87)

———

But there is no doubt that we are semisolitary protagonists, oriented or disoriented, by vast terrains scarcely cultivated, by semicolonial associations, deafened by the tremendous vitality of our nature and by the ancient isolation to which the metropolises of yesterday and today have condemned us.

But perhaps the fact of this longing for nature in the solitude of the city hints at some more-than-human quality he had learned about himself in the wilds of La Araucanía. Neruda's fascination with nature requires immobility, while his social concerns are facilitated by his frequent travels through various geographies. Neruda is both the fast-paced world traveler and the stoic and static observer of the material world. That he recognized this need to remain still, to return to his primordial inspiration drawn from the material world, was due to his growing suspicion that the alienation of human society was perhaps not merely existential but due to an imbalance with nature. In his incomparable study of Neruda Alain Sicard notes that Neruda believed in "a necessary readjustment of human rhythm to the rhythm of the material world [del ritmo humano al ritmo material]. The time has come for men to learn from the earth and to introduce into their own chaotic restlessness that which it denies the earth but is the only thing that will return the earth its fecundity: stillness [inacción]" (169). In this still encounter with physical existence, particularly at a more mature stage of life, solitude is no longer a burden but the beginning of understanding. Sicard explains that solitude in nature provides "a confirmation of human material origins" (330).

Neruda's poetry never fully reconciles the competing demands made upon him by human society and the natural world. Sicard and Saúl Yurkié-vich before him have argued that Neruda's work is bifurcated by two poetics, one found within mythical, cyclical time that is content for human memory to be enfolded within the cycles of nature's rhythms. The other is historical, determined to recover human time and human suffering and intent on progressing and creating a better future. He often faces the choice between "a natural world without history" or a "history reduced to the political" that ignores the human relationship to the material world (Sicard 552).

With extraordinary passion and unmatched willingness to adopt a variety of strategies, Neruda sought poetic means of reconciling these tensions, but he was never satisfied with the results. For this reason, perhaps, he enjoyed a career of staggering production, variation, and enigmatic contradiction. Belitt's description is apt: "[H]e is plainly Ovidian in his metamorphic passion for change as a mode of virility and a dynamic of cosmological love" ("Pablo" 146). Neruda found Whitman's notion of adamic poetry immensely compelling, but, like Whitman, he also understood that to imagine poetry as innocent first-time naming and direct apprehension and appropriation of the named object was too simplistic. As Yurkiévich argues, the facts of New World human suffering prove too much for Neruda: he "cannot be content with a merely natural, primitive, paradisiacal view of things" ("Mito" 207). Perhaps. But he rarely depicted the indigenous history of the land his family occupied, attracted as he was by its allure as a private Eden. That hesitancy to allow the indigenous facts of Chilean southern history to fully shape his poetic consciousness may be explained by his own ethnocentricity. Indeed, this impulse to see Latin America's Western history as having a prelapsarian Edenic origin remains appealing and problematic for many authors. Even late in life Neruda was still attracted to this portrait of La Frontera. In the preface to the 1963 edition of *Memorial de Isla Negra*, for example, he extrapolates from his own frontier experiences and postulates that "el patrimonio de los americanos" [the patrimony of Americans] is that of a relatively empty slate of previous human history, a remark that would later be portrayed in Gabriel García Márquez's *Cien años de soledad*. He explains:

> [N]acimos y crecimos condicionados por la naturaleza que al mismo tiempo nos nutría y nos castigaba. . . . No teníamos a quién acudir. Nadie fue anterior en aquellas comarcas: nadie dejó para ayudarnos algún edificio sobre el territorio ni olvidó sus huesos en cementerios que sólo después existieron, fueron nuestros los primeros muertos. Lo bueno es que pudimos soñar en el aire libre que nadie había respirado. Y así fueron nuestros sueños los primeros de la tierra. (*OC* 2:1401)
>
> ———
>
> Our birth and growth were conditioned by nature, which both nurtured and chastened us. . . . We had no one to turn to. No one was prior to those settlements: no one left any building in the territory to help us nor left behind their bones in the cemeteries that only came into existence later; ours were the first dead. The good thing was that we could dream in free air that no one else breathed. Thus, ours were the first dreams of the land.

The originality upon which he insists here is disconcerting, given the relatively recent history of conquest in the region that facilitated his family's arrival in the area. Such erasure allows him to attribute a seemingly categorical innocence to the endeavors of the new arrivals in the area. Once this Edenic land of originality has been cleared of this past history, all use of natural resources has the blessing of nature: "el serrucho y la sierra / se amaban noche y día, / cantando" [the handsaw and the power saw / loved each other night and day, / singing] (*OC* 2:1144).

Like Whitman's vision of the demise of the redwood, this portrait of innocence would no doubt benefit from some assessment of indigenous presence in the area. Volodia Teitelboim explains that during Neruda's childhood the Mapuche Indians "lived totally apart" from the Chilean settlers due to their recent expulsion to the surrounding countryside (24). This might be an overstatement that serves to diminish the importance of the disturbing absence of Native American life in Neruda's poetry. Nevertheless, Neruda's point seems to be that in such raw and comparatively primitive circumstances the colonial conditions of Latin American society in the nineteenth and into the twentieth centuries have left many societies relatively isolated from the directives of Western modernity and that such societies have the particular advantage of struggling with and learning more directly from nature than in the twentieth century with its technological advances.

The particular geological history of the Chilean south has also isolated many settlements and is arguably one of the most significant factors that made the Mapuche resistance so successful for so long. The area exposes to the naked eye much of nature's raw regenerative forces, such as volcanoes, glacial lakes, and other phenomena that inspire Neruda to declare that the wind of the cordilleras "limpió la creación" [cleaned the creation] and that in this place where "nace el aire / por fin conocimos la tierra / y la tocamos en su origen" [the air is born / finally we came to know the earth / and we touched it at its origin] (*OC* 2:1258). His comments foreshadow Walcott's belief that being born on a small island, far removed from the commotion of metropolitan life, was a blessing for a writer because it taught him to have a more complete "communion with things that the metropolitan writers no longer care about," such as "family, earth, history" (qtd. in Nichols 177).

Sicard argues that Neruda was similarly able to take poetic advantage of such circumstances: "No Eden and no experience of solitude can escape history. That which is uninhabited [*lo deshabitado*] is nothing more than a fiction invented by consciousness in order to imagine the material world" (381). While many such Edens have been invented not just to imagine but to exploit the material world, it is true that Neruda's Edens would not remain untouched by history. In provincial worlds of relative solitude a dialectic begins, akin to Octavio Paz's notion, whereby the poet's self discovers "a confirmation of his material origins" (Sicard 330). This discovery teaches, as does all radical scientific materialism, that there is no opposition between natural and human history, even though it presents a considerable challenge to the poet in being able to name his history and origins in human terms. When developed in direct contact with the material world, poetic naming of our human place in the land, like that of these three poets, may not be the same thing as experience itself, but they provide opportunities for reconnection. As Jonathan Bate argues, poems are like parks: they may be artifice, but that does not make them "unreal"; they simply provide a "re-creational space" to reenact our encounter with nature (63). Neruda provides one such example in *Memorial*:

Las tablas de la casa
olían a bosque,
a selva pura.
Desde entonces mi amor
fue maderero
y lo que toco se convierte en bosque.
Se me confunden los ojos y las hojas,
ciertas mujeres con la primavera
del avellano, el hombre con el árbol,
amo el mundo del viento y del follaje,
no distingo entre labios y raíces. ("Primer viaje," *OC* 2:1143)

—

The boards of the house
smelled of the woods,
of the deep forest.
From that time on, my love
had wood in it
and everything I touched turned into wood.
They became one in me,
lives and leaves,
certain women and the hazelnut
spring, men and trees.
I love the world of wind and foliage.
I can't tell lips from roots. (Stavans, *Poetry* 649)

Boards and tables are not forests, but we should not divorce them from their natural origin by thinking of them as unnatural. The poem insists on the proximity of the natural world that confuses natural and human history (note the subtle shift in sound from *ojos* [eyes] to *hojas* [leaves]), allowing the reader to imagine the common biology of the human and the more-than-human world.

Historical knowledge and political conscience would develop later in Neruda's life, and, as we will see, he attempted to reintroduce those elements into his conception of New World history. However, his point here is that life on the frontier was experienced *as if* it were a raw and untrammeled world. To retroactively introduce historical injustices into those primal scenes of his poetic development would be untrue to his naive childhood experience, which taught him to confuse lips and roots. With these new vistas available to him, everything, including of course the forests themselves, now becomes infinite space by virtue of their silent mysteries and dynamic life.

Neruda is keenly aware of the paradox this presents. As the poet's consciousness of natural process increases, so too does his awareness of his own separability from this natural womb. In "Tierra austral" he writes:

> Suena y se calla el bosque:
> se calla cuando escucho,
> suena cuando me duermo,
>
> . . . .
> Pero, sólo de entonces,
> de los pasos perdidos,
> de la confusa soledad, del miedo,
> de las enredaderas,
> del cataclismo verde, sin salida,
> volví con el secreto:
> sólo entonces y allí pude saberlo,
>
> . . . .
> se decidió mi pacto
> con la tierra. (*OC* 2:1150–51)
>
> —
>
> The forest resounds and falls silent:
> it falls silent when I listen,
> it resounds when I am sleeping,
>
> . . . .
> But only from then on
> from the lost steps,

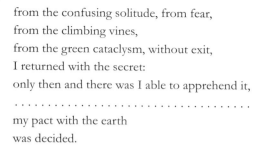

from the confusing solitude, from fear,
from the climbing vines,
from the green cataclysm, without exit,
I returned with the secret:
only then and there was I able to apprehend it,
. . . .
my pact with the earth
was decided.

Neruda's apparent reference to Alejo Carpentier's 1953 novel, *Los pasos perdidos* [*The Lost Steps*], is illuminating. The novel's protagonist is a composer who enters the Amazon jungle in Venezuela, composes his masterpiece as he is drawn closer to the ultimate Muse of all composers, nature itself, but is unable to carry the music back out into civilization. Nature here seems to represent a kind of Jungian subconscious, the source of all art, and yet it cannot be known except as a secret or as silence. To write poetry is to sound the untranslatable depths of the natural history of human being, or, as Bate puts it, "Art is the place of exile where we grieve for our lost home upon the earth" (73).

Instead of being made in the image of a knowable spiritual God, Neruda is "a semejanza, a imagen del misterio" [in likeness, in the image of the mystery] ("La poesía," *OC* 2:1156). He is made in the image of an unknowable physical mystery; he becomes aware of the fact that the same mysteries that present themselves to the mind in contemplation of nature's infinitude are also within him and that poetry is the language that bears witness to this deep kinship with the wild. As he states in "La condición humana" [The Human Condition], "así mi adolescencia / fue territorio, tuve / islas, silencio, monte, crecimiento [and so my adolescence / was landscape, I had / islands, silence, mountains, growing]" (*OC* 2:1163; Stavans, *Poetry* 663). His openness to experiencing his unity with nature prepares the ground within him for poetry: "[F]ui fértil con todo / lo que caía en mí, germinaciones [I was fertile in everything / that happened to me, germinations]" (*OC* 2:1163; Stavans, *Poetry* 663).

His effort to understand the precise meaning of his material unity with the physical world of his youth inspired Neruda to spend considerable effort, arguably more than any poet of his generation, studying natural history. Nature's difference, its elusiveness, did not remain a mythological mystery for Neruda, but, as I suggested was the foundational experience of much natural science in chapter 1, his increasing knowledge of ecological processes only served to increase his adamic wonder, as it had for Whitman. He came to appreciate that nature itself told a story incapable of being captured by language and that this elusiveness was the essence of our own natural history as human beings. His poetry rose to great heights in its expression of mourning over a broken union with the natural world, but, unlike Whitman, he was adamant that this was not romantic longing for poetry to rekindle a spiritual wholeness. There were rational laws that explained our material belonging to the planet and our kinship with animals and the elements. Poetry was still necessary, however, because science, like history, can only explain; they are discourses aimed at the construction of future and better understanding and are therefore able to assess the limitations of previous formulations but ill equipped to assess their own limitations, to avoid fomenting reductive thinking, or to imagine the quality of our human belonging in the natural world.

In his preface to his *Memorias* Neruda explains how poetry plays an adamic role but only because it acknowledges that metaphors are the best way to approximate the strangeness of the natural process. He insists that our memories are inevitably the work of the imagination, a poetic creation, not a documentation of the past. By implication, all thinking is potentially poetic, made new because of the paradoxical inevitability of forgetting whenever we attempt to memorialize what we know. He writes:

> *Estas memorias o recuerdos son intermitentes y a ratos olvidadizos porque así precisamente es la vida. La intermitencia del sueño nos permite sostener los días del trabajo. Muchos de mis recuerdos se han desdibujado al evocarlos, han desvenido en polvo como un cristal irremediablemente herido. . . . De cuanto he dejado escrito en esta páginas se desprenderán siempre—como en las arboledas de otoño y como en el tiempo de las viñas—las hojas amarillas que van a morir y las uvas que revivirán en el vino sagrado. (OC 5:397)*

—

> *In these memoirs or recollections there are gaps here and there, and sometimes they are also forgetful, because life is like that. Intervals of dreaming help us stand up under days of work. Many of the things I remember have blurred as I recalled them, they have crumbled to dust, like irreparably shattered glass. . . . From what I have left in writing on these pages there will always fall—as in the autumn grove during the harvesting of*

the vineyards—yellow leaves on their way to death, and grapes will find new life in the
sacred wine. (Memoirs 3)

His memoirs are themselves simultaneously offered as the sacred wine that
has given new life to old grapes and as a force that kills and drops yellow
leaves of autumn to the ground. Neruda's poetics of oblivion means that
memories are a poetic language that, although promising regeneration, cannot entirely escape the inevitability of continued amnesia and death. That is,
memory and amnesia go hand in hand; everything that is commemorated in
poetry is inseparable from what is also forgotten by the same process. This
paradox is sustained by the nature of Neruda's New World experience,
as this and the following chapter explore, as well as by the fact of our
subjection to the laws of natural history, as his metaphor implies. That is,
the constitution of the self, if it is to be true both to human experience and
to natural history, is by necessity a poetic process of commemoration and
mourning, one that draws the self to natural history to find the reasons for
its untellable story.

Naming the Self

For Neruda, what one learns about the human belonging in the natural
world cannot be generalized beyond what is learned chiefly through one's
senses. Autobiographical metaphors, then, will always be necessary and
insufficient to make the language of the senses intelligible. For this reason,
Neruda's is a much more intensely focused meditation on the poet's direct
experience with a particular locale than we saw in Whitman, with the possible exception of what we find in Whitman's reflections at Timber Creek.
The specificity of his autobiography grounds Neruda in southern Chile,
where he is able to recollect his sensual contact with the world. Neruda
explores this contact the first time he formally tells his autobiography in
verse in the final chapter, "Yo soy," of his 1950 epic, *Canto general*. Echoing the words of the Lord in the Old Testament ("I am"), the God who
spoke and the world was, Neruda is interested in revising our notion of the
constative powers of adamic naming because he recognizes that what has
formed him, more than his own linguistic powers, family origins, or social
relations, is the natural world he came into contact with from the time of
his infancy. The natural world has replaced the Judeo-Christian Creator. In

the beginning was not the Word of the poet but the sensual encounter with physical being, and it becomes poetry's task to capture anachronistically the essence of that encounter.

He announces in the section's opening that "[l]o primero que vi fueron los árboles, barrancas / decoradas con flores de salvaje hermosura [I first saw trees, ravines / adorned with flowers of wild beauty]" (*OC* 1:807; *Canto* 373). In the beginning was not the word but, rather, as David Abram argues, the sensual experience of things; words arrive belatedly to try to recapture this prelinguistic experience of materiality. This material and sensual experience is the essence of Neruda's childhood:

> Mi infancia son zapatos mojados, troncos rotos
> caídos en la selva, devorados por lianas
> y escarabajos, dulces días sobre la avena. (*OC* 1:807)
>
> ——
>
> My childhood is wet shoes, broken trunks
> fallen in the forest, devoured by vines
> and beetles, sweet days upon the oats. (*Canto* 373)

As the poet emerges from these sensual stimuli, he is not Adam seeking to name things but rather a sensual wilderness himself that seeks to be named by the garden:

> Nómbrame, dije tal vez a los rosales: . . .
> cada temblor del mundo conocía mis pasos,
> me esperaba el rincón más oculto, la estatua
> del árbol soberano en la llanura:
> todo en la encrucijada llegó a mi desvarío
> desgranado mi nombre sobre la primavera. (*OC* 1:808)
>
> ——
>
> Name me, I said perhaps to the rosebushes: . . .
> Every tremor of the world knew my footsteps,
> the darkest corner awaited me, the statue
> of the sovereign tree on the prairie:
> everything on the crossroad reached my delirium,
> threshing my name upon springtime. (*Canto* 375)

Abram describes how animistic cultures see nature as a witness, as constituted by seeing, feeling sentient beings. In his comparison to postanimistic societies he notes, "to directly perceive any phenomenon is to enter into relation with it, to feel oneself in a living interaction with another being. To define the phenomenon as an inert object, to deny the ability of a tree to inform and even instruct one's awareness, is to have turned one's senses away from that phenomenon" (Abram 117). To fully engage the senses in our perception of the world is to begin to understand ourselves as perceived by it, what phenomenologists call "perceptual reciprocity" (153). In this instance Neruda's as yet nameless poet seeks the constitution of his self but finds that his objective is scattered throughout the phenomena of the physical world that fill his senses. Thus, he can only be what he sees, smells, touches, and hears, and his senses will thus tell him what to remember about himself and about his people. His very name, then, must become an echo of those sensations of communion with an animated, intelligent world. Neruda's autobiography becomes a series of memories of what his senses can recall and what his body can remember.

When Neruda leaves the south for Santiago and finds himself separated from this garden, his poetry becomes a gesture in behalf of restoration, a reclamation of "las soledades / donde nació [mi voz]" [the solitudes / where (my voice) was born] (*OC* 1:811).[2] The road back to the wilds of his childhood is through sensual experience with material life:

Amé cada materia, cada gota
de púrpura o metal, agua y espiga
y entré en espesa capas resguardadas
por espacio y arena temblorosa,
hasta cantar con boca construida,
como un muerto, en las uvas de la tierra. (*OC* 1:824)
—

I loved every material, every droplet
of purple or metal, water and shock of grain,
and I entered dense strata protected
by space and quaking sand,
until I sang with a ravaged mouth,
like a corpse, in the grapes of the earth. (*Canto* 388)

The paradox of a self founded on sensual experience is that corporeal experience delimits the particularity of the body in time and space. At the same time, however, it opens the self to an almost infinitely broad physical world that disperses the poet's sense of self across a vast geography of biological belonging and brings into question the very utility of selfhood as traditionally understood by Western society. This is why he sings "like a corpse," undone by this new vastness of the self.

The imagery in the above passage recalls the experience Neruda recounts in his 1938 essay, "La copa de sangre" [The Cup of Blood], regarding his father's coffin. Neruda experienced a kind of religious epiphany in the sense that he understood that natural regeneration was the meaning of human yearnings for eternal life. Neruda was never close to his father, but, in order that his parents could be buried together, he and his brother disinterred their father's casket, held within a cemented and sealed niche. They took the casket out,

> pero ya llena de hongos, y sobre ella una palma con flores negras y extinguidas: la humedad de la zona había partido el ataúd y al bajarlo de su sitio, y sin creer lo que veía, vimos bajar de él cantidades de agua, cantidades como interminables litros que caían de adentro de él, de su substancia. (*OC* 4:418)
>
> ———
>
> but [it was] already full of mushrooms and on the top a clump of black and extinguished flowers: the humidity of the area had caused a split in the coffin, and as we lowered it from its place and in disbelief at what I was seeing, we saw cascades of water fall from the coffin, endless liters that fell from within the coffin, from his substance.

This was Temuco's famous rainwater,

> y esta lluvia había atravesado techos y balaustradas, ladrillo y otros materiales y otros muertos hasta llegar a la tumba de mi duedo. Ahora bien, esta agua terrible, esta agua salida de un imposible, insondable, extraordinario escondite, para mostrarme a mí su torrencial secreto, esta agua original y temible me advertía otra vez con su misterioso derrame mi conexión interminable con una determinada vida, región, y muerte. (*OC* 4:418)
>
> ———
>
> and this rain had passed over roofs and balustrades, over brick and other materials and other dead until it arrived at the tomb of the one I had lost. Now, in order to show me its torrential secret, this terrible water, this water

emerged from an impossible, unfathomable hidden place, this original and fearsome water taught me again in its mysterious sudden flow of my perpetual connection to a predetermined life, region, and death.

Becoming a witness in such an intimate way to nature's indifferent regenerative power binds and destines Neruda to his homeland and to his holy task of reaching for this "insondable . . . escondite" [unfathomable . . . hidden place] in order to understand what links his own life and death to the life and death of other beings, human and nonhuman.

The constitution of his self, then, precisely because nature teaches the lessons of interdependence and regeneration, must necessarily also involve solidarity with his fellow beings, human and nonhuman. Only four years later and just a few weeks prior to his visit to Machu Picchu, Neruda wrote that the existential materialism of the great Spanish poet Francisco de Quevedo, not Whitman's transcendental urges or embrace of death, had taught him this "biological lesson" (*OC* 4:457). Quevedo challenged him to ask,

[N]o integramos la muerte en nuestra cuotidiana existencia, no somos parte perpetua de la muerte, no somos lo más audaz, lo que ya salió de la muerte? No es lo más mortal, lo más viviente, por su mismo misterio? (*OC* 4:457)

———

Do we not incorporate death into our quotidian existence, are we not a perpetual part of death, are we not the most audacious thing that has already come forth from death? Is not that which is the most mortal, the most alive, itself a mystery?

As I explore in chapter 9, Walcott's mother's death causes him to question the concept of eternal life and leads him to resolve the dilemma by learning to see death in nature's bounty and bounty in death. Poetry is the language of resurrection, since it sees ecologically. Neruda reflects in similar ways on his mother, who died shortly after giving birth to him. In *Memorial de Isla Negra* he recalls seeing her grave:

[L]a llamé entre los muertos, para verla,
pero como todos los otros enterrados,
no sabe, no oye, no contestó nada. (*OC* 2:1142)

———

I called to her among the dead, to see her,
but like all those who were buried
she does not know or hear, she didn't have an answer.

From the silence of her grave, however, things emerge reborn, including
his own poetic voice, much like his experience at his father's disinterment:

Y de allí soy, de aquel
Parral de tierra temblorosa,
tierra cargada de uvas
que nacieron
desde mi madre muerta. (*OC* 2:1143)

—

And from there I come
from that Parral of trembling earth,
earth bearing grapes
that were born
from my dead mother.

This ecological truth requires a radical reorientation of our human relationship to time. As Neruda explains in "Aquellas vidas" [Those Lives] in *Memorial de Isla Negra*, the mistake is to assume that

teniendo dientes,
teniendo pies y manos y alfabeta
era sólo cuestión de honor la vida. (*OC* 2:1203)

—

having teeth,
having feet and hands and alphabet
life was only a question of honor.

If the full measure of human "history" is so easily measured, one can only
conclude that

sólo le sirvió para morir
la vida: el tiempo para no tenerlo.
Y la tierra al final para enterrarlo. (*OC* 2:1203)

—

life was only useful

for dying: time for losing time.
And the earth, in the end, for being buried.

Shallow time means that the telos of human history is simply death in the
ground, but, once expanded within the context of natural history, human
experience obtains a kind of material perpetuation that gives reason to
earthly joy. In his poem "La gran alegría" [The Great Joy] from "Yo soy"
he explains that his greatest desire is to exult in his earthly destiny: "la
herencia de los bosques, el viento del camino / y un día decidido bajo la
luz terrestre [the forest legacy, the wind of the road / and a determined day
beneath the earthly light]" (*OC* 1:829; *Canto* 393).

A human natural history means that, like Whitman, Neruda has discovered his broad geography of New World solidarity. His adamic imagination
urges him to cross social and political borders, like Temuco's widespread
rain, and speak to the voiceless poor. In an allusion to his father's coffin he
insists that if poetry can promise new life to the suffering minions, it must
be a poetry of nature and natural death:

Quiero que a la salida de fábricas y minas
esté mi poesía adherida a la tierra,
al aire, a la victoria del hombre maltratado.
Quiero que un joven halle en la dureza
que construí, con lentitud y con metales,
como una caja, abriéndola, cara a cara, la vida,
y hundiendo al alma toque las ráfagas que hicieron
mi alegría, en la altura tempestuosa. (*OC* 1:830)

———

At the gates of factories and mines I want
my poetry to cling to the earth,
to the air, to the victory of abused mankind.
In the hardness that I built, like a box,
slowly and with metals, I would like
the youth who opens it, face-to-face, to find life,
and plunging his soul in may he reach the gusts
that spelled my happiness, in the stormy heights. (*Canto* 394)

If the earth is our mortal destiny, for Neruda it is also the promise of our
transformation, since in its embrace human society will find the means to

regenerate and resurrect. Neruda knows that "voy a morir, sin nada más, con tierra / sobre mi cuerpo, destinado a ser tierra [I'm going to die, without more ado, with earth / on my body, destined to be earth]" (*OC* 1:830; *Canto* 394), but this does not mean the end. Again echoing his experience with his father's coffin, he claims a similarly earthly destiny for himself:

Que los sepultureros escarben las materias
aciagas: que levanten
los fragmentos sin luz de la ceniza
y hablen en el idioma del gusano.
Yo tengo frente a mí sólo semillas,
desarrollos radiantes y dulzura. (*OC* 1:831)

—

Let the gravediggers pry into ominous
matter: let them raise
the lightless fragments of ash,
and let them speak the maggot's language.
I'm facing nothing but seeds,
radiant growth and sweetness. (*Canto* 395)

The implication is that natural history is saturated by the sorrows, pains, and joys of human existence and that human action is potentially harmful to the cycles of life. Neruda's understanding of environmental degradation was hampered by the hope inspired by socialist experiments with environmental engineering, feats that he hoped would prove capable of feeding the earth's poor. But late in his life he became more cautious in this enthusiasm because of a growing awareness of potentially irreparable harm done to the natural cycles of regeneration, which in the long run were humanity's greatest source of hope.

Shortly after his sixty-fifth birthday Neruda wrote a small collection simply entitled "Aún," which can be translated as "Still" or "Even Now." The aim of this collection appears to be a reassertion, despite his aging body and a growing sense of world-weariness, that he remains invested in an earthly poetry: "[D]ebo aclarar aún mis deberes terrestres" [I must still clarify my terrestrial duties], he writes, insisting still that "cuando quiero / contar mi vida / es tierra lo que cuento" [when I want / to tell the story of my life / it is earth of which I speak] (*OC* 3:525, 528). He reasserts that these duties begin again with his beloved Araucanía. The book's second poem revisits his birth land, even though now he observes "los alerces rotos, las araucarias muertas" [the broken Chilean redwoods, the dead monkey puzzle trees] instead of a virginal and unnamed forest. The latter years of Neruda's life allowed him to mark the environmental changes that had occurred since his childhood, giving him more pause about a Whitmanian praise of human labor. The land has changed its face, but so too has the ocean been affected:

> Se fueron las ballenas: a otro mar?
> Huyeron de la costa encarnizada?
>
> . . . .
>
> Y nadie defendió a las gigantescas! (*OC* 3:538)
>
> —
>
> The whales have departed: to another sea?
> Did they flee the fierce coast?
>
> . . . .
>
> And no one defended these giants!

His aim, however, is not to remain lodged in a hopeless nostalgia but rather to reckon with history's errors and then find reason for celebration in the context of a sobering account of the detritus of time's passage. Just as Walcott experiences awe in the ordinary despite a regrettable past, Neruda still stands before the day capable of perceiving the news that new light and weather bring:

> Hoy que un día creció para ser ancho
> como la tierra o más extenso aún,
> cuando se abrió la luz mostrando el territorio
> llegó tu lluvia y trajo sus espadas
> el retrato de ayer acribillado,
> el amor de la tierra insoportable,
> con aquellos caminos que me llevan
> al Polo Sur, entre árboles quemados. (*OC* 3:526)
>
> —
>
> Today that a day grew to be wide
> as the earth or even more extensive,
> when the light parted revealing territory
> the rain came and brought its swords

the portrait of yesterday was crumpled,
love of the intolerable earth,
with those roads that carry me
to the South Pole, among burned trees.

Time is wider than space in Neruda's poetics because light is that which frames spaces and makes them measurable and remarkable; light and its passage is the context within which space obtains meaning, and this means that newness with each passing day is always possible, even in the context of a lamentable past.

Neruda provides, for example, a sobering and self-implicating account of the colonial failings that his generation of Chileans is responsible for ("los ladrones éramos nosotros" [we were the thieves], he confesses) after they seemingly spoiled the indigenous innocence of La Araucanía when they introduced policemen, railroads, umbrellas, and books (*OC* 3:527–28). He explains that despite his opportunities to live elsewhere in the world and despite the irrevocable changes in his land he remains determined by the physical environment of his birthplace:

[M]e hizo volver y quedarme y no volver a partir:
que sepa todo el mundo que por los menos en mí
la tierra me propone, me dispone y me embarga. (*OC* 3:533)
—

The earth made me return to stay, not to depart again:
let the world know that at least when it comes to me
the earth proposes me, lays me down, and seizes me.

Despite technological advances and the migratory opportunities of modernity, birthplace "still" remains that which both enables and delimits his being.

The paradox is that Neruda's awareness of time's passage is facilitated by these lamentable changes. If unchanging paradises stand outside of time, time becomes the very narrative structure of inevitable environmental degradation. The only reason why time's passage is not cause for perpetual lament or complicit embrace of degrading changes is because nature brings its own changes as well. That is, the physical world we think we have come to love may have been changed by human hands, but it also changes in its very nature, so to speak, as a dynamic and living ecosystem. The poet, then, must forge the capacity to bear witness to these silent and seemingly obscure transformations. Neruda does not here attempt to write from a position outside of time as the omniscient observer of its ravages; instead, he writes from within time. This means that he is an accomplice to nature's end, but this is a risk he must take if he is also going to be a witness of nature's powers of regeneration. He writes:

> Se va el hoy. Fue una cápsula
> de fría luz que volvió a su recinto,
> a su madre sombría, a renacer.
> Lo dejo ahora envuelto en su linaje.
> Es verdad, día, que participé en la luz?
> Tiempo, soy parte de tu catarata?
> Arenas mías, soledades!
>
> Si es verdad que nos vamos,
> nos fuimos consumiendo
> a plena sal marina
> y a golpes de relámpago.
> Mi razón ha vivido a la intemperie,
> entregué al mar mi corazón calcáreo. (*OC* 3:539)
>
> ———
>
> The day dissipates. It was a capsule
> of cold light that returned to its corner,
> to its mother shadow, to be reborn.
> I leave the day now wrapped in its lineage.
> Is it true, day, that I took part in light?
> Time, am I a part of your cataract?
> My sands, solitudes!
>
> If it is true that we are leaving
> we left in the act of consuming
> in full marine salt
> and in strikes of lightning.
> My reason has lived in the open air,
> I gave my chalky heart to the sea.

The implication here is that the poetic task is to resist the temptations of the linearity of historical time, its teleological seduction, and to succumb to nature's circularity. We will fail to do this unless we gain self-consciousness *within*, instead of in denial of, the flow of natural time and change. The evidence for the poet's participation in light is his own sensual apprehension of the world. If human destiny is circumscribed by the earth and its cycles of time, the poet's "reason" is gained only through his experience of the phenomena the earth makes available to his senses.

The environmental advantage of an imagination informed by circular temporality is that we do not become overcome by nostalgia or by a just as dangerous naive positivism about time's inevitable progress. The key for Neruda is the capacity to acknowledge

> honor del día fresco,
> la juventud del rocío,
> la mañana del mundo,
> lo que crece a pesar del tiempo amargo:
> el orden puro
> que necesitamos. (*OC* 3:540)
>
> —
>
> the honor of the fresh day,
> the youth of the dew,
> the morning of the world,
> that which grows despite bitter time:
> the pure order
> that we need.

This pure order is more profound in its measurements than the naive and narrow-minded "sombrereros que pasaron la vida / midiendo mi cabeza y tu cabeza" [the hatmakers who spent their lives / measuring my head and your head] (*OC* 3:540). It is the order Whitman intuited when he wrote that "to die is different than anyone supposes, and luckier," where death and life can no longer be distinguished (*PW* 30). We might die within time, but time itself continues: Neruda dies "con cada ola cada día" [with each wave each day], but "el día no muere / nunca" [the day does not die / ever] (*OC* 3:541).

Unnaming the Self

In February 1956 Khrushchev revealed Stalin's crimes, and Neruda, a remarkably unbending devotee of the Soviet cause, had finally had his comeuppance. Neruda had consistently praised Stalin and the Soviet Union despite increasing evidence of repression and violence within the party government and despite open differences with anti-Stalinists such as Octavio Paz. Critics have argued that Neruda underwent a significant change in his poetics after 1956, noting a new self-questioning attitude, a less strident Marxist fixation on the future, and a more intent focus on the world around him.[3] It is hard to miss the playfulness and openness of Neruda beginning in his *Tercer libro de odas* [Third Book of Odes] in 1957, in *Estravagario* in 1958, and in *Piedras de Chile* [Stones of Chile] in 1959. However, as I will explain in my analysis of the penultimate book of *Canto general* entitled "El gran océano" [The Great Ocean] in chapter 6, the constitution of the self that is so confidently expressed in "Yo soy" is already contextualized by the perspective provided by Neruda's growing understanding of ecological process and geological deep time. Although his emerging Marxism led him to hail a poetics of "impure poetry" while living in Spain, this interest in material life led him deeper and deeper into mystery, and his late poems, so focused on material life, began to resemble the purity of Rilke he had once rejected. Nearing his own death, Neruda confided in a friend: "I now see that there is no such thing as pure or impure poetry. I had to make mistakes, but I was honest enough to admit it" (qtd. in Feinstein 407). The natural sciences offered Neruda a challenge to his teleological Marxism, and the circumstances of 1956 only spurred him on to develop further a view of the infinite dialogue between human and natural histories that was implicit in his earlier poetry.

Hernán Loyola, the editor of Neruda's most recent and comprehensive complete works, argues that in *Tercer libro* Neruda begins to lose confidence in "that sense of progression and development, of marching toward a desired goal" (*OC* 2:1357). Consequently, he argues that Neruda abandons the modernist project "of pursuing the goal of a final self-portrait [*del autoretrato final*]; he abandoned all illusion of advancing toward the high and ambitious achievement [*ambicioso horizonte*] of the definitive 'I'" (*OC* 2:1357). Loyola describes this as a transition from modernism to postmodernism in Neruda, notable also in *Piedras de Chile*. He explains that in *Canto general* "natural resources . . . needed History so as to conquer a human significance capable of reestablishing the foundation of the (modern) Subject. Now it is the reverse. The Subject, historicized to an excess, seeks to establish symbolically its new (postmodern) poetic of the Stone, the most inert of all Nature" (*OC* 2:1389). Loyola insists, in fact, that what we see in Neruda after 1956 is a "progressive emptying out [*deshabitación*] of history" (*OC* 2:1389).

I agree that a fundamental shift in Neruda's conception of history and of the self appears after 1956, but I do not agree that we have to see this as a modern-postmodern shift. It would be more accurate to call this a shift from an anthropocentric conception of history to a biocentric one. Writing within an imagined temporal scale much deeper than either Whitman or Walcott, Neruda offers arguably the most profound and sustained investigation of the self in deep time, in a truly ancient New World, this hemisphere has ever seen. The self still holds, constituted now by a deeper time and history than what human and specifically Western history afford; the self is given life within a context that can no longer be fully accessed or denoted. Although it would appear that this means the self is postmodern because of its fragmentation and the uncertainty regarding its epistemological limits, these limits are not ontological and are only limits of what can be measured by the insufficient tools of language and culture. Both can be reoriented in order to intuit the wholeness and integrity of the biological world, which thus serves as the new circumscription of the self.

This kind of reorientation has led many nature poets to a kind of neo-romanticism in which, like Whitman, as I argued earlier, they are aware of the limitations of metaphor but seem hesitant to embrace the ironies of linguistic limitation and of the indeterminate boundaries of the self. Neruda rejects the allure of transcendence and the pursuit of a higher realization of the self; instead, he allows the ironies of his ecological condition to feed the fire of his poetic self-dissolution. This is in part because Neruda has lost confidence in the Hegelian trajectory both of historical progression and of self-realization. His relationship to the past becomes more complicated by the fact that what lies ahead is not necessarily preferable or a genealogical succession of what came before. Therefore, his poetic task becomes one of archaeological investigation to discover what was left behind by virtue of having vainly followed the illusion of a teleological narrative to his life. In short, the self's acquired name and learned history must be unnamed.

We see how the poet's autobiographical self is challenged by ecology in several poems from *Tercer libro de odas*. In "Oda al algarrobo muerto" [Ode to the Dead Carob Tree] the poet encounters a fallen *algarrobo*, knocked down by "un golpe de cielo" [a blow from the sky] (*OC* 2:455). He writes:

Me acerqué y era tal
su fuerza herida,
tan heroicas sus ramas en el suelo,
irradiaba su copa
tal majestad terrestre,
que cuando
toqué su tronco
yo sentí que latía
y una ráfaga
del corazon del árbol
me hizo cerrar los ojos
y bajar
la cabeza. (*OC* 2:454)

—

I drew near and such was
its wounded strength,
so heroic its branches on the ground,
its top radiating
such earthly majesty,
that when
I touched its trunk
I felt its pulse
and a gasp
from the heart of the tree
made me close my eyes
and bow
my head.

The life force that the poet still senses in the tree, though wounded, indicates a life in death. This life does not receive the same celebratory treatment it might have elsewhere in Neruda's poetry when he is more persuaded by a Whitmanesque optimism. The tree's dead life is a marvel, for, as the poet notes, "y no lloré / porque mi hermano muerto / era tan bello en muerte como en vida" [I did not weep / because my dead brother / was more beautiful in death than in life], but it still apparently merits the mourning of the wind that "acariciaba su cabeza" [caressed his head] (*OC* 2:455). Like the dead tuna that he describes lying "como una nave, / armado / entre legumbres" [like a ship, / armed / among vegetables], dead things merit the poet's praise for their own sake, not because of what future they might portend (*OC* 2:467). Loyola explains that perished things "have intrinsic worth, even though they will not be recorded by any utopian future celebration. The natural axis proves to be the parameter of the human (and of human history), not the reverse" (*OC* 2:1359).

The poet's growing awareness of this axis results in a more muted and dispassionate openness toward the world, something that tempers the often marked anthropocentrism in Neruda. In "Oda al camino" [Ode to the Way] the poet rides on horseback, it would appear, in a region akin to the coastline of Puerto Saavedra and Lago Budi, to which he referred in his autobiography. He describes his protagonist:

Viajero
dirigido
no a un punto,
no a una cita,
sino sólo
al aroma
de la tierra. (*OC* 2:491)
—
Traveler
aimed
not at a point,
nor at an appointment,
but only
at the fragrance
of the earth.

Far from having his direction unsettled by historical or political circumstances, the traveler is a wanderer among invisible beings, encircled by an animated world:

Yo voy despierto.
Y

como
una nave en el mar
abre
las aguas
y seres invisibles
acuden y se apartan,
así
detrás del aire,
se mueven
y reúnen
las invisibles vidas
de la tierra. (*OC* 2:492)
—

I go awake.
And
as
a ship on the sea
parts
the waters
and invisible beings
come together and draw apart,
so too
behind the air
the invisible lives
of the earth
move
and gather.

This environmental awareness allows Neruda access to the invisible life in the air, the leaves, the wind, and the rain; as Whitman ultimately came to accept, however, what the earth says can never be translated. Translation would make the poet a prelapsarian Adam who could commune with the voices of the earth, so that all he names speaks through his own language without mediation. Neruda was certainly attracted by this possibility as, for example, evidenced in "Oda a la tranquilidad," where he calls for "la boca de los árboles" [the mouths of the trees] to speak and insists that "nada es mudo en la tierra" [nothing is mute on the earth] (*OC* 2:239). In "Oda al camino," however, he merely celebrates the chance to not have to explain himself:

[C]aminar para ser, sin otro
rumbo
que la propia vida,
y como, junto al árbol,
la multitud
del viento
trajo zarzas, semillas,
lianas, enredaderas,
así, junto a tus pasos,
va creciendo la tierra. (*OC* 2:493)

———

To walk in order to be, without any
direction
other than life itself,
and just as, together with the tree,
the multitude
of the wind
brought brambles, seeds,
vines, climbing roots,
just so, together with your steps,
the earth goes on growing.

His sensual and aesthetic appreciation of land appears to make it blossom or joins the fecundity of the earth. Neruda's declaration at the conclusion of the poem expresses this circumscription of natural history that now marks both the limitations and opportunities of poetry:

En cada hoja está mi nombre escrito.

La piedra es mi familia.

De una manera o de otra
hablamos y callamos
con la tierra. (*OC* 2:494)

———

In each leaf my name is written.

The stone is my family.

One way or another
we speak and fall silent
with the earth.

If human beings are kin with the more-than-human world, then our language participates in the sounds of the world. Neruda's adamic longing to speak the language of the trees is rewarded but only as a kind of truce of intermittent silence. Poetic communion with the earth must recognize nature's voice as well as its opacity and resistance to translation.

The push of Neruda's seemingly newfound biocentrism is not enough, however, to rid him of the pull of anthropocentric tendencies, as evident in his "Oda a la mariposa" [Ode to the Butterfly]. His praise for the insect is cut short when he discovers that in large groups the butterflies have been eating the alfalfa intended for the cattle. After insisting that they deserve to be collectively burned, he warns: "No atacarás al hombre y a su herencia, / al campesino y a sus animales" [You shall not attack man and his inheritance, / the farmer and his animals] (*OC* 2:567). Nevertheless, we see again how Neruda consistently measures his praise of human labor against the aesthetic values he so treasures. For example, while he frequently echoed Whitman's praise of woodcutting as a primary symbol of simple agrarian life, of working-class people, and of a kind of democratic promise, in "Oda al carro de la leña" Neruda questions the wisdom of unrestrained logging of quebrachos, *algarrobos*, robles, and pines. While he insists that trees are made for human use, he balances the functional value of wood with the fact that these trees are

sin embargo
tiernos
padres de los follajes,
del susurro, del nido (*OC* 2:500)

—

nevertheless
tender

fathers of the foliage,
of the whisper, of the nest.

Without announcing outright opposition to logging, he presages environmental activism when he queries:

Ay quien
pudiera
detener
el curso
del río de la leña,
desandar el camino
devolverlo a la selva:
enderezar
de nuevo
la majestad
antigua
sobre
la tierra asesinada
y esperar
que regresen
las aves encendidas,
el canto pleno y puro
de las hojas,
la fragante
salud
de la madera! (*OC* 2:501–2)
—
Oh, who
could
stop
the course
of the river of lumber,
turn the way around
return it to the forest:
straighten
again
the ancient

majesty
upon
the assassinated earth
and hope that
the birds aflame
will return
the full and pure song
of the leaves
the fragrant
health
of wood!

The demands of cyclical time here take precedence over those of human historical time. As I have already suggested, however, Neruda's poetry is deeply conflicted by these competing demands, as evident, for example, when in the same book of poetry he praises the handsaw as the "violín del bosque" [violin of the forest] because along with the aesthetic pleasures the labor of logging provides and despite the rivers of fallen trees such business demands, woodworking makes it possible that "penetre a la casa / el río de la luz por la ventana" [a river of light through the window / enters the house] (*OC* 2:609).

At this particular stage of his evolution Neruda is willing to take the risks of this poetics of avowed silence and ignorance before the natural world, even if it compromises the outline of the historical self and a clearly delineated polity. What emerges is what he describes in *Memorial* as a self born "con tantos ojos / como planetas tiene el firmamento" [with as many eyes / as the firmament has planets] (*OC* 2:1203). *Estravagario* represents perhaps the most abrupt departure from the self-assigned prophetic role of the poet that runs throughout Neruda's poetry.[4] Announcing that he is asking for silence in the opening poem, raising questions without answers, and proclaiming that "sé cada día menos [I know less every day]," Neruda explores the aesthetic and ecological vistas that this new epistemology opens (*E* 22). Specifically, he hopes to gain understanding from the paradox he has already explored numerous times before of nature's ironic indifference to death, loss, and change. In the poem "A callarse" [Keeping Quiet] he imagines the fishermen no longer hurting the whales, the warmongers walking as brothers, and the possibility that

tal vez un gran silencio pueda
interrumpir esta tristeza,

. . . .

tal vez la tierra nos enseñe
cuando todo parece muerto
y luego todo estaba vivo.

—

perhaps a huge silence
might interrupt this sadness,

. . . .

perhaps the earth can teach us
as when everything seems dead
and later proves to be alive. (*E* 28)

It is in fact not the stasis or oblivion of death that he desires, but, as he later expresses it in the powerful poem "Cierto cansancio" [A Certain Weariness], the rigidity of norms, the mythologies of the past, and the lifelessness of a predictable society so opposed to natural process. In "The Muse of History" Walcott criticizes the patrician authors who long for ruins and reject the untamed landscape because they yearn for evidence of civilization, what he insists in "The Sea Is History" are "monuments, battles, martyrs" (*CP* 364). Neruda too complains of too much monumentalization of life, which similarly stems from metropolitan expectations:

He visto algunos monumentos
erigidos a los titanes,
a los burros de la energía.
Allí los tienen sin moverse
con sus espadas en la mano
sobre sus tristes caballos.
Estoy cansado de las estatuas.
No puedo más con tanta piedra.

. . . .

Estoy cansado del recuerdo.

—

I have seen some monuments
raised to titans,

to donkeys of industry.
They're there, motionless,
with their swords in their hands
on their gloomy horses.
I'm tired of statues.
Enough of all that stone.

. . . .

I am tired of remembering. (*E* 64)

Echoing Whitman's pleas for an originality untainted by tradition, Neruda calls for a society that will respect the native imaginative freedom of every citizen:

Dejen tranquilos a los que nacen!

Dejen sitio para que vivan!
No les tengan todo pensado,
No les lean el mismo libro,
Déjenlos descubrir la aurora
Y ponerle nombre a sus besos.

——

Leave the newborn in peace!

Leave room for them to live!
Don't think for them,
Don't read them the same book;
Let them discover the dawn
And name their own kisses. (*E* 64)

He later describes a similar hardening of life force and of open sensitivity to the surrounding world that occurs in the Wordsworthian transition from childhood to adulthood in "Al pie desde su niño" [To the Foot from Its Child]. Here he imagines that the naked foot of a boy, innocent still of the habituations of social society, does not know if it is foot, butterfly, or apple. Only through a long process of denial of our embodied natures, beginning with the simple act of wearing shoes and thus denying contact with the earth, does the boy become a man. However, upon being buried, we still do not know if he will fly or become an apple.

Instead of imagining a New World transformation and improvement upon the Old World's Muse, as Whitman does in "Song of the Exposition," Neruda calls for a kind of ecological deference and respect for the perpetually dynamic motions of nature that are so unlike the stillness of immured memories of civilization. While Neruda previously demonstrated his environmental awareness, in *Estravagario* he is less confident in his own prophetic and omniscient powers and embraces instead a new call, in the words of "Sonata con algunos pinos" [Sonata with Some Pine Trees]: "[C]onversemos con las raíces / . . . hagamos profesión terrestre [(L)et us talk with roots / . . . let us make a profession of being earth-bound]" (*E* 156). The hope is that nature will be more vocal, but this requires the poet to quiet his metaphorical energies and learn to "think like a mountain," as Aldo Leopold once put it. Neruda admits in "Desconocidos en la orilla" [Strangers on the Shore] that for the ocean to even begin to take notice of his presence on the beach, "tengo que aprender / a nadar dentro de mis sueños" [I have to learn / to swim within my dreams]. In this way, perhaps, the great motions of water and wind "sabrán quién soy y por qué vuelvo / me aceptarán en su instituto [will know who I am and why I return, / will accept me into their school]" (*E* 219). This requires an abdication of the unique claims of individuality on experience.

It also means that the self must adapt to nature's small deaths and resurrections. While the senses are the vehicles of experience and of memory, as experiences accumulate between moments of amnesia and of nature's changes, the senses construct a self that is layered. Just as geological time leaves its signatures in strata on canyon walls, the self is a series of experiences between which lies no visible evidence of continuity. Autobiography, then, becomes a kind of archaeological dig through the deep time of nature for our human traces. We can only write of the self in interrupted chapters, "hasta que tan tardíos ya somos, que no somos / ser y no ser resultan ser la vida" [until belatedly we are and are not / being and not being turn out to be life] (*OC* 2:1209). This "verdad misteriosa" [mysterious truth] is what such digging reveals, a digging that is inevitably a poetics, since only metaphors can breach the many gaps in the story. In this way poetry imitates nature's own mysterious transitions and regenerations. Neruda's poetry attempts, in the words of Belitt, to "float . . . the burden of the phenomenal world on the unanswerable pathos of a mystery" (*Adam's Dream* 105).

The perpetual motions of change in nature almost become oxymoronic when they are named, since their persistence becomes a kind of stillness and immobile sameness. In "Estación inmóvil" [Still Season] Neruda rephrases the Whitmanian mantra, "to die is different from what anyone supposed, and luckier": "[N]ada se gasta ni se muere / hasta nuestra resurrección [(N)othing is wasted or dies / until our resurrection]" (*E* 134). He describes the paradox

> de lo que yacía perdido
> inacablemente inmóvil
> y que ahora sube desde no ser
> a ser una rama florida.
>
> —
>
> of all that lay deep and lost,
> interminably still,
> and that now swims up from unbeing
> to become a branch in flower. (*E* 134)

This changeability of nature raises doubts about the stasis of human being. Neruda sees change even in the very fabric of his own identity. In "Cuánto pasa en un día" [How Much Happens in a Day] he writes:

> Quién no diría que la tierra
> con su vieja piel cambia tanto?
> Tiene más volcanes que ayer,
> el cielo tiene nuevas nubes,
> los ríos van de otra manera.
>
> —
>
> Who would have said that the earth
> with its ancient skin would change so much?
> It has more volcanoes than yesterday,
> the sky has brand-new clouds,
> the rivers are flowing differently. (*E* 68)

Human labor has changed the environment, but natural change takes precedent and creates the need for the poet to recognize his own perplexing multiplicity. When he greets his lover, "nuestros besos son otros besos / y nuestras bocas otras bocas [our kisses are other kisses, / our mouths are other mouths]" (*E* 68). The singularity and integrity of the poetic voice is thus challenged by the laws of ecological change. Whitman claimed he contained multitudes, and although this was based in part on his knowledge of science, this claim had more to do with Whitman's desire to make his words the meeting point for his readers' democratic imagination. Neruda's awareness of containing multitudes as well as his notion of democracy have a stronger environmental basis. As he claims in "Muchos somos" [We Are Many],

> voy a ver si a las otras gentes
> les pasa lo que a mí me pasa,
> si son tantos como soy yo,
> si se parecen a sí mismos
> y cuando lo haya averiguado
> voy a aprender tan bien las cosas
> que para explicar mis problemas
> les hablaré de la geografía.

> ——

> I would like to know if others
> go through the same things that I do,
> have as many selves as I have,
> and see themselves similarly;
> and when I've exhausted this problem
> I'm going to study so hard
> that when I explain myself
> I'll be talking about geography. (*E* 100)

Arguably, this could be seen as a poem that treats the disintegration of the modern into the postmodern self, but its final lines suggest a different cause than the breakdown of traditional values, coherent stories of human origins, and commonly shared beliefs. There is no doubt that Neruda took full poetic advantage of this modernist crisis, but it seems to have provided him a clear slate with which to reapproach the rawness of the earth. Geography's many faces and moods and its multiple personalities taught him the multiplicity of his human being. The lessons of geography are healing even though they do not precipitate a traditional reunion of the self; wholeness becomes instead an awareness of one's permeable boundaries and an extension into the vastness of the physical world. As he notes in "Aquí vivimos" [We Live Here],

Gracias doy a la tierra

. . . .

porque no es poco, no es así? haber vivido
en una soledad y haber llegado a otra,
sentirse multitud y revivirse solo.

—

I am grateful to the earth

. . . .

for that's no small thing, no? to have lived
through one solitude to arrive at another,
to feel oneself many things and recover wholeness. (*E* 106–8)

The poet has opened himself to the vicissitudes of geography even at the cost of the omniscient narrative authority that constitutes historical memory or autobiography in *Canto general,* for example. The poetic voice doesn't organize geographical matter in biblical, genealogical fashion but is itself infused with each geography with which it has experience. Loyola aptly calls this shift the "desacralization of autobiography" (*OC* 2:1366). This also means that Neruda's poetry undergoes "a systematic reappraisal of the past," including experiences he thought were definitively behind him ("las experiencias pretéritas").

Rethinking the pastness of the past also means, importantly, an opening to the presentness of the environment. He arrives at a poetics of confessed ignorance, of awe before the mysteries of nature, and a resolve to unite with the thingness of things. This is perhaps most powerfully expressed in "Aquí vivimos." Confronted by the perpetual violence of ocean waves before him, his is a lost soul because he does not have to choose between joy and sorrow. He can instead be purified by learning from nature how to encompass both. In a passage that appears to recall his first encounter with the sea at Puerto Saavedra, Neruda writes:

La soledad abierta allí cantaba,
y yo, perdido y puro,
mirando hacia el silencio
abrí la boca, dije:
"Oh madre de la espuma,
soledad espaciosa,

fundaré aquí mi propio regocijo,
mi singular lamento."

—

All that deserted space was singing
and I, lost and awed,
looking toward the silence,
opened my mouth and said:
"Mother of the foam,
expansive solitude,
here I will begin my own rejoicing,
my particular [lament]." (*E* 106)

Alastair Reid translates "lamento" as "poetry," since that appears to be what Neruda is referring to, but the translation loses the sense that his poetry encompasses, like Whitman's sea, the contradictions of joy and sorrow, life and death.

If death is the mother of all beauty, as Wallace Stevens once alleged, then death also stimulates love, and for Neruda, "sólo el amor no gasta [love is the only inexhaustible thing]." His poetry can endure "porque casi soy de tierra pura / tengo cucharas para el infinito [and almost being earth myself / I spoon away at infinity]" (*E* 108). Although there is presumably nothing infinite about things at all, since they are particular, change, and die, as the poet grows more attentive to the life and death of things the love inspired by change and perpetual renewal portends a kind of infinitude embodied in the elegiac voice of poetry itself.

This new vocation as the silent observer of nature leaves him much less interested in history. In "Pastoral" Neruda finds himself interested merely in the task of copying nature: "Voy copiando montañas, ríos, nubes [I copy out mountains, rivers, clouds]" (*E* 118). As a lone wanderer his attention no longer can be bothered by questions of history.

No se me ocurre más que el transparente
estío, no canto más que el viento,
y así pasa la historia con su carro
recogiendo mortajas y medallas
y pasa, y no siento sino ríos,
me quedo solo con la primavera.

—

Nothing else crosses my mind except
the transparency of summer, I sing only of the wind,
and history passes in its carriage,
collecting shrouds and medals
and passes, and all I feel is rivers.
I stay alone with the spring. (*E* 118)

His devotion to natural regeneration is an indifference to the claims of finality that history might make upon him. He also knows, however, that by turning his back on the concerns of cause and effect in historical progression he must change his role in relation to his reader. A voice interrupts the pastoral meditation with a reminder of his public obligations: "Pastor, pastor, no sabes / que te esperan [Shepherd, shepherd, don't you know / they are all waiting for you]" (*E* 118). The wandering shepherd is also the pastor, or priest, whose flock awaits instruction. He responds simply by declaring himself to be an unfinished product and even that the idea of his complete realization as a man of wisdom is comical:

[A]unque me esperen yo quiero esperarme.

. . . .

y cuando llegue donde yo me espero
voy a dormirme muerto de la risa.

——

[A]lthough they are waiting, I want to wait for myself.

. . . .

and when I reach the place where I am waiting,
I expect to fall asleep, dying of laughter. (*E* 118)

The disavowal of self-realization through historical recollection inevitably comes at this cost of forsaking the prophetic role that is especially prominent in *Canto general*, as we will see. But the advantages outweigh these costs because of the potential for perpetual adamic discovery, even rediscovery of the meaning of his past, that this now inaugurates. In his "Carta para que me manden madera" [A Letter Ordering Lumber] Neruda admits that leaving Temuco meant a loss that he can only compensate for by engaging in acts of collection and of devotion to remnant things.

Yo perdí la lluvia y el viento
y qué he ganado, me pregunto?

. . . .
es mi alma que no está contenta
y busca bajo mis zapatos
cosas gastadas o perdidas.

—

I lost the rain and the wind
and what have I gained, I wonder?
. . . .
It's my spirit that's not content
and wants under my feet
things used or lost. (*E* 222)

His desire is no longer to wander the earth but to construct a home of "los fragmentos de la montaña [the shavings of the mountain]" so that "se levantarán las paredes / con los susurros que perdí [the walls are raised up / with the sighs I left behind]" (*E* 223–24). The desire for fragments, for wasted things, would consume him and nurture his poetry for the rest of his life. His three exquisitely constructed homes bear witness to this. Built with the wood of the alerce and the araucaria, among others, and filled with innumerable quantities of collected shells, rocks, bottles, and other items, each home is a monument to his staggering hunger for natural recollection. As he explains in "No me hagan caso" [Forget about Me], to gather "monedas del tiempo y del agua [coins of time and water]" is to "tomar parte en los trabajos / de la soledad y la arena [share in the labor / of solitude and the sand]" (*E* 232).

Later in his poem "Demasiado nombres" [Too Many Names] he suggests that our biological, material belonging to the earth not only alters our sense of self but has transversal biological parallels that transgress national borders and language differences. Nature, in other words, is the foundation of a New World belonging:

Nadie puede llamarse Pedro,
ninguna es Rosa ni María,
todos somos polvo o arena,
todos somos lluvia en la lluvia.
No me hablan de Venezuelas,
de Paraguayes y de Chiles,
no sé de lo que están hablando:

conozco la piel de la tierra
y sé que no tiene apellido.

—

No one can claim the name of Pedro,
nobody is a Rosa or María,
all of us are dust or sand,
all of us are rain under rain.
They have spoken to me of Venezuelas,
of Chiles and Paraguays;
I have no idea what they are saying.
I know only the skin of the earth
and I know it has no name. (*E* 234)

This New World poetics creates communities based on this ecological multiplication of the self:

Yo pienso confundir las cosas,
unirlas y recién nacerlas,
entreverlas, desvestirlas,
hasta que la luz del mundo
tenga la unidad del océano,
una integridad generosa.

—

I have a mind to confuse things,
unite them, make them new-born,
mix them up, undress them,
until all light in the world
has the oneness of the ocean,
a generous, vast wholeness. (*E* 236)

The paradox of poetry's role in forging a sense of New World natural wholeness remains complicated, however, by the fact that the ocean's oneness cannot be circumscribed by language, as Neruda so frequently admits. He was inspired by Whitman's poetics of oblivion in which the poet acknowledges the sea as a space of death but awaits the remnant life of the sea's waste. Neruda names the detritus that the sea casts upon the land and comes to understand human history as one metonymic fragment of the larger natural whole. My reader will recall that this is what Édouard

Glissant describes as a poetics of relation in which the poet, like a postlapsarian Adam, "conceives of totality but willingly renounces any claims to sum it up or to possess it" (*Poetics* 21).

The chief metaphor of Neruda's poetic labors is a gathering of the fragments of nature's wholeness in order to regain an image, however incomplete, of his own wholeness. This is not exactly a disavowal of the immediate concerns of human society, but it is a reorientation of his social concerns within these more specifically biological parameters. In the extraordinary poem "Bestiario" [Bestiary] Neruda questions whether he can be a poet without understanding the language of animals and suggests that the formalities of society and the demands of capitalism have contributed to his hesitancy to take this task seriously:

> quiero más comunicaciones,
> otros lenguajes, otros signos,
> quiero conocer este mundo.
>
> . . . .
>
> Yo quiero hablar con muchas cosas
> y no me iré de este planeta
> sin saber qué vine a buscar,
> sin averiguar este asunto,
> y no me bastan personas.
>
> —
>
> I need more communication,
> other languages, other signs;
> I want to know this world.
>
> . . . .
>
> I want to speak with many things
> and I will not leave this planet
> without knowing what I came to find,
> without solving this affair,
> and people are not enough. (*E* 280)

To speak in other languages, to learn the speech of dumb things, would mean to speak outside of the parameters of human language, something he knows is impossible, but it is precisely Neruda's persistent quest of the unsayable and his consistent acknowledgment of what lies beyond his poetry's grasp that gives his poetry such potency. To express this desire for impatience with what we think we know and understand creates the impetus for new understandings. The wholeness he imagines is not one that incorporates his being or delimits it in any way. If Neruda can escape the seemingly unnatural solitude and otherness he feels in nature, as he says at the conclusion of *Estravagario*, "entonces cantaré en silencio [then I will sing in the silence]" (*E* 302). Until then, silence will impel his poetry in its reach for infinitude beyond words.

In *Piedras de Chile* Neruda answers Gary Snyder's criticism of Whitman for not going deep enough into the New World ancient story. Neruda explores the New World in geological deep time, and although this is a strictly materialist view of the hemisphere, it obtains a religious feeling for the infinite.[5] Neruda understood the relationship of amnesia to New World experience but not with the same insistence as Walcott. We will see his impatience with History's absence, for example, in his construction of the New World story in *Canto general* in the next chapter. But deep time also provides him with a new way to imagine the totality of New World experience without giving in to the temptation to use poetry to recovery its entirety. It is, perhaps, for this reason that Gabriela Mistral once called him "a mystic of matter" (5). He announces, for example, that the historical foundation of the Americas is deeper still than America's indigenous past. Even the indigenous gods are here imagined to have been geologically procreated:

> [T]odos nacieron de la piedra:
> América los levantó
> con mil pequeñas manos de oro,
> con ojos que ya se perdieron
> borrados por sangre y olvido. (*OC* 2:979)
> —
> They were all born of stone:
> America raised them
> with a thousand hands of gold,
> with eyes that were already lost
> erased by blood and oblivion.

He posits here that the natural origins of America's early human history were occluded by the blood of human conflict and its concomitant oblivion.

The eyes that are erased are not the human witnesses of a natural history but a natural witness of the human story, implying a kind of retrogression of nature's procreative energies.

Stone still remains in possession of the story of creation, and with a story it possesses *anima,* or spirit, intelligence, and its own inherent dynamism. It might not be an overstatement to suggest, as does Ben Belitt, that "[n]othing is less static or earthbound than the stones of Neruda's Chile" ("Pablo" 150). The perception of these stony motions is facilitated by the poet's own stillness, as Sicard notes, because "rest has not interrupted the work of matter. It is only made evident in incessant character" (171). The problem is that the story of this incessantly creative dynamism is only cryptically available to the poet. In "La creación" [The Creation] he writes:

[L]a piedra conservó el recuerdo.

. . . .

[Y] hay en la piedra un animal sin nombre
que aún aúlla sin voz hacia el vacío. (*OC* 2:998)

———

Stone preserved the memory.

. . . .

There is in stone a nameless animal
that still howls voicelessly into the emptiness.

Akin to Walcott's Major Plunkett and his search for St. Lucian history, Neruda developed earlier in his career an intense hunger for colonial and indigenous histories so as to adorn the Americas with the historical dignity they lacked in the eyes of metropolitans. Scarce evidence of indigenous history in St. Lucia led Walcott to embrace a pronounced poetics of oblivion and renounce the need for anything but a deep belonging in the natural world as a means of founding a new culture. This attitude may not be transferable in the Americas without some disturbing dismissals of still-thriving indigenous cultures. Neruda's swooning awe in front of the ruins of Machu Picchu was perhaps a sign of his impatience with Chile's own comparatively sparse evidence of a complex ancient history, but, like Achille and Walcott, who renounce Plunkett's historical hunger, Neruda here sees this as Chile's advantage. What is disappointing is his rather impatient dismissal of the relevance of Mapuche culture to his poetic birth in La Araucanía; it was nature, not the indigenous culture, that provided a muse:

"sin otros dioses que el trueno" [without gods, other than thunder] (*OC* 2:979). As I suggested earlier, however, it perhaps would have been false to his own experience to have pretended otherwise.

So he turns to a geological story of the Americas writ large in stone. In *Piedras de Chile,* written in 1959, Neruda has moved beyond his obsession at Machu Picchu for a codified and lost human history he seeks to translate into poetry, a moment I will explore in the next chapter. Because the stone is a story shaped by deep time and not by human hands it cannot be translated into its proper home as historical knowledge. The stone is instead a monument to itself:

> Por eso en las rocas crecieron
> brazos y bocas, pies y manos,
> la piedra se hizo monumento. (*OC* 2:980)
>
> —
>
> That is why the rocks grew
> arms and mouths, feet and hands,
> stone became a monument.

Time ("tiempo") visits the stone with wind, cold, and water until "la piedra iluminó mi patria / con sus estatuas naturales" [stone illuminated my country / with its natural statues] (*OC* 2:980). Unlike the monuments that have exhausted his patience with mythologized History in *Estravagario* (recall his statement, "Estoy cansado del recuerdo" [I am tired of remembering]), Neruda now faces monuments to time, since nature changes "sin otras herramientas / que el tiempo" [with only time as its tool] ("La estatua ciega," *OC* 2:986).

This approach opens adamic possibilities for Neruda. In "Soledades" [Solitudes] he writes of the Chilean coastline,

> despedazada
> por el trueno,
> carcomida
> por los dientes de cada nueva aurora. (*OC* 2:982)
>
> —
>
> broken in pieces
> by thunder,
> eaten away
> by the teeth of every new dawn.

Suggestive of Walcott's similar image of nameless beaches without history, Neruda insists that the natural shapes of the rocky shores are without verbalized signification:

[Y] se sabe que aquí termina el mundo.
Nadie lo dice porque
nadie existe,
no está escrito, no hay números ni letras,
nadie pisó esta arena oscura. (*OC* 2:982)

—

And everyone knows that the world ends here.
Nobody says so because
no one exists,
nothing is written, there are no numbers or letters,
no one has stepped on this obscure sand.

He concludes, therefore, that as a poet confronted by this illegible story of beautiful nothingness, "debo . . . hablar / sin nadie, hablar con nadie, / ser y no ser en un solo latido" [I should . . . speak / with no one, speak to no one, / be and not be in one solitary beat of the heart] (*OC* 2:983). In an existential twist to Adam's destiny as dust, Neruda captures a sense of his own deep time as organized natural matter that was once stone and will again return to its rocky home: "[P]iedra . . . es lo que fui, lo que seré, reposo / de un combate tan largo como el tiempo" [Stone . . . is what I was, what I will be, the peace / of a battle as long as time] ("Casa," *OC* 2:985–86).

Again the poet's search for self is challenged, this time by deep time. In "La estatua ciega" [The Blind Statue] Neruda imagines himself a craftsman of time and stone, learning to build and ultimately therefore to find himself in the shapes of stones:

[M]e costó encontrarme,
hacerme manos,
ojos, dedos, buscar
mi propia sangre. (*OC* 2:987)

—

It was difficult to find myself,
to make my hands,

eyes, fingers, to look for
my own blood.

Self-discovery is only made possible by the challenging imaginative work of readjusting his own sense of time to that of geology, and in so doing he finds a likeness between himself and stone that gives ecological meaning to his poetry:

> [E]ntonces mi alegría
> se hizo estatua:
> mi propia forma que copié golpeando
> a través del los siglos en la piedra. (*OC* 2:987)
>
> ——
>
> So my joy
> became a statue:
> my very form that I copied as I pounded
> on stone across the centuries.

As the Christian story has it, Adam's return to dust is circumscribed by the teleological story of his birth, death, and ultimate resurrection, which thus teaches him dependence on a redeeming God. Neruda's redemption, however, is a departure from the weight of history and entry into deep time, with a larger and more mysterious self to be reckoned with. The self is more mysterious precisely because time, unlike History, cannot be marked by causal links that would suggest a progressive movement from past, present, and future. Instead, the self is held in a tenuous present perfect tense, making the present a memory of the future. The only problem is that time follows no order and cannot guarantee unbroken continuity. The shapes of rock suggest

> un solemne recinto
> de pureza, formas puras caídas
> en un desorden sin resurrecciones,
> en una multitud que perdió la mirada,
> en un gris monasterio condenado
> a la verdad desnuda de sus dioses. ("Teatro de los dioses," *OC* 2:990)
>
> ——
>
> a solemn place
> of purity, pure forms fallen

in a disorder without resurrections,
in a multitude staring blankly,
in a gray condemned monastery
down to the truth stripped of its gods.

When confronted by the stony ruins of Machu Picchu, as we see in the next chapter, Neruda demands to know the story of human suffering that geological time has buried. The ciphers of the stones demand translation in order to get at that history, but Neruda can only forge a feeling of solidarity across time and space out of such eclipsed stories. Here, as he contemplates the ramifications of his discovery of deep time, he seems to speak to his former self at the ruins in order to urge greater patience with the hieroglyphic language in which nature's deep time composes our history:

Por eso, viajero, cuidado
con las tristezas del camino,
con los misterios en los muros.

Me ha costado mucho saber
que no todo vive por fuera
y no todo muere por dentro,
y que la edad escribe letras
con agua y piedra para nadie,
para que nadie sepa dónde,
para que nadie entienda nada. ("El caminante," *OC* 2:1010)
—

For this reason, traveler, be careful
with the sadnesses of the world,
with the mysteries of walls.

I have paid a heavy price to know
that not everything is alive on the outside
and not everything dies from within,
and that the age writes letters
with water and stone for no one,
so that no one knows where,
so that no one understands a thing.

To read the book of nature is to read and translate a language that makes no historical sense because perpetual natural regeneration means that we can no longer be certain what physical appearances hide *or* reveal. So while Neruda might agree with Whitman that "to die is different from what anyone supposed, and luckier," he does not know the human significance of this illusion of eternity.

Neruda concludes his long autobiographical poem, *Memorial de Isla Negra*, still searching for the woods of his childhood. This suggests how compelling the poetic quest to recover the dimensions of this natural genealogy remained for him. There is no final moment of self-constitution by means of a historicized memory of human origins. Belitt explains: "Precisely when all is in readiness for a triumphal affirmation of consciousness, however, the Spirit of the Place materializes like a wraith to reaffirm the poet's total disbelief in the buoyant historicity of his chronicle" ("Pablo" 163). The poet does not name his place in time and space but rather "is invaded" by the material world around him (Durán 185). In "El cazador en el bosque" [The Hunter in the Forest], for example, Neruda seeks to speak with the trees, but he accepts the fact that the forest will remain silent until he learns to dispense with the anthropocentric belief in the unique individual trajectory of one body, from birth to adulthood to death. He must learn to think of himself oxymoronically, like a stone, simultaneously alive and dead, being born and decaying. The earth

> [c]allará hasta que yo comience a ser
> substancia muerta y viva
>
> . . . .
>
> Calla la tierra para que no sepan
> sus nombres diferentes, ni su extendido idioma,
> calla porque trabaja
> recibiendo y naciendo:
> cuanto muere recoge
> como una anciana hambrienta:
> todo se pudre en ella. (*OC* 2:1252–53)
>
> ——
>
> will remain silent until I begin to be
> substance, both dead and alive
>
> . . . .

The earth remains silent so that they will not know
its different names, nor its expansive language,
it remains silent because it is at work
receiving and being born:
when it dies it gathers
like a hungry old woman:
everything decays in her.

Deep time means that life and death are synonymous. The task, then, is to unite his poetry with all that is reborn through such processes, as he explains in "Lo que nace conmigo" [What Is Born with Me]:

[E]stoy unido
al crecimiento, al sordo alrededor
de cuanto me rodea, pululando,
propagándose en densas humedades. (*OC* 2:1261)

——

I'm one
with growing, with the spread silence
of everything that surrounds me, teeming,
propagating itself in the dense damp. (Stavans, *Poetry* 702–3)

His response, then, to the silent forest is, in a later poem called simply "Bosque," answered with the resounding adamic naming of flowers and trees, organized into poetic form by the poet. Naming things is the adamic account of the forest's silent capacity to rejuvenate by means of transcending the life-death binary. For this reason he declares that poetry is the profession of regeneration, of one who comes "enterrar de nuevo / la raíz del árbol difunto" [to bury again / the tree's dead root] and thus participate in the profession of regeneration: "profesión / de empecinado en las raíces" (*OC* 2:1268–69).

The peace of natural regeneration, however, creates a perpetual tension in the poet, especially in a poet who is as socially conscious as Neruda, one who declares in "La injusticia" that "[e]l hambre no era sólo el hambre / sino la medida del hombre" [hunger is not only hunger / but is the measure of man] (*OC* 2:1163). Nature's deep time and its capacity for perpetual regeneration potentially mean that human injustice is not what it appears to be, that action is not urgent, and that peace is not found in political solutions but in the solace of the wild. In the stunning and challenging poem "Para la envidia" [For Envy] Neruda explores this tension. He speaks autobiographically when he queries, "[T]al vez el hombre crece y no respeta, / como el árbol del bosque, el albedrío de lo que lo rodea" [Perhaps man grows and like the tree of the forest, / doesn't respect the agency of that which surrounds him] (*OC* 2:1287). He explains:

> No tuve tiempo en mis preocupaciones
> de ver, de oír, de acechar y palpar
> lo que estaba pasando. (*OC* 2:1288)
>
> —
>
> Preoccupied as I was, I had no time
> to see, or hear, or seek out and touch
> what was happening.

What he failed to sense around him is the process by which nature integrates death. The horrific truth is nature's "secreta voluntad [secret urge]" (*OC* 2:1290; Stavans, *Poetry* 727). Nature violently consumes and regenerates the broken fragments of its own body, the detritus of life, indifferent to the fate of individual lives. The result:

> [Y] todo
> fructificó en la herida de la boca,
> funcionó las pasión generatriz
> y el triste sedimento del olvido
> germinó, levantando la corola,
> la medusa violeta de la envidia. (*OC* 2:1286)
>
> —
>
> [A]nd everything
> flourished in the wounded mouth.
> A web of passions started up
> and the woeful dregs of being forgotten
> gave root to the spreading tentacles,
> the violet medusa of envy. (Stavans, *Poetry* 723)

Nature's indifference to suffering, then, is both intolerable and enviable.

Neruda's penchant for collecting and gathering lost things—his role as fisherman who pulls in "what was lost"—is a feeble attempt to stem the tide of nature's voracious appetite and to bring to light their stories and rescue them from the oblivion of natural regeneration (*OC* 2:1287). His love of these discarded fragments of life and his compassion for human suffering now appear to him to be a disavowal, a turning of his back on nature's promise of regeneration and wholeness. They are signs of his impatience with nature's slow healing.

Neruda admits the possibility that, although nature's fragments have inspired his poetry, his work has scripted the readers' relationship to their own "condición bravía" [wild condition] and thus, like the forest's tree, has perhaps silenced their voices (*OC* 2:1287). That is to say, if we are truly part of natural history, in the life we generate as individual beings light is taken from other beings, meaning that all human happiness comes at the cost of other light and life. In his urgency to sing the song of compassion for the carpenter, the working men and women, Neruda recognizes that this potentially comes at the price of neglecting the "procreative depths" of nature and the lives of those in his own shadow.

In light of this new confession of potential error Neruda asks a fundamental question of his lifelong effort to restore justice to the suffering: "Qué puedo hacer para restituir / lo que no robé? [What can I do to give back / what I never stole?]" (*OC* 2:1289; Stavans, *Poetry* 726). In light of nature's indifference to human suffering his question takes on a deeper anxiety than that inspired simply by the ethical challenge of being accountable for human pains in the past and in the present. In other words, Neruda's capacity to right wrongs is not just limited by the exercise of unjust power that he cannot match or by human indifference. If Walcott, for example, cannot balance the scales of justice in the wake of slavery, it might be due to human indifference and persistent colonial power, but it is limited by the fact that cries for justice will always be, in Neruda's word, "atrasada" [delayed] by humankind's biogeography, which transforms and diminishes the meaning of suffering with the passage of time (*OC* 2:1289). Neruda asserts, however, that his tardiness has nothing to do with an insufficiency of concern for human life:

Fue porque a cada mordedura
el día
que llegaba
me separaba de un nuevo dolor,
me amarraba las manos y crecía

el liquen en la piedra de mi pecho,
la enredadera se me derramaba,
pequeñas manos verdes me cubrían,
y me fui ya sin puños a los bosques
o me dormí en el título del trébol. (*OC* 2:1290)

—

It was because with every taunt
the day
that dawned
detached me from new hurt,
bound my hands, and lichen
grew on the stone of my breast.
I was overgrown by creeping plants,
small green hands covered me,
and I took to the woods, unfisted,
or slept in care of the clover. (Stavans, *Poetry* 726–27)

Even though Neruda's political anger was always considerable, he asserts that nature's bounties slow his urgencies and teach him to be patient and "lento / en la ira" [slow / to anger] (*OC* 2:1290). His duty to human society is both urged upon him and tempered by nature's self-sustaining and self-healing capacities. He has learned from nature what humankind's potential is, but he also has learned that he cannot pretend to accomplish this potential outside the bounds of natural process and time. He determines to enter the wide world of nature

a ser lo que amo, la desnuda
existencia del sol en el peñasco,
y lo que crece y crece sin saber
que no puede abolir su crecimiento. (*OC* 2:1290)

—

to be that which I love, the naked
presence of the sun on the boulder,
and that which grows and grows without knowing
that it cannot stop growing.

This "secret urge" of the physical world has imposed upon Neruda a "wild condition." The deep time of natural regeneration teaches patience, since a merely human scale of time is too shallow to measure the meaning of events, but its ultimate lessons also teach the interdependence and belonging of all things and thus provide an important spur or "alimento" [food] needed in the "trabajos" [labors] waged for social good (*OC* 2:1291). Neruda's reconciliation of natural and human histories is founded on the notion that they are united under the same "bandera verde" [green banner] of biological kinship that represents peace, restitution, and fruitfulness (*OC* 2:101).

Coming to this resolution, as these autobiographical poems suggest, was not an easy process for Neruda, but as socialism seemed to offer fewer reasons for his lifelong, ardent hope of a hemispheric solidarity, he was willing to explore the New World implications of his devotion to the natural world. He was increasingly confident that New World communities had to be founded, above all else, on ecological principles, but that did not cool down his political fervor entirely. The tension between the demands of immediate human suffering and the well-being of nature was perhaps an even more strange and vexing problem for Neruda than it seems today in an age of global climate change if for no other reason than the fact that few were willing to probe both problems as deeply as Neruda. There were few models that could provide him a blueprint of reconciliation. As I have insisted, Neruda's willingness to probe the depths and implications of natural history was not a new development in his later years; he was simply more disenchanted with the socialist blueprint he thought had held the answers. Indeed, nowhere is the unresolved tension between the exigencies of society and nature more evident than in his great epic of the Americas, *Canto general.* Indeed, an ecocritical reading of the poem questions the assumed meaning of Neruda's prophetic recovery of the New World's lost history that lies at the heart of the critical reception of the book.

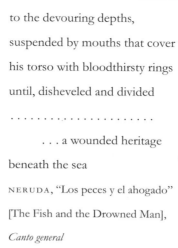

he descended

to the devouring depths,

suspended by mouths that cover

his torso with bloodthirsty rings

until, disheveled and divided

. . . .

. . . a wounded heritage

beneath the sea

NERUDA, "Los peces y el ahogado"

[The Fish and the Drowned Man],

Canto general

CHAPTER 6

Hemispheric History as Natural History

Neruda began to search the roots of his own autobiography at the same time that he became more aware of the greatest threat to the survival of human community: the rise of fascism, World War II, and the birth of the cold war. This was the context, of course, in which the modernist hope in the redeeming powers of art was threatened. Roberto González Echevarría notes that "while these developments produced an existentialist gloom in post-war Europe and some regions of Latin America and the United States, neither Neruda nor Carpentier . . . fell prey to its doleful allure. It was instead a heady *nuevomundismo*, based on the New World's ever-renewed promise of a fresh start, that nourished the hope of Neruda" (1–2). This *nuevomundismo*, or New Worldism, stimulated Neruda's social *and* ecological conscience, and the early result in *Canto general* is a heightened tension between his desire to restore historical memory of human suffering and to celebrate nature's dynamic capacity to make the world new again. That is to say, Neruda was not yet able to define a relationship between human and natural history that would easily reconcile his poetic impulse to foreground ecology *and* to decry human injustice. But precisely because of his unwillingness to force a facile reconciliation the grand epic poem of human history on the American continent remains today one of the century's most powerful expressions of the emerging sense that the high demands of human justice cannot be addressed independently of the challenges posed by ecology and its increasingly threatened status.

Critics have wrestled with the seemingly dissonant claims of natural and human histories in the poem, but most of that work was undertaken prior to or in apparent ignorance of the most salient developments in environmental studies and environmental philosophy. In 1980 Saúl Yurkiévich provided the most useful model for understanding this nature-culture tension in the poem, one that I wish to develop further. In his view Neruda has two almost antagonistic poetic visions that interplay throughout the poem. On the one hand, Neruda is attracted to a poetics of mythic expression. This poetics, argues Yurkiévich, "postulates a turning back [*retroceso*], a turning back to the womb, a return to origins that privileges the past; it is a nostalgic vision [that] places us in natural, cyclical time, without progress . . . where everything is transferable, reversible, recoverable, where birth and death are interchangeable" ("Mito" 201). The result is a style that is metaphorically dense, expressionistic, and informed by a mythical imagination. On the other hand, Neruda consistently turns to a "historicist poetic [that] presupposes a prospective time of continual advance, arrow-like [*vectorial*], directed at a future where we find fullness. . . . History is a motor that drives . . . toward the consequential realization [*consecución*] of this ventured objective" (201). The style here is mimetic and, contrary to the density of his mythic expression, transparently realist and elemental in expression. These poles do not coalesce, according to Yurkiévich, until the final section of the poem, where Neruda articulates the constitution of his poetic self, which is simultaneously born adamically in the forests and shorelines of La Araucanía and yet also answerable to the sufferings of others.

González Echevarría insists that there is no such reconciliation of these two poles, if for no other reason than the fact that the world Neruda inhabits (and that we still inhabit) has not rid itself of continual betrayals of trust and of violence against the sacred order that dictates the bounds of human possibility and happiness. Until that happens, poetry must continue to play this dual, even contradictory role of resorting to a mythical space of boundlessness from which to reflect upon and critique the plight of men and women. But this would assume, as do the vast majority of Neruda's critics, that the well-being of nature is secondary to and at inherent odds with the well-being of human society. While Neruda wrestles with the possibility of this irreconcilability in the poem, and while human history tells a long story of conflict between the plight of humans and the more-than-human world, Neruda's epic poem operates on the assumption that the New World's natural history has a different story to tell, one that holds the secret to human peace and to human survival within the nurturing care of the more-than-human world. Rediscovery of this New World, then, is paramount for human sustainability, an objective Neruda's poetics seeks.

Critics uniformly recognize the importance of nature and natural metaphors in Neruda, but they consistently bypass the possibility that as he became both more intimately and scientifically familiar with natural history he began to challenge his own rather pronounced anthropocentrism and to unveil a world that was founded on ecological processes and delimited by the laws of ecosystems. This raises the possibility that Neruda's metaphors are not merely significations of some more pressing personal, psychological, or human historical claim but rather the beginnings of a poetics that sought to engage with nature on its own terms. In so doing Neruda risks undermining his own sense of social urgency (and Neruda will fight this risk repeatedly with calls to political action until the very end of his career) but with the result that the reader emerges with a more ecologically informed vision of both human misery and human potential. The reader is thus empowered rather than agonized by the tensions between the exigencies of human and natural histories.

Even a brief glance at the literary sources that inform the poem and the latter stages of Neruda's career would suggest the seriousness with which Neruda embarked on familiarizing himself with the natural history of Chile and of the Americas. We know, for example, that during his year spent in internal exile in Chile Neruda went from house to house, all of them belonging to people he had never met, and that one Álvaro Jara was put in charge of Neruda's clandestine passages. Jara was studying to be a historian at the time and was a vital source of books that provided Neruda with the social and natural history of Chile. Neruda collected hundreds of such books over the course of his lifetime from the ancients to more contemporary publications that described everything from the life of birds, oceanography, marine biology, botany, reptiles, fossils, indigenous history, astronomy, cosmology, and more. To be sure, Neruda was perhaps more fond of collecting than of reading these books. When he donated them to the University of Chile he admitted, "I'm not a thinker, and these collected book are more reverential than investigative. Here is a collection of beauty which dazzled me" (qtd. in Feinstein 295). Enrico Mario Santí documents that although Neruda was primarily motivated by his own aesthetics, he made explicit use of the *Enciclopedia hispanoamericana, El compendio de la historia de América* by Diego Barros Arana (written in 1865 by a pupil of Andres Bello), and *Aves de Chile* [Birds of Chile] by Rodulfo Amando Philippi, a Chilean naturalist who also wrote other books in Neruda's possession on Chile's deserts, dolphins, and fossils ("Introducción" 67–71).

What characterizes these books on the whole—and there are a great number of them in Neruda's library—is an integrative approach to the study of flora, fauna, geology, oceanography, and ancient and more recent human history, an approach clearly adopted in *Canto general*. They are, however, much more explicitly restricted to national borders than Neruda's poem, and this is due to the fact that the late nineteenth and early twentieth centuries were a time of national consolidation (and indeed of determining the exact location of national borders), of growing interest in natural resources, and hence of government-sponsored expeditions into previously little known or understood landscapes, such as one of Neruda's favorites, Philippi's *Viage al desierto de Atacama*, from 1860. They are also books that exhibit a very marked Darwinian racism that Neruda was not always successful in shedding, despite his sympathy for indigenous cultures.

In sum, Neruda's library is a monument to his interest in the natural world. This interest was fueled by his childhood experiences but also by the growing Marxist confidence that scientific knowledge of the physical environment would lead to successful environmental engineering for the benefit of humans. Since the appearance of Friedrich Engels's own incomplete but ambitious *Dialectics of Nature*, written between 1872 and 1882, it had been a Marxist creed that nature could be successfully exploited for the benefit of all people and that capitalism was one of the chief wasters of natural resources vital to the poor. Neruda owned a 1947 Spanish translation of the book, in which Engels argues that the dialectic that has shaped human economic history has also shaped natural history. The evolution of the human hand, for example, is, according to Engels, the result of a process of discovery of its uses for work; the hand is a product of human labor as much as it was its instrument. As humans began to develop a self-conscious understanding of their dialectical relationship to nature they began to develop the technological means to withdraw from it. Engels writes: "[T]he further men become removed from animals, however, the more their effect on nature assumes the character of a premeditated, planned action directed towards definite ends known in advance. The animal destroys the vegetation of a locality without realising what it is doing. Man destroys it in order to sow field crops on the soil thus released, or to plant trees or vines" (290). His argument implies that the only reason we have seen environmental waste is because capitalism has alienated humankind from the products of their labor and from the natural world. Engels cites the degradation caused by Cuban plantations as his example.

Engels fails to recognize any limitation to our ability to understand and manipulate the natural world to our advantage without unforeseen consequences. We will see in Walcott's *Omeros* the poetic difference this awareness can make, but the telos of this kind of Marxist thought was prevalent among natural scientists over the span of Neruda's lifetime up to the point of writing *Canto general* and does not account for this possibility. The naturalism and positivism of much of the science Neruda studied articulated a simplistic and somewhat naive conception of indigenous harmony with the natural world that often resembled the social Darwinism that Marxism was presumably out to defeat.

This confidence in the future is expressed vehemently by Alejandro Lipschütz, a brilliant intellect in Chile who influenced an entire generation of Marxists and whom Neruda once called the "most important man in my country." Neruda kept copies of Lipschütz's books, including works on indigenous cultures in Chile and one small book, *La ciencia en la Unión Soviética*, that included a lecture Lipschütz delivered in 1944 and a poem of praise to the Soviet Union by Neruda. His lecture also praises the USSR, specifically, its scientific achievements, which have "brought to light a New World of social possibility" based on the premise that "intense labor" can and should "remake nature to serve man; to remake human life so that it is enjoyed by all [*sea goce de todos*]" (Lipschütz 20, 26). Caught in the cold war battle over bragging rights regarding the engineering of the planet, he offers categorical praise for advances in geology and mineralogy as evidence that nature is waiting to be exploited to serve human social ends.

We find no expression whatsoever of caution or awareness of the possibility that in the process of making these advances humans might turn back the clock and do irreparable damage to fragile ecosystems. Neruda's own visit in 1949 to the Soviet Union inspired admiration for "the magnitude of its plans, the infinite possibilities that seemed to open up to 'Soviet man'" (Soto 21). Long before Chernobyl, the possibility that environmental engineering might lead to environmental disaster had not yet registered. As Hernán Soto argues, Neruda was also likely influenced by Aníbal Ponce's book *De Erasmus a Romain Rolland: Humanismo burgués y humanismo proletario*, a book that celebrated the "Soviet man" who "changes the course of rivers, renews the soul of ancient tribes, transforms flora and fauna before their eyes" (qtd. in Soto 22). While Neruda's poetry always reflects what Renato Martínez calls his "poetics of things," as I argued in the previous chapter, his disillusionment with Communism and his growing understanding of ecology caused him to reexamine the distance between the world of things and the work of human hands (Martínez 748).

Shortly after the publication of *Canto general* Neruda returned to this notion of nature's social utility in the first books of odes. Despite his belief that Western civilization could learn from Eastern philosophies of nature, he writes in a vein similar to the simplified and perhaps erroneously Christian notion that nature's purpose alone is to serve humankind and to submit to his divinely sanctioned rule. Neruda writes praises in "Oda al edificio" [Ode to a Building], for example, to edifices that embody a "unidad vencedora" [conquering unity] of cement, steel, and wood (*OC* 2:89). The smell of fallen trees from his childhood was the smell of the future: "la construcción, la forma, / el edificio, / de las manos del hombre" [the construction, the form, / the building, / of human hands] ("Oda a la madera" [Ode to Wood], *OC* 2:154). His "Oda al mar" [Ode to the Sea] likewise demands of the sea:

[A]yúdanos, océano,
padre verde y profundo,
a terminar un día

la pobreza terrestre.
Déjanos
cosechar la infinita
plantacíon de tus vidas. (*OC* 2:159)

—

Help us, ocean,
our green, deep father,
to put an end someday
to earthly hunger.
Let us reap the infinite
plantation of your lives.

His overestimation of the sea's capacities is almost exuberant; he looks forward to the day when the feminine sea will succumb to masculine man, who will be "montándote, domándote, dominándote el alma" [mounting you, taming you, dominating your soul] (*OC* 2:161). Even the sands of the coastline are "para servir / la voluntad del hombre" [to serve / the will of man] (*OC* 2:273).

At this stage of his thinking, however, Neruda was capable of lamenting excess and abuse of nature, but his concerns are still human centered and blind even to the excesses of natural engineering. His "Oda a la erosión en la provincia de Malleco" [Ode to Erosion in the Malleco Province] calls for sustainability

a detener el hambre
de mañana,
a renovar la selva
prometida,
el pan
futuro
de la patria
angosta! (*OC* 2:311)

—

to hold back the hunger
of tomorrow,
to renew the promised
jungle,
the future

bread
of the narrow
country!

Poetry is to be a voice of conservation but only so that natural resources more effectively meet social ends. This utilitarian vision will give way to something much more aesthetic, but, as the above evidence shows, Neruda was slow to follow the implications of his own ecological masterpiece and to disavow a Marxist environmental imagination.

This anthropocentrism, of course, was not just true of socialist thought in the middle of the past century but of so-called free market societies as well. Only after the use of the atomic bomb and a growing awareness of unforeseen global environmental damage in the 1960s and 1970s do we see the emergence of a new environmental ethic of caution and restraint coming from the capitalist West. My point is not to condemn Neruda for buying into the dominant ethos of his time with regard to the environment but to suggest that despite his great hope for environmental engineering Neruda's poetic obsession with natural history would bring him closer than he anticipated to an environmental reason for caution.

One book, for example, that seems to have helped Neruda in this regard was Philippi's *Los fosiles terciarios y cuartarios*, from 1887. Philippi was at the cutting edge of his time, following Darwin's lead in exploiting the considerable evidence found in contemporary Chile of evolutionary change and of deep prehistory (the first fossils were studied in Chile in 1842). Neruda's interest in fossils, shells, and stones, aided by this literature, opened up to him a broad and deep perspective of time that extended well beyond the bounds of even pre-Columbian human history, itself still a relatively new science in Chile during Neruda's lifetime. What we see, then, in *Canto general* is the beginnings of a transformation of this worldview of nature as exploitable material to a philosophy of confessed ignorance and limitation in the face of nature's vast and ultimately unfathomable mystery, a mystery that for Neruda eventually extended into the expanse of the heavens as well as into the complexity of stones.

Before he arrives at the conclusion of nature's ultimate mysteries, however, in the middle of his career Neruda shifts away from mourning over the loss of his austral roots to a brief but intensive effort to reconstruct the natural and indigenous history of Chile and, ultimately, of the New World.

The result of *Canto general* is an epic account in poetry of what Lipschütz was accomplishing in the sciences, but one that contains the seeds of its own epic undoing. This reconstructive impulse was forged by his experiences with the Spanish Civil War, the rise of fascism in Europe, and World War II. More specifically, however, it is his sojourn as ambassador to Mexico from 1940 to 1943 and his 1943 visit to the ruins of Machu Picchu that inspired Neruda to situate his growing political vision within the context of the American hemisphere—a New World poetics that started with an interest in Chile and then included the hemisphere's vast and diverse geography and its rich and largely neglected indigenous history (Santí, *Pablo* 109, 117; Loyola 178). As his biographer, Volodia Teitelboim, notes, "it was Mexico that truly gave him the disturbing sensation of an almost unknown America. He felt himself in her debt because he hadn't yet really come down to his own soil. . . . The notion was maturing within him that beneath his feet was a buried universe over which he passed almost in complete ignorance" (271).[1]

Neruda himself once called Mexico "the touchstone of the Americas" (qtd. in Suárez 8). The visit to Machu Picchu expanded Neruda's awareness of a broader Americas back to his southern region. Specifically, what the visit opened to Neruda was the fact of deep historical memory that had become erased from contemporary Latin American civilization. As José Martí had earlier argued and Walt Whitman and Henry David Thoreau before him, Neruda was initially convinced that indigenous history was so little known or understood simply by virtue of a contemporary misguided value placed on America's European heritage:

> [N]uestro desconocimiento o silencio era no sólo un crimen, sino la continuación de una derrota. El cosmopolitismo artistocrático nos había llevado a reverenciar el pasado de los pueblos más lejanos y nos había puesto una venda en los ojos para no descubrir nuestros propios tesoros. (*OC* 4:932)

> Our ignorance or silence was not only a crime but the perpetuation of a breach. Aristocratic cosmopolitanism had carried us to the point of reverencing the past of the most distant peoples and had blindfolded us and thus prevented us from discovering our own treasures.

He understood that his task now had to be that of a chronicler in the colonial tradition of an all-encompassing history of nature and man, that his job was not only to tell the story of "pueblos" [peoples], but the story of "nuestras plantas y nuestras flores deben ser por primera vez contadas y cantadas" [our plants and our flowers should be told and sung for the first time] (*OC* 4:890). In a 1953 essay he cites Whitman's *Democratic Vistas* and its call for a New World poetry that would reject mimesis in favor of poesis, of natural-born metaphors. He places *Canto general* in the company of many of his predecessors—Ercilla, Bello, Darío—and his contemporaries who "sintieron primordiales deberes hacia la geografía y la cuidadanía de América . . . [a] unir a nuestro continente, descubrirlo, construirlo, recobrarlo" [felt primordial duties toward America's geography and citizenry . . . to unite our continent, to discover, construct, and recover it] (*OC* 4:889).

The experience of starting over in the wake of the conquest informs this poetics of newness, but, unlike Bello and others, Neruda understands that the difference is that "[s]omos los cronistas de un nacimiento retardado. Retardado por el feudalismo, por el atraso, por el hambre" [we are chroniclers of a retarded birth. Retarded by feudalism, by backwardness, by hunger] (*OC* 4:890). As discussed in chapter 3, Neruda embraced Whitman's notion of the poet's adamic task of "creerse el primer descubridor de las cosas y su primer dueño al entregarles nombre" [believing himself to be the first discoverer of things and that he is the first owner to give them names] (*OC* 4:310). However, as his career advanced and his knowledge of prehistory and natural history deepened, he became aware of the fact that he was postlapsarian or even more like Noah than the Edenic man, since naming was now, in the words of Santí, "an effort of post-diluvian reconstruction" ("Introducción" 72). As I have insisted, this important distinction means that his poetry carries the weight of a past it cannot know in its entirety and that as he names and praises nature he cannot escape the suspicion that it holds secrets it will not tell. This opacity of nature, enhanced by a buried human history, helps Neruda to coalesce a private and individual journey with a cross-cultural and historical journey back to the past.

The seeming impossibility of his historical quest, or at least its immense monumentality, demands explanation, however; otherwise the poet must accept injustice and amnesia as both inevitable and irrevocable. Since Neruda initially felt that this historical ignorance was criminal, he couldn't embrace the ironies of New World amnesia with the sober pleasure of Walcott, but neither could he pretend, like Whitman, that indigenous cultures only needed a few modest celebrations of native words to satisfy this breach. In 1949 in Mexico Neruda outlined his New World ambition to overcome the colonial condition of fragmented solitude in which American nations found themselves. Drawing inspiration from the recent death of José Clemente Orozco, he insisted rather emphatically that

> tenemos en nuestra América un mundo por hacer, y no somos aban-
> donados náufragos de una isla tenebrosa. . . . [N]i nuestras creaciones ni
> nuestra lucha son actitudes solitarias, sino partes solidarias de una fuerza
> constructora. (*OC* 4:768)
> ———
> we have in our America a world to make, and we are not shipwrecked
> and abandoned on some dark island. . . . [N]either our creations nor our
> struggle are solitary attitudes but fraternal pieces of a constructive force.

As it had for Whitman, nature teaches Neruda the meaning of this New World solidarity, except that Neruda's hemispheric community becomes more genuinely transnational. His many travels, wide hemispheric popularity, and broad network of political and literary allies helped him build a New World solidarity unparalleled before or since. Walcott's hemispheric ambition is much more modest and only superficially familiar with Latin America by contrast. There are problems with Neruda's New World community, as I will show, but it is important to recognize that Neruda figures among the most monumental literary figures who attempted to speak across the Americas. Although initially Neruda was interested in a poem of national scope, his visit to Machu Picchu helped him realize the need for something much more ambitious:

> [Q]uise extenderme en la geografía, en la humanidad de mi país, definir
> sus hombres y productos, la naturaleza viviente. Muy pronto me sentí
> complicado porque las raíces de todos los chilenos se extendían debajo de
> la tierra y salían en otros territorios. (*OC* 4:931)
> ———
> I wanted to extend myself through the geography, through the humanity
> of my country, to define its men and its products, its living nature. Soon
> enough things got complicated because I learned that the roots of
> all Chileans extend underneath the earth only to come forth in other
> territories.

His reconstruction of the New World is short-lived because these subterranean New World parallels ultimately lead him to a confrontation with a nonhuman scale of time that paradoxically shrinks the significance of the very story he wishes to rescue from oblivion.

Neruda came to call his book *Canto general* in order to express his desire to amend Whitman's notion that a song of oneself can become a song of all; he aspired to a more genuine and aggressive transnational *nuevomundismo* that connected the individual to the collective as well as natural and human history, as the word *general* implied.[2] The word was also used in the titles of colonial chronicles that ambitiously sought to depict both the human and natural histories of the places they described. In this ambition he was much more serious than Whitman; his historical coverage is significantly more broad and more specifically focused on particular injustices and acts of heroism enacted by named individuals, and his natural history shows the mark of serious botanical, geological, and oceanographic study.

Although he rejects Whitman's facile optimism that risked political inertia or indifference in the face of naked injustice, Neruda is nevertheless frequently guilty of his own Whitmanian overreaching. In a direct echo of Whitman, Neruda declares his hope that his poetry will sing to all people: "A todos, a todos, / a cuantos no conozco, . . . al que sin saberlo me ha esperado, / yo pertenezco y reconozco y canto [To all, to all, / to whomever I don't know, . . . to the one who unknowingly has awaited me, / I belong and acknowledge and sing]" (*OC* 4:715; *Canto* 286). These gestures in the poem risk failing to demarcate the limitations of poetic knowledge, of subjectivity, and of a very human apprehension of all things natural. These risks are all attendant in a worldview such as Neruda's that was often tempted by the seductions of a dialectical Marxism wherein the future promised to harmonize today's contradictions.

Neruda makes his share of mistakes in this regard not only in *Canto general* but throughout his career. However, I wish to suggest that Neruda is moving, from *Canto general* forward, toward an ambitious desire for a poetic celebration of mystery rather than toward a triumphant expression of mastery. This deference toward nature and natural processes contextualizes Neruda's preoccupation with social justice and gives enough pause to wonder about either the urgency or the legitimacy of his cries for retribution. Although he ostensibly wishes to write a totalizing story of human and natural histories, the key to this emergent environmental ethic is his growing awareness of nature's elusiveness and opacity. He describes an early and persistent ambition in his writing, inspired by the poetry of Carlos Sabat Ercasty, whose work was characterized by a "voluntad cíclica" [cyclical will] that "englobara no sólo al hombre sino a la naturaleza, a las fuerzas escondidas, una poesía epopéyica que se enfrentara con el gran misterio del universo" [would circumscribe not only man but also nature, the hidden forces, an epic poetry that would confront the great mystery of the universe] (*OC* 4:1202). The global and totalizing scope of Neruda's own ambition is kept in check by this aesthetic inspired by "the great mystery of the universe."

The consequence of this important admission regarding the natural world is that a deeper sense of irony regarding the ruptures of history and its stories of broken promises pervades Neruda's work in a way that never touched Whitman. For this reason I disagree with Peter Earle's assertion that both Whitman and Neruda share more in common with the romantics than with the moderns in that they preferred analogy to irony (192–93). As I hope to show, the seeds of irony are more latent in Whitman than in Neruda and especially Walcott, but tracing this ironic play of language is ecocritically vital, since it betrays poetry's sense of its own constructedness and deference to nature's opacity.

If Whitman lacked the will to confront human evil, as Walcott argues, Neruda is a postdisillusionment Whitman, trying to restore, not merely find, a sense of wholeness lost to language and history. González Echevarría insists that the calamities of New World history for Neruda are not "visited on humanity by an angry god but by wicked acts committed against the collective by evil men. . . . The utterance of the words themselves is already the beginning of a restoration. . . . This prophecy is, however, dependent on betrayal, the break at the origin that must be bridged by figures, by the figural quality of poetic language" (11–12). While Whitman will hope that history's wrongs will take care of themselves, Walcott will opt for a form of healing that happens aesthetically *despite* history's unanswered wrongs. Neruda attempts to heal New World wounds, but he does not accept the inevitability of either the betrayal or its healing without a politicization of poetry and its readers. This is a seduction that will strain his own ecological awareness, since if all human suffering has a political cause and solution, he must disavow even natural pain. He recognizes a poetic urgency necessitated by historical amnesia, but he begins to suspect that the fall from

Eden—a place for Neruda where memory is continuous and people possess land naturally and in equality—is the result not just of human injustice but also of ecological process. This presents Neruda with the dilemma that human injustice and amnesia might be conditions of an unnecessary fall, but they might also be the necessary conditions of humanity. Hence, his poetry fluctuates between a distinction drawn by Jonathan Bate of political writing, which is to motivate social change, and ecopoetics, which is "to engage *imaginatively* the non-human" and to serve as a "revelation of dwelling" on the earth (199, 266).

As discussed in the previous chapter, this ambiguity is manifest in the way Neruda describes his own memoirs as rife with failed acts of recovery. His poetry might seek to unite with natural processes of regeneration, like Whitman's leaves, but he also understands that this will mean forsaking the belief in a totalizing recovery of lost or elusive knowledge. The irony that results from this poetics of oblivion, as is evident in *Canto general*, more fully enables poetry to fight against the end of time and the environment, as I argued in the introduction. While both poets seek buried realities and establish relationships between differences, Whitman's poetry errs on the side of overstating the reconciliation or synthesis of opposites (north/south, black/white, life/death) of which he writes. This is a temptation to which Neruda is particularly vulnerable in his more political moments in the poem, a vulnerability we can understand if we remember the extraordinary pressures of clandestinity and exile under which the poem was written. Neruda nevertheless manages to capture those buried relationships between natural and human histories without conceding their ultimate unification and thus provides a deep ecological context for his political exigencies.

America's Vegetal Beginnings

In the inaugural poem, "Amor americano (1400)," the poet announces his biblical ambition to speak as what the Spanish poet Gabriel Celaya once called him, "the poet of the third day of creation."[3] His intention is to speak an as yet untranslated story that has been buried by colonialism, a story of intimacy between man and the earth. Neruda dates this time of intimacy as taking place "*[a]ntes de la peluca y la casaca [(b)efore the wig and the dress coat]*" (*OC* 1:417; *Canto* 13). The depth of this story of primordial intimacy is signified by the "ríos arteriales" [arterial rivers] that preexisted the trappings of modern Western civilization. These trappings, according to Mario Rodríguez's reading of this opening, divided the world between the natural and the artificial, between nature and culture, a divide Neruda's poetics seeks to bridge by means of the materiality of his own writing (131). Man, in this pre-Columbian beginning, "*tierra fue . . . forma de la arcilla [was dust, . . . the shape of clay]*," in accordance with a great many indigenous creation legends (*OC* 1:417; *Canto* 13). Significantly, this earth-man carried on his weapon "*las iniciales de la tierra [the initials of the earth]*," which are presumably the birthmarks that indicate the earthy origins of both man and his technology, but

> *[n]adie pudo*
> *recordarlas después: el viento*
> *las olvidó, el idioma del agua*
> *fue enterrado.* (*OC* 1:417)
>
> ———
>
> *[n]o one could*
> *remember them afterward: the wind*
> *forgot them, the language of water*
> *was buried.* (*Canto* 13–14)

Neruda's task is to "contar la historia [to tell the story]" that has been buried in oblivion (*OC* 1:417; *Canto* 14). Poetry must emerge from silence, from "amnesia, lost keys, the burial of language" (Rodríguez F. 136). Like Whitman's hieroglyphics, nature is a cipher, a buried language of the human story, and the poet can only become the translator by tactile experience with the material world. As Rodríguez explains, "without tactile apprehension of matter there is no word, or, to state it more clearly, without a hand there is no voice" (141). Neruda's adamic poetics relies not so much on a landscape emptied of history as on a regeneration of meaning through immediate sensual contact with the earth. His revelations come from below, not above. He announces, like Moses, "[T]oqué la piedra [I touched the stone]" and awaits his believers in his unearthed letters and words (*OC* 1:418; *Canto* 14). González Echevarría argues: "Neruda's poem is monumental in the sense that it covers a vast span of history and focuses on transcendental persons and deeds as well as on the humble masses. One has the sense of being in a crowd when viewing one of Rivera's great murals. The self is dwarfed by the size and the transcendence of the historical figures" (7). It would seem, however, that what dwarfs the self is not so much the epic human figures but the grandness of Neruda's vision of our indebtedness to the earth. In ironic biblical fashion, he does not place paternal names and begats to launch a genealogy of the New World but instead foregrounds the land, rivers (in this case four of them, like the four rivers of Eden), animals, birds, and vegetation, as if nature were the progenitor of human history.

He does date the New World's natural beginnings because they do not reside in some prehistory outside of time, even though they do lie in a chronology before the "fall" of 1492. Neruda's postlapsarian ambitions are historical, but because of history's ellipses he has to resort to myth and metaphor to mount a counternarrative to Western colonial explanations of the New World. Unlike Whitman's hieroglyphics, then, nature's indecipherability is not only the inevitable result of ecological process but often has a political explanation. Walcott announces his disavowal of nostalgia from the beginning of *Omeros*, but Neruda seems more profoundly ambivalent. The political import of his epic history is hard to miss, but because the poem opens with an epic *natural* history, Neruda raises the possibility that hope lies not in corrected history and balanced scales of justice but perhaps in a corrected balance between human and natural history. Because of the intimacy implied between those two histories, in order to "tell the story" the poet must stay closely attuned to nature's dynamism. Such attention allows the poet to catch glimpses of the deeper story of a painful human past but also ultimately to turn away from the task of chronicler to the task of knowing and praising nature.

In the poem "Vegetaciones," for example, we see an "América arboleda" [arboreal America] populated by numerous trees, among which Neruda highlights those of legendary greatness throughout the hemisphere, such as the alerce, araucaria, mahogany, rubber, and other trees as well as native plants such as wild tobacco, corn, and jacaranda. But more than simply a litany of great trees, the poem is a description of a second creation or second Eden, which is nothing more than a metaphor for nature's capacity for perpetual renewal. Neruda describes, for example, a providential wind that comes "desde otros dominios . . . [que] devolvía las flores y las vidas [from other domains . . . (that) restored flowers and lives]" and a "nuevo aroma propagado [newly propagated aroma]" by new growth (*OC* 1:418, 420; *Canto* 15). The scene is summarized as a "[ú]tero verde [(g)reen uterus]" (*OC* 1:420; *Canto* 16). Significantly, the procreative powers of nature stand in a dialectic relationship to a past of human suffering. As the corn emerges, for example, Neruda notes that it "tuvo / muertos bajo sus raíces [had / corpses beneath its roots]" (*OC* 1:419; *Canto* 15).

The subsequent sections build on this theme of creation story as historical recuperation. As the rivers come forth Neruda clarifies their role as shapers of their beloved ("amada"), or the land. Indeed, their shaping action is seen tattooing the land's skin, "rompiendo en el camino / toda la sal de la geología, / apartando los músculos del cuarzo [shattering on your way / all the salt of geology, / sundering the quartz's muscles]" (*OC* 1:424; *Canto* 19). The beloved land is fallen Eve ("tu espectro / de diosa oscura que muerde manzanas [your specter / of a dark goddess that eats apples]"), and yet Neruda's point is quite the reverse of the Unfortunate Fall (*OC* 1:423; *Canto* 19). Neruda's fallen world is violent, omnivorous, and oblivious to human memory, but it is not a signification of our alienation from God and of our need for redemption and return to him. For Neruda it is the site of our renewal and beginning. The eating of the apple signifies participation in dynamism and rebirth, the "espesura madre [maternal density]" of nature (*OC* 1:424; *Canto* 19).

The cutting action of rivers is a violence that signifies change and hence death but also new life. Thus, in his descriptions of the rivers they are consistently given parental and generative attributes, and Neruda here invokes for the first time the image of the plunging hand that will later be used in his encounter with Machu Picchu in order to recover the human story nature has buried: "[D]éjame hundir las manos que regresan / a tu maternidad [(L)et me immerse my hands that return / to your maternity]," he tells the Orinoco (*OC* 1:424; *Canto* 19–20). Mixing his gender metaphors, as he often does, Neruda says the Amazon is full of "esperma verde [green sperm]" and is the "padre patriarca, . . . / la eternidad secreta / de las fecundaciones [patriarchal father, . . . / the secret eternity / of fecundation]" (*OC* 1:425; *Canto* 20). The poet must ally himself with this procreative force if he hopes to "tell the story" that nature has buried, but he soon learns that nature teaches the language of hope, awe, and praise, not the language of history, before an always newly created world. The Bío Bío of Chile is the river that in its fecund powers first gave Neruda his voice:

[S]on tus palabras en mi boca
las que resbalan, tú me diste

el lenguaje,   ·

. . . .

me contaste el amanecer
de la tierra,

. . . .

                        murmurando
una historia color de sangre. (*OC* 1:425)

——

[Y]ours are the words that
roll off my tongue, you gave me
language,

. . . .

you told me about the dawning
of the earth,

. . . .

                        murmuring
a tale the color of blood. (*Canto* 20–21)

The images of dawning and of blood suggest that this watery language hints at unspeakable and violent secrets of nature and of human history but also at the promise of renewal.

As nature renews itself historical memory recedes and loses its significance. Neruda concludes the first section, "La lámpara de la tierra" [The Lamp of the Earth], with the arrival of man, but he ends the final poem with a description of the Mapuche Indians disappearing into the jungle. In comparison to the civilizations of the Maya, the Inca, and the Aztecs, here "no hay nadie, sólo son los árboles. / Sólo son las piedras, Arauco [there's no one. It's just the trees. / It's just the stones, Arauco]" (*OC* 1:433; *Canto* 27). The landscape emptied of a human presence can be read as a kind of lament regarding this absence of memory or perhaps even as a disturbing willed erasure of the Mapuche Indians, but it also suggests that the human story is embedded in and delimited by the natural story. The implication that nature empties history of its meaning and that human suffering loses significance drives the poetic force of "Las alturas de Machu Picchu" [The Heights of Machu Picchu], which follows this natural beginning to the poem.

The Buried Heights

The second chapter jumps us from 1400 to the 1940s, when Neruda contemplates the ruins of Machu Picchu, a religious sanctuary of the Incan elite built in the late 1400s and abandoned shortly thereafter. While the reasons for the sudden departure are not known, we know that smallpox and civil strife ravaged a large percentage of the Inca population in the early 1500s in advance of the European arrival to Cuzco in 1532. Santí notes that "the presence of the ruins presupposes a passage of time in which the city was built and also saw its decline. The ruins bespeak the time [*son ellas los que delatan que el tiempo*] that has transpired between the first and second sections" ("Introducción" 82). He insists that the following sections detail the crimes and heroism of the colonial period that help to explain this time lapse. Similarly, González Echevarría argues that the poem responds to the betrayals of the New World's colonial history.

What both critics ignore, however, is the insufficiency of history and political ideology to explain the presence of the ruins. Even historically speaking the ruins were not the direct result of Spanish colonial violence or of Inca suppression of their subordinate classes. Latin America inherited a violent and dismissive attitude toward ancient cultures, to be sure, but another chief reason the ruins were not discovered until 1911 by Hiram Bingham, a Yale professor of archaeology, was because of the natural protection provided by the steep mountains, dense vegetation, and apparently intended obscurity of the location. If it is also true that smallpox played a role, it would appear that the biological realities of the conquest, the transferal of disease, and the European encounter with a radically new and unfamiliar climate and terrain had more to do with the city becoming a ruin than any original sin of social injustice on the part of the Inca or the Spanish. There is no admission in any criticism on the poem that nature has aided the erasure of historical memory in the Americas, which would mean that oblivion is not necessarily the categorical crime Neruda's critics want to make it. While contemporary American citizens are answerable to the crimes of the past and present, they are also answerable to nature and natural process.

Santí argues that Machu Picchu provided Neruda with an opportunity to establish his prophetic role, which undergirds the entire structure of the poem. As prophet, his role is to become the mouthpiece for the dead and the sufferers and to clarify the human reasons for history's gaps and memory's lapse. According to Santí, the ruins provide "dramatic evidence of the violation that the prophet discovers in his ascension to the ruins that, from then on, he must denounce as he reconstructs the details of the crime, bringing the criminals to justice and restoring the rights of the victims" ("Introducción" 83). The possibility that nature has played an antagonistic role of its own in relation to the survival of human memory would change Santí's suppositions about Neruda's prophetic role. Undoubtedly, Neruda seeks to display his desire to play the role of prophet, but he also stages the ecological reasons for his failure to fulfill the role. Second, he does indeed attempt to bring to judgment those villains of America's history, but the poem provides ample evidence that Neruda recognizes the limitations of his pursuit of perfect human justice, dictated not by unjust powers alone but by the laws of nature, and suggests that such justice cannot be obtained independent of a profound environmental awareness and ethic.

Nature provides a model against which human efforts at renewal and sustainability compare poorly. Neruda writes, for example:

> Si la flor a la flor entrega el alto germen
> y la roca mantiene su flor diseminada
> en su golpeado traje de diamante y arena,
> el hombre arruga el pétalo de la luz que recoge
> en los determinados manantiales marinos
> y taladra el metal palpitante en sus manos. (*OC* 1:435)
>
> ———
>
> While flower to flower gives up the high seed
> and rock keeps its flower sown
> in a beaten coat of diamond and sand,
> man crumples the petal of light he picks
> in the deep-set springs of the sea
> and drills the pulsing metal in his hands. (Felstiner 205)[4]

The soul of man, consequently, dies from modern indifference and injustice ("con papel y con odio [with paper and with hate]") and from the suffering human ineptitude creates, leaving the poet wondering "en cuál de sus movimientos metálicos / vivía lo indestructible, lo imperecedero, la vida? [in which of his metallic motions / lived the indestructible, the imperishable—life?]" (*OC* 1:435–36; Felstiner 207). What, in other words, is it in human life that is "natural," that might demonstrate obedience to the same laws by which nature regenerates itself from flower to flower and even in the slow life of stones?[5] Neruda's ambivalence stems from the fact that while nature is to be admired, its regenerative capacities stand in the way of knowing the decidedly "unnatural" history of oppression and violence that led to natural ruin and obscure an ancient human story that predates colonial injustice.

While Whitman only rhetorically nodded to native signs of New World originality, Latin Americans historically proved more deeply invested in recovering the indigenous roots of the continent. Similar to Alejo Carpentier's contemporaneous visit to the ruins of San Souci in Haiti, Neruda's discovery of this past presents him with the opportunity, long dreamed of by Latin American creoles over the past century, to lay the grounds for a New World originality. However, because of his own invariable Westernization, a process that long ago erased so much historical continuity between the pre-Columbian and colonial eras in Latin America, the Inca ruins can only signify to him something fantastic, otherworldly, and disturbingly foreign. The ruins appear to Neruda, as Santí argues, as symbols of "the union of history and nature," but as emblems of erosion they also express "transience" and "irresistible decay" (*Pablo* 140). I wish to push Santí's point to its ecological conclusions: natural erosion and regeneration contribute significantly to the ruins' precariousness, a fact that causes Neruda to measure the distance that "separates sign and meaning, knowing full well that their original sense has been suspended, and perhaps even lost, all the while we re-create a second meaning attesting to the loss of that original sense" (*Pablo* 171).

For this reason, the god who touches his mouth, as happened to Isaiah, is not Jehovah or even an indigenous deity but oblivion itself, a most ironic Dantesque blessing of poetic prophecy. As Neruda notes in the final section of *Canto general*,

> subió por mis venas el olvido
> recostado en el tiempo, hasta que un día
> estremeció mi boca su lenguaje. (*OC* 1:819)

———

and oblivion recumbent in time

rose through my veins, until one day

its language shook my mouth. (Felstiner 384)

Neruda expresses exultation and praise upon discovering the ruins only to encounter the oxymoronic irony of dead stone remainders of life. He writes: "Pero una permanencia de piedra y de palabra . . . vivos, muertos, callados, sostenidos / de tanta muerte, un muro, de tanta vida [Yet a permanence of stone and word . . . living, dead, silenced, sustained, / a wall out of so much death, out of so much life]" (*OC* 1:440; Felstiner 219). And finally, there is "una vida de piedra después de tantas vidas [a life of stone after so many lives]" (*OC* 1:440; Felstiner 219). These ironic, natural remainders of a human story leave him little choice but to read nature as one would a photographic negative. That is, he must avoid the temptation to see nature—wind, water, lightning, and geological events—not only as expressing its own story but as suppressing a human story it hides and cannot speak. The prophetic role demands that he bypass the ecology of nature in the interest of the human core. Looking at the stones, he writes: "Miro vestiduras y las manos, / el vestigio del agua en la oquedad sonora, / la pared suavizada por el tacto de un rostro [I look at clothes and hands, / the trace of water in an echoing tub, / the wall brushed smooth by the touch of a face]" (*OC* 1:439; Felstiner 215).

Although these stones have been painstakingly shaped by human hands, they are also signs of how the elements have conspired to reclaim them within their deep, primordial geological story. Neruda has to admit, at least, that "ropaje, piel, vasijas, / palabras, vino, panes [clothing, skin, jars, / words, wine, bread]" do not appear to constitute the imperishable life of human beings he seeks, since "todo . . . se fue, cayó a la tierra [everything . . . is gone, fallen to earth]" and has become soil, water, and air (*OC* 1:439; Felstiner 215). Stones and human beings, then, share the same destiny. Their brief interaction cannot compare to the shaping forces of "mil años de aire . . . lustrando el solitario recinto de la piedra [a thousand years of air . . . polishing the lonely boundary of stone]" (*OC* 1:439; Felstiner 217). It is as if to say that a recovered human memory must lose intelligibility and tautologically join the very elemental substance that erased it from visibility.[6]

What is valuable here is that the ecological destiny of man at least obligates the poet/prophet to be attuned to ecology in order to rescue the stories of the past. His inquiry leads him down the mountain slopes following the natural flow of rainwater to the Urubamba River below and eventually to the sea. He does so, interrogating the river as he goes:

> Qué dicen tus destellos acosados?
> Tu secreto relámpago rebelde
> antes viajó poblado de palabras?
> Quién va rompiendo sílabas heladas,
> idiomas negros, estandartes de oro,
> bocas profundas, gritos sometidos,
> en tus delgadas aguas arteriales? (*OC* 1:442)
>
> —
>
> What do your tormented flashings say?
> Your secret insurgent lightning—did it
> once travel thronging with words?
> Who goes on crushing frozen syllables,
> black languages, banners of gold,
> bottomless mouths, throttled shout,
> in your slender arterial waters? (Felstiner 223)

Neruda's language communicates a more profound sense of tragic loss than we see in Whitman. All natural life, although presumably procreative, potentially signifies the ruin and death of human memory. But Neruda is not happy with an ecological explanation alone and cannot escape the need to find someone to blame for this oblivion. Hence the frequent iteration of "Quién?" as the poet's task is to personify and thus indict the perpetrator of this massive burial of an American past. His recriminatory line of questioning finds no answers, however, and he is left with the resignation that recovery of historical memory will have to wait.

In the waiting he must pay greater attention to nature as protagonist, not merely as antagonist. For this reason he warns himself against an overzealous interest in America's human past that his American love has inspired:

> [N]i adores la cabeza sumergida:
> deja que el tiempo cumpla su estatura
> en su salón de manantiales rotos,
> y entre el agua veloz y las murallas,
> recoge el aire del desfiladero . . .

y sube, flor a flor, por la espesura,
pisando la serpiente despeñada. (*OC* 1:442)

—

[D]o not worship the sunken head:
let time extend full span
in its hall of broken wellsprings,
and between ramparts and rapid water
gather the air in the pass . . .
and climb through the denseness flower by flower
trampling the serpent flung to the earth. (Felstiner 223)

As if anticipating Walcott's refusal of the Muse of History, the snake in Neruda's garden is the seduction of History, inspiring him to worship a broken past, a temptation that will only lead to perpetual nostalgia and a failure to apprehend nature's bounty before him. He is talking himself into accepting that time cannot be undone and must be allowed its forward and amnesia-producing course. If the ruins say anything at all, they declare themselves as a paradoxical layout of "manantiales rotos [broken wellsprings]," points of origin that are interrupted but nevertheless emit a flow of time that cannot be reversed. This does not have to mean abdication of responsibility toward that past. Ecological process teaches him his duty: to learn to think like wind and water, to think like the pollen that moves from flower to flower he had earlier observed in order to learn from its regenerative powers, even though this means following nature patiently toward its mute conclusions.

This resignation to oblivion does not lead to silence, however, but instead becomes the very fount of adamic renaming. Neruda invokes at the outset of *Canto general* an "amor americano" that surfaces again here in section 8 of "The Heights." In the first instance he describes an Edenic garden in which emerges earth-man, whose earthly signature is erased with time. Although he explains that this loss of knowledge regarding our intimate earthly origins was the moment in which "se apagó una lámpara de la tierra [the lamp of the earth was extinguished]," it is also the moment at which the poet arrives with the task of telling this obscured story. This love, then, is compassion not only for human suffering but also for American nature; it is the search for the common origin of both histories. Such love must work upward, following the erosion caused by the "agua salvaje [wild water]" that falls from the snowmelt (*OC* 1:441; Felstiner 221). As it works itself back up to the tops of the mountains, to the site of "manantiales rotos [broken wellsprings]," this love must bypass the serpent. Although Neruda's natural world of America is raw and Edenic, the site of the original Eden is where human and natural histories are unified and where recovery of the human story is simultaneous with, rather than at the cost of, knowledge of nature.

As this love rises to the ruins it must partake of the fruit of the tree. The difference from the biblical account is that eating the fruit of this world brings us back to an Eden of the lost foundations of human belonging in the natural world, where "el reino muerto vive todavía [the dead realm lives on still]" (*OC* 1:442; Felstiner 225). This prodigal return to the garden is suggested by Neruda's phrase, "Mantur estalla como un lago vivo / o como un nuevo piso del silencio [Mantur breaks out like a living lake / or a new ledge of silence]" (*OC* 1:442; Felstiner 223). Neruda's living lake suggests the phrase "agua viva," which echoes Christ's allusion but refers instead to springwater, the mountains' "manantiales." "Mantur" is Quechua for the red fruit of a tree. Thus, his reworking of the Edenic tale here implies that the effects of the Fall—lost knowledge of our origins, our brotherhood, and our natural inheritance—can be reversed through direct experience and exploration of the life of the human body and the physical world it inhabits. If the Fall brought human awareness of the physical senses, as he develops the idea further in *La espada encendida* [The Flaming Sword], it is through physical senses that we can return to primordial energies. This idea was first suggested by William Blake, whom Neruda translated in his youth, in *The Marriage of Heaven and Hell*, where he asserted that "man has no body distinct from his soul. For that called body is a portion of the soul discerned by the five senses, the chief inlets of soul in this age" (164).

Neruda's growing suspicion that natural history contains the secrets of the human past he seeks brings him little solace. On the level of political exigency, human and natural histories appear to remain separate and even antagonistic, and the result is that the promise the ruins held of a desired ancient past, a Glissantian sacred root to situate Americans more firmly in the New World, proves insubstantial. The ruins do not bespeak nature's victory over human memory alone. They also intimate the triumph of oppressors who have obliterated the pains of the poor within the very structure that remains behind. Neruda queries: "Piedra en la piedra, el hombre, dónde estuvo? / Aire en el aire, el hombre, dónde estuvo?" [Stone upon stone, and man, where was he? / Air upon air, and man, where was he?] (*OC* 1:444). He refuses to be seduced by the discovery of a past if it means he must forsake his impassioned solidarity with all human beings. Note here how he invokes the same image of the plunging hand he hoped could plumb the depths of the Orinoco's maternity:

> [D]éjame hundir la mano
> y deja que en mi palpite, como un ave mil años prisionera,
> el viejo corazón del olvidado!
> Déjame olvidar hoy esta dicha, que es más ancha que el mar,
> porque el hombre es más ancho que el mar y sus islas
> y hay que caer en él como en un pozo para salir del fondo
> con un ramo de agua piedra secreta y de verdades sumergidas. (*OC* 1:445–46)
> —
> [L]et me plunge my hand
> and let there beat in me, like a bird a thousand years imprisoned.
> The old forgotten human heart!
> Let me forget today this joy that is broader than the sea,
> because man is broader than sea and islands
> and we must fall in him as in a well to rise from the bottom
> with a branch of secret water and sunken truths. (Felstiner 235)

By the time we get to "The Great Ocean" in *Canto general* it appears Neruda has reconsidered this bold claim about the comparative breadth of human suffering and the sea, and the scales have tipped back in favor of the all-engulfing reach of deep time and natural regeneration. Whether or not humankind is wider than the sea, the net effect of Neruda's rhetoric here is that it establishes a parallel between his search for the source of the human story in the New World and his search for the depths of nature's mystery. By sustaining instead of prematurely reconciling this tension between ecological and human ethics, Neruda's poetic reach allows us to begin to imagine the reasons for their deepest connections.

What stands in the way of both worthy quests are the claims of History, symbolized by the geometrical forms of the ruins, which have come to offer the opportunity to construct a New World genealogy based on exact chronology, sacred origins, and foundational myths, all of which are notoriously elusive for the New World writer. For this reason, Neruda understands that he must "olvidar . . . la proporción poderosa [forget . . .

the sovereign symmetry]" and instead seek the suffering upon which these stones were built (*OC* 1:446; Felstiner 235). His "American love," then, encompasses, case by case, the suffering of the most poor and oppressed upon whose backs the foundational claims of civilizations are erected:

> Devuélveme el esclavo que enterraste!
> . . . .
> Dime cómo durmió cuando vivía.
> Dime si fue su sueño
> ronco, entreabierto, como un hoyo negro
> hecho por la fatiga sobre el muro. (*OC* 1:445)
> ——
> Give me back the slave you buried!
> . . . .
> Tell me how he slept while he lived,
> tell me if his sleep,
> was snoring, gaping like a black hole
> that weariness dug in the wall. (Felstiner 233)

Compassion leads to the urge to speak on behalf of the voiceless. Whitman had felt the possibility that dumb voices coalesced in his own séance with the dead. As we saw, however, he always seemed aware that such ventriloquism was more rhetorical than real and that consequently he was left with metaphors that expressed a poetics of oblivion, expressing a *wish* to translate the hints about the dead. A similar awareness of failure fuels Neruda's poetics, as evident in his opening declaration of the final section:

> No volverás del fondo de las rocas.
> No volverás del tiempo subterráneo.
> No volverá tu voz endurecida. (*OC* 1:446)
> ——
> You won't come back from bottom rock.
> You won't come back from time under ground.
> No coming back with your hardened voice. (Felstiner 237)[7]

These lines are particularly significant, since they are followed by what many critics have noted is evidence of Neruda's prophetic or shamanistic role. Neruda explains: "Yo vengo a hablar por vuestra boca muerta" [I come to speak through your dead mouth] (*OC* 1:447). The Spanish is ambiguous, since "por" can mean "for," "in behalf of," "instead of," and "through." This range of meanings indicates a poetics that allows him to overreach, to try to be the mouthpiece of the dead, and also acknowledge his mere wish to do so. He is not the prophet/priest or the shaman but the modern poet who must stand in the stead of such figures.

This ambiguity is further reinforced in the poem's final line, which commands, without answer, "Hablad por mis palabras y mi sangre" [speak through (for, instead of) my words, and through (for, instead of) my blood] (*OC* 1:447). In recordings of the poem Neruda's voice seems to end in melancholic defeat. Precisely because we are left wondering whether he is asking the dead to speak instead of him or if he will speak for them, all we can know is that he remains the poem's sole voice; the poem is a tribute to the suffering of the dead and a lament at its failure to speak adequately for them. In the end, the poem's failure is a New World poetics that stirs the reader's affections and imagination on behalf of eclipsed pasts and untold sufferings. The poem moves us because of its audacious love and its relentless pursuit of the past despite the reality of amnesia. He does not accept that memory no longer has to do its work, but he understands that memory must cede to metaphors that can only bridge the gaps of New World history with imagined affection for imagined lives.

As we saw in Whitman's deliberations about the meaning of grass and as we will see in Walcott's meditations on the sea, a tenuous balance between amnesia and recuperation also holds human and natural history together in a relationship beyond simple dichotomies. To the extent that the poet refuses to consider any political explanations for the muffled dead, as Whitman tends to do, the nature-culture binary is not as richly confused, since all of history becomes naturalized. This confusion, when exploited as it is here, means that nature and the past lie just beyond the reach of language, eclipsed but not unnoticed, like haunting ghosts, reminding us that we are not fully independent of human choices or of nature even if we cannot adequately explain the terms by which either makes its claims on us. What is therefore highlighted by virtue of this distance between poetic language and what it signifies is the power of poesis, of adamic world making. Neruda does not deny the claims of the New World past, but this past does not overshadow the power of new New World myths. Because they cannot fully bring "real" history into representation, his myths of origins are not self-deceived about the truth of their historiographic role. In this way Neruda's poetry, even more than Whitman's, proves anti-Hegelian, since it acknowledges the inevitability of forgetting in any realization of self-consciousness in relation to the past. Such forgettings serve as a reminder of memory's inevitable failure, but they also liberate the imagination to begin again in the wake of an apocalyptic end. Because Neruda relentlessly maintains that balance between oppositions, he forges in his reader an "American love" that is more likely to cherish the past, our natural environment, and the entirety of human society.

New World History: Betrayal and Vengeance

Natural regeneration is a sign of hope for a devastated landscape, but it also inspires Neruda to believe in New World possibility in the wake of colonial wreckage. In his description of the desolation of Cuba in "Los conquistadores," for example, he explains that the violence shook the island

hasta que te hiciste pureza,
soledad, silencio, espesura,
y los huesitos de tus hijos
se disputaron los cangrejos. (*OC* 1:449)

—

until you became purity,
solitude, silence, dense growth,
and the little bones of your children
were fought over by the crabs. (*Canto* 45)[8]

Although a fallen world, Cuba still retains its innocence and purity, and it therefore still has the capacity to reestablish justice. Neruda later invokes the devouring mouths of crabs who resist the conquest instead of merely devouring the evidence of its wreckage; he petitions them to devour "los pulmones / y los labios" [the lungs / and lips] of the conquistadors (*OC* 1:459).

This amnesia of natural process erases the dead, but for Neruda this implies that access to nature's purity is not an escape from but rather an entry into the past and its wrongs. Much in the vein of William Carlos Williams's view of an open history in which things are not declared dead but can be perceived remaining within time, Neruda speaks to the victims of Cortés's violence as if he were present: "[D]esde el musgo te hablo, desde las raíces de nuestro reino [I speak to you from the moss, from the roots of our kingdom]" (*OC* 1:451; *Canto* 46). This union with the roots of American soil retains a hint of irony, however, that is not as fully developed in Whitman's *Calamus*. Neruda interrupts his narrative of historical figures with an elegy. The poem pauses to reflect on the poetic and procreative nature of the history he constructs, since, despite his solidarity with and compassion for human suffering and natural devastation, Neruda remains ignorant of the full story: "Estoy hecho de tus raíces, / pero no entiendo, no me entrega / la tierra su sabiduría [I'm made of your roots / but I don't understand, the earth / doesn't grant me your wisdom]" (*OC* 1:464; *Canto* 58). All that he knows is what historiography—the "general" histories he has been reading—tells him were the actions of the so-called protagonists, and so once again he pleads to be led down into the very belly of the earth "hasta llegar / a la boca del oro" [until / I reach the mouth of gold], where he hopes that the natural oracle will speak the tale of "la desdicha" ("unhappiness" or "misfortune") of New World history (*OC* 1:465).

In a section entitled "Se unen la tierra y el hombre" [Land and Man Unite] the violence against the New World continues, and the Amerindian people and their natural environments find a perhaps more self-conscious union one with another. This newfound alliance is the birthplace of the "patria," according to Neruda. His Chilean forefathers "esperaron en las profundidades / de la soledad indomable [waited in the depths / of the indomitable wilds]" (*OC* 1:468; *Canto* 61). This last phrase indicates that the silence and solitude of the forest are the result of colonial violence but also its own source of resistance to it. Neruda concludes: "Así nació la patria unánime: la unidad antes del combate [That's how the country was born unanimous: unity before combat]" (*OC* 1:469; *Canto* 61). Even though physical resistance so often failed and the arrival of Europeans meant "the blood of three centuries," common men and women and nature quietly record the injustices: "Lo supo el árbol fronterizo, / . . . lo supieron las aguas madres / del Bío Bío [The borderland tree heard it / . . . the maternal waters / of the Bío-Bío]" (*OC* 1:470; *Canto* 63).

Nature's mute witness of history's violence is not only the birthplace of the "patria" but also, not coincidentally, of poetry. Ercilla, a one-time conquistador, Chile's first poet, and one of the most important precedents set for the epic range of Neruda's poem, finds himself overrun by the seductive reach of the Chilean landscape. Rocks, flowers, roots "[i]nvaden su armadura con gigantesco liquen. / Atropellan su espada las sombras del helecho [(a)ttack his armor with gigantic lichens. / The fern's shadows invade his sword]" (*OC* 1:471; *Canto* 64). Nature's peace corrodes his arms, almost in a time lapse, as lichen advances quickly enough to help Ercilla lay down his arms and become a conduit of nature's silent story of time. Ercilla's story demonstrates the vanity of human energy expended in the name of conquest and settlement of the region, since everything, victims and victimizers, "vuelve al silencio coronado de plumas [returns to the feather-crowned silence]" (*OC* 1:472; *Canto* 64).

Indeed, such are the oblivious forces of nature that Neruda's earth is a tomb large enough for all history, a "planeta carnívoro" [carnivorous planet], as he calls it in the section "Todos han muerto" [All Have Perished], wherein all life is absorbed, leaving only the silent witness of the sea. And yet this devouring planet does not mean that human stories are lost and gone forever or that the past is sealed off from us. Rather, this dialectic of oblivion and natural regeneration means that the past is always just dying and thus close to the present, despite the eventual erasure of its traces. It also means that history is not a series of events that lie outside of time and change. In the spirit of Williams's call for a living history, Magellan is remembered not as a mythic hero or as a man whose death is final but rather as a man with "barba llena de gusanos [a beard crawling with maggots]," still subject to the decaying and transformative force of the elements (*OC* 1:475; *Canto* 67).

What such perpetual dying leaves behind in its wake is adamic newness. Neruda writes in "A pesar de la ira" [Despite the Fury]:

Pero a través del fuego y la herradura
como un manantial iluminado
por la sangre sombría

. . . .

se derramó una luz sobre la tierra:
número, nombre, línea y estructura.

Páginas de agua, claro poderío
de idiomas rumorosos, dulces gotas
elaboradas como los racimos,
sílabas de platino en la ternura
de unos aljofarados pechos puros,

y una clásica boca de diamantes
dio su fulgor nevado al territorio. (*OC* 1:476)

—

But through fire and horseshoe,
as from a fountain illuminated
by the somber blood,

. . . .

a light was cast over the earth:
number, name, line and structure.

> Pages of water, transparent power
> of murmuring languages, sweet drops
> shaped like clusters,
> platinum syllables in the tenderness
> of some pure breasts bathed in dew,
> and a classical mouth of diamonds
> gave the territory its snow-clad splendor. (*Canto* 68–69)

In other words, colonial conflict and ruin and natural oblivion have created the circumstances for a second creation, a new book of nature the poet can read and translate into new significance. The New World of Pablo Neruda is not the New World the explorers and conquistadors thoughtlessly saw as territory without history and therefore as a land that could uphold European innocence but rather the beauty that survives colonialism and the watery and reborn story of its wreckage.

Because of this paradox, tasting New World fruit leaves a bitterness on the tongue, as it does for Walcott's Adam. In the introductory poem to the section "Los libertadores" [The Liberators] Neruda writes of a tree of life that can provide redemption, but it is a tree "*nutrido por muertos desnudos, / muertos azotados y heridos* [*nourished by naked corpses, / corpses scourged and wounded*]" (*OC* 1:478; *Canto* 71). Unlike that of the tree in Genesis, this tree's life stands in dialectical relation to the destruction that has preceded it:

[S]us raíces comieron sangre
y extrajo lágrimas del suelo:
las elevó por sus ramajes,
las repartió en su arquitectura. (*OC* 1:478)

—

[I]ts roots consumed blood,
and it extracted tears from the soil:
raised them through its branches,
dispersed them in its architecture. (Canto 72)

This Edenic tree blooms because of the labors of people who have cared for it, despite the agony of colonialism. They have protected *"the fragments"* of the primal Eden, the vestiges of what came before 1492, in order to express the voice of freedom contained in this new *"inmenso árbol repartido / diseminado en todas partes [immense divided tree, / disseminated everywhere]"* (*OC* 1:479; *Canto* 72).

What enables this reseeding of the tree is the people's capacity to perceive nature's beauty "despite the fury." To join the liberators, one must partake of the fruit of this new tree not to commence in a fallen world but to redeem the one we are already in. For this reason Neruda urges his readers to be Adam-like, aesthetically sensitive to be able to hear the tree's message:

Levanta esta tierra en tus manos,
participa de este esplendor
toma tu pan y tu manzana. (OC 1:480)
—

Raise this earth in your hands,
partake of this splendor,
take your bread and your apple. (Canto 73)

To partake of the splendor of a new day is as much a political act on behalf of the liberation of people as it is an aesthetic act on behalf of the well-being of the physical world. The apples of the garden will bring not the Fall but renewal.

If human injustice is written into the very beauty of nature, does suffering become naturalized to the point that its perpetrators are freed from accountability? As we recall, Whitman's Hegelianism struggles with this dilemma unsuccessfully in part because of his reluctance to acknowledge evil. As implied in his chapter "La arena traicionada" [The Sand Betrayed], *Canto general* portrays a fundamental breach that lies at the very foundation of New World history, which is not without authors. Neruda takes the implications of Whitman's New World vision of democracy to the level of political exigency. Like Whitman, Neruda extends himself into others, believing that he cannot separate himself from the suffering and the life matter of other living beings. Like Whitman, he says, "[T]oqué las puertas [I knocked on doors]," and seeks communion with others (*OC* 1:603; *Canto* 181). Whitman sought unification of a divided nation by means of overpassing the tribunals of justice and instead appealed to a sense of common humanity and dignity and a generalized suffering, a poetics of forgiveness drawn from the lessons of natural regeneration. The difference in Neruda is his belief that suffering cannot be generalized and that traitors must not go unnamed. Walcott will warn that this pursuit of justice can lead the poet to neglect praise for the untamed and empty landscapes of the New World, but *Canto general* argues that the poet can and must do both.

If the pursuit of justice is a risk, so too is its neglect. Neruda resorts to his share of archetypes (e.g., the "American beggar" or "Juan Stonecutter"), but he still insists that suffering and injustice always wear individual faces and cannot be generalized or ignored for Panglossian reasons. Correction of the course of human events must begin with identification of wrongs and wrongdoers, with the objective of moving history toward a different future, one in which poverty is no longer accepted as inevitable. In his portrayal of the "American beggar" Neruda undermines the generalizing effect of his own type:

[N]o voy a poner marfil antiguo,
barbas del rey en tu escrita figura,
como te justifican en los libros,
yo te voy a borrar con esperanza. (*OC* 1:604)

———

I am not going to put ancient ivory
or a regal beard in your written image,
as they justify you in books,
I'm going to expunge you with hope. (*Canto* 182)

He is not, in other words, interested in representation of poverty as much as he is in action on its behalf, which is the real substance of hope. Walcott is less political in his depictions of poverty, but in *Another Life* and *Omeros* in particular he is equally aware of the dangers of aestheticizing suffering for the sake of a good postcard.

Neruda's naturalized history does not mythologize the past because his ethics of accountability renders it subject to change in the present. It is not enough to feel compassion: one must make new choices. In reference to a massacre of six people during a demonstration on behalf of miners on January 28, 1948, Neruda writes:

> Yo no vengo a llorar aquí donde cayeron:
> vengo a vosotros, acudo a los que viven.
> Acudo a ti y a mí y en tu pecho golpeo. (*OC* 1:608)
>
> —
>
> I don't come to weep here where they fell:
> I come to you, I repair to the living.
> I appeal to you and me and I beat on your breast. (*Canto* 186)

Neruda's ethics of answerability override the passivity deep time might inspire. We hear this expressed in this powerful assessment of the massacre:

> Pero entonces la sangre fue escondida
> detrás de las raíces, fue lavada
> y negada
> (fue tan lejos), la lluvia del Sur la borró de la tierra
> ·
>
> nadie sabe dónde están ahora,
> no tienen tumba, están dispersos
> en las raíces de la patria. (*OC* 1:609)
>
> —
>
> [T]heir blood was hidden
> behind the roots, it was washed
> and denied
> (it was so far away), the South's rain expunged it from the earth
> ·
>
> nobody knows where they are now,
> they have no grave, they are dispersed,
> in the country's roots. (*Canto* 187)

The ubiquity of human suffering and loss means that we cannot allow nature's preeminence to anesthetize our reflections on the past and on human suffering. Neruda's dialectic of natural and human histories is not Hegelian, since it does not appear to mean synthesis is inevitable or even desirable. Poetry's task is not to aid in this premature healing of wrongs but rather to revisit the past in order to instill in the reader appreciation for natural beauty as well as compassion for those who suffer from the unjust actions of others. In Neruda's cosmology human trials are not accidents, and neither are they ontological conditions of human being. While this may have served as a powerful retort to the passivity Christian morals seemed to inspire in his society, however, it is not clear where or when vindictiveness or retribution can or arguably should come to rest. For this reason, Walcott's response to the crimes of New World history warns that a litigious approach to the past may lead to perpetual regret and an endless cycle of retribution.

Neruda reaches the excesses of his own litigious approach to the past and to contemporary suffering in "Que despierte el leñador" [Let the Wood-cutter Awaken], a poem that draws inspiration from Whitman's "When Lilacs Last in the Dooryard Bloom'd" and seeks to appeal to the best impulses of U.S. culture, embodied in the person of Abraham Lincoln.[9] Neruda's prototype of Lincoln is the woodcutter, a common laborer, not "un imperialista, sino un fundador original" [an imperialist, but an original founder], like his own grandfather on the Chilean southern frontier (OC 5:404). Like a poet, the woodcutting pioneer makes of his wooden materials another work of nature. He transforms nature's death into new life and, as in the various elegies of Whitman, brings forth new forms, new shapes worthy of praise that amount to, in Whitman's words, "the new society at last, proportionate to Nature" (LG 177).

Neruda invokes Whitmanian rhetoric to establish common ground in the Americas and suggests that the Americas share "el fraternal subsuelo / de América purísima, los sencillos / hombres de los caminos y las calles [purest America's / fraternal subsoil, humble / humanity of the roads and streets]" (OC 1:694; Canto 266). His appeal to Whitman facilitates this vision of brotherhood that includes not only all of Latin America but, in one of only a few instances in his poetry, potentially North America as well. However, Neruda's Whitmanian rhetoric cannot disguise the ideological battlegrounds of the cold war. As I suggested in chapter 3, southern readings of Whitman reflect their own limitations even if they also manage at times to liberate a more broad potential in his vision. On this basis of a vague understanding of his northern neighbor and of Whitman's romance with U.S. imperialism Neruda only divides the New World further into socialist and capitalist camps and between contemporary Euro-American society and a long-dead indigenous past (Brotherston 125–26).

These divisions are symptomatic of a problematic binary in this particular poem between civilization and the wild. Written simultaneously from the western frontier of the United States and the frontier of the Ural Mountains in the Soviet Union, the poem emerges from the silence of an Edenic untamed forest in the moment just before the axe begins to make trees into wood and industry turns wood into paper and, of course, into books of poetry. That is, to suit his ideological purposes Neruda's poetry here is Adamic, not adamic, in that it predates the beginnings of history. In mythological language Neruda begins the poem by invoking such a space in the U.S. West:

Al oeste de Colorado River
hay un sitio que amo.
Acudo allí con todo lo que palpitando
transcurre en mí. (*OC* 1:682)

—

West of the Colorado River
there's a place that I love.
I hasten there with every pulsing thing
that transpires in me. (*Canto* 255)

He goes on to praise the America of "el pequeño hogar del *farmer* [the farmer's little house]" and of "sangre laboradora [your laborer's blood]" (*OC* 1:683; *Canto* 256). His America is the place of innocent Whitmanian industry and development, "tu ciudad, tu substancia, / tu luz, tus mecanismos, la energía / del Oeste [your city, your substance / your light, your mechanisms, the West's / energy]" (*OC* 1:684; *Canto* 257). He concludes: "Es tu paz lo que amamos, no tu máscara. / No es hermoso tu rostro de guerrero [It's your peace that we love, not your mask. / Your warrior's face is not beautiful]" (*OC* 1:683; *Canto* 256).

Similarly, in a telling passage the Ural frontier lies where human and natural history have an innocent beginning:

Trigo y acero aquí han nacido
de la mano del hombre, de su pecho.

Y un canto de martillos alegra el bosque antiguo
como un nuevo fenómeno azul.
Desde aquí miro extensas zonas de hombre,
geografía de niños y mujeres, amor,
fábricas y canciones, escuelas
que brillan como alhelíes en la selva
donde habitó hasta ayer el zorro salvaje.
Desde este punto abarca mi mano en el mapa
el verde de las praderas, el humo
de mil talleres, los aromas
textiles, el asombro
de la energía dominada. (*OC* 1:688–89)

—

Here wheat and steel were born
of mankind's hand and breast.
And a song of hammers cheers the ancient forest
like a new blue phenomenon.
From here I see extensive zones of humanity,
geography of children and women, love,
factories and songs, schools
that glow like gillyflowers in the forest
where only yesterday the wild fox thrived.
From this point my hand on the map embraces
the meadowland's green, smoke
from a thousand workshops, textile
aromas, the wonder
of harnessed energy. (*Canto* 261)

Here we have a tamed nature brought into harmony with the industry of
proletarian man. Perhaps we read this now, in the age of environmental
anxiety, with some disappointment that Neruda does not seem to note the
irony of his vacated wilderness now thriving with factory smoke and urban
development. The results of human engineering of nature is as natural as
the "wild fox," which has departed; he can make no distinctions between
wheat and steel.

A poetics that cannot recognize the otherness of wilderness on any
terms runs this risk of sanctifying human economy. In Neruda's socialism

this leads to sanctifying the proletarian legacies of what he describes in America as

el canto de la maquina que hila,
la cuchara de hierro que come tierra,
la perforadora con su golpe de cóndor
y cuanto corta, oprime, corre, cose:
seres y ruedas repitiendo y naciendo. (*OC* 1:683)
—

the song of the spinning machine,
the iron scoop that eats earth,
the drill with its condor's blow
and whatever cuts, presses, runs, sews:
beings and wheels repeating and being born. (*Canto* 256)

One thinks of the great Detroit mural by Diego Rivera, who attempted to naturalize and harmonize the proletarian energies of the United States' greatest car plant, a plant that produced what now poses one of the greatest environmental dangers of the modern age.

Whitman makes similar use of the western frontier in his poetry, despite his similarly superficial knowledge of the West. As discussed in chapter 4, "Song of the Redwood-Tree" gives expression to America's Manifest Destiny by depicting the West as "[t]he fields of Nature long prepared and fallow, . . . / At last the New arriving, assuming, taking possession" (*LG* 177). And the New was intent on "[c]learing the ground for broad humanity, the true America, heir of the past so grand / To build a grander future" (*LG* 177). Neruda adapts Whitman's vision of this seemingly inevitable and patriotic violence against nature so that it now serves transnational socialism. He fails to see this violence as a precursor to or as the seedbed of an expansionist tendency that would come to fruition at the end of World War II or even as an ominous expression of willed environmental degradation. Neruda's innocent Whitman becomes a rhetorical guarantee of his own innocent appraisal of human labor. He calls upon Whitman in the Ural forest and asks:

Walt Whitman, levanta tu barba de hierba,
mira conmigo desde el bosque,
desde estas magnitudes perfumadas.

Qué ves allí, Walt Whitman?
Veo, me dice mi hermano profundo,
veo como trabajan las usinas,

. . . .

Veo desde la planicie combatida,
desde el padecimiento y el incendio,
nacer en la humedad de la mañana
un tractor rechinante hacia las llanuras. (*OC* 1:689–90)

—

Walt Whitman, raise your beard of grass,
look with me from the forest,
from these perfumed magnitudes.
What do you see there, Walt Whitman?
I see, my deep brother tells me,
I see the factories run,

. . . .

I see [from the embattled plain
from the agony and ashes]
rising in the morning moisture,
a tractor whirring toward the prairies. (*Canto* 262)

Whitman serves rhetorically as the American counterpart to Neruda's socialist vision; his implication is that once the common cause of feeding the human community is acknowledged and celebrated, we would see an end to cold war differences and New World differences alike. It was his conviction that "sobre ellos la misma aurora del hemisferio arde / y de ellos está hecho lo que somos [above (U.S. authors) burns the same dawn of the hemisphere / and what they made of it is what we are]" (*OC* 1:684; *Cantos* 257). Consequently, he pleads with the American bard:

Dame tu voz . . .
. . . .

para cantar estas reconstrucciones!
Cantemos juntos lo que se levanta
de todos los dolores, lo que surge
del gran silencio, de la grave
victoria. (*OC* 1:690)

—

Give me your voice . . .

. . . .

to sing these reconstructions!
Let's sing together whatever arises
from all the sorrows, whatever surges
from the great silence, from the solemn
victory. (*Canto* 262)

The cold war becomes a kind of civil war between brothers. Just as Whitman's poetry attempted to heal a nation divided against itself, Neruda's poetry takes on a more global ambition to sing of the common plight of soldiers in the postwar United States and the Soviet Union.

Neruda's vision is flawed in at least two important ways. First, the poem trusts Russian innocence and only warns of what will happen if the United States becomes too aggressive. Neruda has nothing but categorical praise for Stalin's vigilance for his people and chillingly and almost unpardonably condones whatever use of nuclear weapons might become necessary if the United States crosses the line:

Y desde el laboratorio cubierto de enredaderas
saldrá también el átomo desencadenado
hacia vuestras ciudades orgullosas. (*OC* 1:697–98)

—

And from the laboratory covered with vines
the unleashed atom will also set forth
toward your proud cities. (*Canto* 269)

The poem is meant to be a call for peace, but peace can only be secured, it would seem, if the spirit of the woodcutter of the United States awakens to calm the violence of U.S. aggression. No mention is made of any aggression on the part of Stalin and the Soviet Union. Without any self-implication, Neruda's poem becomes propagandistic and ineffective in shaping a mentality of peaceful coexistence either between human communities or with the environment.

The second problem, which I wish to argue is related to the first, is the Adamic temptation to write from an imagined space of innocence, absent of prior history. As is true in many of Neruda's more politically impassioned moments, there is little self-distrust in the poem because his world is simplified by binaries that allow his poetry to wander about the world decrying injustices and celebrating nature without ever questioning the apparent contradictions and competing aims of, say, social and environmental justice or Soviet and U.S. interests. Hence he adopts a kind of socialist antinomianism that allows him freedom from the laws that govern the rest of his world. Speaking from the Ural pine forests, Neruda observes the industry that is converting wilderness into settled and conquered nature, but he remains just outside of this space in what appears to be a liminal poetic wilderness. While nature's energy must be "dominada" [tamed] for the sake of communal well-being (hence the labor of the woodcutter invoked in the latter section of the poem), it remains wild in the poet's garden, from which he observes the world. Nothing, in other words, changes in this garden by virtue of his presence and poetic activity, as if he never needed heating and food or never produced waste. He has so thoroughly sanctified the hand of labor that he can equate writing poetry with the activity of woodworking, fishing, and other rudimentary forms of alimentary labor, all without accountability for the history that results from such activity. Due to the increased evidence of degradation in the Caribbean islands, Walcott will try to make a similar equation between writing and craft but with an understanding that the point of danger lies when one's signature on the land is no longer legible.

In his description of the rebirth of the Soviet Union after World War II Neruda writes from the "antigua noche de los pinos / y el silencio como una alta columna [pines' ancient night / and silence like a towering column]" (OC 1:688; Canto 261). He does not note the difference his human presence makes in this natural space but instead naturalizes his poetic authority. Note the directional speech of the section: "[d]esde aquí miro [(f)rom here I see]" and "[d]esde este punto [(f)rom this point]" (OC 1:688; Canto 261). In each case we see him just on the outside of the man-made world he describes. And when Neruda invokes Whitman he invites Whitman to speak from this same space: "[M]ira conmigo desde el bosque, / desde estas magnitudes perfumadas [(L)ook with me from the forest, / from these perfumed magnitudes]" (OC 1:689; Canto 262). What Whitman and Neruda together observe are "reconstrucciones" in the wake of violence and World War II, but there is no such prior history that occupies the space whence the poet writes; he writes, in other words, a history without history, as natural as leaves of grass.

I do not wish to argue that every form of violence against nature is equally deplorable or that every tool is a symbol of environmental degradation. Precisely because distinctions between sustainable and nonsustainable forms of interaction with nature need to be made, all discursive activities must have some means of registering their relationship to the inevitable and perhaps in some cases necessary signatures of violence on the land. As I argued in my discussion of Whitman's "Song of the Broad-Axe," Aldo Leopold's dissection of human violence on nature is instructive. Just one year prior to the appearance of *Canto general* Leopold wrote that trees are books that tell the story not simply of human error or tragedy but also of their own natural story. The paradox is that "woodsmanship is the translation of the book" (Leopold 81). Tools such as the axe, the wedge, and the saw wield a violence against trees, but they yield both "good wood, and . . . good history" (17). Leopold explains:

> I have read many definitions of what is a conservationist . . . but I suspect that the best one is written not with a pen, but with an axe. It is a matter of what a man thinks about while chopping, or while deciding what to chop. A conservationist is one who is humbly aware that with each stroke he is writing his signature on the face of his land. Signatures of course differ, whether with axe or pen, and this is as it should be. (68)

Any reading of a tree's history inevitably tells the story of the violence that made its telling possible. The impulse to write adamic poetry implicitly runs this risk of ignoring the environmental history that enables the poet's metaphors. In Judeo-Christian terms it is not possible to speak of the garden's innocence with innocent language; nature's ambiguous and liminal position within human history can only be outlined with language that bears witness to our estrangement from the physical world and its deep time.

Precisely because some violence is necessary in order to feed ourselves, a woodcutter is an apt metaphor for how we can assess what kind of violence we wage. Only those forms of violence that are visible and legible as stories are going to be useful to this end. Neruda's woodcutter exists in a mythologized natural realm, however, where there is no distinction between the tree and the woodcutter's language about the tree.[10] An entire society emerges from the poet's garden, seemingly unaware of or at least unconcerned by the violence necessitated by its birth. The rhetorical figure of Lincoln, who embodies Neruda's notion of the woodcutter, exhibits an innocence sustained by such naturalizing language:

> Que su cabeza de corteza,
> sus ojos vistos en las tablas,
> en las arrugas de la encina,
> vuelvan a mirar el mundo
> subiendo sobre los follajes,
> mas altos que las sequoías. (*OC* 1:698)

> —

> Let his head of bark,
> his eyes seen in the boards,
> in the oak's wrinkles,
> return to the world
> rising above the treetops,
> higher than the sequoias. (*Canto* 270)

My point here is this: human conceptual and physical activity, when seen independent of a natural world to which it refers and for which it must be accountable, becomes hopelessly solipsistic, an image of nothing but itself. We enter into a world of pure illusion and representation, not unlike the world in which Don Quixote finds himself in the second half of the great novel, in which the world is now imitating his imagination. It is perhaps unfortunate that Neruda felt he gained more from Whitman than from Cervantes, as he claimed in his speech to the PEN Club in 1972 discussed in chapter 3, since it was the latter who understood more clearly the dangers of solipsistic representations and the need for answerability to a multiple world outside the world of the self. Precisely at the moment he discovers his imagination made flesh, Quixote can no longer take pleasure in his dreams. Carlos Fuentes observes:

> Don Quixote has no trouble coexisting with what is outside his own
> universe: the very fact that reality does not coincide with his readings
> permits him, again and again, to impose his vision of his readings on
> reality. But when what only pertains to his univocal readings finds an
> equivalent in reality, the illusion is shattered. . . . [There is no denying]
> the permanent divorce between words and things, [but] literature is the
> utopian operation that would like to reduce that distance. When it simply

disguises the divorce, it is called epic. When it reveals it, it is called novel or poetry. (61, 70–71)

Because he is more careful to reveal the divorce, Walcott is more hesitant than either Whitman or Neruda to call his great American poem *Omeros* an epic. Neruda is too unsettled by the American hemisphere's political plurality and gives in to the temptation here to will his socialism on his reader with a disturbingly epic intolerance. I hope it is not too impatient to suggest that an alternative communion in the American hemisphere might have been and indeed might still need to be forged by an ecological ethic that is far less ideological and divisive. If there is still an epic story of the Americas to tell, it must begin with such an ethic. It will be, of necessity, transnational and global but perhaps more willing to conserve the diversity of places and peoples because it demands an aesthetic openness to an immanent natural world that can neither be fully known nor controlled and yet certainly not ignored. As environmental history teaches us, social injustice almost always results in environmental injustice as well. While words and things might be divorced, their common fate is not; we can no longer afford to pretend otherwise.

The Great Ocean of Nature: The Bridge Between

One of the unusual advantages of studying a poet as prolific and experimental as Neruda is that one often finds answers to dilemmas his poetry presents from . . . his poetry. He does indeed contain multitudes, and his self-contradictions disallow facile and categorical readings of his ideological impulses. This is no more true than when he turns his poetic attention to the natural world. Just prior to the "Woodcutter" poem we find "Canto general de Chile," the section of the poem that precipitated the writing of *Canto general*. This poem demonstrates that "making a start out of particulars," in the words of William Carlos Williams, is the foundation of a relational model of New World poetics, one that connects the hemisphere ecologically without collapsing its various sites of uniqueness. The poem portends the elemental poetry that will follow in Neruda's career and an empirical aesthetic toward nature that would seem to offer temperance in the demands for immediate justice.

"Canto general de Chile" includes a wide variety of celebrations of the aesthetic qualities of the botanical and other natural wonders of Chilean landscapes. There is little metaphorizing here, little interest in transforming the trees, waters, and stones into some sign of the human story in the land. The poet approaches the natural world with an openness that simplifies his task to that of naming and praising. There are brief reminders of the social world the poet inhabits, such as the moving depiction of the floodwaters that carry the detritus of the poor:

> estas ruinas que nadan
> con tus muertos vagando dulcemente hacia el mar,
> entre las pobres mesas y los perdidos árboles
> que van de tumbo en tumbo mostrando sus raíces. (*OC* 1:646)

———

> these ruins that swim
> with your dead, gently drifting to sea,
> amid humble tables and lost trees
> that tumble downstream displaying their roots. (*Canto* 221)

But this poem seems to be an exception to an otherwise focused attention on flora and fauna. His poem "Drimis Winterei" describes a tree known as *canelo* in Spanish that is of sacred and magical significance in Mapuche culture—its branches are used as symbols of peace, its shade was often used as the site for treaty negotiations. Neruda merely describes it as consisting of "plantas sin nombre, hojas / y cuerdas montañosas, / ramas tejidas de aire verde [nameless plants, leaves / and mountainous tendons, / branches woven with green air]" (*OC* 1:650; *Canto* 225). Similarly, he praises an ocean without historical metaphors; it is simply Chile's "cielo oscuro . . . esta fruta universal, toda esta delirante corona [dark sky . . . this universal fruit, all this delirious crown]" (*OC* 1:644; *Canto* 219). He imagines himself to be the tree upon which the wrens can rest—"un canto mío me sostiene / como un tronco arrugado, con ciertas cicatrices [my song sustains me / like a wrinkled trunk, with certain scars]"—but pleads simply: "[Q]uiero ser más pájaro cada día [(E)very day I want to be more bird]" (*OC* 1:652–53; *Canto* 226–27).

This desire does not appear to be allegorical, as many of his natural metaphors are in other contexts throughout *Canto general*. It seems rather an expression of an emergent biocentric yearning. "Botánica" [Botany] is a litany of praise for Chile's varieties of trees, including the *ulmo*, the *canelo*, the *avellano*, the roble, and so on, but again without double significance as signs of Chile's human history. Even the famous araucaria, also important to the Mapuche culture, is ennobled simply by virtue of its aesthetic beauty and biological traits:

> Llanto erizado, eternidad del agua,
> monte de escamas, rayo de herraduras,
> tu atormentada casa se construye
> con pétalos de pura geología. (*OC* 1:655)
>
> —
>
> Bristling tears, eternity of water,
> scaly mount, thunderbolt of horseshoes,
> your tormented house is built ·
> with petals of pure geology. (*Canto* 229)

In the poem "Zona eriales" [Untilled Zones] he turns to the southernmost reaches of Chile, and while these more raw regions of Chile appear to be without significant evidence of a pre-Columbian history, Neruda's temporal reach is much more profound. When measured ecologically, human history is faint and shallow and challenges the poet's Adamic impulse to believe in inaugurating history by virtue of naming the world. The first lines set up a contrast between his shallow capacity to observe time in the natural forms before him:

> Aquí estoy, aquí estoy,
> boca humana entregada al paso pálido
> de un detenido tiempo como copa o cadera,
> central presidio de agua sin salida,
> árbol de corporal flor derribada.
> únicamente sorda y brusca arena. (*OC* 1:651)
>
> —
>
> Here am I, here am I,
> a human mouth abandoned to the pale passage
> of a time arrested like a wineglass or hip,
> a central penitentiary of impounded water,
> tree of a demolished corporal flower,
> nothing but deaf and brusque sand. (*Canto* 226)

The poet's mouth seeks a language that will be lost on the deafness of nature, even though he then suggests that this unique and oddly Edenic opportunity is the chance for his poetry to help found his "patria." Nature nurtures itself on death, but its beauty is without the hint of bitter irony that haunts the poet elsewhere in the epic.

While Neruda's politics attracted him to Hegelian notions of synthesis whereby history's conflicts move history toward a brighter future and the creation of what Santí calls "an authentic Latin American writing," his penultimate poem, "El gran océano," problematizes this search in its explorations of the historical and poetic implications of ecological process, regeneration, and deep time (*Pablo* 186). The poem's unusual appeal to environmental science creates a "textual texture between science and mythology" and serves to disrupt the facility with which Neruda's poetics aspires to arrowlike teleology. Instead, the poem implies the need for a constant revisitation of and a circling back to the ocean's radical temporal otherness (Yurkiévich, "Génesis" 386). Nature's challenge of deep time renders rhetorical and ironic the apocalyptic direction of biblical prophetic writing that informs the poetics of Whitman's *Leaves of Grass* and *Canto general*.[11] In order to understand the significance of this poem it is instructive to cite Derek Walcott's observations about the particular dilemma that the ocean represents to a New World poet:

> The strength of the sea gives you an idea of time that makes history absurd. Because history is an intrusion on that immensity. History is a very, very minor statement; it's not even an intrusion, it is an insignificant speck on the rim of that horizon. . . . If you are on land looking at ruins, the ruins commemorate you. They more commemorate than lament the achievement of man. They may contain a moral lesson but underneath that there is still praise of the tyrant or hero. And that's what the ruins of any great cultures do. In a way they commemorate decay. That's the elegiac point. The sea is not elegiac in that way. The sea does not have anything on it that is a memento of man. Somehow the motion of the sea enters the motion of the mind. The mind itself tries to absorb part of that immensity, and realizes that its own contributions to the immensity of that thing are simply a bubble, one of many bubbles in an infinite area. ("Interview" [White] 158–59)

Walcott's assessment of ruins suggests that Neruda's attractions to Machu Picchu, although not guilty of praising the tyrant by any means, run the risk of focusing too exclusively on the heroism and centrality of the human story. Unless Neruda is willing to let go of the pull of America's buried past, his poetry will be characterized as nothing but elegiac epic. Highly elegiac in tone, "Alturas" nevertheless begins to raise questions, as we saw, about the meaning of the watery grave that renders the human story insignificant in the way Walcott describes. Neruda finds himself gravitating in the direction of deep time, probing its depths and exploring the wonder of its mysteries, and the result is a vital qualification, even softening, of the recriminating tone of his political poetry.

Because Neruda is clearly indebted to Whitman's writings on the ocean, it could be said that for Neruda the ocean marks the limits of all knowledge and of all life. It not only literally circumscribes all terrestrial life, but it is the site of nature's majestic and sacred work of destruction and re-creation. Although in the poem "Nacimientos" Neruda indicates his understanding of an astrological origin of earth life, he generally places the sea at the center of earth's ongoing procreativity; the earth is laved and rebirthed in water, and what appears solid is merely a temporary way station for the liquidity of all life-forms. Even stones, as he will later assert in *Piedras de Chile* and *Piedras del cielo,* are, in the context of geological time, drops of liquid metal on their way to future transformations.

Some debate has concerned the location of this chapter in a poem rife with biblical, epical reach. Coming toward the conclusion of the poem, it might appear, as Alain Sicard notes, that Neruda "introduces a parenthesis into the book in which he would express a poetic project fundamentally distinct from that which inspires the historical chronicles" in the poem (459). Sicard reconciles the chapter's presence in the poem by arguing that Neruda's intention is to reconcile the natural with the historical. He explains that by 1945 Neruda began to depict the ocean in historical terms: "[O]ceanic time adopts the character of historical time. . . . When the poet faces the sea, he only appears to turn his back on history" (459). Sicard does not explain why Neruda would explore a fundamentally different register of time with such reverence, one that would become increasingly important to his atheistic mind for understanding the concept of eternity and his own impending death, if he only intended to discard it. I agree that Neruda may have wanted a reconciliation between natural and human histories if for no other reason than to resolve his anxieties over the indifference ecology implied to human problems, but it is not clear to me that he succeeds. His failure proves instructive because it suggests an ethic in which nature must not be circumscribed by the human story.

What saves the epic from its own overt ideological impulses is Neruda's willingness to grant to nature something akin to gnosis, a knowledge that is both superior to what his historical imagination is able to muster and ultimately beyond the expressive reach of his poetry. It is far from the case, then, as Loyola claims, that Neruda is merely expressing in this chapter "a *personal* cosmogony" instead of a more "general or American" vision (*OC* 1:1206). Nor is it the case that the eternity of oceanic time is merely an extension of human meaning to the physical world or the "infinite permanence of history," as Sicard insists (487). Neruda's oceanic cosmogony intends to be both totalizing and universal, as we shall see, but also an ever-important acknowledgment of the limits of human understanding. Since the ocean challenges human and, more specifically, linguistic meaning, the poem's polysemic aspect is apt. As Yurkiévich explains, "the unstable polysemy is the figurative recourse, par excellence, to represent natural mutability in its full dynamism" ("Génesis" 393).

The ocean is not the negative type or the yin to the yang of human historical time. History is embedded and recycled in the sea, but it is only knowable in fragments. This means the poet must forsake, or at least radically reconceptualize, his ambition to recover the past, but it also means the New World in some sense is always new, always asking to be reconstructed from the fragments of the past that its compelling natural beauties reveal. No poet can be too disappointed by such adamic obligations. Sicard is right to insist that just because oceanic time empties history ("se deshabita") of its location in place and time, Neruda does not "reject or negate history" (455). We can accept that the material world becomes the means by which Neruda builds the world and "reaffirms history" if it is also true that this process does not guarantee historical continuity, as Sicard is intent on arguing. Reconstructing historical memory in the context of ecological process resembles what Édouard Glissant calls the New World writer's paradoxical obligation to remember on the basis of a "series of forgettings" ("Creolization" 273).

The ocean's most important characteristic in the chapter is that it functions both as tomb and womb for all life. Neruda chooses to highlight the ocean's capacity to internalize destructive and creative forces into one singular entity,

> la energía de tu idioma blanco
> que destroza y derriba sus columnas
> en su propia pureza demolida. (*OC* 1:767)
> ——
> the energy of your white language
> that destroys and topples its columns
> in its shattered purity. (*Canto* 337)

Oceans, of course, are most frequently observed from shorelines, where the action of their waves "tritura costas y produce / la paz de arena que rodea el mundo [pulverizes coasts and produces / the sandy peace that envelops the world]," but this might obscure the ocean's

> central volumen de la fuerza,
> la potencia extendida de las aguas,
> la inmóvil soledad llena de vidas. (*OC* 1:767)
> ——
> central volume of force,
> the extended potency of waters,
> the motionless solitude brimming with life. (*Canto* 337)

This internal force appears to have no telos, no destined location such as a shoreline, and it can only be observed as waves. The poet cannot access the ocean's depths, except of course through the imagination, but on the sea's surface waves are visible evidence of the sea's "raíces / hijas del firmamento sumergido [roots, / offspring of the submerged firmament]" (*OC* 1:783; *Canto* 351). The reading of the story they contain becomes one of seeing the world upside down, implied in the term "firmamento sumergido." Waves bear the marks of all of the sea's "nacimientos y derrotas [births and defeats]" and shine forth with "toda la luz que fue abolida [all the abolished light]" (*OC* 1:783; *Canto* 352). Death expresses itself as watery swells, as a "manantial de la blancura [fountain of whiteness]" that paradoxically "subió a la muerte [ascended to death]" (*OC* 1:783; *Canto* 352).

The ocean's chaotic "biodynamic animism," as Yurkiévich calls it, blurs the distinction between life and death and therefore nullifies the relevance of history ("Génesis" 396). The ocean is, rather, itself

> [t]iempo, tal vez, o copa acumulada
> de todo movimiento, unidad pura
> que no selló la muerte. (*OC* 1:767)
>
> —
>
> [t]ime perhaps, or accumulated cup
> of all movement, pure unity
> unsealed by death. (*Canto* 337–38)

The cyclical action of oceans means that there is no end or death, and thus the waters become the sign of unending time. Neruda explains:

> [T]u energía
> parece resbalar sin ser gastada,
> parece regresar a su reposo.
>
> . . . .
>
> Toda tu fuerza vuelve a ser origen.
> Sólo entregas despojos triturados
>
> . . . .
>
> lo que expulsó la acción de tu abundancia. (*OC* 1:767)
>
> —
>
> [Y]our energy
> seems to flow unconsumed,
> seems to return to its repose.
>
> . . . .
>
> All your force becomes origin again.
> You only deliver crushed debris,
>
> . . . .
>
> whatever the action of your abundance expelled. (*Canto* 338)

What is observable, in other words, on the shore is merely the fractional detritus of an otherwise perpetual regeneration of life, the "trails of debris" that also seemed to call to Whitman for translation of their broken meanings (*PW* 180). These castaways—shells, sand, seaweed—obsessed Neruda throughout his life but especially in his last decades living on the coast at

Isla Negra, as they seemed to be metonymic ciphers, the only language the sea's procreativity spoke concretely to the discerning poet's ear. The only other language is that spoken to the fisherman, the ocean's poet, for whom

sólo sube al hilo de las redes
el relámpago muerto de la escama
un milímetro herido en la distancia
de tus totalidades cristalinas. (*OC* 1:768)

———

nothing rises to the nets' thread
but the dead lightning of a fish scale,
a wounded millimeter in the distance
of your crystalline totalities. (*Canto* 338)

Within the ocean the detritus of time's passage, "el trascurso sumergido [sunken flux]," survives, "y la magnitud creada mantiene / las mismas esmeraldas escamosas [and the magnitude created maintains / the same scaly emeralds]" (*OC* 1:770; *Canto* 340). These buried fragments of time, which include "ojos ahogados [drowned eyes]" as well as an "acumulada cantidad desnuda [accumulated naked quantity]," find their way into the very procreativity of the ocean. Consequently, the magnitude and variety of submarine forms, like Walcott's submarine cathedrals in "The Sea Is History," turn us away from a search for monuments of the past toward nature itself. Neruda comments: "Se contruyó la catedral sin manos / con golpes de marea innumerable [The cathedral was built without hands / by blows of innumerable tide]" (*OC* 1:770; *Canto* 340).

This is a stunning disruption to those moments in *Canto general* when Neruda appeals to genealogical and biblical rhetoric and poetry's Adamic powers. Just as Walcott reads the chapters of New World history under the sea as a deconstruction of the historical determinism of biblical time, Neruda points to alternative, more strange and monumental cathedrals in the sea.[12] Although he, like Whitman before him, does not make the explicit link between the particular historical qualities of New World experience and ecology that Walcott does, it is nevertheless clear the poets share a similar appreciation of the fact that natural history is both aide and obstructer to an access to the past and that nature's monumental qualities present rich poetic opportunities in the context of such amnesia for the creation of New World cultures. As Neruda suggested earlier in "The Heights," human beings typically think of themselves as outside of the claims of deep time, and they tend to act as disruptive forces to the integrity of nature's ongoing procreative force. As Yurkiévich puts it, "[W]hile life protects the purity and integrity of the sea's capacity for renewal, earthly man suffers a nefarious tendency that turns him into an unnatural and unnaturalizing predator [*depredador desnaturalizado y desnaturalizante*]" ("Génesis" 395).

Neruda once explained that he came to live by the sea in Isla Negra because it is generally untainted by injustice and, at least to his eyes, by pollution:

[E]l mar me pareció más limpio que la tierra. No vemos en él los crímenes diabólicos de las grandes ciudades, ni la preparación del genocidio. A la orilla del mar no llega el *smog* pustulario, ni se acumula la ceniza de los cigarrillos difuntos. El mundo se oxigena junto a la higiene de las olas. (*OC* 5:273)

—

The sea seemed to me cleaner than the earth. We don't see in it the hellish crimes of great cities or plans for genocide. The pustular smog doesn't reach the seashore, nor do cigarette butts accumulate there. The world is oxygenated in proximity to the waves' cleanliness.

The erasure of human life that drowning in the sea portends becomes an aesthetic opportunity for Neruda. In the poem that follows, "Los peces y el ahogado" [The Fish and the Drowned Person], Neruda describes the death and dismemberment of a drowned man with impressive calm inspired by the promise of ecological regeneration. He insists that this ecological reality establishes aesthetic value:

Hermosa fue la mano o la cintura
que rodeada de luna fugitiva
vio trepidar la población pesquera
. . . .
y sometió su sangre descendiendo
a la profundidad devoradora,
suspendido por bocas que recorren
su torso con sortijas sanguinarias
hasta que desgreñado y dividido
. . . .

       . . . una herencia herida
bajo el mar, en el árbol numeroso. (*OC* 1:771–72)
—

Beautiful the hand or waist
that, enveloped by a fleeting moon,
saw the denizens of the deep tremble
. . . .
and submitting his blood he descended
to the devouring depths,
suspended by mouths that cover
his torso with bloodthirsty rings
until, disheveled and divided
. . . .
       . . . a wounded heritage
beneath the sea, on the numerous tree. (*Canto* 341)

I cited this passage in my epigraph to this chapter because it captures
Neruda's delicate understanding of how ecological death functions. In a
rare moment of generalization he does not give the drowning man a name
or his death a political cause, but by this manner of forbearance we see "a
wounded heritage / beneath the sea" that is strangely beautiful even if also
mournful.

Neruda avoids aestheticizing all death and injustice, however, by contrasting this ecology of dying with the violent injustice of human-inflicted
suffering. The Yámanas, an indigenous people who live in the southernmost
regions of Patagonia, have their plate full with struggles against the forces
of nature in this untamed region. They work for their survival, even though
they are "azotados / por el látigo antártico . . . en la erizada / enemistad
de témpanos y lluvias [lashed / by the antarctic whip . . . in the bristling
/ enmity of icebergs and rain]" (*OC* 1:777; *Canto* 347). When vegetal life
and human beings alike struggle with natural forces of this kind they are
beautiful and receive the poet's admiration. The human causes for suffering,
however, are ugly. He knows that "el exterminio [extermination]" sometimes comes "no . . . de los ríos de la nieve [not from the rivers of snow]"
but from "el hombre [man]" (*OC* 1:778; *Canto* 347). This human violence
is an unnatural "ola / nacida en las rupturas, dirigida / como el amor
herido bajo el viento [wave / born in ruptures, driven / like love wounded

beneath the wind]" (*OC* 1:778; *Canto* 348). To die from such human waves of oppression, as Neruda later describes the fate of the impoverished and marginalized "hijos de la costa [children of the seacoast]," is to die "sin ataúd, mordidos / por las últimas olas y desdichas [without coffin, / bitten by the last waves and calamities]" (*OC* 1:782; *Canto* 350).

While ecological cycles obtain an inherent beauty and teach us to see the human story in a broader and less finite context, Neruda cannot accept the implicit indifference toward human injustice that this context might transmit. For this reason he differentiates between natural and human causation of human suffering and death and seems to imply that the latter attempts to function as an arrogant substitution for natural force. Human injustice arrives like waves and wind but with the intent to destroy territories and nature's rhythms. He understands, for example, that, once it arrives, the poor and indigenous peoples of the sea are destined to something other than a watery death,

> no a la muerte del mar, con agua y luna,
> sino a los desquiciados agujeros
> de la necrología. . . .
> Antes la muerte tuvo territorios,
> transmigración, etapas, estaciones,
> y pudisteis subir bailando envueltos
> en el rocío diurno de la rosa
> o en la navegación del pez de plata. (*OC* 1:781)
>
> —
>
> not a sea death, with water and moon,
> by the unhinged holes
> of necrology. . . .
> Formerly death had territories,
> transmigration, stages, seasons,
> and you could rise dancing enveloped
> in the diurnal dew of roses
> or in the silver fish's navigation. (*Canto* 350)

The implication is clear: once the rhythms of nature and death are disrupted, so too are the rhythms of culture, which should have allowed death only on ecology's terms.

Neruda returns immediately in the next poem to the drowned man and to death, adding emphasis to the contrast between ecological death and human injustice. The dark forms of oceanic life, although foreboding to the sailor, move beneath the waters "como el amor que invade la garganta [like love invading the throat]" (*OC* 1:782; *Canto* 351). Like Walcott's omnivorous Caribbean rainforest and also echoing Whitman's whispering Long Island Sound, the Pacific awaits with "ramos / de brazos, bocas, lenguas que rodean / con undulante flor lo que devoran [clusters / of arms, mouths, tongues that envelop / whatever they consume with an undulating flower]." An apt metaphor for the sea's capacity for death and regeneration, mouths and tongues, of course, both speak *and* devour. This delicate balance between oblivion and speech is why "[e]n la mínima gota de la vida / aguarda una indecisa primavera [(i)n the slightest droplet of life / awaits an indecisive springtime]." This means that death, although containing "la agonía negra del perdido [the black agony of the lost]," will become a new web of life,

> el tapiz del ahogado recubierto
> por un bosque de lanzas y murenas
> temblorosas y activas como el telar que teje
> en la profundidad devadora.
>
> ———
>
> the tapestry of the drowned man covered
> by a forest of lances and lampreys
> trembling and busy as a loom that weaves
> in the devouring depths.

Even the pain of lost love loses its force in the context of the sea's "coro de movimiento y mundo [choir of motion and world]" (*OC* 1:793; *Canto* 360). Neruda tells of a sailor haunted by memories of love left behind and finds himself "buscando tierra [seeking earth]." The poet contrasts the weakness and insufficiency of human-generated instruments of solidity and solace with the ongoing song of the sea:

> Es orgullo de arcilla que morirá en el cántaro,
> quebrándose, apartando las gotas que cantaron,
> amarrando a la tierra su indecisa costura.
>
> ———
>
> It's pride of clay that will die in the jug,

breaking, scattering the drops that sang,
binding its indecisive stitchwork to the earth.

The aural contrast between "cántaro" and "cantaron" helps us to sense the ultimate futility of human labor to create a sense of permanence or sustainability (the "pride of clay") that can compare with that embodied in the ocean. For this reason, Neruda counsels the pained lover that solace does not lie in a return to land, in individual dreams, or in recourse to lifeways that would seek to deny our biological and ecological foundations as human beings. Instead, in an incantatory pentameter, he urges a kind of Jungian communion with the collective soul of nature:

No busques en el mar esta muerte, no esperes
territorio, no guardes el puñado de polvo
para integrarlo intacto y entregarlo a la tierra.

Entrégalo a estos labios infinitos que cantan,
dónalos a este coro de movimiento y mundo,
destrúyete en la eterna maternidad del agua.

—

Do not seek this death in the sea, do not wait for
territory, do not save the fistful of dust
to integrate it intact and deliver it to the earth.

Deliver it to these infinite singing lips,
donate them to this choir of motion and world,
destroy yourself in the eternal maternity of water.

Neruda assigns himself this same task in the section's stunning concluding poem, "La noche marina" [The Marine Night], and expresses his hope that in this way his poetry can become a medium of communion between human sorrows and the ocean's "pureza y destrucción contra toda la muerte, / distancia que no puede gastarse [purity and destruction against all death, / distance that cannot be consumed]" (*OC* 1:806; *Canto* 371). Nature's solace does not, in this way, bypass the need to redress wrongs, but it at least promises perspective and strength. As he declares earlier in the "Alturas," he sees that human societies have been their own worst enemy by virtue of having shut nature out of the rhythms of their lifeways, that they have denied their own natural inheritance. Simply by refusing the solace that nature's infinitude can bring, man condemns himself to solitude:

Cerró la noche para que tus ojos
no vieran su reposo miserable:
quiso proximidad, abrió los brazos
custodiado por seres y por muros,
y cayó al sueño del silencio, bajando
a tierra funeral con sus raíces. (*OC* 1:804)

——

Night closed in so that your eyes
wouldn't see his miserable repose.
He wanted closeness, he opened his arms,
safeguarded by beings and by walls,
and fell into the dream of silence, sinking
into funereal earth with his roots. (*Canto* 369)

What is available to man is the mystery of the ocean, the stars, and the seemingly eternal expanse of the universe that can be contemplated on dark shorelines. Neruda hopes that the marine night, like a lover, will bestow upon him

                     un solo
minuto de extensión, y más que todos
los sueños, tu distancia. (*OC* 1:805)

——

                     a single
minute of extension and, more than all
dreams, your distance. (*Canto* 370)

His epic New World imagination moves him beyond political borders and ultimately to contemplate what constitutes the boundaries of the natural and the human. As he becomes aware of the illusory quality of this particular boundary he realizes the need for his poetry to embrace an ecological possibility for the New World, one that will renew poetry and renew hope. He wants his New World song to be a song of the sea; he wants

tener tu frente simultánea,
abrirla en mi interior para nacer

en todas tus orillas, ir ahora
con todos los secretos respirados. (*OC* 1:805)

—

to possess your simultaneous brow,
to open inside me in order to be born
on all your shores, to set forth now
with all the secrets inhaled. (*Canto* 371)

Armed with this infinitude of space and distance, he can return to society
with the multiplicity of nature, "con tantos ojos / como los tuyos [with
as many eyes / as you have]." The multitudes the poet will then contain
will not be those of people alone but those of our vast and interconnected
biology. We are left with the hope that this cosmological vision of the human
place in nature can serve as a mediator between the political necessity of
considering one human life at a time, singularly and individually, and the
ecological exigency of nature's unlimited expanses. Ecological awareness
for all Americans is the ultimate import of Neruda's "general" song because
of the way it simultaneously moves us beyond the bounds of the human self
and returns us back again. We discover an attenuated solidarity with one
another and with the infinitude of nature. With soberness, he declares that
the New World is yet to exhaust its promises of renewal and that poetry
teaches the necessary skills of reinhabitation. As if to expand Whitman's
song of the self in this ecological way, Neruda writes: "[Q]ue me toquen
/ hasta el agua total que no se mide [(M)ay they touch me / to the total
immeasurable water]."

Part Three

A nature reduced to the service

of praising and humbling men,

there is a yes without a question,

there is assent founded on ignorance,

in the mangroves plunged to the wrist . . .

there are spaces

wider than conscience.

DEREK WALCOTT, *Another Life*

CHAPTER 7

The Muse of (Natural) History

Derek Walcott's poetics of the environment developed in the context of
a small geographical space of extraordinary beauty. Born in 1930 on the
island of St. Lucia, he was offered a dual education in his youth; his mother
and other mentors and teachers exposed him to the great poetic traditions
of English, European, and American literature while he and his friend
Dunstan St. Omer drew inspiration from the raw and untamed qualities of
the St. Lucian landscape and its local populace (Baugh 10). From his earliest
contacts with the beaches, hillsides, and backstreets of the island, Walcott
and St. Omer thought of themselves as among the island's first artists.
Land, sea, and sky were the building blocks of Walcott's formidable and
pervasive sense of himself as an artist and the inheritor of a blessed land of
raw beauty. Given the opportunity to leave the Caribbean for England in his
college years, he very likely would have taken it, as did many other talented

students throughout the region. He only went as far as Jamaica, however, and eventually found himself working in theater in Trinidad, where he founded the Little Carib Theater. Although he receives invitations to read in places as distant as Taiwan, Italy, and elsewhere in Europe and the United States, and although he spends four months of the year in New York City, he has remained in the Caribbean, where he finds persistent nourishment for his poetry and painting from the local natural and social qualities of St. Lucia within a very small geographical space. His career has consistently taken advantage of the provincialism of his island experience, as he once put it, so as to have a more complete "communion with things that the metropolitan writers no longer care about," such as "family, earth, history" (qtd. in Nichols 177).

Pablo Neruda is the most well traveled of the three poets, including long stays in other countries and in other hemispheres, but, as his poetry demonstrates, his travels did not move him too far away from the nurturing soils of his native land, even if he never again lived in the southern regions of Chile where he was born and raised. Just as Whitman's leaves became a metaphorical gateway to exploring the possibility of a cross-cultural New World poetry, the local, the particular, and the singular remained the foundation of Neruda's rather pronounced transnational New World poetics. Walcott is a much more reserved poet than either of his precursors, not given to their tendency for overstatement or a sometimes overreaching generosity of spirit. Nevertheless, he too found that the more he rooted himself in the particulars of his island experience, precisely because of its geographical insularity the more he tended to reach across American cultures by expressing those particulars as metonyms of a broader New World experience.

It became increasingly evident to him that his island situation was a challenge not without risks, however. Cosmopolitan norms from elsewhere consistently degrade, either explicitly or implicitly, the seemingly barbaric qualities of peoples and the tropical landscapes they inhabit because of their lack of the markers of civilization—the monuments, great edifices, and spaces saturated with history—that characterize Western civilization. Rather than striking a purely defensive pose, however, Walcott has negotiated his autonomy on the basis of assaulting the adjudicators of civilization with his own abundant and extravagant naming of his New World.

As Walcott's star continued to rise in the 1960s, the implicit dialogue he had begun with Western tradition in his earliest poetry became even more explicitly pronounced. His contacts throughout the Caribbean and in New York City helped him forge friendships with the likes of Robert Lowell in the late 1960s and early 1970s and exposed him to the idea that his poetry belonged to a New World tradition of writing that of course included all of the Caribbean but that also extended north to the United States and south into Spanish America. As Sandra Pouchet Paquet puts it, Walcott's "celebration of his Caribbean roots . . . links him functionally to Césaire and Guillen on one hand and to continental poets like Whitman and Neruda on another" (195). He began reading Gabriel García Márquez, Alejo Carpentier, Carlos Fuentes, Octavio Paz, Jorge Luis Borges, Pablo Neruda, and Cesar Vallejo, all of whom have figured as important influences on Walcott's work during this period I call his American phase. Patricia Ismond insists on the term "Caribbean phase" to describe Walcott's career up to 1979, after which his longer stays in the United States began to result in a more self-conscious reflection in his poetry on his role as itinerant world traveler. The term "American" is meant to highlight his interest during the 1960s and 1970s in inter-American themes beyond the Caribbean islands; Walcott is certainly not less interested in New World themes after the 1970s, but his expressed interest in placing his work within a hemispheric tradition in the Americas becomes less pronounced as he becomes more internationally recognized and more identified as a cosmopolitan writer. This period was an extraordinarily fruitful time for Walcott, as he honed his thesis regarding the New World Adam in a variety of poems and essays, a process that resulted in the publication in the 1960s of *In a Green Night* (1962), *The Castaway and Other Poems* (1965), *The Gulf* (1970), and his salient essay "The Figure of Crusoe" (1965). The 1970s amplified the New World themes of this work in *Another Life* (1973), the essays "What the Twilight Says" (1970), "The Muse of History" (1974), and "The Caribbean: Culture or Mimicry?" (1974), and the extraordinary collection of poems, *Star-Apple Kingdom* (1979).

American allies in a New World quest for authentic and honest gratitude for the benedictions of American environments were vital to Walcott's defense of West Indian culture. As he wrote in "The Caribbean: Culture or Mimicry?" he saw the Atlantic as the great divide between the present condition of the New World and the Old World, divided by what he calls "the meridian" and "mirror" forged by European colonialism

(Walcott, "Caribbean" 53). Charges such as those launched by V. S. Naipaul of Caribbean inauthenticity and derivativeness implicated all New World cultural activity, "all endeavor in this half of the world . . . : the American endeavor." But if Caribbean literature was derivative, so too was U.S. and Latin American literature, since "we share this part of the world, and have shared it for centuries now, even as conqueror and victim, as exploiter and exploited" (51).

Of course, the Latin American "boom" of the 1960s and 1970s, itself indebted to Pablo Neruda's efforts in *Canto general*, was forging a community of authors who saw themselves as part of a hemispheric phenomenon. Their articulations of the New World's historical and cultural conditions resonated with Walcott's perception of West Indian reality, particularly their accounts of the colonial legacies of the Old World, political corruption, the baroque New World tropics, and the search for new language.[1] In Walcott's private papers one finds articles on Brazilian modernism and the anthropophagist movement, Spanish American authors, and other signs of his curiosity regarding his New World neighbors. In a 1977 interview he claimed that learning Spanish would be more useful to him than learning Swahili, a rhetorical statement, of course, since there is no evidence he has ever learned either. The point, however, underscores the profound New World conditioning of the Caribbean despite its African roots: "I have found more of an affinity in Spanish-American poets than I have found in poets in England, or in America. We have a similar historical origin, similar problems of self-resolution, and I can recognize a sensibility as being very close to mine. . . . I probably am a stranger to the African, whereas I am not a stranger to Marquez, or Fuentes, or Paz" (Walcott, "Reflections Before" 46–47). The sensibility he refers to is an awareness of the pressing need for new expression and new apprehensions of the New World in the context of cultural discontinuity from the various lands of the Americas' origins. Disagreeing with T. S. Eliot's formulation of the unbroken arc of the West, Walcott explained, "I don't think there is anything 'pure' on this side of the world; the whole feel of it is multitudinous, several races with various ancestral ties. Does not America—and I mean the land from Greenland right down to Tierra del Fuego—argue against this unbroken arc, particularly in light of the African experience, in light of the conditions in which he was brought to the New World?" (42).

Although the New World is not pure or its history innocent, it nevertheless offers itself to be named and apprehended as if for the first time. The danger of forgoing direct apprehensions of nature is that one will remain ignorant of one's own home and place in the world. As Walcott wrote in "American, without America," "To deprive a people of factual knowledge about themselves and their environment is probably the most powerful weapon available. . . . How can they describe their home when they only see it through the colonizer's mirror? . . . How can natives express their feelings about a Virgin Island home when all the facts speak of an American paradise" (5). Walcott has consistently asserted that the New World's beauty and newness are still available to the determined poet despite its despoliations and ruin. Seeking this beauty without naïveté and without apology is the primary task of the poet; recrimination is not. Drawing his inspiration from Shelley, who once said that "[r]evenge is the naked idol of the worship of a semi-barbarous age" (431), Walcott's career has consistently upheld his aphorism that "revenge is uncreative" ("Caribbean" 57).[2] The gift of being able to apprehend that newness is to be enjoyed, even though it inevitably means the poet repeats what has been done so many times before; indeed, the mimetic task that suddenly becomes the poet's labor in his relationship to the environment as well as to literary models becomes a childlike delight in repetition. The paradise lost may be the Caribbean's historical origins or the innocence of believing in oneself as the first man but not the opportunity for originality.[3] A poetics of oblivion facilitates this newness of the New World because of an illumination regarding what has undeniably come before but what can no longer be retrieved.

A New World Sense of Place

One trait of Spanish American literature that attracted Walcott was its willingness to confront the tough problems of New World history without forsaking the elemental task of celebrating and naming the New World. This was a facet of U.S. literature Walcott often found missing, despite his open admiration for such U.S. authors as Walt Whitman, Emily Dickinson, Ernest Hemingway, and Robert Frost. As I discussed in chapter 1, his 1995 critique of Frost's reading of "The Gift Outright" at JFK's inauguration provides important insight in this regard. Walcott reminds us that this "augustan moment" lacked vital historical memory of New World sins: "No slavery, no colonization of Native Americans, a process of dispossession and then possession, but nothing about the dispossession of others that this destiny demanded" (*What the Twilight* 193). A sense of place cannot be forged at the cost of erasing the memory of violent human displacement that enabled Euro-Americans' pretension to their own "innocent" westward relocation in the New World.

As I detailed in my discussion of a New World poetics in chapter 2, historical recuperation cannot become the chief task of the poet as well because of the particular violence of New World history. Walcott's embrace of the adamic task does not make him immune to despair over this fact. In "Air," written in 1969, he complains bitterly that "there is too much nothing here" because the "jaws of this rain forest . . . never rest, / grinding their disavowal of human pain" (*CP* 114, 113). They devoured the native inhabitants of the Caribbean, Caribs and Arawaks, and half of the black race in the Middle Passage. Nature devours human history as a "faith, infested, cannibal, / which eats gods" and "leaves not the lightest fern-trace / of his fossil" (*CP* 114). All that remains is "nothing: milling air" heard in the conch shell, the same echoes we will see are heard by Walcott's child in *Another Life*. There is one untranslatable testimonial to this history, in stark contrast to Whitman's singing bird in "Out of the Cradle Endlessly Rocking," and that is the utterly indifferent and untranslatable "rusting cries of a rainbird" (*CP* 114). Whitman struggled more overtly with the delimiting effect of historical oblivion because of his hesitancy to let go of his own prophetic ambition to translate the cosmos. The crisis of disunion even after the Civil War prodded him further into this role of the ventriloquist. When we hear birdsong in "Air," we hear the bird's indifferent noise and the irony of amnesia, which may be just one way of expressing what Whitman said was the fundamental message of the sea: death. While the oblivion of nature fuels the metaphors of both poets, the difference in Walcott is that nature does not speak our language; we own our own metaphors.

The poem clearly exaggerates the absence of historical markers, and one might argue that it does so to a dangerous extreme, since not only do indigenous people exist in the Caribbean, but archaeological finds have revealed sufficient "fern traces" as to make Walcott's claim of absolute erasure seem to border on willed ignorance. Walcott has spent considerable energy in his career working against the grain of the kind of gleefully willed erasure of the past he sees in Frost's poem, but "Air" pushes to the other extreme. The lack of ruins, of fossils, or of any kind of documentation of the genocide of the native inhabitants of the islands or of those enslaved is documented by the silent and persistent "nothing" of nature, making nature nothing more than a mere elegy of the New World past.

The need to confront oblivion propels his poetry beyond the binaries "Air" implies. The poem argues that history's events are known but not properly remembered because human violence has obliterated evidence of the crime and also because of nature's prodigious and indifferent growth in the Caribbean. Walcott is more willing than Neruda to acknowledge the amnesia of New World experience. His nature does not merely ensconce the past and the suffering of the oppressed. It will never be the political ally that Neruda sometimes sees because it will refuse to give up its secrets; in this sense, nature is more radically other. Remembering history impels the Nerudian task to read back into nature what its indifference cannot tell us, but the poet must then accept what cannot be known and begin again as if for the first time. Nature is culture's ally, since it asks for this new, natural foundation of elemental praise.

Walcott's nature is therefore never entirely Edenic because beneath its virginal untamed appeal lurks the suspicion of its "disavowal of human pain." This concept is radically different from that which operates in the Americanist critique of the American Adam I discussed in chapter 1. An Eden haunted by this disavowal means that, as David Mikics explains, "an Edenic image of nature, though at first a deeply attractive prospect, proves futile exactly because it means denying the cultural complexities that make up the New World" (383). To view our natural surroundings as an uncontaminated virginal space that provides us respite from the relentlessness of human history would be an immoral identification with nature's indifference toward that history. But this does not mean that we must forsake all notions of Edenic possibilities in the New World. "Air" is a lamentation for what cannot be named and an expression of desire for connectedness to the land while simultaneously providing a caution: it expresses the inevitability of its own failure to establish a static sense of place and historical belonging in the landscape. Walcott does see some human trace in the nothing of natural history and even goes so far as to name it in the void; he names the genocide of Native Americans and of Africans. However, there is a lingering sense of incompletion. Walcott debunks nature's apparent ahistorical position by resurrecting a history that haunts its scenic edges, but he does not pretend to totalize that history; rather, like Nature, the poem is also haunted by what it cannot tell.

Walcott pointedly denotes the forest's but also the sea's unnatural story as a signifier of an illegible history of New World death and violence. In his 1979 poem "The Sea Is History" Walcott begins with the question:

Where are your monuments, your battles, martyrs?
Where is your tribal memory? Sirs,
in that grey vault. The sea. The sea
has locked them up. The sea is History. (*CP* 364)

We should recall that Whitman acknowledged the New World's paucity of monumental history, particularly in his own evocation of a New World Muse in "Song of the Exposition." He had written that the New World's response to Notre Dame was "Thy great cathedral sacred industry." In the wake of Reconstruction's failings, he hoped that *Leaves of Grass* could be a New World bible that gave account of a genealogy that would be forged in a new partnership between human history and the natural world. The sea proved a recurring site for Whitman to imagine this commingling. Neruda also encountered Machu Picchu's enigmatically silent and partial record of America's ancient past, a record that ends up in the sea, and concluded that the Muse of nature, more than the Muse of History, was crucial to build solidarity across the Americas. Walcott's sea is an important repository of the human stories that natural erosion and water cycles have brought to it, but for Walcott natural history's oblivious relationship to the New World past renders the ironies of the poet's epic ambitions for a new American bible much more pronounced. If epics are still possible in the New World, they must embrace the ironies of New World amnesia, center on nature and not history, and avoid the trappings of nationalism.

In "The Caribbean: Culture or Mimicry?" Walcott writes that nations mistakenly think of history "as a succession of illuminations, lightning moments that must crystallize and irradiate memory if we are to believe in a chain of such illuminations known as history" (54). As if to portray and then undermine the genealogical thrust of such a chain, "The Sea Is History" proceeds to list its chapters according to the books of the Bible. Genesis is "the lantern of the caravel" of Columbus; Exodus is "the packed cries, / the shit, the moaning" of the Middle Passage; the sounds of wailing drowned women are the Song of Solomon (*CP* 364). The irony of this exegesis is particularly keen. The historical events he recites clash with the traditional meanings of the biblical books. The Bible's story as an archive of the legal and genealogical memory of a diasporic people is challenged by the New World's experience of amnesia:

> Bone soldered by coral to bone,
> mosaics
> mantled by the benediction of the shark's shadow,
>
> that was the Ark of the Covenant.

Here the bones of Africans thrown overboard have been soldered into coral, and the very covenant of the word of God, so carefully preserved to bring the Israelites to the Promised Land, is the power by which these black bodies are enslaved and fed to the sharks. If there is a bible for New World peoples affected by the hemisphere's history of slavery, it will not be a New World epic poetry of historical recovery that "redeem[s] race in ancestral history" but the ironic emblem of nature's strange indifference to human suffering (Ismond 115). The "text" the poem's voice seeks to read is not in fact textual or historical; it is an illegible natural record. Seeking the historical roots of a place becomes an impossible, perhaps even an undesirable task when the past is ridden with events that waged a war against historical memory itself.

In the context of diaspora and racial mixture, seeking historical rootedness in the landscape may lead to perpetual nostalgia, either for the original colonial land, which is marked by monuments and other colonial signs of "civilization," or for the "Eden" of alternative exotic soils, such as Europe or Africa. In either case, colonial history leads us away from our contemporary place. The Muse of History is a powerful temptation, especially for Neruda, who was more keenly aware than Whitman of the tragic losses of New World history and the consequences of amnesia. As I have argued, however, they both eventually turn to the kind of adamic poetics that we find more fully pronounced at the outset of Walcott's interest in the setting of the New World for his poetry. He wryly remarks that "the ocean kept turning blank pages / looking for History." The coral, the sharks, the sea sands, the barnacles are "our cathedrals," ironic and submarine monuments to a buried human suffering. Neruda's submarine "wounded heritage," my reader will recall, similarly included a "cathedral . . . built without hands" (*Canto* 340). In light of such natural irony, the real monument is forged in the reader's mind by poetry's capacity to inspire an imagination of what has been forgotten. Unlike monuments' tendency to mythologize the past by means of consolidated and embodied figures, poetry serves to acknowledge that the stories of the past can never be entirely unlocked because of nature's capacity to absorb wounds and erase history's sins and achievements.

It would appear that if nature is unwilling to yield the full narrative account of New World history, then the poet has two choices. He can forever lament the New World's apparent paucity of a monumentalized history and suffer an "oceanic nostalgia for the older culture and a melancholy at the new, and this go can as deep as a rejection of the untamed landscape, a yearning for ruins" (Walcott, *What the Twilight* 42). Or he can pretend to a kind of Adamic innocence in the new landscape and demonstrate his own indifference toward its prior history of violence and dispossession and thus reenact a colonization of place. The mood of "The Sea Is History" refuses these choices. Whereas a more Whitmanian response would be to choose the optimistic mood and celebrate the Caribbean society that emerges in the context of these choices, Walcott sees contemporary Caribbean society as an imperfect realization of Caribbean possibility that still delays a realization of its potential:

> [T]hen came the synod of flies
> then came the secretarial heron,
> then came the bullfrog bellowing for a vote,
>
> fireflies with bright ideas. (*CP* 367)

We sense we are in the midst of a history trying to emerge from the vault where it was buried by genocide, slavery, and colonialism. But the political noise of this society misses its aim, just as nature continues to hide Caribbean origins:

> [A]nd in the salt chuckle of rocks
> with their sea pools, there was the sound
> like a rumour without any echo
>
> of History, really beginning.

Although tempted by the cynicism of this poem's conclusion throughout his career because of the political impotency of Caribbean nations, Walcott rejects the false choice between nostalgia and revenge. The poem still reflects a belief, as Ismond puts it, in an "invisible history" and thus "amounts to a rediscovery of the root, human levels at which history is made" (55). I would only add that this history lies at the deeper human *and* ecological levels at which history is made. Nature's refraction of the fragmented traces of the past seems to provide the grounds for a sobering, tough-minded, but hopeful beginning in the land. Walcott's strange coupling of the fragmentation and loss of history with natural processes allows him to find an ambiguous solace in the emptiness around him and to hone his eye and ear to perceive what he calls the "subtle and submarine" future possibilities contained in the natural present.

In an essay entitled "Where I Live" Walcott explains that "local color is what moves over the blackened galleons of rocks, the skulls of pervious coral, the mossed ropes of seaweed and the little flags of fish escaping battle" (30–32). Even though natural beauty disguises the traces of a former historical battle of empires, it simultaneously surprises the artistic eye with awe. Ultimately, "blue is the color of oblivion here, but it also creates shadows" that conceal the "rusted cannon, broken ships and who knows what treasures" of history (32). Nature signifies a possibility yet-to-be, a "future that can stand against history," not a past to which the poet yearns to return (Mikics 383). Glissant similarly argues that in Caribbean literature, when the poet confronts nature's opacity and the history it hides, "landscape in the work stops being merely decorative or supportive and emerges as a full character. Describing the landscape is not enough. The individual, the community, the land are inextricable in the *process of creating history*" (*Poetics* 105, emphasis added). The search for history, then, is not "teleological" but "implies the plasticity of human experience as on-going"; it is a search, in other words, for the best metaphors to capture an elusive past and an ambiguous present (104).

To remember the history of the Caribbean or that of the New World we must look to our contemporary place and attune ourselves to its historical voices, which, like ghosts, emerge partial, ephemeral, wasted, but nevertheless still "singing from the depths of the sea," to quote Walcott's character Shabine in "The Schooner *Flight*" (*CP* 361). Shabine represents Walcott's attempt to give voice to the stories that the sea contains in its vault, but rather than simply indicating poetry as a kind of translation of forbidden or otherwise encoded tales, as Whitman is tempted to do, Shabine's song represents a creation of a voice that emerges "out of the depths" and "after the storm," to quote from the final two section titles of the poem. Shabine's postapocalyptic voice remains after the wreckage of New World history: "[W]e sang how our race / survive the sea's maw, our history, our peril" (*CP* 359). Although he witnesses the phantasms of the Middle Passage, Shabine's voice is not historical recuperation but rather poetic acknowledgment of oblivion and the forging of new meaning; it is a song of survival.

This singing is most productive in relationship to the landscape that surrounds the poet, even if that landscape bears unmistakable markers of the same kind of bastardization that has been the Caribbean's political and cultural legacy. Shabine's words, "either I'm nobody or I am a nation," are frequently cited to address the postcolonial challenges of the Caribbean, but critics have ignored how deeply tied this bastard condition is in Walcott's poetry to the Caribbean's environmental history. Trees in the Caribbean largely come from outside the region, due to the massive transformation of the environment following the discovery and the development of the plantation complex. Trees from Asia, including the casuarina, the bread-fruit, the cedar, and others, were brought to the islands to provide fuel and food for the slave and peasant populations, who suffered most acutely the ravages of the plantation economy. Simply identifying a tree's name is a complex process that cuts through layers of pre-Columbian, colonial, and postslavery history. Caribbean trees often have a scientific name, a creole name, and names in different modern European languages. This explains Shabine's difficulty in identifying the object of his praise when he attempts to sing to the casuarina. A member of the pine family, the coastline tree imported from Australia is easily confused with cedars and cypresses, something that Shabine himself appears to do:

> Once the sound "cypress" used to make more sense
> than the green "casuarinas," though, to the wind,
> whatever grief bent them was all the same,
> since they were trees with nothing else in mind
> but heavenly leaping or to guard a grave;
> but we live like our names and you would have
> to be colonial to know the difference,

to know the pain of history words contain,
to love those trees with an inferior love,
and to believe: "Those casuarinas bend
like cypresses, their hair hangs down in rain
like sailors' wives. They're classic trees, and we,
if we live like our names our masters please,
by careful mimicry might become men." (*CP* 353–54)

The trees, in other words, suffer the same indignity of having to prove their belonging in the world, in this case in the science of natural history, by means of proper denomination that ensures their genealogical place in the "tree" of Western knowledge. But these trees, interestingly, have suffered the same history of transplantation and adaptation as the human populations of the Caribbean; indeed, few environments are as anthropogenic today as the Caribbean. Casuarina trees are mongrel survivors like Shabine: originally from Australia, they are recognized for their adaptability to a wide range of climates and circumstances and have provided firewood and vital strength to prevent soil erosion in many areas of the Caribbean (see National Research Council). The "inferior" love of the poet does not seek to sort out the proper taxonomy of the trees but instead uses the multiple layers of their origins and names and the lore of folk biology with all of its risks of denominational error as the means of poetic creation. The trees' natural and aesthetic functions here have nothing to do with the claims or interests of history; they have "nothing else in mind" but to serve as metaphors, as signs of local meaning for a local population, as equally displaced and mixed as the metaphors and trees they use. To see a "casuarina" as "like a cypress" is no different a stretch of the poetic imagination than to see their thin branches and needles moving in the wind "like sailors' wives." That is, taxonomical and historical ignorance becomes a poetic opportunity, even a necessity.

As he once explained in his 1964 poem "Origins," standing between cultures, "[b]etween the Greek and African pantheon" as a "lost animist," Walcott "rechristened trees" (*CP* 14). Rechristening is also misnaming, and that is precisely the point of poetry, as Walcott sees it: to take possession by means of renaming. The overly structural critique of the Adamic impulse I criticized in chapter 1 might mistake this for Columbus's arrogant presumption of his Christian right to name the New World as it lay before him like a blank page. Despite his attempt to claim the New World as Asia, the difference nature makes explains his error. The true history of Columbus is not contained in his letters and diary but in the sky of "[c]louds, log of Colon" where "a gap of history closes, like a cloud" (*CP* 12–13).

Poetry is a rechristening that sees the New World as a palimpsest and poetry as the adamic task of turning away from the allure of fading names, histories, and meanings in order to keep language fresh and alive to the demands of the natural present. Just as the full significance of the trees is lost on anyone interested merely in taxonomy, the Muse of History can also lure the poet away from this adamic responsibility. Renaming in the adamic imagination implies at least a nod to what has come before, but to confuse this notion with the American Adam's pursuit of innocence is to miss the difference between finding and founding a home. In "Origins" Walcott explains:

> The mind, among sea-wrack, sees it mythopoeic coast,
> Seeks, like the polyp, *to take root in itself.*
> Here, in the rattle of receding shoal,
> Among these shallows I seek my own name and a man.
> As the crab's claws move backwards through the surf,
> Blind memory grips the putrefying flesh. (*CP* 14, emphasis added)

Blind memory here feeds itself on history's detritus, and while Walcott insists that detritus is the material of poetic naming, the crab's desperation here is blind to the reality that "sea-wrack," not wholeness, defines New World experience. Colonial violence and diasporas leave "*seeds of / islands dispersed by the winds,*" shattering memory of a monumental past. Wisdom lies in accepting the sea's oblivious power, which "*razed that / memory from / our speech,*" and that New World origins, therefore, are not historical but environmental; they begin with speaking the elemental and simple facts of sensual experience in the present, when "*a single raindrop irrigates the tongue*" (*CP* 15).

"Ruins of a Great House," produced by Walcott after a visit to plantation ruins in Jamaica in 1953, explains how nature's capacity for regeneration offers an alternative to nostalgia and revenge. The first line, echoing Neruda's encounter with Machu Picchu, where he found "a life of stone after so many lives," begins: "[s]tones only, the disjecta membra of this Great House" (*CP* 19). As in Neruda's poem, the stones signify a natural conclusion to a human history, but in Neruda's case they hint at the New World's ancient past, which colonial amnesia has erased. Even though he recognizes the limitations of his historical search to recover this past, Neruda sees the stones themselves as native reminders of a New World heritage in which history and ecology are blended. Plantation ruins, on the other hand, signify a New World of diaspora, racial mixture, of no center in the past. The stones, the "disjecta membra" of a larger body, remind Walcott of history's natural conclusions, but they are not signs of a lost nativity but of adaptation after rupture. Neruda's attempt to read suffering into the ruins' beauty is perhaps more unexpected than Walcott's insistence that plantation ruins are metonyms of the evils of empire and slavery, "the abuse / Of ignorance by Bible and by sword" (*CP* 20).

In reference to both Blake and Keats and their meditations on the universality of death and the passage of time, Walcott declares in ironic quotation: " 'Farewell, green fields, / Farewell ye happy groves' " (*CP* 19). The pastoral green of the past here is an ironic symbol of the ephemeral and fading reality of slavery's past. Only the stony remainders of that life remain, "Marble like Greece, like Faulkner's South in stone, / Deciduous beauty prospered and is gone" (*CP* 19). Greek statues that have lost their glory but whose stone remains to inspire admiration stand in a provocative tension with "Faulkner's South," a place haunted by the dual sins of slavery and Native American displacement. The suggestion seems to be that all societies hide their sins beneath the stony remainders of its tangible forms of civilization. All societies and all art dream of permanence, just as Walcott and Anna, in *Another Life*, dream of staring at one another with "stone eyes" (*CP* 230). Nature changes, erodes its surface as readable text of History, and leaves the poet imagining what lies under the surface of the stone. Whitman's "This Compost" had been a particular favorite poem of Robert Lowell, one of Walcott's significant influences at this point in his life. In an apparent echo of the poem Walcott writes:

> But where the lawn breaks in a rash of trees
> A spade below dead leaves will ring the bone
> Of some dead animal or human thing
> Fallen from evil days, from evil times. (*CP* 19)

Walcott does not rush to Whitman's optimism and insist on the green grass as triumphant symbol of nature's transformation of disease; instead, he insists that "the rot [of colonial history] remains with us," like pollution (*CP* 20). Like Neruda, he recognizes that the water cycle leaves him facing nature's indifference to human suffering: "[T]he river flows, obliterating hurt." Accepting this erasure of injustice is a bitter pill, but instead of inspiring in Walcott an indifference to the past, it suggests something more akin to Whitman's wide democratic embrace, even if he resists Whitman's romanticization:

> Ablaze with rage, I thought,
> Some slave is rotting in this manorial lake,
> But still the coal of my compassion fought
> That Albion too was once
> A colony like ours, "part of the continent, piece of the Main." (*CP* 20)

Because the old empire suffered similar rage and "the vain expense / of bitter faction," it would be better to accept that "All in compassion ends / So differently from what the heart arranged: 'as well as if a manor of thy friend's'" (*CP* 20–21). The slave and slave owner alike are men subject to death and must be imagined as friends. We hear an echo of Whitman's declaration that "to die is different from what anyone supposed," but Walcott here is more openly indebted to John Donne than to Whitman. The citation of Donne on these two occasions in the poem offers Walcott an opportunity to affirm the need for universal compassion for the dead as well as to extend a more profound cultural meaning to Donne's ethics. By transplanting Donne's words into his own poetic confrontation with the rage and hurt the New World's past inspires, Walcott both quiets his own rage so as to avoid "bitter faction" and tests Donne's idea to grant it a more robust meaning. Unlike Whitman and Neruda, Walcott offers no instruction or hortatory discourse regarding our ethical duties, and neither are the dead speaking to or through him. This allows him to expose and exercise with the reader the full range of emotions that such a resolution demands from us. As Bruce King notes, Walcott "blends Christian notions of fall and compassion with those of New World exceptionalism and the restoration of Adamic innocence. What prevents it from becoming a cliché [or a reinvention of exceptionalism, for that matter] is that the tensions never settle, the hurts and anger continue to erupt" (102).

What prevents the adamic imagination from becoming a license to perpetual vengeance and nostalgia, however, is the presence of beauty. In

"Verandah," written in 1965, slavery's past is significant because of its relationship to present beauty. As we have seen already, nature's transformation of the New World past into a beautiful present is ironic, not inevitable, and its implications of condoning the past are as repugnant to Walcott as it would be to allow rage to turn him away from the present. Walcott does not see Hegelian evolution at work, moving history along a series of genealogical links or facile and forgiving syntheses. His use of genealogical metaphors in the poem suggests Caribbean discontinuity both in family lines *and* in natural history. He invokes his own English past:

> A ghost steps from you, my grandfather's ghost!
> Uprooted from some rainy English shire,
> you sought your Roman
>
> end in suicide by fire.
> Your mixed son gathered your charred blackened bones
> in a child's coffin. (*CP* 89–90)

The grandfather invoked here is Walcott's paternal grandfather, Charles Walcott, who arrived in St. Lucia from Barbados and by posterity from England in the late nineteenth century to buy plantation land. Charles's wife, Christiana, was a dark brown St. Lucian who delivered five children, including Derek's father, Warwick, who was the oldest. Warwick buried his father after an apparent suicidal fire killed him shortly before Walcott was born (King 7–8). What is most significant about this rather frankly autobiographical passage is the somewhat oblique reference to a ghost that "steps from" the ghost of the grandfather, as if to suggest an echo that is not caused by an original sound. The poem's opening lines already hint at "grey apparitions," some motion, like smoke, that emerges from the fallen structure and "coherence" of the age of slave plantations. These "ghosts" are the substance of new cultural possibility in the wake of slavery's history. Their potential for beauty is not a symptom of genealogy but rather of genealogical rupture and natural regeneration. Walcott asks, as if to anticipate the need to explain the genealogical logic of the poem:

> [W]hy do I raise you up? Because
>
> Your house has voices, your burnt house
> shrills with unguessed, lovely inheritors,

your genealogical roof tree, fallen, survives,
like seasoned timber through green, little lives.

I ripen toward your twilight, sir. (*CP* 90)

The poet finds himself ripening in direct proportion to the growing incoherence of the plantation age, but this is not simply because the past has left a clean slate. It is precisely on the rotting stuff of plantation history that his poetic imagination feeds. What happens in this process of (de)composing proves antithetical to genealogical causation and any notion of historical indebtedness. The house "shrills with unguessed, lovely inheritors"; the possibilities of the present are neither intended nor guessed, and just as fallen timber provides ironically fertile ground for "green, little lives," so too the poet must give his "strange and bitter and yet ennobling thanks" for the world that slavery's history has bequeathed him (Walcott, *What the Twilight* 64). Similar to his conclusion of "Ruins of a Great House," Walcott's return to the ruins of the plantation calls to his mind Donne's embrace of all human life:

> I climb the stair
> and stretch a darkening hand to greet those friends
> who share with you the last inheritance
> of earth, our shrine and pardoner,
>
> grey, ghostly loungers at verandah ends. (*What the Twilight* 90)

He hints at the possibility of his grandfather's pardon even though he himself does not do the pardoning, and this is because the natural destiny of all human life challenges the efficacy of the tribunals of history. His greeting is for the slaves, not for the slave master, despite the "pardon" he assumes the earth has granted him, since their voices provide the inspiration for his poetry. Walcott opts neither for a Whitmanian translation of the unspeakable nor even a Nerudian desire for translation. He merely acknowledges the fertile qualities of their elusive memories and experiences.

Walcott's poetry consistently searches for the merger between human and natural history, and he suggests that the only human voice where those disparate histories unify is either the voice of the dead, which is no longer accessible, or the voice of those who speak about and from what they do, those whose actions are intertwined with the material of the earth: peasants, "the fishermen, the old women behind their trays of fruit in monumental patience" ("Where" 34). Because his own lived experiences do not involve the same earthly labors, as a poet he can only talk *about* this voice; he cannot assume it.

In "The Muse of History" Walcott acknowledges this awkward position of the poet: "Fisherman and peasant know who they are and what they are, and when we show them our wounded sensibilities we are, most of us, displaying self-inflicted wounds" (*What the Twilight* 63). The "we" he refers to here are those who become alienated from the places they inhabit. To become conscious of place is to become conscious of our separation from it, a separation that is implied in the term "environment"; to be conscious of how human and natural histories merge is to be conscious of their difference. Such self-consciousness would appear to be the result of an awareness of the ruptures and discontinuities of history in the New World, which begs the questions, Do not fishermen and peasants experience a self-conscious relation to place? Are they not capable of aesthetic experiences? He will answer these questions in the affirmative in *Omeros*, but the distinction he draws between himself as poet and the laborers of his island is meant to call attention to the perhaps more specialized work of poetry, which runs a higher risk of betrayal of the local by virtue of its aim to communicate with an offshore audience. Moreover, unlike fishing or harvesting, writing poetry is not an action that so directly and physically practices a nature-culture marriage but is rather a symptom of a divorce. Even if it has origins in the experience of intimacy with the natural world, poetry becomes necessary when a society begins to lose that intimacy. For Walcott, it behooves the poet to use his voice as a kind of confession of this betrayal and a plea for reconciliation. In this sense his poetry maintains a *historicized* rather than a merely *historical* knowledge of place because his attempts to identify history's ruptures and to name the nature that surrounds him are fraught with perpetual error. Poetry misses the mark, but in so doing and so acknowledging it heightens awareness of the ironies of New World history and therefore facilitates adamic renewal.

Walcott is adamant that he is not arguing for a new version of the old naive notion of the noble savage but rather for a postapocalyptic Adam, one who has survived the wreckage of history. He writes in "The Muse of History":

The myth of the noble savage would not be revived, for that myth never emanated from the savage but has always been the nostalgia of the Old World, its longing for innocence. The great poetry of the New World does not pretend to such innocence, its vision is not naive. Rather, like its fruits, its savor is a mixture of the acid and the sweet, the apples of its second Eden have the tartness of experience. In such poetry there is a bitter memory and it is the bitterness that dries last on the tongue. . . . For us in the archipelago the tribal memory is salted with the bitter memory of migration. (Walcott, *What the Twilight* 40–41)

In the 1965 poem "Crusoe's Journal" Walcott describes how the prose of Defoe's Robinson Crusoe stimulated in his young imagination this kind of bittersweet apprehension of nature. Crusoe is Walcott's example of the kind of writer he fancies himself: someone who indigenizes the wreckage of the Old World in an environment that, for a Caribbean native, must be defamiliarized and reapprehended through a poetics of renewal (Ismond 47). He learned from Crusoe's journal that a New World writer could be a constructionist, taking the pieces of the Old World's shipwreck on American soils and, like a woodcutter who understands what life has been taken in order to facilitate his creation, hewing a new biblical prose of the world:

> [L]ike those plain iron tools he salvages
>> from shipwreck, hewing a prose
> as odorous as raw wood to the adze;
>> out of such timbers
> came our first book, our profane Genesis
>> whose Adam speaks that prose
> which, blessing some sea-rock, startles itself
>> with poetry's surprise. (*CP* 92)

Crusoe's language is biblical, but only because it is a creation, not because it has epic historical reach. His language is not simply *about* landscape but involves a refashioning of the wrecked material of the Old World in order to create the chance to speak *as if* for the first time from within the landscape. In his Crusoe essay Walcott articulates this elemental role of art: "Where have cultures originated? By the force of natural surroundings. You build according to the topography of where you live" ("Figure"

56). Like Whitman's poetics of the open road, "the authorizing, validating presence" of Walcott's poetry is not found in libraries or institutions but is "autochthonous, telluric, and oral in its outward manifestations" (Paquet 199). Because it draws its inspiration from intimate elemental awe before the physical world, Crusoe's prose carries the sensual echoes of nature. Walcott's poem itself suggests the motions and sounds of the sea in its shape of alternating lines of pentameter and trimeter and with all lines ending in different versions of an "ess" sound. Awe before the natural world is the beginning of poetic imagination, which is why Crusoe's journal is "our profane Genesis." Like all adamic poetry, Crusoe's book sanctifies nature's profane stimulation of the senses.

Walcott's New World poetics takes a page from postmodernism *and* from his own biocentric yearnings. Paradoxically, in the very act of sanctifying the senses the poet discovers that he stands apart from the environment with which he labored to unify himself, for as soon as Crusoe blesses the sea-rock with his refashioned language and discovers the newness of the world around him, he also discovers his language as a thing apart from that which it names. As Walcott states in the Crusoe essay, "awe is deeper than the articulation of awe. To name is to contradict. The awe of God or of the universe is unnameable" ("Caribbean" 57). Crusoe's poetry "startles itself" and becomes aware of itself as metaphorical language about things, not the thing itself. His is a language of pretension, an *as if* primordiality that, by virtue of its conscious fictionality, does not aspire to the status of revelation. The poet perpetually discovers his solitude and separation from his environment as much as he strives to place himself fully within it. The Adamic fantasy is to find oneself in the pure space of natural history, "somewhere else, / sharing with every beach / a longing for those gulls that cloud the cays," but it also

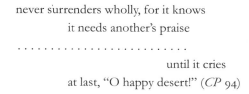

never surrenders wholly, for it knows
        it needs another's praise
. . . .
                    until it cries
        at last, "O happy desert!" (*CP* 94)

In his Crusoe essay Walcott explains that "we live not only on happy, but on fertile deserts, and we draw our strength, like Adam, like all hermits, all dedicated craftsmen, from that rich irony of our history. It is what feeds the bonfire. We contemplate our spirit by the detritus of the past" ("Figure" 40). In the end, poetry remains a human, not a natural, voice, and as such it risks "dramatiz[ing] ourselves at nature's cost" (*CP* 94). The very moment of most intense longing for another's praise is paradoxically when the world's beauty imposes itself on the poet and beckons him back. Crusoe praises his "desert" as he drifts away from his island in search of human community; similarly, the poet is between others and nature, and his metaphors keep in tenuous balance these irreconcilable dual longings. Although he shares Whitman's hope that all things, both human and natural, are united under the shadow of divine light, he cannot assert this faith, as Whitman did; he can only create metaphors that intimate such communion.

The poem concludes that the poet is adamic, but he is not innocent:

> [A]ll of us
>   yearn for those fantasies
> of innocence, for our faith's arrested phase
>   when the clear voice
> startled itself saying "water, heaven, Christ,"
>   hoarding such heresies as
> God's loneliness moves in his smallest creatures. (*CP* 94)

Like all acts of creation, poetry acts against the fear of loneliness, and in this sense, as Walcott implies in the poem's final line, its faith is that the separateness and particularity of things in nature are really manifestations of God's loneliness moving through all of creation, seeking rest in communion. The poet's attempt to clear the slate of history and begin anew will never come to an end because ultimately he writes to conquer individuation caused by history's ruptures, the same condition that is the inspiration of his adamic imagination.

This trap is perhaps what Walcott means to suggest in another 1965 poem, "Crusoe's Island," when he writes that "men fail / according to their creed" (*CP* 69). Crusoe's solitude enabled him to create an Eden from the wreckage of the Old World, but he had "all the joys / But one / Which sent him howling for a human voice" (*CP* 69). The paradox, then, is that poetry will always act as a balm for the wounds of being a poet. The poet will never be able to forge community between people or between people and nature in the way that Whitman had hoped:

And nothing I can learn
From art or loneliness
Can bless them as the bell's
Transfiguring tongue can bless. (*CP* 72)

So he must keep writing in commemoration of the communion he fears he may be losing. Friday's progeny here walk with stunning beauty, and the poet, as Mikics remarks, "stands aloof, frightened, and entranced by his image of the folkloric powers that surround him" (399). Walcott's New World poetics renders ironic whatever prophetic rhetoric is available to him, since the distinction between commemoration and mourning is so attenuated.

A Natural History of the Self

As Neruda had done before him, Walcott found himself in his forties at a geographical remove from his early life, living in Trinidad and traveling with greater frequency to the United States and Europe as he approached middle age. Walcott had consistently expressed his understanding of himself as indebted to his native landscape, but a request to revisit his upbringing in an essay for *London Magazine* in 1965 precipitated a breach of the dams of memory. He began writing a prose autobiography in which he attempted to understand the terms of his natural origins on his native island. The account fell into verse in midstream and resulted in a remarkable autobiographical poem, *Another Life*, published in 1973, a poem that "maintained a special artistic relationship to autobiography, to the epic, to the novel, and to the art of painting" (Baugh and Nepaulsingh 164).[4]

The poem's multiple forms, wide-ranging allusions, insistence on amnesia at the root of New World experience, and self-conscious metaphorizing articulate the foundations of Walcott's New World epic vision, which had come to maturity for Walcott in recent years. Epic poetry of the Americas for Walcott must avoid the excesses of Whitman's wide embrace; it must be autobiographical and epiphanic, telluric and yet ironic, forged in direct apprehensions of the particulars of St. Lucia's natural environment and in awareness of other cultures and the recession of History. It is a foundational poetry, but not in the sense of beginning for the first time; instead, it has a perpetual need to return again and again to the elemental task of naming, evident in the poet's admission at the poem's outset that "I begin here again" (*CP* 145). This New World vision explains why, like James Joyce in *Portrait of the Artist as a Young Man*, Walcott sees the work of memory as inherently artistic. Walcott exploits the latent postcolonialism of the Joycean concept that recollection is self-creation, especially because he finds himself on the outer margins of the centers of power that promulgate and assign genealogies of historical meaning to their subjects and because he inherits radically different cultures.

The advantages of the margin are often depicted in the poem by the waning light of empire, which enhances the beauties of the local landscape. This cannot be an Eden before history, but it is Edenic because of what emerges as History fades. As Walcott describes in the opening lines of the poem,

> Begin with twilight, when a glare
> which held a cry of bugles lowered
> the coconut lances of the inlet,
> as a sun, tired of empire, declined. (*CP* 145)

As the sun sets, the amber light climbs until it arrives overhead:

> [T]he sky
> grew drunk with light.
> There
> was your heaven! The clear
> glaze of another life,
> a landscape locked in amber, the rare
> gleam. (*CP* 145)

The Old Masters of the sixteenth century had learned to seal their paintings and thus heighten and preserve their colors with a transparent resin that gives their work to this day a distinctive amber shade (Baugh and Nepaul-singh 223–24). The implication here is also that the environment itself seems locked in amber and thus haunting in its opacity and distance from the gaze of a loving and nostalgic admirer. The student of the local depends upon the declining light provided by the metropolis's distance from the island in order to catch rare glimpses of a local Eden.

The adamic task of the poet is thus tinged with betrayal and loss even in the act of claiming and praising the local qualities of the island. As a result of his colonial education he was caught in the dilemma of loving by comparison:

> [F]rom childhood he'd considered palms
> ignobler than imagined elms,
> the breadfruit's splayed
> leaf coarser than the oak's. (*CP* 148)

Even though art teaches him how to see, it also blinds him to the reality that surrounds him. It is not long before he realizes the error of this inferiority complex, an error Walcott's mentor, Harry Simmons, was intent on correcting. Initially, he turns away from the whiteness and temperate climates of European norms and toward Africa. His longing to become "the natural man, / generous, rooted" almost makes him miss the opportunities before his eyes, however. He keeps looking beyond the mark toward "some ancestral, tribal country, / I heard its clear tongue over the clean stones / of the river, . . . and multiplied the bush with savages" (*CP* 184).

But his willingness to search for his roots in the roots of his own soil eventually leads Walcott to the epiphany that appears to have shaped his poetic mission. As a young thirteen year old he finds himself climbing where "afternoon light ripened the valley" below.[5] He writes:

> I was seized by a pity more profound
> than my young body could bear, I climbed
> with the labouring smoke,
> I drowned in labouring breakers of bright cloud,
> then uncontrollably I began to weep,
> inwardly, without tears, with a serene extinction
> of all sense; I felt compelled to kneel,
> I wept for nothing and for everything,
> I wept for the earth of the hill under my knees,
> for the grass, the pebbles, for the cooking smoke
> above the labourers' houses like a cry. (*CP* 184–85)

He discovers that his artistic duty is to be "fasten[ed] . . . forever to the poor." He kneels in Joycean prayer to the deities of art history, Michelangelo, Raphael, Turner, and others, and thus he "fell in love with art, / and life began" (*CP* 186).[6]

Drunk with ambition, Walcott and "Gregorias," his friend Dunstan St.

Omer, plunge headlong into the task of claiming the island's environment as material for art:

> But drunkenly, or secretly, we swore,
> disciples of that astigmatic saint,
> that we would never leave the island
> until we had put down, in paint, in words
> as palmists learn the network of a hand,
> all of its sunken, leaf-choked ravines,
> every neglected, self-pitying inlet
> muttering in brackish dialect, the ropes of mangroves
> from which old soldier crabs slipped
> surrendering to slush. (*CP* 194)

The adamic elation of discovering the artist's obligation is fueled by an awareness that "no one had yet written of this landscape," even if it is not prehistoric. The depth of time for Walcott is not measured by geology, as it was for Neruda, but it does contain a "life older than geography" because of its buried layers of human history, which have fallen into oblivion (*CP* 196). He writes:

> For no one had yet written of this landscape
> that it was possible, though there were sounds
> given to its varieties of wood;
>
> the *bois-canot* responded to its echo,
> when the axe spoke, weeds ran up to the knee
> like bastard children, hiding in their names,
>
> whole generations died, unchristened,
> growths hidden in green darkness, forests
> of history thickening with amnesia. (*CP* 195)

Walcott's natural history is deep because it is itself a bastard child, just like the Caribbean islands, cut off from its own genealogy in History as dictated by colonial reason. Nature, then, becomes a potential ally to the island boy as he seeks to use art like "conquerors who had discovered home" (*CP* 195). Unlike the conquerors, however, the impulse of the poem "resists the amnesia which would otherwise be required by the successful arrival of a new, apocalyptic, dispensation" (Christiansë 202). The amnesia he has to accept is that rendered by human and natural history. The ancient life of the earth and the vault that it has become for the stories of the faceless indigenous and African dead leave the poet in an almost existential vacuum. Traces of the human story of the islands dissolve with the green growth: "[T]he lost Arawak hieroglyphs and signs / were razed from slates by sponges of rain, / their symbols mixed with lichen" (*CP* 196).

In Walcott's papers there is a photograph of Simmons tracing the recently eroded outline of an Arawak hieroglyphic with chalk in the presence of some of his students (Baugh and Nepaulsingh 264–65). However, Walcott appears more taken by the idea of irrecoverable indigenous origins than by the romance of a Caribbean culture newly oriented toward its native past. In this sense, "hieroglyphics" assumes a more Whitmanian meaning of an unintelligible sign that signifies multiple and fragmented origins rather than the promise of historical recovery through translation. The archipelago of islands is itself "like a broken root," and each island, each man, each tree strives "silently to become / whatever their given names resembled" (*CP* 196). Poetic knowledge of natural and human history in the New World for Walcott is the result of a series of approximations and echoes that never arrive at the Ur-language of rooted meaning. This is not the condemnation of perpetual poetic exile but rather the poet's procreational opportunity for generative metaphors that organize the broken roots of New World experience into new meanings. After an attempt to capture the motions of the landscape in front of him, Walcott concludes:

> I have toiled all of life for this failure.
> Beyond this frame, deceptive, indifferent,
> nature returns to its work,
> behind the square of blue you have cut from that sky,
> another life, real, indifferent, resumes. (*CP* 200)

Nature's elusiveness means that painting cannot engage metaphors like poetry to capture this ironic slippage between reality and representation that results from amnesia. The "another life" of poetry is also the other life of the natural world that defies crystallizations into images. Painting misses "the sociological contours" of history's ironic layers within the same geographical spaces and is also less likely to express these ambiguities of Caribbean experience. In his youth Walcott could paint what he saw, but he could not resist the tendency to seek "the paradoxical flash of an instant / in which every facet was caught / in a crystal of ambiguities" (*CP* 200). While his poetry often yearns for painting's ability to reach for what he calls in *Omeros* a "light beyond metaphor," the poet cannot look on nature without an awareness of the Caribbean's violent and multiple historical legacies. He writes that "my hand was crabbed by that style, / this epoch, that school / or the next"; consequently, writing poetry was both literally and figuratively a kind of "sideways crawling" as a result of "this classic / condition of servitude" (*CP* 201). Gregorias, on the other hand, "plung[ed] whole suit in the shallows, / painting under water, roaring, and spewing spray" (*CP* 193). Unlike painting, which implies a more immediate apprehension of the environment, poetry strives for communion with nature but cannot do so without at least implicitly addressing the relevance or irrelevance of history. The next chapter explores how Walcott seeks a reconciliation of these distinct impulses through more elaborate moments of ekphrasis in *Tiepolo's Hound*.

Walcott's poetic impulse was to see nature for what it hid. He had hoped to find "epochs" in the sea, "an undersea museum," something that would provide documentation and the reason of his past (*CP* 208). As he had earlier noted in "Origins," however, Walcott only finds "sea-wrack" as his genealogical promissory note:

Crouched there,
like a whelk picker,
I searched the sea-wrack for a sea-coin:
my white grandfather's face,
I heard in the black howl of cannon,
sea-agape,
my black grandfather's voice,
and envied mad, divine Gregorias
imprisoned in his choice. (*CP* 208)

Nature comes to signify the New World's history of transplantation, confused genealogies, and amnesia, since that history was never properly documented but rather written "on [a] slate of wet sand," waiting for the next wave to erase it (*CP* 209). If Walcott could collapse nature into a metaphor for stories it appears to hide, his own metaphors would cease to have reference to the world; his poetry would become existential, procreational, and it would have no mimetic function at all. In essence, he could be anywhere.

Fortunately, nature's other life, its indifference to the colors he cuts also signifies its presence and reality, which means that failed art is the truest.

Walcott confesses that his awareness of his own racial plurality caused him more self-doubt about failure than Gregorias ever felt:

> How often didn't you hesitate
> between rose-flesh and sepia,
> your blood like a serpent whispering
> of a race incapable of subtler shadow,
> of music, architecture, and a complex thought.

But he concludes that this was instead his opportunity:

> [B]e happy
> in every uncertainty. Cherish the stumbling
> that lashes your eyes with branches,
> that, threatened with rain,
> your sorrow is still uncertain. (*CP* 251)

The stumbling here enables the poet to perceive the contours of the indifferent reality rather than running the risk of its headlong appropriation of nature for artistic purposes and thus missing the point of nature's otherness.

In his imagined dialogue with his teacher and master, Harry Simmons, who committed suicide while Walcott was in the process of writing *Another Life*, the poet insists on this value of nature's otherness. Simmons was himself a painter, literary critic, folklorist, amateur archaeologist, and naturalist (Ismond 200). He helped to turn Walcott toward his island duties, advocating art that exhibited "the spontaneity, the primitiveness in creations that bear the imprimatur of the people" (qtd. in Baugh and Nepaulsingh 211). Although Walcott understood the limitations of this Whitmanian nativist pose, he nevertheless understood that Simmons's curiosity and humility, which he related to Crusoe's awe, helped to create works that emerged within a numinous cosmos of deep time. Walcott describes a presence that is beyond language, a lesson that poetry can still learn from painting:

> A nature reduced to the service
> of praising and humbling men,
> there is a yes without a question,

there is assent founded on ignorance,
in the mangroves plunged to the wrist . . .
there are spaces
wider than conscience. (*CP* 280)

The poet accepts his failures as symptomatic manifestations of these wide spaces of the natural world that are greater than the anthropomorphic imagination can capture; they draw us to them, assent to our praise of them, but do not reveal all of their secrets.

The paradox of Walcott's New World poetics is that he consistently resorts to descriptions of history's withdrawal in order to try to make an argument for nature's more-than-human breadth. Because of his awareness of the New World's history of amnesia, direct appraisals, like that of Simmons described above, are not his luxury. In the penultimate chapter of *Another Life* Walcott articulates in verse his poetics of oblivion that informed the discussion in chapter 2. He sees the natural world as at best a site of compromise between the nostalgic pull of the Americas' various nations of origin and the Edenic longing to be beyond history's claims. The chapter, first published separately in the *New Yorker* in 1972, was initially titled "The Muse of History at Rampanalgas." Rampanalgas is a small fishing village in Trinidad frequented by Walcott and his family in those years and a place whose negligible historical significance and exceptional raw natural beauty Walcott fully exploits. As the initial title suggests, the poem also formed the basis of his later essay, "The Muse of History." The poem provides, then, a philosophical examination of the significance of Walcott's natural metaphors throughout the poem, allowing us to see how the poem's exploration into the poet's life "gains a wider significance as a confrontation not only with the history of the Caribbean region as a whole but with the very concept of history" (Baugh 72). Ismond likewise explains that the provincial beauty of the place becomes the foundation "of a unifying, re-humanizing cross-culturalism within the multicultural environment of the region" (220). As I outlined in chapter 2, however, it is amnesiac nature that leads to this cross-culturalism and radically transforms the progression of "illuminations" in Western History. Describing a shoreline of mangroves, hidden red herons, and "too green acid grasses," Walcott writes:

[L]et the historian go mad there
from thirst. Slowly the water rat takes up its reed pen

and scribbles. Leisurely, the egret,
on the mud tablet stamps its hieroglyph. (*CP* 283)

The allusion to grass and to hieroglyphs (recall that he had earlier referred to the hieroglyph of the Arawak erased by natural processes and "mixed with lichen") evokes Whitman's phrase regarding the child's riddle regarding the leaves of grass. My reader will recall that Whitman answers the child with a series of tentative answers that suggest Whitman's belief that natural regeneration signifies both a figurative and literal transformation of human life and suffering. The grass seems to symbolize a synthesis of contradiction, inequality, and injustice into a higher form of democracy: "Or I guess it is a uniform hieroglyphic, / And it means, Sprouting alike in broad zones and narrow zones, / Growing among black folks as among white" (Whitman, "Song of Myself," *PW* 37). Walcott pushes the ironic implications of this idea further than Whitman, implying that precisely because grass could become the "beautiful uncut hair of graves," as Whitman says, it means that natural regeneration and its beauty are a cruel irony. History is buried by New World nature, and this will force a difficult choice: either the poet turns away from nature's historically blank slate in search of the past, or the poet fashions a poetics of oblivion that simultaneously acknowledges history's absence and praises natural beauty. In the latter case, which is certainly Walcott's choice, this does not result in naive dreams of empty Edens but a New World poetics that gives a sobering account of what stories nature will not tell and a bittersweet acceptance of the merely natural history that remains.

If the poet cannot accept the untranslatable language of nature, he will be seduced by the Muse of History, like the "Mediterranean accountant, with the nose of the water rat, / ideograph of the egret's foot, / [who] calculates his tables" (*CP* 283). Writers become accountants when they cannot tolerate the fragmentation of historical memory under New World slavery and colonialism and, rather than awaking to the wonder and awe of nature, find themselves captive to desires of nostalgia and revenge. Walcott pushes the ironies of Whitman's poetics further in order to establish a preferable poetics of bittersweet elation:

The astigmatic geologist
stoops, with the crouch of the heron,
deciphering—not a sign.
All the epics are blown away with the leaves,

blown with the careful calculations on brown paper;
these were the only epics: the leaves. (*CP* 284)

New World epics of biblical history are rendered natural signs, leaves of
grass, as it were, by the violence of New World history. This is certainly a
more bittersweet irony attributed to the meaning of leaves than Whitman
may have intended, but Walcott has returned to Whitman's metaphors, not
to rewrite him so much as to reread him, in order to tease out of them their
New World lessons, which Whitman himself perhaps could only intuit in
his age.

The ironies are deeper because Walcott does not minimize the depth of
the violence and suffering that lie hidden beneath nature's beauty. Whitman's poetic vision was undoubtedly enriched by his direct exposure to
the Civil War's violence, but he was never willing to confront fully Native
American injustices, the growing evils of U.S. imperialism, the conflict between northerners and southerners in the Civil War, or the violence itself
of slavery and the Middle Passage. So while he rejects a facile Hegelian
synthesis of past wrongs, Walcott's more aggressive willingness to tackle
the problems of that history is nevertheless paradoxical, since his objective
is to move us away from a juridical reasoning of historical inquiry that seeks
to balance accounts, a temptation that sometimes seduced Neruda. But, as
Neruda ultimately brings himself to do, Walcott refuses to romanticize
the indigenous past nostalgically;[7] hence we have a decidedly unromantic
reference to the New World indigenous injustices ("the entrails of disem-
bowelled Aztecs") that recalls Neruda's accusation that the Inca practiced
a form of slavery.

Walcott's Caribbean is a place of tremendous and ironic beauty, without
horsemen, armor,

> no fork-bearded Castilians,
> only the narrow, silvery creeks of sadness
> like the snail's trail,
> only the historian deciphering, in invisible ink,
> its patient slime. (*CP* 284)

Those victims of the Muse who want to balance accounts wind up "gild[ing]
cruelty" and "fascinated, / in attitudes of prayer, / by the festering roses
made from their fathers' manacles" (*CP* 286). Had he known Neruda's

political poetry in more depth, Walcott may very well have concluded that Neruda is at times among those who hunger for history, not naked nature, because historical markers allow them to say "at least here / something happened" (*CP* 286). These tribunal poets and politicians, then, seek to legitimize their place in the discourse of Western History even if it also means their place is one of dishonor. While this historical impulse chases empty signifiers with an impotent pen, Walcott's own child hears more New World history in a conch shell:

> [A] child without history, without knowledge of its pre-world,
> only the knowledge of water runnelling rocks,
> . . . .
> that child who puts the shell's howl to his ear,
> hears nothing, hears everything
> that the historian cannot hear, the howls
> of all the races that crossed the water,
> the howls of the grandfathers drowned
> in that intricately swivelled Babel,
> hears the fellaheen, the Madrasi, the Mandingo, the Ashanti. (*CP* 285)

Unlike the assumptions about the American Adam, this child's adamic approach to a world perceived as new paradoxically allows him to hear in what Walcott in "Air" calls "milling air" (*CP* 114) the very history the accountant and historian seek. The child remains in an Eden and not in a fallen world, however, because an insubstantial history echoes its own loss where it lies embedded in the natural world. This allows the poet to turn away from those echoing cries and adamically "to write of the wind and the memory of wind-whipped hair" (*CP* 289). As I argued in chapter 1, this New World poetics is unlikely to leave nature vulnerable to willed claims of innocence on the land because the poet is always looking over his shoulder, aware of the ironies that have bequeathed him this garden. Unlike a merely Hegelian notion of synthesis, Walcott's landscape is riddled by ghosts of "simultaneity and multiplicity" (Christiansë 203). The environment offers an adamic opportunity because it contains multitudes that no one poem, no one book can synthesize. This means he can confront the past without becoming obeisant to it, and he can appraise nature without appropriating it. Walcott is thus safeguarded from a naive sanctification of the landscape before him:

> [H]oly is Rampanalgas and its high-circling hawks,
> holy are the rusted, tortured, rust-caked, blind almond trees,
> your great-grandfather's, and your father's torturing limbs
> . . . .
> and the tireless hoarse anger of the waters
> by which I can walk calm, a renewed, exhausted man. (*CP* 289)

His description of his Eden here is rife with irony. The tree of knowledge is tortured and blind and a reminder of ancestral death, and the sea, the very repository of slavery's nameless dead, speaks with anger and yet renews an "exhausted" man. This insistent fusion of natural and human history is what Walcott refers to when he writes that "the great poetry of the New World does not pretend to such innocence, its vision is not naïve. Rather, like its fruits, its savour is a mixture of the acid and the sweet, the apples of its second Eden have the tartness of experience" (*What the Twilight* 40–41).

Although Walcott includes Whitman among the most prominent examples of this "great poetry of the New World," his vision here leaves little room for Whitman's leaves of grass, because they are simply not tainted by the bitterness Walcott describes. Walcott has revised Whitman's initial call for New World poetry to such an extent that Whitman's Hegelian confidence that "all goes outward and onward, and to die is different from what anyone supposes, and luckier" seems embarrassingly naive. This is especially true if such a declaration is offered as a salvo to the slaves thrown overboard in the Middle Passage. Walcott has shifted his tone regarding Whitman in recent years, noting that Whitman has only a superficial vision of tragedy or evil, but, as I suggested in chapter 4, Whitman's poetry on the whole holds up to scrutiny from Walcott's more annealed perspective on the New World.

If we think of Walcott's gesture here as a way of reintroducing the history of slavery into Whitman's poetics, it allows us to see the voices of the dead beneath the grass as those who have suffered at the hands of the founders of many American nations. As previously noted, Whitman had in fact witnessed the dead bodies of soldiers who fought in the Revolutionary War washing to shore near his home in Brooklyn and had come to imagine the sea as a great space of death, an image undoubtedly of no small influence on Walcott. As we saw, Whitman wasn't always rosy in his views of nature's regenerative power to transform human death into natural living forms of green grass. Walcott's ability to extend the reach of Whitman's poetics demonstrates a poetics of reading that I earlier outlined in chapter 3. Just as Glissant learns to read Faulkner despite the possibility of his obtuseness on racial questions as revealing fissures in his own culture, so too Walcott hears in Whitman an expression of a composite America that was perhaps broader than Whitman may have realized but that had to be accessed with greater humility than Whitman could muster. Walcott remakes Whitman in this kind of relational reading and thus demonstrates that literature's force cannot be "mapped" according to geography or simplistic identitarianism by focusing on its lands or authors of origin; poetry's power is that it can expose the fissures, the liminal spaces between communities, but only if that is what we are interesting in reading.

There is a similar moment in *Another Life* in which Walcott rereads his own life and suggests that his epiphany on the hill at thirteen has become something much more significant than it seemed at the time. If nature offers "spaces / wider than conscience," then our deepest encounters with it bring us into contact with buried realities that poetry can only intuit. As they did for Joyce, personal epiphanies experienced in the open air function as alternatives to the "illuminations" of successive, genealogical History; they "become one way of steadying personal identity on the unstable sea of cultural history" (Nichols 184). This is especially true because of the way in which Walcott's epiphanies are often modes of imagination in which "conflicting sides of his cultural identity" are brought together in a strange kind of reconciliation (186).

The New World's overlapping histories of diaspora and racial plurality are the reasons for the generosity of a Glissantian reading—to bring out these spaces in our interpretive practices—and are also the basis for not rejecting outright the limitations of a Whitmanian cosmology of the democratic self. Walcott is cautiously attracted to nature's immensity of space, where "there is something which balances," but he never assumes Whitman's tone of triumphal announcement of what that "something" is or that one need only feel optimism for the future. Nevertheless, Walcott does not deny the possibility of Whitman's faith. In chapter 21 Walcott revisits the epiphany:

And on that hill, that evening,
when the deep valley grew blue with forgetting,

why did I weep,
why did I kneel,
whom did I thank?
I knelt because I was my mother,
I was the well of the world,
I wore the stars on my skin,
I endured no reflections,
my sign was water,
tears, and the sea,
my sign was Janus,
I saw with twin heads,
and everything I say is contradicted.

I was fluent as water. (*CP* 281)

This Whitmanian moment of unification with the wider spaces and multitudes of historical ghosts found in nature inevitably means, as Whitman himself once so famously confessed, that the poet will contradict himself in his attempts to give expression to such experiences. The poet moves beyond conscious speech and into the realm of natural energy, signified by the fluency of water and the "linear elation of an eel" (*CP* 281).

It is in this space without reflection, so unlike the self-conscious space of poetry, that Walcott is also able to experience a kind of solidarity with the dead, specifically, the "Sauters," the leaping Carib Indians who committed suicide in 1651.[8] He celebrates the fact that the normally insular personality of the poet discovers a Whitmanian capacity to feel compassion. Echoing Whitman's declaration in "Song of Myself" that "I am the man . . . I suffered. . . . I was there" (*PW* 71, ellipses in original), Walcott writes that he discovered

an urge more than mine,
. . . .
let it be written, I shared, I shared,
I was struck like rock, and I opened
to His gift! (*CP* 281–82)

This strikes a different tone than the despair over the "too much nothing" of Caribbean indigenous history Walcott lamented in "Air," but this is not the resurrection of a buried past intended to overturn the fundamental problem of Caribbean amnesia.[9] Like Neruda's "American love," the triumph is the discovery of his own sympathies.

Communion with spirits of the past not only connects him to the broader spectrum of New World history buried beneath the sea and the vegetation he so loves, but it also consoles the lover who has long since left his beloved Anna behind. Instead of being stuck with stagnating nostalgia, he has learned Rilke's assertion that lost love transforms into something far more deep: "I have loved all women who have evolved from her" (*CP* 281). Continuity is possible, even if this fact does not provide facile comfort for what is lost.

Earlier in the poem Walcott was impatient for immurement and stasis when he was with Anna:

We sit by the stone wall

All changes to grey stone,
stone hands, stone air,
stone eyes, from which

irisless, we stare,
wishing the sea were stone. (*CP* 230)

Their desires seem to freeze them in time like irisless Greek statues, and they find themselves for the moment in a Garden of Eden: "[W]e were the first guests of the earth / and everything stood still for us to name" (*CP* 231). Instead of learning to be "fluent as water," the poet wishes the "sea were stone, / motion we could not hear" (*CP* 230). He can never be Adam in such a garden, however, since nothing stands still, least of all the other life of nature. Poetry betrays its objects of devotion, as Walcott will explore more extensively in *Tiepolo's Hound*, because of its inherent incapacity to give representational fixity to the fluidity of time and dynamic change in nature. But this failure allows the poet to escape the illusions of the false and stony Eden haunted by young love and nostalgia and to be adamic in a second garden, one that admits to "the noble treachery of art" (*CP* 236). Walcott writes in an unpublished essay from 1987, entitled "Inside the Cathedral": "The only hope that artistic failure offers is, in fact, stronger than success; it is the nocturnal failure of the saint at prayer, the repetition of 'I am not worthy.' Repeated enough, a strange strength can grow as it does out of the mesmeric Litany. The subject's subjection" (11).

The stillness of objects in Walcott's memories is not the symptom of nostalgic pull toward the past but rather the function of memory's limitations. As he writes of his recollections of the old house where he was a child,

Finger each object, lift it
from its place, and it screams again
to be put down
in its ring of dust. (*CP* 157)

Memory is itself a form of artistic remembrance, and the stasis of things in the past is a function of art's inability to remember things *in time*. Moments are pulled out of time, encased, and thus unable to be moved again. The best we can do is to create new works of art that seek to plumb the depths of those stationary things, as Walcott does here. Like the smell of the forest in Neruda's home, a remembered house "bears the depth of forest, of ocean and mother," and poetry thus becomes a form of "weep[ing] for dumb things" (*CP* 155). Poetry for Walcott is not ventriloquism, nor is it compensation for lost things, but neither do these two facts render poetry merely existential. As he once claimed: "History is irrelevant, not because it is not being created, or because it was sordid, but because it has never mattered, what has mattered is the loss of history, the amnesia of the races; what had become necessary is imagination, imagination as necessity, as invention" ("Caribbean" 53). As I explore in the last chapter, Walcott is as agnostic about his faith as he is about his doubt, thus leaving us with expressions of tentative hope, possibility, and elation of a more sober order than Whitman or Neruda.

Because of his own dual legacies of African pantheism and Methodism, Walcott is never willing to define the precise nature of the numinous presence he experiences in Caribbean landscapes. This cultural agnosticism functions similar to Whitman's adopted combination of natural science, such as it was in his age, and Swedenborgian spiritualism. It becomes a kind of ecumenical poetics of animism. In another unpublished portion of his essay "American, without America," a manuscript he worked on contemporaneously with *Another Life*, Walcott acknowledges that for those interested "there are very boring epochs of genocide and greed" that lie beneath the Caribbean's natural history. As he looks to his own beloved Morne Coco in Trinidad he admits that the "imagination can people it with ghosts from Asia, from India, from Africa and from Europe" (Walcott, "American" 26). But the truth is, the mountain "has never held these mythologies. We will never know what it held for the lost, vaporous, wailing races of the Arawak and the Carib, but we can claim them, each of us, separately, and the separations can blend with the anonymity of smoke." His point here is to suggest that poetry fills the vacuum created by the Caribbean's absence of mythology, and even though poetic imaginings of natural and human histories are idiosyncratic, they reach beyond the limitations of the self and have the potential to blend with the poetic dreams of other New World exiles, thus granting the poetry "the force of revelation" even as it refuses the kind of faith this would require (Paquet 206). When they are willing to forgo the search for buried epochs and instead learn "to see every daybreak as a tentative beginning," New World poets are engaged not merely in perpetuating tradition or mimetically representing culture but in creating it (Walcott, "American" 26).

It seems to me to be increasingly difficult, more and more difficult, to render light. . . . That's what I consider to be the peak of effort. Not to render things as they are exactly, but to somehow illuminate them by the simplicity of what the vocabulary may be, or the thought may be. The simplicity I am talking about is a striving—it's the same principle actually as the Adamic idea of renaming.

DEREK WALCOTT, "Interview with Derek Walcott"

CHAPTER 8

Impressionism in the New World

If poetry is the ideal medium for seeking a conceptual balance between natural and human histories, it also runs the risk, as the discussion in the last chapter implied, that it will always need to historicize and humanize nature. It may be insufficient, in other words, on its own to reach for an adamic apprehension of nature, or what Walcott calls in *Omeros* the "light beyond metaphor." If painting is less metaphorical than poetry, it is at least more capable of seeing light without historical echoes. This raises the possibility that a partnership between the two can establish a deeper and more genuinely adamic relationship to the physical world. Such was, after all, Walcott's earliest suspicions given his intense interest, unique among these three poets, to name *and* paint the garden of St. Lucia that history had bequeathed him. His intense interest in visual art perhaps contributes to Walcott's more focused obsession on the transatlantic influence of European culture on the New World. Neither Whitman nor Neruda spent so much energy in this regard, in part because they lived in geographies more immediately affected by the presence of Native American cultures. Although only Neruda came close to Walcott's prodigious knowledge of European culture, Walcott's knowledge, paradoxically forged in a markedly marginalized colonial context in the Caribbean, was far more pronounced than either Whitman's or Neruda's. Walcott's hyperconscious awareness of Western literary tradition is manifested in his frequent and overt nods to literary precursors. But what is perhaps more compelling to explore for the purposes of this study is how his intense interest in painting raises important questions regarding the effect of visual culture, exported by imperialism, on the local landscape. He raises the possibility that seemingly innocent first-time apprehensions of New World nature are already largely predetermined by the viewer's internalization of Western visual discourse, but he also suggests that those very artistic frames, impressionism in particular, can provide solutions that preserve the usefulness of the adamic imagination.

While his career as a painter has never reached the levels of achievement of his poetry, in his later years he has become more intensely interested in developing his painting. This interest led him to finally publish twenty-five of his paintings within the book-length poem *Tiepolo's Hound*, an extensive exploration of the parallels between Camille Pissarro's impressionism and Walcott's own New World poetics of nature. The net effect of this inclusion and the art historical themes of the poem suggests a multigenre approach to a New World poetics, one that moves between the triangulated relationship of nature, metaphor, and image in order to exorcise finally the ghosts of history. Triangulation, as I suggested in the introduction, allows for comparisons beyond hierarchies and the historical claims implied by a strict chronological approach to comparative study. As this chapter demonstrates, triangulation proves liberating not only for nature itself in relation to the claims of human history but also for the poet's adamic imagination as he seeks to appraise home landscapes free of the claims of History.

Triangulation and the New World Eye

When the Franco-Prussian War broke out in 1870 Pissarro was peacefully situated in the city of Louveciennes, some eleven miles from Paris. Otto von

Bismarck had laid siege to Paris in an attempt to consolidate Prussian power within the newly united North German Confederation, and the winds of war eventually chased Pissarro, Claude Monet, and many other refugees across the Channel to England. It was there at London's National Gallery that Pissarro and Monet engaged in a fruitful visual dialogue with the great landscape artists of England, most notably John Constable and J. M. W. Turner. Although they admired Gainsborough, Lawrence, and Reynolds, among others, Pissarro commented to a friend that "we were struck chiefly by the landscape-painters, who shared more in our aim with regard to 'plein air,' light, and fugitive effects" (qtd. in Adler 45). Pissarro took special note of Turner's capacity to depict the effects of light on snow and ice "by using a number of brushstrokes of different colours placed next to each other, rather than white alone" (Adler 46).

The image of these two great impressionists standing before the work of their English compatriots of art has fascinated art historians because of the influence it suggests that Turner and Constable may have had on the impressionist movement, but the fascination of this encounter for Derek Walcott is more personal. Turner's 1838 painting, *The Fighting Téméraire*, hung in the National Gallery before the eyes of Monet and Pissarro, but it also appeared in Thomas Craven's book *Masterpieces of Art*. Walcott inherited a copy of the book from his father, who died in Walcott's infancy and who had left behind amateur copies of Turner and other painters to fascinate and haunt his son's painterly imagination.

Monet and Pissarro would have likely taken note of *The Fighting Téméraire* because it was prominently displayed in the National Gallery, was referred to by Turner as "my darling," and was known to have been one of the only paintings Turner refused to sell (Egerton 10). The work depicts the famous retirement of the ship that had helped England to victory in the 1805 Battle of Trafalgar during the Napoleonic Wars against Spanish and French warships. A steam tugboat pulls the famous warship into port to be dismantled, and, like many of Turner's paintings, the image seems to vacillate between nostalgia for the past and an acceptance of the inevitability of change. It exhibits the most outstanding visual trait of Turner's work: the sunset reflected on the water, splitting the light into halves by the horizon of the sea, shining in decline directly into the eyes of the viewer. The moon also appears in the image, further suggesting the dividing line between what was and what will be. Judith Egerton argues that since it is unlikely that a tugboat would pull a ship at twilight through a heavily used river, it is important to see the work as imaginatively and metaphorically addressing the inevitability of decline, change, and continuity rather than as historical documentation; indeed, it "defies [the event's] realities" (75). Turner enables his viewers to contemplate the sun as the protagonist of so many of his works, infiltrating and affecting every aspect of the historical drama that he depicts, subordinating the event's significance to the sun's movement.

Turner's aesthetics of temporality, which is also central to the later impressionists, including Pissarro, have interested Walcott since he was a boy, as evidenced by his references to Turner's work in *Another Life*.[1] Seeing historical events through the lens of time's protagonism, in its small but relentless shifts and changes, has allowed Walcott to explore the various dualities that constitute his world, dualities of racial difference, Caribbean and European cultures, human and natural histories, poetry and painting, without falling into the logic of hierarchies or false dichotomies. His reference to Turner's painting in *Tiepolo's Hound* has little to do with his interest in repeating the art historical claims of influence, of aesthetic cause and effect, that would explain the development of impressionism. Even despite his own intensely historical interest in Camille Pissarro's place in the history of impressionism and his relevance to Caribbean culture, ultimately Walcott is uninterested in "History." What Walcott means by this term is a discourse of Western civilization that establishes patrimonial claims of inheritance, that aligns cultural figures and geographical areas in relationships of center and margin, authority and dependence, by means of affiliation and chronology. Similar to the simultaneity with which Walcott's child experiences the past at Rampanalgas, Walcott prefers to imagine the encounter as an anachronistic triangulated meeting of disparate places (France, England, the Caribbean) and times (early 1800s, late 1800s, early twentieth century). He writes:

Triangulation: in his drawing room
my father copies *The Fighting Téméraire.*

He and Monet admire the radiant doom
of the original; all three men revere

the crusted barge, its funnel bannering fire,
its torch guiding the great three-master on

to sink in the infernal asphalt of an empire
turning more spectral, like the mastodon. (*TH* 76)

As I remarked in the introduction, triangulation is a spatial order used in surveying to delimit a location by means of measuring its distance from two distinct spots. Triangulation not only confirms the distance by means of two witnesses, but it also implicitly and relationally places the three locations on a similar plane, allowing us to use any two of the points to determine the location of the third. No single location, then, exists without relation to the other two, and hence there is no center or margin, only relation. This kind of relation is precisely what ekphrasis aims for. Murray Krieger once argued that a fundamental distinction between literature and painting was the difference between temporal and spatial order, respectively. Consequently, ekphrasis is that moment when literature attempts to defy this binary and establish a spatial plasticity (Krieger 285); ekphrasis is more than literary representations of visual works of art but is instead the "sought-for equivalent in words of any visual image, in or out of art" and includes "every attempt, within an art of words, to work toward the illusion that it is performing a task we usually associate with an art of natural signs" (Krieger 9).

In Walcott's poem what appears to be a primary interest in describing works of art becomes a more broadly conceived obsession with breaking down the spatial and temporal binaries that shut down adamic possibility and bind Caribbean landscapes in hierarchical relationships to European art. Although a priority in time could be established between the European masters and the Caribbean acolyte, in Walcott's ekphrastic triangulation they are synchronized. The triangulation of Turner, Monet, and Pissarro already highlights the differences between Pissarro's more mundane and ordinary beauty and Monet's penchant for close studies of color and light and disrupts the unilateral causal relation between English landscape art and French impressionism. This hierarchical implication of priority is what Édouard Glissant describes as Western civilization's faith in "the absolute of ancient filiation and conquering linearity, the project of knowledge and arrowlike nomadism" (*Poetics* 56). One could, of course, determine the meaning of Walcott's father's imitation of Turner by deciding how far from the original his sketches are (and, by implication, how inferior he is as an artist, how inferior the Caribbean is, etc.) simply by means of a chronological comparison between him and Turner. However, when Walcott introduces Monet and Pissarro facing the canvas of Turner, they join Walcott's father on the same plane of space as acolytes, learning not so much from Turner as from the motion of the sun. Ekphrastic spatial seeing, in *Tiepolo's Hound*, is what Walcott calls "Time"; it is a temporal equalizer that frees the artistic imagination before a present landscape from the chronological constraints and demands of History. This liberation in turn means that the artist, no longer constrained by cosmopolitan aesthetic norms, can practice unfettered an adamic art of seeing in the Caribbean.

Regardless of how revolutionary they may have first been, works of art in museums and in catalogs have a tendency to become conventions of seeing and, when these works are landscapes, clichés of natural beauty. The risk is that a colonial admirer of European art will look around at the local landscape and disparage these particulars of light, vegetation, and vistas as signs of inferiority. Metropolitan norms internalized in this fashion by the locals result in what Walcott once called the "insulted landscape." In an unpublished lecture from 1980 of this title from which portions were adapted in "The Star Apple Kingdom," he commented about the enigma of the Caribbean vegetation, whose "adlib inimical shapes seem to lack concepts and divinity" to eyes trained by the masterpieces. The temptation is to want to reject the messiness and chaos of tropical growth in favor of the "god-given cartography of empire, which is always dead ahead, Roman style . . . in which the road stops arguing with the bush, does not observe the contours of the landscape but heads as strict and radial as the fronds of that exemplary palm, out of the center of an imaginary capital" (Walcott, "The Insulted Landscape").

We need only think of the baroque landscaping at Versailles to understand Walcott's comparison here. The preferable and more liberating alternative would be a naturalistic artistic and political culture that follows "the flow of exploration as a river does, both shaping and obeying where it runs, changing its mind or course into an oxbow lake, cascading into the penitential torrent of a waterfall, even admitting the fertilizing algae of stagnation." What Walcott describes here is nature's inherent spatial and temporal dynamism, a conception of which painting has often struggled to represent because of the need to fix its subject in space and time. Insulted landscapes are the result of false binaries between there and here, centers and peripheries. Triangulations that compare both with the temporal dynamism that all art tries to capture will avoid these pitfalls.

If it is simplistic to believe in the universal standards of "masterpieces," it is equally excessive to think of them as having the power to subjugate the colonial's environmental imagination simply by virtue of being admired. The risk of betraying one's own local reality increases, according to Walcott, only when we reify art and divorce it from its relationship to time; we fetishize masterpieces if we worship *or* reject them simply because they are Western. And the victim is the local landscape, which suffers a similar fate of being either disparaged or mistakenly praised merely because it is seen as out of step with the march of time.

What is important to remember, for Walcott, is "Time, petrified in every classic canvas, / denied the frailty of the painter's hand" (*TH* 43). Without an understanding of the ongoing task of responding to a dynamic and ever changing environment, its other life, we will forget the anguish all artists experience about what their hands and ultimately their art fail to capture. In contemplating art we must imagine Time's refusal to collapse into an ordered plot—a History—with a final ending. Once freed from the imperatives of History, the New World landscape becomes the vital source of inspiration for a New World art. As Whitman had argued, this means that the value of adamic artistic expression is not determined by means of determining its place in Western history but by its ecological place of origin, the physical and temporal particulars of each local landscape that impelled it into existence. In order to become more deeply attuned to the natural world the New World poet must learn to exorcize the specter of the past.

The Specter of the Past

Similar to what he previously intimated in *Another Life*, Walcott insists that Turner's image demonstrates that an empire in decline "turn[s] more spectral" because the focus is no longer on history but on light (*TH* 76). For a painter the word "spectral" suggests the effects of a declining sun, spreading the spectrum of color out across the water and the sky, precisely what the impressionists found so inspiring in Turner. The declining light of empire in the former colonies provides an added advantage for the artist:

> Separation only brings
>
> sharper definition, sun-startled angles
> of trunks over a small stream, bright corners
>
> we had not thought preserved. (*TH* 99)

But "spectral" assumes a more metaphorical meaning to a poet, since it implies that the possibilities for local beauty and wonder increase to the degree that the empire fragments. As discussed in the previous chapter, this interest in the "unguessed lovely inheritors" of colonialism's decline foments poetic opportunity in the Caribbean. This requires a detached interest in the past and a focused attention to present visual beauty, which is determined by time's shifting hand. To appreciate the present is to avoid the logic of what Glissant calls the West's linearity or what Walcott explains is the "idea of history which justifies and explains and expiates" (*What the Twilight* 64). If the detritus of the past, as Walcott argued about Crusoe, has provided the material for present beauty, appreciating such beauty is not an homage to that past but rather a way to root oneself in a particular place in the wake of a fragmented past and to lay the foundation for the future.

But a spectral empire has a third meaning; Walcott has here named the kind of disembodied ghost or visage that haunts Whitman when he contemplates the leaves of grass or Neruda when he rhapsodizes about ruins. The specter of the past promises a sacred root in the land but simultaneously sows seeds of uncertainty about New World authenticity and ownership of the present. A spectral past has the capacity to diminish one's metaphorical imagination in relation to one's home environment because of its call to document an undefined, unreachable, but necessary past. This additional meaning of "spectral" is suggested in the first book of *Tiepolo's Hound*, where Walcott introduces us to the nineteenth-century town of Charlotte Amalie in St. Thomas. He imagines the smells and sights of Dronningens Gade and Pissarro's Jewish childhood there, including "The Synagogue of Blessing and Peace and Loving Deeds," which Pissarro presumably attended. He also introduces us to the "mongrel" that he later contrasts with the hound he remembers seeing in a painting by Giovanni

Battista Tiepolo, an eighteenth-century Italian rococo painter. This opening poem concludes, however, by confessing the artificiality of Walcott's reconstructions:

> Their street of letters fades, this page of print
> in the bleached light of last century recalls
>
> with the sharp memory of a mezzotint:
> days of cane carts, the palms' high parasols. (*TH* 4)

His metaphors here suggest that whiteness of the page, in contrast to the black letters of his poetry, serves to make his memory legible. Like Neruda's comment regarding the fallen leaves and the new wine of his own memoirs, Walcott's point is that the past is unknown and forgotten. The letters, signs, and maps that would tell the story of the past on its own terms have faded, and the blank space of the past can only be filled with the imagination of art, like a white canvas with paint, or a printing plate engraved by memories, as in mezzotint.

In the next poem of this first section Walcott, who is in Trinidad thinking about Pissarro, witnesses a hauntingly similar scene. Through "wooden window frames" he notes that "a black dog crosses into Woodford Square," and he hears "tribal voices" emerging from a "stone church" nearby (*TH* 5). Given Walcott's location in Woodford Square in downtown Port-of-Spain, this is likely the Greyfriars Presbyterian Church, a church with "walls as bare as any synagogue / of painted images" (*TH* 5). He asserts:

> There was a *shul* in old-time Port of Spain,
> But where its site precisely was is lost
>
> In the sunlit net of maps whose lanes contain
> A spectral faith, white as the mongrel's ghost. (*TH* 5)

The Jewish past of Port-of-Spain is only vaguely recollected, and a black Protestant analogy must take its place because of the relentless forces of amnesia against which the brilliant confidence of a "sunlit net of maps" struggles.[2] This "exact perspective of loss" means that time's passage breaks experience into seemingly unrelated metonymic fragments of a lost whole, and the work of the artistic imagination becomes necessary, even inevitable (*TH* 8). Unlike art, maps and chronicles of the past exhibit historians' "spectral faith" by virtue of a confident reconstruction of the past. Their work points to a fixed reality that belies their own fictionalization of the irretrievable past. Time's movement makes history possible, but it also makes amnesia inevitable, since the significance of the present will never be fully captured or rescued from time's relentless flow.

Art becomes necessary, but it must not fall prey to the "spectral faith" of historiography. It can pursue the past as long as it recognizes the illusions of its imaginative work, or else the local landscape will suffer. Walcott seeks Caribbean roots and relations, Glissant's "concealed parallels in history," only to insist ultimately that roots are forged in the imagination, not discovered (*Caribbean* 60). The parallels he explores between Pissarro and himself, between Europe and the Caribbean, between the West and its colonies are attempts to make transparent connections, but they also demonstrate opaque failures. *Tiepolo's Hound* consistently explores its own spectral faith, but in the end, after an exorcism of these specters of the past, it abandons the pursuit and embraces the present landscape. "Spectre" then returns to its original register of meaning as aesthetic opportunity in the present made possible by a receding empire.

Ut Pictura Poesis I

As we saw in *Another Life*, Walcott's turn to poetry as his primary art was in part due to his growing conviction that painting alone cannot capture "the sociological contours" and the ambiguity of history's ironic layers within the Caribbean landscape (*CP* 148). In *Another Life* his turn to metaphor was the result of his incessant need to compare what he saw in the present environment with what had transpired in the past and elsewhere. His darting imagination led to the "crabbed" and "sideways crawling" expression of poetry (*CP* 201). In order to avoid the possibility of insulting the landscape by incessant comparisons, however, *Tiepolo's Hound* turns back to painting in order to transform this condition of "servitude" by means of ekphrasis. Ekphrasis, for Walcott, is aspiration for the union of word and image, which tends to portray the past and present as anachronistically simultaneous. Through ekphrasis he triangulates his relationship to land and can explore the dualities of his world with greater subtlety and freedom.

As Walcott continues to look out on Woodford Square on an empty and quiet Sunday he cannot keep his mind from wandering through several spaces and moments in time:

a frilled child with the hoop

of the last century, and, just as it was
in Charlotte Amalie, a slowly creaking sloop.

Laventille's speckled roofs, just as it was
In Cazabon's day. (*TH* 6)

Three images, apparently from the past century, converge here: a child with a hoop skirt, a sloop in the capital of St. Thomas when Pissarro lived there, and the image of Laventille, a neighborhood of Port-of-Spain in the time of Jean-Michel Cazabon, Trinidad's only painter of international acclaim from the nineteenth century. Walcott later describes the naturalism of Cazabon's work as "embalmed *paysages*" that "were all we had, / our mongrel culture gnawing its one bone" because Pissarro and so many other talented artists have chosen not to remain in the Caribbean (*TH* 154). Laventille's "speckled" corrugated roofs of today would seem to belie its continuity as a *sight* from the last century, unless we remember that Laventille is the birthplace of steel drumming in the hills of Port-of-Spain and thus the *site* of an invisible continuity of cultural memory. These "sociological contours" are made evident by the triangulated relation between Walcott's view from the window overlooking the square, Cazabon's depictions of the beauty and quaintness of colonial island life, and Pissarro's early development as a painter in the Caribbean. Walcott relates the present and the past, images and words, and what Pissarro became and what he might have been had he stayed in the Caribbean.

Chronology would suggest that Walcott's powers of perception have been colonized. He cannot resist, for example, seeing "brush-point cypresses / like a Pissarro canvas" (*TH* 6). He even seems to complain about the fact that "I kept seeing / things through [Pissarro's] eyes," and, by comparison, the Caribbean seems to "withdraw before his dream" (*TH* 154). But he is saved from the inferior servitude implied in such admiration by shifting from the chronological impulse of History to the synchronicity of Time. This involves triangulating Cazabon, Pissarro, and himself, which allows Walcott to share "the conviction their work carries" (*TH* 155). Using the same triangular logic, he asserts that "[l]earning / did not betray [his father's] race if he copied a warship's / berth, a cinder from a Turner sunset burning" because of the unifying fact of Turner's and his father's mutual devotion to rendering light (*TH* 13). In a recent interview Walcott explained this interest in light:

My theory about painting is principally light, the theory of light, physical light. This may certainly not apply to abstract representation at all, and therefore I can be a dinosaur in terms of what my opinion is, in terms of the kind of painting that I like to do. There can be a name for it which can be representational, or something. But all that vocabulary comes from the centers. That vocabulary comes from London and Paris and Berlin and wherever. Therefore, when I encounter that vocabulary I feel anger at the fact that my choices are being defined in decades, in centuries, by people who[m] I have nothing to do with, nothing in common with, basically. If someone in Berlin says "nobody paints like that anymore in Berlin, and what we are doing [is a new technique]," whatever that technique is, that is a chronological concept from history that includes art. In other words, "we have exhausted representation." Therefore I am supposed to fall in line, chronologically, with the evolution of an art, and I am old-fashioned in the sense that I am staying in the kind of a context that may be nineteenth century, that may be eighteenth century, or whatever. What I resist is the definition and chronology imposed on me by the center. . . . I consider myself blessed that I was never a part of that, being aligned to a particular school. ("Interview" [Handley] 99–100)

A hard-line postcolonialism might likewise dictate Walcott's choices by suggesting that he can only express himself outside the bounds of accepted tradition. He is not unaware of the risks of servitude that admiration of European art might imply:

Paintings so far from life fermenting around us!
The skeletal, scabrous mongrels foraging garbage,

the moss-choked canals, back yards with contending odours
purifying in smoke, then turn to a sepia page

from the canals of Guardi, from a formal battle with banners,
the carnival lances of Uccello's pawing horses,

to the chivalric panoply of tossing green bananas
and the prongs of the ginger lily. (*TH* 14)

The fifteenth-century historical frescoes of Paolo Uccello and the eighteenth-century landscapes of Francesco Guardi cause a clash of visual comparisons between the apparent paucity of "monuments, . . . battles, martyrs" in the natural and primitive Caribbean, to quote from "The Sea Is History," and the glory of European art (*CP* 364); St. Lucia's "moss-choked canals" contrast the beauty of Guardi's Venice, as do its "tossing green bananas" in comparison to the "lances" in Italian Renaissance depictions of war. But Walcott does not apologize for creating these colonial ironies because, as he asserts, "[n]o metamorphosis / was required by the faiths that made all one" (*TH* 14–15). The "faiths" are those of painting and poetry, which, although limited in different ways, share the calling to express exhilaration before present land and light.

Walcott's ekphrasis involves a fusion of these faiths to make this argument for unity. Paintings help us to see what his poems cannot reveal to us, and his poems help us to hear what the mute paintings fail to communicate. The couplets throughout the poem demonstrate this stitching together of worlds, as demonstrated in the following verse, tightly knit in meter and rhyme but seemingly undisturbed by its variety of geographical images:

> A hill town in Mantegna, afternoon light
> Across Les Cayes, and dusks of golden wheat,
>
> As pupils we need both worlds for the sight:
> A Troumassee's shallows at the Baptist's feet. (*TH* 14)

An image of a hill town in a painting by Andrea Mantegna, another fifteenth-century Italian fresco painter, flows into the afternoon light of Les Cayes, a port in Haiti, to the still darker twilight falling upon wheat fields, presumably in Europe, and finally to the Troumassee River and its pools located in St. Lucia near the Piton Peaks on the south end of the island. This last image is creolized by acting as an imagined setting for John the Baptist, which might be an image more appropriate for Mantegna, but it is not uncommon in the Catholic murals, for example, of Dunstan St. Omer. The faith that makes all these things one is the artist's faith in the joy that responds to light, hence the tight rhyme between "light" and "sight."

Not all of Walcott's couplets are so closely rhymed, however, and that becomes the real aural strength of the poem's unvarying metrical couplets. In the above example images that are perhaps on one level incongruous are reconciled harmoniously through sound. Later in the same section, however, we find an example of what becomes quite common throughout the poem, a kind of playful, loosely associative rhyme that helps to expose the artificiality of the poet's imagined harmonies. He writes:

[M]y joy would shout

to the stained air, my body's weight through it
lighter than a spinning leaf, my young head

chattering with birdsong, a bird-pecked fruit;
I saw how the dove's wings were eyed and spotted. (*TH* 15)

The rhyme here is creatively slant and relies on the word's visual appearance to complete the harmony that falls short aurally ("young head" and "spotted," "through it" and "fruit"). The fact that language's unique medium of sounds turns out also to be visual is a useful breakdown of the border between media that facilitates the fusion of the Caribbean's disparate fragments. The effect is one of loose association between a Caribbean dove— of which there are many native species, some with spotted wings—and the traditional biblical symbol for the Holy Ghost. This dove, in inspiring Walcott's natural joy, also instills in him a "lightness until my sins / crippled and caged me" (*TH* 15). Thus it is loosely paired with God's blessing after Jesus's baptism (also invoked with the earlier mention of the "Baptist"). Like the rhymes, the looseness suggests relation, but it neither redeems nor subordinates the bird by recalling its possible Old World meanings.

The unifying factor among competing artistic faiths, in sum, is art's subjection to Time. Walcott explains that the naive young artist at first believes in his own historical evolution into a master painter:

[Y]outh

feels it has the measure of Time, that there is a plot
and metre to Time, structured as if it were fiction,

with a beginning, a middle, and an end, except Time is not
narrative, triumph resolved by ambition,

and Time continues its process even for the masters
whose triumph astonishes us, but they are still learning

with arthritic fingers and shovel-wide beards, their disasters
our masterpieces. (*TH* 94)

Instead of imagining that one can climb a ladder of progressive triumphs, one must submit oneself to reality's inevitable triumph over art at all stages. Pissarro himself similarly once commented: "What good is it to look backwards and never at nature, so beautiful, so luminous and so diverse in character? Always in the dust of the old masters, which one pretends not to notice, on the pretext of venerating them. It seems to me that it is better to follow their example and seek those elements in that which surrounds us, with our proper senses" (qtd. in Adler 123). If the young artist understands himself to be an apprentice of light and not merely an apprentice of the masters, his work is no longer condemned to a permanently derivative status. This is one way to reimagine art history biocentrically or, if you will, heliocentrically. All art is understood in relation to Time's inevitable movement, which is marked by nature's changes both when the work was being painted and since its completion.

Such natural apprenticeship also rescues the work of art from becoming a mere artifact of history. As my discussion in chapter 2 of a New World poetics demonstrates, history will not prove interested in its own dynamic medium of time as long as it ignores the amnesiac force of natural ecological processes on human memory. To the extent that history wants conclusion and narrative structure and that it wants to be able to stand apart from the ongoing flow of time, history crudely concludes that the past is dead, as William Carlos Williams argues. To foster Williams's poetics of history, as we have seen in both Whitman and Neruda, it is not enough to remember the context of ongoing human choices and changes in human conditions; a poetics must include both social *and* ecological changes. This is especially important when art strives to offer a response to an elusive, living, and changing ecological reality. Walcott reverses the stultifying and stereotyping effects of art when it becomes conventional and cliché by portraying the masters still painting the landscape, with their "shovel-wide beards," as if they never died. The image recalls Neruda's similar historicization of Magellan with his "beard crawling with maggots" (*OC* 1:475; *Canto* 67).

Works of art, as Walter Benjamin once argued, risk this reified status when they are mechanically reproduced in catalogs of art, such as Craven's, which lay in Walcott's childhood home, and then seen in a transplanted context.

The tendency is for the works to become surrounded by an almost mystical aura. Landscape art obtains nothing more than a partial, fragmented, and incomplete response to a broader whole that surrounds and overwhelms an artist, but through repetitious promulgation the work is reduced to a visual cliché. These clichés then perpetuate habits of seeing nature that blind viewers from ever understanding the particulars of the places they inhabit. For Walcott liberation from such entrapments lies in remembering the "subject's subjection," which is the subjection of the eye to the temporality of natural change; if art's truest subject is the reality of nature's constant change, which it seeks to artificially arrest, art will of necessity fail, but fail meaningfully, since it engages in a hopeless fight against death. Even if one feels the determination, as he and St. Omer once did, to "get [the] true tints someday" (*TH* 94), it would be mere spectral faith to believe such truth is achievable. The lessons of time mean that success only lies in the "beat of a brush reaching / into its creamy palette, oranges, ochres" (*TH* 94); as impressionism exemplifies, what matters more than finished achievement is the *devotion* itself to rendering light.

For this reason, Walcott's interest in impressionism is not a symptom of the colonial's anxiety of influence but rather its self-healing solution. He comments that Cézanne's art, available in "museum missals" to the aspiring colonial,

> opened the gates of an empire
> to applicants from its provinces and islands,
>
> in the old argument that the great works we admire
> civilise and colonise us, they chain our hands
>
> invisibly. Museums seen as magnetic prisons
> for the gifted exile, the self-diminishing ceiling
>
> of a baroque glory more humbling than the sun's
> predictable blue,
> . . . .
>
> the paint is all that counts, no guilt no pardon,
>
> no history, but the sense of narrative time
> annihilated in the devotion of the acolyte,

> as undeniable as instinct, the brushstroke's rhyme
> and page and canvas know one empire only: light. (*TH* 57–58)

Or, as he puts it later in the poem, "[t]here is no history now, only the weather, / day's wheeling light, the rising and setting /seasons" (*TH* 71). The apprentice's devotion to light annihilates narrative time and its interest in plot and historical consequence. As Whitman discovered in his meditations on natural regeneration, devotion to cyclical, ecological time paradoxically frees the mind from the chains of servility. The "masters" become contemporaries in a world triangulated by light. The local landscape stands little chance of being ignored or insulted because the acolyte has now become servile to the contours of one's place in time and in the land.

Impressionism as New World Poetics

Because it is known for this kind of servility, impressionism provided an apt model for Walcott of how the New World artist can be freed of the constraints of the West. Impressionism grew out of a certain fatigue with the demands of nineteenth-century naturalism, which expected the artist to copy the natural world but with an allegorical aim. The impressionists generally did not worry about painting stories, allegorical or historical, or about producing painstakingly elaborated and self-contained compositions. Instead, they found their art in the perception of light in their immediate environment and sought to expose the prismatic quality of light when closely observed through brief passing moments. Time, for the impressionists, is the great law of nature, since it is what dictates change and shapes our perception of things in space. And in order to capture the play of light on the human eye in an instant, it was necessary to contemplate objects deeply and quickly, leaving aside the need for elaboration and even completion.

This desire for what Henri Bergson and others referred to as sensation or pure perception was expressed by Monet: "I have no other wish than a close fusion with nature, and I desire no other fate . . . than to have worked and lived in harmony with her laws. Beside her grandeur, her power, and her immortality, the human creature seems but a miserable atom" (qtd. in Goldwater and Treves 313). Monet's statement is a bit misleading because he and the other impressionists well knew that such an obliteration of the cultural baggage that we all carry from education, socialization, and memory was well nigh impossible. The impressionist painter had to work duplicitously, desiring, on the one hand, to fuse with nature while recognizing, on the other, the inevitability of making things conform to the work of the imagination.

Perhaps it is inevitable that impressionism did not have a very long life as an artistic practice, since this tightrope act of walking between realism and expressionism was bound to lose its balance. Impressionism wants pure perception, but it is aware, as the science of the day was beginning to discover, that the eye cannot see light as light per se but only as the reflection of light on the mind. As the late-nineteenth-century German scientist Hermann von Helmholtz put it, "If you like paradoxical expressions, you could say: light becomes light [only] when it meets a seeing eye; without that it is merely a movement of aether" (qtd. in Barasch 38). A growing sense of meaningful failure is the cumulative impression we gain of Monet's haystacks, or of Cézanne's Mont-Sainte-Victoire series from 1902 through 1906, which explores color and geometrical forms playing in the same physical space, or of the more aggressively varied attempts in Pissarro's work to depict the small rural village of Pontoise from all its infinite angles and climates in the 1870s.

So if we can at least understand Walcott's interest in impressionism and its usefulness in his context, why, then, Pissarro, of all the impressionists? Is it simply the convenient historical fact of his birth in St. Thomas in 1830, fully one century before Walcott's birth? His early artistic formation in the Caribbean? His identity as a Jew, a racial and Caribbean outsider in Paris? While these are of expressed interest to Walcott, Pissarro's particular aesthetics is of most value to the argument of *Tiepolo's Hound*, an aesthetics of "awe of the ordinary" that is perhaps more striking in Pissarro than in the other impressionists (8). Pissarro was a painter of enormous industry who painted thousands of works, drew thousands more sketches, and, despite his wide-ranging curiosity about various styles and techniques, was almost compulsively consistent in motif. He emerged from the nineteenth-century landscape traditions of France having inherited the belief once promulgated by the naturalists of the Barbizon school that nature, not the tradition of art, should determine one's style and that it was the artist's duty to find that *coin de la terre*, that corner of the earth, that would transmit its unique formal imprint to the work of the artist (Brettell 2). In Cézanne's opinion, Pissarro "had the good fortune to be born in the Antilles; there he learned to draw without a master" (qtd. in Adler 18). In that raw setting Pissarro "made many an excursion on foot, exploring his surroundings and sketching what he saw" (Adler 15).

When Pissarro first arrived in Paris in 1855 he caught the Exposition universelle, an exhibition of enormous size, and he was particularly struck by the modest landscapes of Camille Corot, whom he immediately sought out for guidance. Corot, unlike members of the Barbizon school, believed in the importance of painting directly in response to what one sees in plein air, as he later encouraged Pissarro to do. In his old age Pissarro later echoed to one young painter Corot's advice: "Don't proceed according to rules and principles, but paint what you observe and feel. Paint generously and unhesitatingly, for it is best not to lose the first impression. Don't be timid in front of nature: one must be bold at the risk of being deceived and making mistakes. One must have only one master—nature; she is the only one to be consulted" (qtd. in Adler 23).

But what perhaps sets Pissarro even farther apart from other impressionists is his dogged determination to pursue this faithfulness to immediate nature within a relatively small geographical space. One of his critics, Richard Brettell, writes in his assessment of Pissarro's years in Pontoise during the 1870s: "No landscape painter of the nineteenth century was more bounded, less geographically adventurous, than Pissarro" (37). He concludes: "Pissarro's landscape of the 1870s is among the most physically constricted in the history of art, rarely extending more than 500 meters from his doorstep" (Brettell 100). These Pontoise landscapes reveal a consistent refusal to depict landscapes within a totalizing frame or with any rhetoric of moralizing or allegorizing. They are simple, almost abrupt images of locations, chaotically organized, that refuse facile narrativization. As Brettell explains, "the lack of passion in Pissarro's landscapes underlies another reason for his preference for *coins* [corners] more than motifs. The *coin* lacks strong meaning: it is an odd, framed portion of an environment and is, by definition, part of a larger whole" (105). Walcott's own frequent iterations of praise for the trees, beaches, and ravines of his neighborhood in Gros Islet bear some resemblance to Pissarro's pointed devotion to provincialism.

Walcott explained his interest in Pissarro in this way:

The inner thing in him was not modest in the wrong sense, it kept its celebration, but it did not do it with distortion or with some thing that came out of an egotistical source. The category you would have to put him is a category in which the search is not for the true thing, or for an expression of identity, but as an absolute search for anonymity. That is what's there in Wordsworth, the annihilation of the "I" that is there in the presence of nature. ("Interview" [Handley] 105)

Walcott insists that Pissarro developed this adamic sensitivity to common, unanticipated beauty in the untutored outdoors of the Caribbean and that this Caribbean influence not only informed his work but spread to the many artists Pissarro tutored, including, of course, Cézanne. He writes:

Cézanne stayed close to two years in Pontoise,
attentive to his older friend's advice

to change his dingy palette to colours
brightened by his tutor's tropical eyes,

a different language for a different light,
more crystalline, more broken like the sea

on island afternoons, scorchingly bright
and built in prisms. He should learn to see. (*TH* 56)

Walcott further claims that this tropical sensibility influenced the "visible syntax" of Cézanne's own remarkable postimpressionist formalism, a style that would open the doors to visual modernism (*TH* 57). But Pissarro remained faithful to his humility: "There is something uxorious in Pissarro's landscapes / as if his brush had made a decorous marriage / with earth's fecundity" (*TH* 64). This excessive telluric devotion contrasts the overt expressionism of Cézanne, "whose / canvas rants at the subject it has chosen" (*TH* 64). Pissarro's art consistently avoids "[n]arrative excess" that "had made theatrical melodrama of great art," a virtue of anonymity in art that grows "with the acceleration / of time" (*TH* 64, 65). Eventually,

in moderation
of self, of fame, the art of being bored

diminishes conceit, and cherishes the plain
and the repetitive: light in the kitchen,

> cats coiled on chairs, and sunlight shot with rain,
> things without grandeur in their modest shine. (*TH* 65)

Time valorizes the modest self because what shines through the art is the paradoxically immortal value of transient and mundane nature. Walcott's and Pissarro's shared "awe of the ordinary," then, manages "to heighten the commonplace into the sacredness / of objects made more radiant by the slow gaze of time" (*TH* 98).

At the same time that he celebrates the possible Caribbean influence in the history of impressionism in France, Walcott is equally concerned with what the Caribbean lost when Pissarro decided to leave:

> My question was: What might have happened to his painting had he stayed
> in the Caribbean? Inevitably he would have produced masterpieces. And
> if those masterpieces were masterpieces of the Caribbean landscape,
> first of all wouldn't we be eager to grasp them as something belonging
> to us? And what might they have looked like if they were painted in the
> Caribbean? . . . I've always found it necessary to a Caribbean artist to
> remain rather than to go somewhere else. I don't insist on it, but I just
> have a feeling that if location of your gift is specific in terms of where
> you are, particularly in the visual arts, and painting, or even prose, but
> if every tendency is to finally abandon where you are from, then in a
> way you are denying your gift and what you might have made of it.
> There are practicalities . . . [but] it is not a matter of financial pressure or
> stuff like that; it is a matter of where you feel you belong. ("Interview"
> [Handley] 104)

The irony is that despite Pissarro's undeniable raw talent and seemingly native humility, his work in the Caribbean up to his departure for France did not exhibit much of the more creative and experimental expression that he learned from his contact with many of the more successful artists of France of the time. His humility, in other words, may have had its origin in the Caribbean, but it needed French training to realize itself. One work of particular interest that he painted during his first year in France is a depiction of the Caribbean, *Two Women Chatting by the Sea, St. Thomas,* from 1856. The work suggests a lingering fascination with Caribbean light even in his first months in France, but it also exposes the discrepancy between his rather overt moralistic naturalism in the Caribbean and the less allegorical impressionism he would develop later in France.

Walcott insists that Pissarro's origins were transmitted into the aesthetic triumphs of impressionism, but his departure from the Caribbean still causes us to wonder what were the costs of impressionism, what it ignored, betrayed, or abandoned in order to come into being. Walcott recognizes that not all Caribbean artists leave, that "others took root and stood the difference" that New World dislocation can make to an artist (*TH* 143). These were those who made themselves native to their second garden because they

> achieved a gratitude
> beyond their dislocation, saw what was given
>
> and seized it with possessed delight,
> . . . .
>
> and let the ship go, trailing its red banner
> out of their harbor, like *The Téméraire*.
>
> St. Thomas stays unpainted, every savannah
> trails its flame tree that fades. That is not fair. (*TH* 143)

Walcott uses Turner's portrait of the great ship heading to retirement to tell this story of departure, only this time it has been transformed into a symbol of a journey back to empire. Although the empire may be in decline and its art worthy of admiration and emulation, the problem of the Caribbean's artistic paint-drain still needs redressing. As Whitman had intuited over a century earlier, the adamic imagination can become alienated and drawn out of New World gardens of ordinary and local awe because of metropolitan charges of backwater provincialism; the result is a culture failing to realize itself.

The Mad Impressionist in the Attic

The power of this line of questioning is akin to Jean Rhys's portrayal of the Caribbean origins of Rochester's mad wife in *Jane Eyre* in her own brilliant tale, *Wide Sargasso Sea* (1966). The novel demonstrates the subtle ways European faith in narrative truth relies on a suppression of colonial relations. Similarly, Walcott undermines confidence in art history's narrative of impressionism by highlighting the movement's Caribbean origins and by triangulating Pissarro's art with Walcott's own paintings and with what "[Pissarro] would have made" had he remained (*TH* 143). This specter of what might have been loosens the solid ground upon which History makes its claims about Western masterpieces. This disruption occurs because Walcott's ekphrasis depends on triangulation between nature, the word, and the image and thus helps to destabilize the certainty of narrative truth, even Walcott's own. Visual references in his poetry rarely serve his texts, "literally, with a one-to-one correspondence" (Hamner 77), nor do they function merely as a way to "advance some aspect of the narrative" as complements to the literary (Terada 23). His use of ekphrasis is not simply aimed at using a linguistic metaphor for a visual representation; paintings by Turner, Pissarro, and others are themselves in turn already "textualized" by the traditions of museums, art history, and the subtle discourses of coffee table books and calendars like Craven's book, all of which "*usually* control the interpretation of images*" (Loizeaux 85). Walcott insists, however, that all art must be measured against Time, not History, which is to say it must be measured against the changing flux of its chief subject: the natural world.

One important example of how Walcott accomplishes this is when he anachronistically places himself within a painting by Pissarro and his Danish friend, Fritz Melbye. Walcott recalls his own visit to St. Thomas and imagines their presence in the landscape during the past century; he then transforms himself into one of the black figures that may have been their subject in the landscape: "I felt a line enclose my lineaments and those of other shapes around me too" (*TH* 140). He conforms to the demands of their artistic vision ("I shrank into the posture they had chosen") and becomes "a young slave, mixed and newly manumitted / last century and a half" (*TH* 141). This unusual maneuver triangulates the relationship in ekphrastic theory between word and image with a textual consciousness that lies behind the image and a visual consciousness that lies behind the word.[3] The binary of word and image is disrupted by imagining that the viewer is also the viewed Caribbean subject with its expressive qualities that cannot be reduced by objectification. In his poetic conflation of subject and object, past and present, and word and image Walcott exposes the betrayal of representation. He notes that despite the "kindness" of Pissarro's brush, "yours may just be love of your own calling / and not for us, since sunshine softens pain, / and we seem painless here." He finally pleads, as one of the subjects lost in the translation of Caribbean reality onto the artist's canvas, "do not leave us here, / for cities where our voices have no words" (*TH* 141). His ekphrastic moment here exposes how the betrayal plays itself out three times: first, because the subjects will not have a voice by virtue of being painted onto a silent, two-dimensional canvas; second, because this image of the Caribbean will then be transferred to a different light and environment in France; and third, because Walcott has himself relied on the same limitations of his own poetic representation to make this argument.

Triangulation introduces the specter of a haunting, unheeded subjectivity that undermines the solidity and fixity of Pissarro's painted image. This introduction of temporality within the image challenges conventional wisdom that visual representation is a more readily natural sign than metaphor. Poetry and painting are both subject to Time, so neither can ultimately satisfy "our semiotic desire for natural sign[s]" (Krieger 11). The Rhysian rhetorical effect of introducing an underlying Caribbean temporality in Western art, a haunting presence of margins at the very center of empire, keeps visual signs honest about their spatial and temporal limitations even if it means too that poetry must confess its own fictions.

We are led to ask, along with Walcott, "Are all the paintings then falsifications / of [Pissarro's] real origins, was his island betrayed?" (*TH* 143). And the answer is yes, because slippage is inevitable, of course, in all art, including Walcott's own. He admits that Pissarro's "drawing / is edged with a kindness my own lines contain" because he too shares a love of his calling that is perhaps greater than his love of the particulars of people's lives (*TH* 143).

But the answer to his question about betrayal is also no, since something truthful still manages to be transmitted across contexts and geographies in the work of an artist devoted to nature. In Walcott's imagined conversation with Pissarro the impressionist responds to the accusation of betrayal:

He said, "My history veins backwards
to the black soil of my birthplace, whose trees

are a hallowed forest; its leaf words
uttering the language of my ancestors,

> then, for ringed centuries, a helpless dimming
> of distance made both bark and language fade
>
> to an alphabet of bats and swallows skimming
> the twilight gables of Dronningens Gade." (*TH* 142)

Rootedness, signified so frequently in Walcott's poetry by the presence of talking ancestral trees, is weakened by the passage of time, by the experience of sometimes violent transplantation, and consequently the ancestral voices dim to the sound of birds. Nature, in other words, is all that remains of ancestral memory, whether one is a displaced African in the New World or a twice-displaced Jew who in his journey to France crosses "the deep reversing road / of the diaspora, Exodus" (*TH* 30). Walcott suggests that Pissarro's continued devotion to painting the natural world with kindness and humility in France was a tribute to the "black soil of [his] birthplace." The untranslatable language of nature and the elusive shifts of the sun's light form genealogy links without hierarchies among the Americas and between Old and New Worlds.

Ut Pictura Poesis II

The relationship between painting and poetry has not always implied the kind of openness to raw and ordinary nature that we find in Walcott's New World view of impressionism. Since the classical world the relationship between the two arts has been debated. By the nineteenth century some romantics asserted that both poetry and painting shared a common devotion to capturing the best of nature, even to compensate for nature's imperfections. This idea, most strongly advocated during the late eighteenth century by the painter Sir Joshua Reynolds, president of England's influential Royal Academy, and before him by the seventeenth-century poet John Dryden, led to a romantic tendency to allegorize nature, to depict it typologically rather than to expose its more mundane, natural state. This defense became necessary because, as Reynolds explained, if painting is understood merely as an imitation of nature, "painting must lose its rank and be no longer considered as a liberal art and sister to poetry, this imitation being merely mechanical, in which the slowest intellect is always sure to succeed best" (qtd. in Landow 52). The anthropocentrism in this critique denigrates humanity's attention to the contours of place. Reynolds understands "nature" as scenery, as a flat, timeless object that needs History and allegory to dignify it.

Walcott's New World poetics prefers to think of imitation of raw reality as the dynamic moment in which the artist always and forever remakes himself in the context of a reality that cannot be reduced, demythologized, or objectified. For this reason Walcott insisted in "The Caribbean: Culture or Mimicry?" that "awe is deeper than the articulation of awe" and that "a pygmy is better than an atheist" (57). The romantic desire to elevate painting to the level of poetic expression of inner states of noble thought and feeling eventually proved contradictory because of its reliance on this kind of flattened and ultimately knowable nature, a reality that in the end many romantics deemed not worth knowing. As Landow explains, "the gradual shift from the imagination as maker of images to the imagination as creator of emotional states or sympathies tended to divide the two allied arts" (74).

Walcott returns to the more traditional idea of the imagination as creator of images that, it must be confessed, fall short of "another life, real, indifferent, [that] resumes" after the work of representation (CP 200). Nature's independence and elusiveness, in other words, stimulates more intensive artistic searching and, in his case, greater interdependency between the two arts. This fundamental fact of nature's independent motions can only be observed when the artist is determined, against all odds, to follow the motions of light. I quote Walcott at length on the centrality of nature in artistic production:

If you took certain poets out of their locale, if you uprooted them, then you would really be deracinating them from something very profound in their spirit. If you took Hardy out of his countryside and Faulkner out of his acres, then you would have a different person. So the growth that happens in terms of a poet and a place is not quite the same as a painter and a place, but it's close, and it's unlikely that you would feel a severe detachment if one was a painter only. Or that I, even as a poet, would feel that if I lived somewhere else I don't have to remember the landscape or even the streets I grew up in when I was younger. It is really, ultimately, in everything that is provincial, that the area that is around an artist is really a very small area, although he can have a world vision, a huge vision of things that can happen, the intimate experience remains very strict and very provincial. . . . It seems to me to be increasingly difficult, more and more difficult, to render light, and by light, to render lineaments. That is one of the toughest things in the world, and it looks like one of the easiest. Because, why is it that a prose passage from Hemingway next to a prose writer using almost the same words, almost in the same order, doesn't catch it? That's what I consider to be the peak of effort. Not to render things as they are exactly, but to somehow illuminate them by the simplicity of what the vocabulary may be, or the thought may be. The simplicity I am talking about is a striving, that Rilke described in terms of saying that if I had the ability to name things over, I would be able to say "loaf," "bread"—it's the same principle actually as the Adamic idea of renaming. That is a poetic principle. To name something. It takes a particular instant of illumination that might make those words suddenly have a clarity and a validity and a presence that they didn't have before, even if they still sound the same, come from the same vocabulary. And that is what is the greatness and it is a gift actually. I think it is a special, and I think I am brave enough to say, almost divine gift that that illumination can happen with the simplicity of what we are given. ("Argument" 139; "Interview" [Handley] 99–100)

The paradox is that the more devoted one is to rendering light and lineaments in the physical environment, the more the artist discovers his own outline, the precise dimension of his own separation from the world. This is true especially when the artist has committed to being shaped profoundly by place. As Whitman had urged in *Democratic Vistas*, Walcott insisted on nurturing his own poetry in those years on the physical extravagances of Caribbean skylines, the moods of the sea, and the island's villages. This aided him in avoiding strictly mimetic results in his willingness to absorb metropolitan influences. He became more creative and original, and ultimately more expressionistic, to the extent that he turned his imitations away from literature and toward the physical world.

If one's aesthetic is like that of the impressionists, who refused to allegorize nature into a symbol of the past, it also means turning away from Old World orientation and from History in the interest of the present. Neruda faced the dilemma of orienting himself according to the implications of natural regeneration and deep time, and while this offered him adamic poetic renewal, it also implied the difficult choice of choosing the present over a lamentable or neglected past. Similarly, for Walcott, if the painter needs to pay close attention to light, Time unburdens him of History but also limits the painter's ability to capture the "sociological contours" of society.

Pissarro's decade-long stay in Pontoise demonstrates this point. Brettell recounts that the medieval history of the historical Pontoise was largely ignored until the late nineteenth century, when several historical tourist guidebooks were published that encouraged locals and visitors alike to become more familiar with the town's deep history. The only problem was that there was little visual evidence of this ancient history, allowing the so-called historians to exaggerate and mythologize this past and leading Brettell to conclude that there were "two separate Pontoises: an historical Pontoise and an actual or 'new' Pontoise" (16). Only the latter interested Pissarro, but, paradoxically, this resulted in his carefully measured distance from the life of the town. Brettell explains: "Pissarro was a hoverer on the edge of activity, much like his more intensely isolated pupil-colleague Cézanne. . . . He looked *at* Pontoise rather than *into* it," and this "in spite of more than a decade of intense interaction" (55–56, 201). So even though Pissarro had the potential to become intimately familiar with his *coin de la terre*, it was only an environmental and visual intimacy that ultimately had little to do with the "sociological contours" of the place. Even such devotion to see the land on its own terms, however, moved the artist to become more idiosyncratic. Brettell explains: "It is clear that he tried to abandon himself to the reality of Pontoise. . . . Yet the remainder of his career in that town had progressively less to do with Pontoise and more to do with various concepts of construction and order" (201).

The lesson in Pissarro's paradoxical failure to abandon himself to a place is that presentism not only turns away from history but also eventually evolves away from nature as its subject. This perhaps explains the historical evolution in art toward greater abstraction and self-referentiality. Poetry has a similar self-alienating tendency but for different reasons. Its element is metaphor, and therefore it arguably is not as directly tied to the environment as painting. Its tendency is to compete with History for formulations of the deep past that inform the present. This can reach the point, as Walcott has argued, where the present becomes totally uninteresting and irrelevant to the poet. The past becomes a phantasm and an obsession, a haunting other that forever escapes the grasp of the poet. This raises a crucial and fundamental question: Can culture retain its most profound connections to the physical environment, or must increasing alienation be the rule? For Walcott, impression is only useful as a New World poetics if the artist can sustain a dialectic between painting and poetry.

In *Tiepolo's Hound* these binaries blur, and their extreme effects are tempered. Impressionism's sweeping indifference to history is given expression in the poem's ekphrastic descriptions and simultaneously contextualized by the poem's historical interrogations. Additionally, the poet's own paintings serve as reminders of the Caribbean present his poetic musings must not forget. The American edition of the book is both a book of poetry and a catalog of paintings (the British edition contains no paintings), complete with painting titles, one-sided offset images, and headings of each book and section with both words and a gray brushstroke, signifying the merger of image and word. The paintings have varied levels of relevance to the passages that surround them, but, generally speaking, their connection to Walcott's poetic language is loose; they are never entirely independent of his metaphorical work, and they are never mere visual illustrations of the text.

With the exception of the paintings by Gauguin, which strive more overtly for metaphorical meaning, and perhaps Walcott's own self-portrait, the paintings are mundane scenes, framed with as little self-consciousness as possible and imbued with honest gratitude for the moment and place before him. Twenty-one of the twenty-six paintings are scenes in St. Lucia, and more than half are watercolors, a medium that Walcott argues in the poem expresses "reticence" and a "fragile delight" (*TH* 12). They are largely hymns to his own Pontoise. They echo the words about Walcott's home in St. Lucia that also accompany a seascape painted from his backyard: "This is my peace, my salt, exulting acre: / There is no more Exodus, this is my Zion" (*TH* 162). They signify his own prodigal return to the place of his origins, to that black soil and to those Caribbean trees that, though transplanted and bearing the weight of a broken past, are "true to their sense of place" (*TH* 62). From the very beginning of the poem the paintings interrupt the story with evidence of its conclusion, evidence of a conviction and a determination to paint the visible beauty of the Caribbean that Pissarro left behind.

Most of the poem's ekphrastic moments act "like a sort of unapproachable and unpresentable 'black hole' in the verbal structure, entirely absent from it, but shaping and affecting it in fundamental ways" without reliance on visual images (Mitchell 3). The paintings likewise do not rely on verbal work; they present themselves as a parallel but distinct aesthetic world. They resist the logic of the narrative because they have no narrative, they tell no stories, and they have no apparent chronology or narrative order. Walcott simultaneously insists on the inherent limitations of the different media and yet questions facile and essentialist assumptions about those differences. Just when we sense a narrative logic between the paintings and the poem, as, for example, in the case of Walcott's first painting of Gauguin, which appears precisely when he portrays Gauguin in verse, or the painting of his daughter Anna that appears when he re-creates the imagined death of Pissarro's daughter, we find ourselves searching again. For example, Walcott's 1992 watercolor, *Musicians*, an informal portrait of St. Lucian musicians playing indoors (we only know it is St. Lucia because a cut-off painting on the wall of the room in which they are playing portrays half of the Pitons), appears in the middle of Walcott's recounting of Pissarro's sense of failure. The apparent disjuncture is jarring, but precisely for this reason it provides fruitful insight. In this case, Pissarro's internal doubts are placed opposite the painting:

> Banish the island from your mind completely,
> its zebra patterns of palm light and shade,
>
> the rain-glazed drizzles of Charlotte Amalie,
> and the slave voices down Dronningens Gade.
>
> The slaves practiced obeah. Was he cursed
> For abandoning the island? (*TH* 80)

The often seemingly unrelated images create the impression of a New World aesthetic and cultural life that Walcott himself has pursued as a disciplined plein air painter and that might have been available to Pissarro. The contrast between the poetry and the paintings is particularly powerful, for example, when we compare the simplicity of the Gros Islet church, close to Walcott's home and twice portrayed in his paintings, with the "secular luxury of vice" that he imagines Tiepolo before him witnessed everywhere in the religious architecture and setting of Venice, "a beauty . . . so far beyond nature in her artifice" (*TH* 118). By contrast, the image shows how the late afternoon yellows and oranges of the sun suffuse the entire scene, reflecting off the clouds behind the palms and emerging in the palm leaves, the grass and dirt, and even the trunks of the trees. While light and color are radiant and purify the scene with their blessing, the foreground is littered with a rusted garbage can and broken and scattered appliances on the grass and an unfinished cinder block building on the right. Unlike the idea of a Tiepolo cathedral, the church is embedded in an environment that is neither luxurious nor completely natural but altogether familiar and intimate as a place.

Some paintings have their references, it would seem, in other parts of the poem, creating a kind of stitched, pastiche effect in the relationship between the images and the words. For example, we see the painting *Doctrine*, a watercolor from 1991 depicting two Rastafarians teaching two white women in their bathing suits, almost forty pages before we read a reference to Rastafarian preachers, a delay that allows us to recall the image seen earlier. The poetry is not directed at the painting per se, as they never are, but draws upon it and seems to justify its presence in the book. In this later section Walcott's poetry functions as a way of ascribing more historical and metaphorical significance to the New World religion and the ironic clash between such native newness as Rastafarianism and the tourist trade. He writes of the contrast between the image of these self-made priests, who "have not seen Dürer's panels: Four Apostles, / not the Moorish princes of the Renaissance" (*TH* 132). Their ignorance of European art and their absolute originality is what he praises; they are, more to the point of the poem, "figures not Veronese's or Tiepolo's" (*TH* 132). That is, they are not echoes, nor are they haunted by European spectres. Walcott also sees

> [o]n the beach a young tourist with her head inclined
> toward an infant she cradles in her arms
>
> is a Fra Angelico in a blue wraparound, as the wind
> begins the incantations of pliable palms. (*TH* 132)

The tourist, perhaps because of her presumably non-Caribbean origins, lends herself more easily to European parallels, and while this initially seems like a contrast of irony, Walcott concludes that the priests and the tourist and everything surrounding them are all New World subjects worthy of his art:

> [E]verywhere a craft confirming images,
> from a nosing mongrel to a challenging ceiling

of cloud. The mind raised on mirages
sees my father's copy of storm gulls wheeling. (*TH* 132)

The "mirages" are the paintings of European masters, like Turner, reflected through the lens of his own father's admiration for them. European masterworks are not haunting spectres because Walcott first came to know the imitations and reproductions, not the originals, and consequently the only question that interests him is whether art is true to the subject, not to its models.

Again we see how triangulation disrupts otherwise demoralizing binaries. Walcott continues:

Vessel, apprentice and interpreter,
My own delight, before the frames of Time,

Was innocent, ignorant and corruptible
Monodic as our climate in its sublime

Indifference to seasonal modulations,
To schools, to epochs. (*TH* 132)

Unlike the "crabbed" work of writing poetry, which made him feel he had to choose between schools and epochs in *Another Life*, the monody of the Caribbean environment before the easel, its redundant seasons of drought and rain, its stark tropical distinctions allow Walcott freedom to be anachronistic rather than submitting himself to the chronological evolutions of a culture of four seasons. The visual evidence of the achievements of such innocence is his *Pasture, Dry Season*, an oil from 1998 that lies on the opposite page from this passage. It depicts a scene of a coastal stretch that includes Pigeon Point very near Walcott's home during the Caribbean's dry season. The colors are muted browns and blues, with traces of the evergreen of casuarinas in the distance. Like so many of his paintings, it is ordinary and uneventful, but, paradoxically, its emptiness is precisely what elates; cows relax in the hot sun, and there is a faint trace of a dirt road.

The movement from "vessel" (Craven's book and other transmitters of tradition) to "apprentice" (Walcott's father's and his own imitation of those reproductions) to "interpreter" (his own poeticization of European art and his paintings of the Caribbean landscape) is not an evolution but a triangulation, since all three roles are filtered through his poetic imagination, acting equally and simultaneously on each other. The innocence he stresses here is not without risk because his openness to tradition also meant that he was "corruptible." Walcott's safeguard is to recall art's adamic purpose, which is not to civilize but to function as "an index of elations; / it ignored error, it trusted its own eyes" (*TH* 132). His own historical fascination with Pissarro, like his obsession with the hound he remembers seeing in a painting but can never place in art history, ultimately leads him to denounce history, since in playing the three roles simultaneously

> what is crucial was not the true ascription
> to either hand—rather the consequence
>
> of my astonishment, which has blent this fiction
> to what is true without a change of tense. (*TH* 133)

A change of tense implies priority and evolution, but instead he has subjected himself to Time, to an eternally changing, ever present physical world that communicates to the senses. This New World poetics allows him to join tradition but also to create something new. In the end he is uninterested in the creator of the hound that has haunted him, since he knows the creator is his own poetic imagination. This signifies the alleviation from the weight of such historical questions about Tiepolo and the sixteenth-century Italian artist Paolo Veronese or about Pissarro's Caribbean traces and the development of impressionism.

The poem resists becoming historical or merely narrative in its trajectory because it points us to what must be seen. What we see, however, is not what the poem refers to. Because we never see images of the great masters (and we, like Walcott, certainly never catch sight of that dog!), we must conjure their images by means of a poetic imagination; we learn to read with a visual imagination, in other words, and see with a poetic one. The paintings accrue value from their context within Walcott's frequently reiterated aesthetic values and his historical explorations. We come to see his paintings within a more deeply conceived sociological and temporal context.

In the midst of a discussion of his own efforts at painting in St. Lucia and his awareness of "the old result / of vigorous approximation" (*TH* 97) Walcott places an oil of the Gros Islet church, this time from the front. One senses the motion of wind in the scattered and wispy clouds, the angles of greens and yellows in the trees, the slanting shadows of the sun, and the figure leaning to the left in the foreground as she sits on a crooked piece of concrete. Another moment of stillness captured in the midst of uneventful but constant change in light, air, and perspective. Directly facing the image on the opposite page we find these confessional lines:

> More failures stare through their frames, accusing corpses
> erect in their coffins, a dead light in their eyes,
>
> as you, their silent murderer, conduct your autopsies.
> Outside them the ocean is mixing its different dyes. (*TH* 98)

The play on the word "dyes" here encapsulates the aesthetic theory of the poem, since getting it right, finding the right colors to express the temporal reality before him, leads inevitably to a kind of death or dying of that reality. Nature—here the ocean's blues—continues its own mixing of colors and rearranging of elements, which betrays the "vigorous approximation" of Walcott's final product. In this sense, all paintings are still lifes or, in the French, *nature morte*, "dead nature," and express the fragile temporality of life. So art is a response to nature's perpetual dying, but it also perpetually dies as an effort to forestall change. Adamic renewal is perpetual and inevitable. Walcott stresses this point:

> I painted this fiction
> from the hound's arch, because over the strokes and words
>
> of a page, or a primed canvas, there is always the shadow
> that stretches its neck like a spectral hound, bending
>
> its curious examining arc over what we do,
> both at our work's beginning and at its end
>
> a medieval *memento mori*, or a bow with his arrow
> at a dog-eared page or blank canvas, for every artisan
>
> a skull and a pierced heart. This was true for him now, Pissarro,
> as it was in the still lifes of his friend Cézanne. (*TH* 50)

The spectral hound, like a spectral history, haunts by implied comparison to an original that can't be found. The hound is a sign of self-doubt, but it is not an incapacitating doubt because Walcott transforms it from a spectre of an original, of a source or model that is to be imitated and against which one is measured, to a spectre of doubt caused by the inevitability of death and change. Artists doubt themselves not because of the masters they fail to match in achievement but because of the inevitability of failure dictated by natural change. One paints precisely because of that awareness, since the evanescence of things inspires love even if it results in death. We love and cherish what we know is only temporary and passing. Walcott depends on this love in his moving plea for mercy at the poem's conclusion:

> There is another book that is the shadow
> of my hand on this sunlit page, the one
>
> I have tried to write, but let this do;
> Let gratitude redeem what lies undone. (*TH* 158)

The shadow of his hand is created by the light behind him, the temporality within which he moves and within which the scene before him moves. Note the pairing of the "shadow" with "do," signifying that what is done, the "one," must be measured against what is "undone." His own temporality is the one thing he cannot represent; it is the space that light and art cannot illuminate. Rather than hide behind this curtain, he confesses his hand, literally, in the work he has produced. Like Shakespeare's Prospero, Walcott confesses the artificiality of his art and hopes that gratitude for what he has been able to accomplish, gratitude for the awe the light inspires, will redeem his artistic failures.

This could be considered an absolutely brilliant poetic flourish to excuse or cover up the weaknesses of Walcott's visual art, most notably, his rather predictable color schemes, his routinized stylizations of sea almond trees, and his seemingly unbending stylistic variation. Walcott has not denied the likelihood that his art does not match the brilliance of his poetry, but perhaps precisely because his art has not been canonized, he is allowed to at least argue against the logic that would criticize his art, or that of any other Caribbean artist, simply on the basis of certain European biases and preferences determined without regard for the particularities of Caribbean experience.[4] Historical debates rob us of "the whole / delight of action"

(*TH* 97) in the artistic process and shield from our view the keen anguish of every artist who, like Walcott, "settle[s] before an easel to redeem the fault / that multiplies itself in desperate survival" (*TH* 98).

Art is both its own wound and balm, particularly as artists accept the adamic task of rendering the world as if seen for the first time. The inevitability of natural change and death was certainly the subject of Caravaggio's and Cézanne's still lifes and presumably of Walcott's own landscapes. However, his poetic discourse on the limitations of art and on history stimulates our capacity to imagine the paintings as expressions of self-questioning and anguish before the fragility of the natural world. Akin to Neruda's hesitant embrace of the implications of deep time, the fragility of the world is made evident because of a cautious dismissal of the claims of the past. Walcott achieves this by playing with the possibility of a collapse between image and word, fact and fiction, present and past, Old World and New, culture and nature. The differences remain, however. When nature is our central desire and obligation as a culture, we can begin to find reasons for elation because the boundaries that separate these dichotomies temporarily blur, without being collapsed, in the garden of the world. As Walcott writes:

These little strokes whose syllables confirm
an altering reality for vision

on the blank page, or the imagined frame
of a crisp canvas, are not just his own.

I shift his biography as he shifted houses
in his landscapes. (*TH* 70)

If such mergers are disallowed, if we would judge such transgressions as violations, as arrogant or naive pretenses, we condemn New World places, its people, and its art to secondary status or, worse, to oblivion, since we imply they are unworthy of our gaze. Such a stance prohibits the possibility of elation and of finding a home in the New World. The dialogue between these binaries throughout the poem is always triangulated by time, allowing us to see this third possibility. We see Walcott's painting, for example, of Gros Islet church and see in the mind's eye a painting that could have been in addition to the one we see; in the discussions of Pissarro's St. Thomas and Pontoise we imagine a possible Pissarro who did not come to pass in the Caribbean. But since all spaces, all light are made worthy by the "gaze of time" and the heightened awareness of evanescence that it inspires, they are worthy of the gaze of the artist. Learning to see nature as if for the first time makes art not only possible but necessary, but never more necessary than nature itself.

The worst crime is to leave a man's hands empty.

Men are born makers, with that primal simplicity

in every maker since Adam.

DEREK WALCOTT, *Omeros*

CHAPTER 9

Death, Regeneration, and the
Prospect of Extinction

Derek Walcott's persistent interest in visual art is just one of the many facets of a wide-ranging eclecticism that is characteristic of his New World poetics. This poetics democratically cannibalizes multiple influences in the name of simplifying the poet's elemental adamic contact with the natural world. While Walcott's poetry has always been difficult to define in terms of periodization and style, those who believe that this is a flaw in his poetry typically know little about the various strands of Caribbean culture that make its culture so difficult to place within neat chronologies of "isms" and manifestoes or so difficult to settle on a unitary vision of land and history. The influence of geography is paramount, as Paula Burnett explains:

A region such as the Caribbean, fragmented as its communities are, geographically on small islands, historically by dislocation from ancestral communities, and culturally in terms of language, race, class, and background, nonetheless also exhibits shared sensibilities, its hugely various people having more in common than they have dividing them. It is therefore a case of both difference and sameness, simultaneously. It involves the recognition of otherness specifically as the point of sameness, of identification—of what I choose to call the sharedness of difference. (18)

Caribbean geography itself manifests this paradox of shared difference with its diverse and mutual isolation of lands. The sea provides the only link of commonality among the islands, but this potential unity is forged by an intuitive connection to the immensity of nature that the sea expresses. It will be remembered that Chile's insular geography and culture was similarly part of what motivated Neruda to seek communion across the Americas. The difference, however, is that much of the racial, religious, and cultural contributions to the New World is evident internally on the Caribbean's various islands. This means that a New World cultural unity can be imagined locally. The seemingly limitless physical environment evident in the sky and sea surrounding the islands provides the context within which Caribbean cultural diversity is projected, making for a rather pronounced geographical and biocentric notion of cultural possibility. While he begins with a more keen awareness of the ironies of New World transplantation of diverse peoples than do Whitman or Neruda, Walcott comes to similar conclusions regarding the sea as the radically expansive, regenerative natural space within which to imagine our human place. As I discussed in chapter 6, Walcott insists that the sea "is not elegiac" and that it "does not have anything on it that is a memento of man." He adds: "There is a strength that is drawn from island peoples in that reality of scale in which they inhabit. There is a sense both of infinity and acceptance of the possibility of infinity, which is strong. And in a way that provides a kind of endurance" ("Interview" [White] 159).

Under conditions of geographical isolation, marine circumference, and cultural fragmentation it is understandable why, as Paul Breslin argues, we find elements of romanticism, Victorianism, modernism, and postmodernism in Walcott's work, a kind of "transhistorical simultaneity" that allows him to absorb and borrow from various influences (292). This simultaneity parallels the effect of triangulation articulated in *Tiepolo's Hound*, as I have just discussed. In reference to Romare Bearden's work, Walcott explains that comparisons to earlier artists are helpful, but only if "they are *simultaneous* concepts, not *chronological* concepts. . . . If you think of art merely in terms of chronology, you are going to be patronizing to certain cultures. But if you think of art as a simultaneity that is inevitable in terms of certain people, then Joyce is a contemporary of Homer (which Joyce knew)" ("Reflections on Omeros" 240–41).

My reader will recall my discussion of a New World poetics of reading in chapter 3. I suggested that this poetics means understanding literature as a dialectic between creation (*poiesis*) and revelation. Walcott's Borgesian notion here of simultaneity is one way of articulating the requisite search that leads us back not to a notion of the author's authentic creations but to literature's fissures and gaps, which will possibly reveal glimpses of the reality of New World nature and experience. For this reason Walcott "seeks wholeness by including everything; it is not surprising that so many Caribbean readers, from José Martí to Walcott himself, have forgiven Walt Whitman his journalistic cheerleading for the Mexican War and admired him as the North American poet of inclusion" (Breslin 293). This openness to the simultaneity of tradition springs from an appreciation of the mixtures of the Americas. Walcott notes: "What religion is not a mélange? What culture is not a mélange? In that sense, the first impulse is referential—what I have called the free-form choice—is not to verify the sources, but to accept the references, however 'wrong' they may be. And that to me is very 'New World'" ("Reflections on Omeros" 243).

This New World poetics of inclusiveness, which informs this study, stems for Walcott from his tentative but persistent faith in some form of transcendent meaning. Although a skeptic mind, Walcott is sufficiently skeptical regarding what Breslin calls the self-congratulatory and insistently "cool ironic comfort with the impossibility of truth" implied in postmodernism to have developed something akin to religious faith. "Walcott includes in his work," Breslin writes, "a longing for unity, authoritative truth, and poetic transcendence, but also a knowledge of all the reasons why those things turn out to be illusory" (294). Walcott was raised by a devout and believing Methodist mother and, as discussed in chapter 7, experienced something of a religious calling at a young age in relation to his artistic aspirations.

Throughout his life, albeit with marked reticence, he has referred to the act of writing poetry as a form of internalized spiritual meditation and focus, in short, as a form of prayer. Although incapable of Dunstan St. Omer's plunging faith in God and in art, as discussed in chapter 7, Walcott nevertheless found nature's silent indifference a space where his poetry could intuit the reconciliation of things. In a 1987 unpublished autobiographical essay entitled "Inside the Cathedral" Walcott recounts that even though he did not share St. Omer's more sectarian devotion, which resulted in several church murals, "I had this to believe in: light and nature. We lived on an island with a light that had never been painted, and I had for my freedom, my universality, a larger cathedral than any St. Omer could enter, the sky and the moving floor of the sea. My unpainted walls were not the bored stones of the cathedral, but the virgin zinc of huge clouds, sunsets larger than Tiepolo's" (12–13).

As was the case for Whitman and Neruda as well, imagining himself as the poetic Adam in the garden of the world allowed Walcott to avoid the exclusivity of sectarian belief. Neruda never stated any belief in a deity during his life, but, as we saw, his nature poetry became so deeply infused by his mysticism that it is hard to miss his own intensely spiritual sensibilities. It seems to have been one of Walcott's first poetic impulses to be Adam seeking the divine in the profane world of nature instead of on the pew, as evidenced in his first published poem at the age of fourteen. In the poem Walcott wrote of his wish that "my wanderings among the quiet woods / Be my first lesson from the Holy book! . . . In what happy state I would then be / As our first father was—alive and free" ("Offending" 3). A subsequent sharp criticism was published, in verse no less and notably inferior to Walcott's adolescent attempt, by a local Catholic priest. A priest chided the boy for failing to recognize that "God wills that man should hear from man / The truths of faith that led above" (3). The incident stung the young Walcott and only increased his conviction, as he wrote in "Inside the Cathedral," that, given the Joycean "forked road: that of becoming either an artist or a priest," he would choose the more heretical route. His notion of an adamic poetics, then, though borrowing from the language of sacred literature, is a revision of the Christian myth, one that allows the poet an openness beyond any singular cultural and religious tradition (Walcott, "Inside" 4).

It became increasingly apparent to Walcott that, once unmoored from the sectarian pew, the particulars of his belief would become more and more difficult to define even as he remained committed to cultivating a spiritual sensibility in his work. In the conclusion of "Inside the Cathedral," for example, he finds St. Omer finally painting inside the cathedral of Castries, an act that had been dreamed of by the two when they were much younger and that was imagined to be simultaneously an act of high devotion and a usurpation of the priest's exclusive control over religious sensibility and meaning. Walcott ends the essay by noting, "I could feel that he felt my pride and joy in his standing on the rail of the loft, looking down with his grin of eternal friendship on the pews, the altar, and the years we had worked hard together, believing in the same thing: AMDG." These initials, signifying "ad majorem Dei gloriam" [to the greater glory of God], are frequently found in Walcott's notebooks and indicate his abiding belief in the necessity of the "subject's subjection," as he put it in the same essay. But subjection to what exactly?

As the previous chapter suggests, Walcott opted for subjection to light, to the temporal dynamism of a natural intelligence. His religious sensibility includes an abiding skepticism that nevertheless does not lead to a disavowal of belief. Walcott's frequent doubts, in Emily Dickinson's words, are what keep "believing nimble." His skepticism functions as a decidedly antidogmatic approach to religiosity that allows his poetry to speak rhetorically on behalf of the many beliefs and cultures in the Caribbean and in his own genealogy. But what is more, and this is more to the point, his doubt simultaneously stimulates a view of nature as infused by mystery and awe. He seeks immanence in nature and instead finds imminence; that is, while he holds forth the notion that the divine, whether God or the gods, stands above or behind what Calvin once called the shining garment of the world, it is also true that nature conceals this supernatural story. In its immense finitude nature holds an infinity always about to be revealed but not yet vividly apparent or decided. Walcott wants to believe in the idea of the divine in nature but not in any sectarian sense; the point is to see it for what it can only tantalize us with but cannot reveal. This imminence also means that nature can function as an ambiguous repository and memorial site of the past as well as the starting point for bringing the New World's plurality of cultures together. The lessons of ecology, as we have already seen, become the structure of his historical vision. Many critics have noted how Walcott refuses the false choices presented by binaries and how he instead seeks "fluidity, metamorphosis, the imperceptible shading of one thing into another" (Breslin 266). The ecological process that blurs and integrates differences appeals to Walcott and explains why he wishes his voice to join that of nature. Nature's integration and reformulation of the past is a kind of strange healing whereby the past can be acknowledged but, more important, newness becomes possible. As Walcott explored in *Tiepolo's Hound*, when art is responsive to natural time, human culture is no longer chronological and facing what has come before but simultaneous and oriented toward future possibility.

Strange Chemistry in *The Bounty*

The death of Walcott's mother, Alix, in 1990 forced a direct confrontation with the facts of his own mortality and agnosticism. The result is an intensely personal poem, "The Bounty," from his eponymous collection, and it is one of Walcott's most powerful articulations of nature's strangely healing powers. Although he does not engage the same broader questions of New World history in the poem, my analysis here will provide a foundation by which to read Walcott's view of the dialectic between the New World's natural and human histories in *Omeros*. The opening lines explain:

> Between the vision of the Tourist Board and the true
> Paradise lies the desert where Isaiah's elations
> force a rose from the sand. The thirty-third canto
>
> cores the dawn clouds with concentric radiance,
> the breadfruit opens its palms in praise of the bounty
> *bois-pain*, tree of bread, slave food, the bliss of John Clare. (*Bounty* 3)

Walcott situates the labor of poetry between the Christian notion of Paradise and the tourist version of the Caribbean Eden. The labor of the poet—here the models are Isaiah, Dante, and John Clare—is to take place in the mundane world or the "desert," eschewing the world beyond (the "true Paradise") and the virtual world created by the market and technology ("the vision of the Tourist Board"). The power of this labor is such that it is capable of forcing roses from the sand. Walcott suggests that such "roses" are not the technologically enhanced results of human impatience with nature's imperfections, as Carolyn Merchant has suggested is the result of Edenic discourses. The poet is in an Edenic garden only because of an internal imaginative adjustment that allows more clear perception of the bounties of the actual physical world.

This poetics is implied in the movement from Isaiah, a poet/prophet who first announces the millennial notion of the desert blossoming as a rose, to Dante. Dante plays the role of a more secularized poet/prophet of the Renaissance whose thirty-third canto of *Paradiso* ends with his confession that his earthly senses and language cannot adequately describe his vision of God (his terza rima is the model for Walcott's title poem). Finally, we arrive at John Clare, the mad nineteenth-century peasant poet who ended up writing poems in praise for the most elemental expressions of earth's bounty while he was in an asylum for the mentally ill. Walcott describes these elations: "[H]e stands in the ford / of a brook like the Baptist lifting his branches to bless / cathedrals and snails, the breaking of this new day" (*Bounty* 3). Later he also introduces Shakespeare's poor Tom, an inarticulate madman who wanders in communion with natural subjects. The progression of poets moves from praising God and unseen verities to praising the visible and tangible beauty of the earth to, finally, madness. The point is to understand literature's efforts to plumb the depths of the natural world vacillating along this spectrum, which is cyclical rather than linear. We do not know how to distinguish between creation and revelation, nor do we have sufficient grounds to reject a presence beyond the physical world.

Isaiah is the poet/prophet who imagines a millennial transformation of the earth whereby the desert is made to blossom like a rose through the power of God's Word transferred to human beings in the form of poetic prophecy. In the biblical context the very mundanity of the world, its signification of our alienation from the true Paradise, will be transformed, beautified, and redeemed by divine will. This kind of biblical poetry becomes prophecy because it is backed by the tangible force of God's power and therefore represents his voice. It is a poetry, then, that has a direct correspondence to things for the simple fact that things will be forced to conform to words. It is God's primordial generative word that creates the substantial world through utterance; finite matter conforms to the infinite word, not the other way around. In this prophetic model we are forced to choose between creation and revelation. We do not have to accept the substance of our natural environment, since such substance is an illusion;

what we should believe in and subject ourselves to is the Word and its transcendent reality, which overrides nature's transmutations.

On the other hand, we have the mad poet, John Clare, or, even more extreme, the dumb poet, Tom, both of whom are overwhelmed by the substantial world and whose poetry is a weak attempt to describe the spiritual weight of the physical world: "I am moved like you, mad Tom, by a line of ants; / I behold their industry and they are giants" (*Bounty* 4). This is the bounty of life that "returns each daybreak"; this "madness" apprehends things simply and perceives the smallest miracles of nature. Walcott describes this poetic task as a focus on the finite, as a "praise in decay and process, awe in the ordinary / in wind that reads the lines of the breadfruit's palms" (7). The subject is subjected, then, to what the senses can teach us about the natural environment, and by implication, unlike the recovery plot that seems inherent in Isaiah's blossoming desert, it would seek to honor and protect natural process. This model also implies that the substantial world of nature is placed a priori to language and that poetry is mimetic, not procreative.

The paradox of this circle of poets is that as the poet approaches the muteness of a mad Tom and moves farther away from the generative function of language, nature owns and generates the word as God does in Isaiah's model. An additional paradox is that precisely because the miracles of the ordinary are a function of an always-dying natural world, an awareness of bounty easily slips into existential mourning. Walcott relates the sorrow of his mother's passing to Clare's madness:

> [T]here is grief, there will always be, but it must not madden,
> like Clare, who wept for a beetle's loss, for the weight
> of the world in a bead of dew on clematis or vetch. (*Bounty* 5)

In other words, the deeper the awe in the ordinary, the more frightful natural process becomes for the simple fact that its only story seems to be that of perpetual death and finitude. This evanescent natural world begins to resemble the eternal light of God witnessed by Dante, who wrote:

> [W]hat I could see was greater
> than speech can show: at such sight, it fails—
> and memory fails when faced with such excess. (299)

The point of the poem, however, is not to speak abstractly about nature; it is also a very intimate and personal reflection on the death of Walcott's mother. He cannot reject the notion that she, for whom this poem functions as an elegy, is no longer present in some form after her death. At the same time, however, he cannot accept the idea that his poetry can somehow claim her or claim to know of her afterlife. So he remains agnostic, as resistant to knowing of her existence and her inexistence alike: "But can she or can she not read this? Can you read this, / Mamma, or hear it?" (*Bounty* 9). He later admits uncertainty in his expectation that he will see her again: "I half-expect to see you no longer, then more than half, / almost never, or never then—there I have said it" (12). Then he reverses his thinking because he knows that there is something that draws him to her in death, like tears and like his own poetry, that suggests in the end something more than language and mourning can express:

> [B]ut felt something less than final at the edge of your grave,
> some other something somewhere, equally dreaded,
> since the fear of the infinite is the same as death,
>
> unendurable brightness, the substantial dreading
> its own substance, dissolving to gases and vapours. (*Bounty* 12)

What lies beyond the grave is feared, whether it is God or nothing, because it represents dissolution of the material substance we now are. He implies that existential atheism makes the same mistake as dogmatic Christian belief, since both respond to what cannot be known with equally unpoetic certainty.

A poetic response must admit to being a simultaneous expression of faith *and* treachery because, like nature itself, it incorporates and perpetuates the meaning of human bodies even as it also absorbs and inters their stories with indifference. Walcott feels that his poetic deliberations about his mother are inherently treacherous because his metaphors only seem to make more evident the immateriality of that to which they refer. For that reason he remarks that "[f]aith grows mutinous" and asks for pardon "as I watch these lines grow and the art of poetry harden me / into sorrow as measured as this, to draw the veiled figure / of Mamma entering the standard elegiac" (*Bounty* 9, 5). Measured lines of poetry "harden" him, making his own materiality more evident and more aware of the self-referentiality and self-consciousness of his own measured lines and, hence, of his betrayal. Poetry fails to be elegiac in the same way Walcott describes the sea's erasure of human mementos.

But he is also betrayed by this indifferent bounty of nature around him. No matter how hard he tries to relish in the taste of earthly things he cannot forget that the dead have become "part of earth's vegetal fury . . . ants carry the freight / of their sweetness, their absence in all that we eat" (*Bounty* 13–14). Whitman expressed similar ambivalent admiration for the soil's "strange chemistry" that renders foul flesh sweet, as I discussed in chapter 4. Whitman's "This Compost" was a favorite of Robert Lowell and may have gained influence over Walcott through their friendship. The similarity is evident in the irony in nature's bounty:

> [A]nd here at first is the astonishment: that earth rejoices
> in the middle of our agony, earth that will have her
> for good: wind shines white stones and the shallows' voices. (*Bounty* 14)

The last phrase, "wind shines white stones and the shallows' voices," is comforting as a source of elation precisely because of its beautiful opacity and the Zen-like nothingness of the shallows' voices, and yet its emptiness also proves indifferent to Walcott's suffering.

Earlier he wrote of a similarly troubling peace in common sights and objects in his environment and states:

> My mother lies
> near the white beach stones, John Clare near the sea-almonds,
> yet the bounty returns each daybreak, to my surprise
>
> to my surprise and betrayal, yes, both at once. (*Bounty* 4)

The dynamic, ever changing, ever emerging substantial world of nature offers elation in the wake of sorrow and yet also mockery in its indifferent march forward in time. As Neruda discovers in his meditations on the sea's omnivorous qualities, nature represents both the possibility of continuation of meaning, from death and beyond, and the perpetual end of meaning. Is not its perpetual rebirth also perpetual death? Is it a New World this adamic imagination confronts or a dying one? It is this uncertainty about nature that characterizes what this book has been arguing is a New World poetics. Precisely because the poet remains undecided about this question means that his apprehensions of the world's newness are always tainted by a touch of sadness and withdrawal from the death of the past. And this is nothing short of the primordial lesson of the earth's own ecological transformations. This strangeness of the earth attracts Walcott, as it did Whitman and Neruda, because the resultant metaphysical uncertainty fuels the fire of his poetry. The enigma of nature's meaning is the same as that of his mother's death. He can never be sure that nature's continual dying and regenerating signifies immortality and cause for hope, just as he can never be sure that it does not. Continuity from life to death and back to life is a cycle of adamic resurgence of language, seeking to greet what called it forth, finding itself divorced from what it names, and then beginning over again. As I suggested was the case with Neruda's indecisive pose as the poet/prophet, the implication of a New World poetics is that poetry is both a language of commemoration, in its anticipation of joining a transcendent elation, and mourning for what it fails to signify.

Ultimately, Walcott asks how poetry can be both responsive to transcendent light and life without assuming the authority of prophecy *and* responsive to death without overwhelming the poet with madness and reducing poetry to perpetual elegy. If the poet admits a divine transcendence in nature, must this mean nature is beyond the bounds of human history? Or if nature is defined by its historicity and its ultimate death, on what basis can we identify hope for renewal? Hope, like faith, is found paradoxically in Walcott's persistent indecision between these two poles. As much as Walcott would like this cycle of life to remain below the radar of religious language and meaning, he cannot help finding a resemblance between both forms of awe. He writes of awe

> in the sun contained in a globe of the crystal dew,
> bounty in the ants' continuing a line of raw flour,
> mercy on the mongoose scuttling past my door,
>
> in the light's parallelogram laid on the kitchen floor,
> for Thine is the Kingdom, the Glory, and the Power. (*Bounty* 7–8)

He hears the church bells, sees Christ's story in the vegetation of his St. Lucia, in the "feathery palms that nodded at the entry / into Jerusalem" (8). Even though he describes his childhood religious experience as characterized by a now questioned faith "in His Word," Walcott's dead faith has been rekindled in his celebration of the bounty of life and by his resurrection of memories of his mother. In the "rustling hymnals" he hears

> the fresh Jacobean springs, the murmur Clare heard
>
> of bounty abiding, the clear language she taught us,
> "as the hart panteth," at this, her keen ears pronged
> while her three fawns nibbled the soul-freshening waters,
>
> "as the hart panteth for the water-brooks" that belonged
> to the language in which I mourn her now, or when
> I showed her my first elegy, her husband's, and then her own. (*Bounty* 8)

Here Walcott cites the language of Psalm 42, a poem that continues "[a]s the hart panteth after the water brooks, so panteth my soul after thee, O God." Walcott's lines here coupled with the verse from the Psalm imply a correlation between yearning in nature and a yearning for God.

Despite his gratitude for learning this correlation, Walcott knows he has betrayed his mother. He acknowledges the treachery of a self-conscious measured sorrow and the failure of his own faith, but the power of the elegy is this confession of failure, something not lost on Walcott. Nature's bounties are

> nettles of remorse
> that shall spring forth from her grave from the spade's heartbreak.
> And yet not to have loved her enough is to love more,
>
> if I confess it, and I confess it. (*Bounty* 7)

His insufficient love for his mother while she was alive now deepens his love for nature. Walcott's rose forced up from the sand is the poem itself, the words of commemoration and mourning that respond to his mother's death:

> There on the beach in the desert, lies the dark well
> where the rose of my life was lowered, near the shaken plants,
> near a pool of fresh tears, tolled by the golden bell
>
> of allamanda. (*Bounty* 5)

While the rose of her body is buried in the ground, it is simultaneously disinterred in the form of this commemoration of nature's life. The power of poetic language to force the rose up from the sand is not the same power of God's Word to resurrect the dead literally and, like Isaiah's words, to transmutate the phenomenal through linguistic mandates. Walcott's metaphors, like all metaphors, are unstable. His adamic imagination does not make equations that collapse the differences between words and things or between nature and culture, but neither do they ignore the possibility of some transcendent reason why such unlikenesses might be equal. Newness is always possible even if it is never stable. The rose, then, is a metaphor that brings into relation the immaterial and material worlds, words and things, life and death, commemoration and mourning, the timeless and the timely.

The poem concludes with his resolution to learn again

> my business and duty, the lesson you taught your sons,
> to write of the light's bounty on familiar things
> that stand on the verge of translating themselves into news:
>
> [T]he crab, the frigate that floats on cruciform wings,
> and that nailed and thorn-riddled tree that opens its pews
> to the blackbird that hasn't forgotten her because it sings. (*Bounty* 16)

Her life is continued, ironically and movingly, in the bounty of nature but also in the bounty of the word of the poet as he responds to nature's motions. But that continuation is always tenuous and therefore inevitable because it emerges moment by moment in the transition between what lies beyond nature and time to what becomes news by virtue of being written. So the poet must keep writing just as assiduously as nature regenerates in its apparent indifference to human perception.

As we have seen in Walcott's argument in "The Muse of History" and in his earlier poetry, the "light's bounty on familiar things / that stand on the verge of translating themselves into news" shows us a cyclical rather than a linear relation between human and natural history. Nature, always dying and being born again, brings its light onto those "familiar things" that have presumably already been adopted into the human story, breathing new life into them and consequently making metaphors adamic. And when those metaphors become "familiar" clichés, the "breaking day" will provide another opportunity to start over. This is not a redundant circle but perhaps more like a helix, since it can never be predicted what story new light, or the poet, will tell. While we might suspect that we have heard Adam's story before, there is no way to predict what Walcott's Adam will say. This means that new futures, undetermined by the past, are always possible, that is, unless the cycle is somehow broken by toxic disruption.

Skeptical Faith in *Omeros*

At the conclusion of his essay "Inside the Cathedral" Walcott notes that art has this capacity to make substantial the insubstantial affections of the heart. He writes that art teaches that "there is an earthly paradise, that there is no ambition that cannot be fulfilled, no faith that is not rewarded, in the exact manner that, desired hard enough, is prayed for. But only if it was good, and by good I realized I meant something that could bear pride but was not selfish, that could learn to love itself as it loved others" ("Inside" 27). Art, when capacitated in this way to make a world, does not "write back" to the empire, as Paula Burnett explains, but "writes home"; that is, it expresses "faith in the individual's power of creation, the power to defeat alienation by creating a symbolic 'home,' in whatever external conditions life may be lived" (27). In the absence of his own father and in the absence, more broadly, of the Caribbean's genealogical ties to its past, such a resurrectional power of poetry proves crucial. As this study has consistently argued, a New World poetics allows an alternative to the binary of vengeance for a lamentable legacy or nostalgia for a lost one that New World history bequeaths the poet. In *Omeros* we see how the poetics of Isaiah's elations functions in the broader context of this hemispheric quandary.

Walcott raises similar questions in *Omeros* about his father as he does about his mother, which perhaps may be the "first elegy" to which he refers in "The Bounty." Warwick appears at the conclusion of book 1 and speaks to his son's doubts about an afterlife:

> "Along this coal-blackened wharf, what Time decided
> to do with my treacherous body after this,"
> he said, watching the women, "will stay in your head
>
> as long as a question you have no right to ask,
> only to doubt, not hate our infuriating
> silence." (*O* 74)

These lines puzzle us with their rich ambiguity. Walcott is told that he has no right to ask what happens to the dead because the dead are silent, but he is also told he has the right to doubt. But doubt what? Doubt that the dead live on? Perhaps. But the syntax of the line implies that he must also doubt the reality of "our infuriating / silence," and this doubt is implicitly manifest in the fact that these are words Walcott has Warwick speak. I remind my reader that Whitman's translation of the birdsong in "Out of the Cradle Endlessly Rocking" was framed by the word "death" that the sea whispered to him. In other words, Whitman's pretense of translating the language of nature is framed by nature's grand space of oblivion and silence, which only highlights the rhetorical nature of the translation. Neruda similarly attempts a séance with the dead at Machu Picchu only to end with the sound of his own voice. Writing poetry, as is the case with Walcott here, becomes an expression of doubt about the nothingness that presumably awaits us after death, as Warwick's words imply: " '[y]our pose of a question waiting, / as you crouch with a writing lamp over a desk' " (*O* 75). He chides his son:

"O Thou, my Zero, is an impossible prayer,
utter extinction is still a doubtful conceit.
Though we pray to nothing, nothing cannot be there." (*O* 75)

In the context of uncertainty about metaphysical matters, the best poetry can do is to offer itself as a work, a creation of a world, what Hans-Georg Gadamer calls a "pledge of order," but that does not exclude the possibility that it also establishes some correspondence to things as they really are (36). This provides a theological dimension to what Walcott calls the "reversible world," since the distinctions between imagination and history, the present and the past, human and nonhuman, begin to blur. The important task is to disavow the need to decide these matters and instead " 'kneel to your load,' " as his father counsels, and accept the duty of giving voice to the laboring men and women of his island as an act of love, of crafted language enclosing "the loved world in its arms" (*O* 75). John Elder argues that when poetic language is imbued with this kind of "imaginative energy, then it may take on the power of Saint Paul's 'faith': 'the substance of things hoped for, the evidence of things not seen' " (*Imagining* 110).

Because of the undecided nature of what he writes, Walcott is able to dramatize the Caribbean past as a vision that ultimately fades, like Prospero's plays, as "an insubstantial pageant," leaving us, along with Achille, able to embrace the strange gift of the Caribbean's literally and figuratively substantial inheritance of natural beauty. The poem recounts the struggle of two St. Lucian fishermen, Achille and Hector, for the love of one woman, Helen. Achille's agonized passion for Helen, who at times appears to symbolize the island, results in a search for his African past. A parallel search is undertaken by Major Plunkett, a white retired military man who seeks to grant Helen her dignified place in history. Ultimately, the poem renounces their and its own epic ambitions in the interest of fidelity to the present. Walcott's dialogue with his father bears similarities with Achille's encounter of his African heritage as well as Major Plunkett's research into St. Lucia's European past. The parallel suggests that crossing the geographical meridian of the Atlantic is not unlike striving to cross the meridian between mortality and postmortem life, and this is evident in Walcott's depiction of Africa as a kind of phantasm. The African and European pasts are genealogical explorations of the plurality of Caribbean origins, and, like Walcott's father, they are imagined resurrections, a rose in the sand, as it were, fictional but also no less real. Africa and Europe, then, must also be resurrected through the imagination but only so as to establish a home for Achille and Plunkett in their present inheritance, just as Warwick teaches his son to stop worrying about what happened to his father's body and "kneel to his load." The Caribbean's African and European pasts require similarly skeptical faith, lest facile acceptance of or entrenched mourning over loss inspires rejection of the bounties of the present. Historical research or mythical returns to lands of origin do not offer returns to home but rather moments of uncanniness, a "paradoxical recognition and misrecognition" that betrays the passage of time and stimulates the need to remain faithful to the present conditions of the New World (Christiansë 217). As Yvette Christiansë further argues, "what has come to pass, then, is the *stalled* apocalypse and the possibility of a true transcendence of history. There is no past to rewrite as the future, only the eternal present of resignation to make a home out of the place in which one finds oneself" (218).

The parallel also highlights the role poetic memory plays in performing encounters with ancestors so as to essentially liberate the present from any accusations of inauthenticity that a Hegelian conception of History might wish to make on the present. Poetry, as opposed to historiography, provides a rhetorical turn to the past, a kind of self-conscious performance rather than an endeavor of linguistic disinterment lacking all irony. The presence of irony suggests that Walcott's history is haunted by skepticism even as it moves us. Indeed, poetic irony is arguably what makes Achille's encounter with his ancestors so moving. Like Neruda's *Canto general*, Walcott's poem performs a desire to recover what the Caribbean has lost but insists, albeit more overtly than *Canto general*, that history will remain interred. Neruda concludes his epic with a return to the oblivious and regenerating space of nature and the provincial ecological beginnings of the poet's imagination, but he does not see this as necessarily contradicting his historical objectives. For Walcott the embrace of the sea and of his provincial beginnings is markedly more prodigal. Achille's prodigal moment is not his arrival on African shores but his longing for the Caribbean sea he loves. Achille is, of course, disappointed that he cannot provide Afolabe and his tribe a reason for his name and is terrified by the horrors of enslavement, but he is nevertheless unapologetic about his need to return home.

This is particularly perplexing, since Achille's lost Africa offers a culture, language, and genealogy that are thoroughly embedded in the natural world. Similar to his depictions of the native inhabitants of the Caribbean, Walcott imagines the African ancestors as inhabiting a world in which all their senses are highly attuned to ecology, and consequently their language is itself part of nature. Achille's ancestral tribe rustles and mutters "like cedars at sunrise," and when they learn of how much of Africa has been forgotten in the New World they grieve "as branches sway in the dusk from their fear / of amnesia" (*O* 137, 138). When the griot speaks the genealogical roots of the culture, Achille hears the sounds of nature:

And every night the seed-eyed, tree-wrinkled bard,
the crooked tree who carried the genealogical leaves
of the tribe in his cave-throated moaning,

traces the interlacing branches of their river-rooted lives
as intricately as the mangrove roots. (*O* 140)

When Achille witnesses the dead body of the griot following the capture and enslavement of the village, the seer is nothing more than a gaping "toothless mouth," a silence where "trees and the spirits that they uttered were rooted" (*O* 146, 144). Akin to the hole left by the fallen tree with which

Omeros begins, the griot's death leaves an empty space, "like a felled cedar's whose sorrow surrounds its bole" (*O* 147). The griot, like the Caribbean griot, Seven Seas, has become an unused "caved-in canoe" (*O* 147), and Achille's only weapon to express his rage is his oar and his life as a fisherman.

Walcott's vision of Achille's Africa echoes David Abram's descriptions of the intimacy between language and nature forged in aboriginal cultures. Abram's *The Spell of the Sensuous* argues that Western civilization has lost its rootedness in place, that its language and culture have divorced themselves from ecology, a fate that is increasingly likely to happen to the remaining oral aboriginal cultures left that still have something vital to teach us about our human intimacy with the environment. Abram notes that "the linguistic patterns of an oral culture remain uniquely responsive, and responsible, to the more-than-human life-world, or bioregion, in which that culture is embedded" (178). In its increasing abstraction of language from its natural context Western civilization has uprooted not only itself but the native cultures it has colonized from their local ecologies, thus occluding human understanding of our own natural histories and how to live sustainably within the environments we inhabit. He argues: "[T]he local earth is, for [oral cultures], the very matrix of discursive meaning; to force them from their native ecology . . . is to render them speechless—or to render their speech meaningless—*to dislodge them from the very ground of coherence*" (Abram 178).

What Abram leaves unanswered, however, is how we will be able to recover this more-than-human understanding of ourselves within written cultures, given the fact that this uprooting has become the fate of the vast majority of the world's populations and that going back to this world before the "fall" seems unlikely. Walcott's poem insists that we must acknowledge the loss of intimacy of which Abram speaks, but we must also be cautious about underestimating the human capacity to adapt to new environments, to renew language through renaming, and to thus forge new homes in the context of violent diaspora, otherwise we run the risk of being overcome by despair and nostalgia. Abram suggests that the development of alphabetic culture began Western civilization's self-abstraction from nature and ecological fall from grace because nature was no longer the primary text that vivified words. Walcott's vision of the New World Adam, on the other hand, would seem to admit that even though the spell of alphabetic language might have caused the initial wound that alienated us from the spell of the sensuous, language—more specifically, poetry—is an essential component of the cure.

It is significant, for example, that Achille's African past is envisioned poetically. The tragedy of an uprooted language is signified by Achille's name, which derives from literature, not from nature and genealogy. Afolabe, ironically, is a name Walcott borrowed from a Nigerian playwright as a tribute and because of its African sound, but the poem offers no signification for the name (Afolabe merely touches his heart when he pronounces his name), despite Afolabe's complaint about Achille's meaningless name. Achille explains that his name is merely a sound: "In the world I come from / we accept the sounds that we are given. Men, trees, water" (*O* 138). Afolabe wonders if language is a mere shell of its original value, since it would appear that in Achille's world words used to describe men and trees result in empty sounds, and "every sound [would] be a shadow that crossed your ear / without the shape of a man or a tree" (*O* 138). Achille defends himself by noting that his world is full of shadows and echoes from other worlds but that ultimately his name, like his language, is a "gift / of this sound whose meaning I still do not care to know" (*O* 138). The uprootedness of his language from its original ecological context is an adamic opportunity to allow language to echo anew in its rawness and dislocation from place. His name means only its sound, and it is the spell, not the spelling, of this sound that offers the chance to return to one's senses. This is what Walcott means to suggest when he writes of "that green sunrise of axes and laurel-trees" at the poem's conclusion. He remarks: "Like Philoctete's wound, this language carries its cure, / its radiant affliction" (*O* 323).

The Self-Healing Island

The poem's opening scene tells us something of Walcott's intention to suggest multiple origins for Caribbean language and culture, since the ecologically harmonious language and culture of Africa or of Native America are no longer viable. This "green sunrise of axes and laurel-trees," as he refers to it at the poem's conclusion, serves as a kind of Caribbean creation story, but, unlike Adam's moment in the garden, a wound has already been suffered, and its chief action is the wounding of a tree. This sense of being in medias res conveys Walcott's New World adamic cosmology in which craftsmanship in close proximity to a sensate natural world means recognizing loss and death as well as the birth of new possibility. Walcott portrays poor men cutting down a *laurier-cannelle* tree for the purposes of crafting a canoe, an elemental task demanded by a simple economy. The *laurier-cannelle*, a member of the cedar family, is today near extinction on the island, so it is a somewhat ironic choice, since it raises the problematic question of sustainability I will discuss below. We find Achille, Philoctete, Hector, and others performing this "sacrifice" while tourists look on and Philoctete provides the explanatory narrative (*O* 5). Philoctete is aware that the natural world surrounding the tree is sensate, responsive, and watching. The wind blowing through the ferns seems to give voice to the ferns, who assent: " 'Yes, the trees have to die.' " Rum aids the men in their task because of their awareness of the subjectivity of the trees. As Philoctete puts it, " '[I]t give us the spirit to turn into murderers' " (*O* 3). The murder is witnessed by an iguana, the totem animal of St. Lucia and the island's first indigenous name:

> Although smoke forgets the earth from which it ascends,
> and nettles guard the holes where the laurels were killed,
> an iguana hears the axes. (*O* 4)

The mute witness stands by while the pillars of trees fall, "leaving a blue space / for a single God where the old gods stood before" (*O* 5). The trees "endured the decimation / of their tribe without uttering a syllable / of that language they had uttered as one nation" (*O* 6). So too are the indigenous gods "down at last" (*O* 6), left to be a blank page upon which the Caribbean's history will write itself in the form of a palimpsest.

So far it reads more like a fall from Eden than a creation story. Unlike Whitman's giddy view of the redwoods' demise, nature is murdered, its voice of protest is silenced, the animistic beliefs and lifeways of the Arawaks are fragmented and replaced by Western civilization, and a lizard watches in ironic silence. These would all seem to be elements of the Caribbean's first fall from its indigenous Eden at the arrival of colonialism, but it is instructive that this is a contemporary scene of St. Lucian fishermen. This might suggest that Walcott wishes to condemn contemporary culture for carrying forward the same patterns of environmental degradation and the destruction of indigenous cultures with which modern Caribbean experience began. That is no doubt a very real possibility, but seeing the initial colonial contact in stark binaries runs some risks, not the least of which is the implication that any subsequent use of natural resources on the island categorically will have the same results. And Walcott has consistently resisted such polemical positions, particularly on the grounds that they offer no hope for postcolonial, postdiaspora peoples. Instead, I believe that Walcott is highlighting in this opening scene the difficult but necessary balance that must be struck between necessary acts of human creation and craftsmanship and the inevitable losses that attend human use of natural resources.

The facts that indigenous gods are still receding into the background and that trees are seen to endure decimation "without uttering a syllable" are themselves components of an ecologically open poetics whereby human labor is contextualized by a sensate physical world. We return, then, to the question raised by Whitman and Neruda regarding the use of the axe and Leopold's notion of necessary and acknowledged violence. Walcott suggests that while craftsmanship brings the wielder of the tool closer to the physical world, it does not facilely solve the problem of the ongoing risk that any art of the Caribbean will incur loss. There is no pure relation to nature, just as there is no pure culture. No art, no craft, no language is without risk, so the best we can do is attune our language to the sounds of nature to hear its record of losses, to try to see as the iguana sees (as Walcott does in this opening scene), and to learn from how nature appears to heal from its own wounds. As Gadamer expresses it, craft and art once shared more in common before the onset of rapid technological innovations in modernity, and this led to a growing distinction between works of human hands that control natural forces and those that conform to the particular contours of those forces' chaotic flow (15–16). The latter category describes both canoe making (and other elemental crafts) and poetry making for Walcott. Such a poetics enables us to imagine sustainable forms of human action as well as to discover new possibilities for joy in the wake of history's devastations.

As the opening scene continues it becomes more apparent that nature teaches a lesson about how the New World might heal from its own violent transplantations. Achille contemplates

> the hole the laurel had left.
> He saw the hole silently healing with the foam
> of a cloud like a breaker. Then he saw the swift. (*O* 6)

The swift proves to be an important harbinger of how ecology refashions the meaning of death and a foreshadowing of what will heal the losses of Caribbean history later in the poem. This healing does not represent forgiveness or a righting of the balances of justice, however, like the Hegelian syntheses that so attracted Whitman. Nor does unifying culture to natural process promise a kind of militant resistance to colonialism that Neruda sometimes finds appealing. Walcott pushes the irony of Whitman's and Neruda's suspicions of irony that lay at the New World's natural foundations. Natural regeneration is the ironic result of its indifferent perpetual transmutations, like passing clouds or lapping waves, by which human actions participate in the flowing of the world. What results from the human violence is neither a fall nor a restoration but a mysterious transformation, one that does not justify the violence acted upon the trees but nevertheless accepts what the violence made possible. Walcott implies that our own sense of justice regarding the Caribbean's past could learn from this ecological process:

> [T]he logs gathered that thirst
>
> for the sea which their own vined bodies were born with.
> Now the trunks in eagerness to become canoes
> ploughed into breakers of bushes, making raw holes
>
> of boulders, feeling not death inside them, but use—
> to roof the sea, to be hulls. (*O* 7)

The narrative further explains: "After Mass one sunrise the canoes entered the troughs / of the surpliced shallows, and their nodding prows / agreed with the waves to forget their lives as trees" (*O* 8).

Nature would appear to be acquiescing to its human purposes, calling to mind Whitman's depiction of the redwoods, another endangered tree today, and their submission to their destiny in human hands. What is different, however, is Walcott's more bittersweet recognition of human labor as a kind of wounding, suggesting what is lost in the translation of tree to canoe. His reticence in translating the trees' language is evident in his repeated insistence on their silence. Whitman, it will be recalled, spoke of the trees' death as "clearing the ground for broad humanity," whom he also called the "culminating man" (*LG* 176, 175). Even though he depicts their souls and speech announcing their own fall to silence, he raised little doubt about the suitability of human westward expansion to fill the space once filled by nature. This is, perhaps, an example of Walcott's frequent complaint that there isn't enough reckoning with human evil in Whitman. By contrast, Walcott refers repeatedly in the poem to holes left behind by labor, both in Achille's voyage to Africa and in the Caribbean. The repetition of the pattern of wounding nature in the poem suggests that there is no first original wound but that every subsequent one recalls a prior history, a notion absent in Whitman's depiction of Manifest Destiny.

This more sobering adamic appraisal of the New World raises another problem: if every wound recalls a prior one, the primordial wound of Caribbean environmental history is potentially opened with every subsequent action taken. Slavery and indigenous genocide act as open wounds in the poem and signify the New World's perpetual self-injuring mirrored in Philoctete's wound. Of course, New World environmental history makes it clear that environmental and human wounds of the Caribbean have gone hand in hand, which is perhaps one reason why it is an appropriate use of metaphor for Walcott to speak of Philoctete's wound in both historical and ecological terms.[1] Though caused by a "rusted anchor," "it puckered like the corolla / of a sea-urchin" (O 4). Ma Kilman searches for the root that will heal his open wound: "Where was this root? What senna, what tepid tisanes, / could clean the branched river of his corrupted blood, / whose sap was a wounded cedar's?" (O 19). Senna, a shrub from North Africa, and tisanes, infusions used to make tea, are both used in herbal teas with healing qualities, and both originate from elsewhere. As Philoctete later says to his yams, also originally from Africa, while he pulls them up from the soil:

"You all see what it's like without roots in this world?"
Then sobbed, his face down in the slaughtered leaves. A sap
trickled from their gaping stems like his own sorrow. (O 21)

As tubers, yams are their own roots, an understanding Philoctete does not yet have about himself. Instead, he seems possessed of the idea that "the swelling came from the chained ankles / of his grandfathers. Or else why was there no cure?" (O 19). Philoctete's premise is that the history of slavery introduced a trauma, eruption, or fissure of such range and depth that to speak of healing from such a wound would simply ignore the horrific reality of that past. Philoctete demonstrates his wound to tourists for money, noting: " 'It have some things'—he smiles—'worth more than a dollar' " (*O* 4). The open sulfur pits of St. Lucia's remainder of a volcano, Soufrière, resonate as a geological reference point to Philoctete's suffering, a condition posited in the poem's opening chapters as an ontological problem of Caribbeanness.

If there is a cure for the history of slavery in the Caribbean, it would seem to trivialize the suffering, especially if the cure is offered as a political or economic one. Walcott's cure, however, is ecological; it is the indifference of natural regeneration. Philoctete comes to a self-healing resolution regarding his wound, facilitated by the same flight of the harbinger swift that had healed the hole left by the dead laurel tree. Achille's prodigal return to the Caribbean following the transatlantic migration of the swift inspires him to consider

> the stitched, sutured wound that Philoctete
> was given by the sea, but how the sea could heal
> the wound also. (*O* 242)

The very conditions of Caribbean pain anticipate the wound with a cure that can only occur in an embrace of the ironic beauty of the Caribbean, a circumstance Walcott refers to as a "self-healing island" and emblematized here in the chiasmus of wound/sea, sea/wound (*O* 249).

The biogeography of the Caribbean becomes its greatest hope. The transplantation of flora and fauna along with peoples from various ge-ographies has triangulated the human and nonhuman New World to their foreign origins and thus placed them on the same temporal plane. They share the same ironic condition of seeking rootedness not through history but through finding home in the present condition of diaspora, a word that literally refers to the spreading of seed. The swift inexplicably flies the east-west vector instead of its usual north-south pathway. Known for its speed and high flying, the swift is capable of never touching ground for years after its departure from the nest and is thus itself a displaced cruiser that has carried with it the "cure / that precedes every wound," a seed of an "unknown weed" that will cure Philoctete's wound (*O* 239, 237). Late in the poem, his wound is described as having less to do with the Caribbean's history of slavery as with how that history has led to an unnecessary disposition of homelessness. Achille contemplates the faces of the fisherman surrounding a fire "under the horned, / holy peaks" of the Pitons and notes "that obvious wound / made from loving the sea over their own country" (*O* 302).

While this love is initially experienced by Achille, Philoctete, and others as a betrayal of home, it is also the journey back. Indeed, it is the sea's constant reminder of ecological immensity within which tiny human stories take place that "changed the cedars / into canoes" (*O* 47). Their lives as fishermen necessitate an ecologically aware devotion to craft, and this in turn makes possible the making of the world. In his reflections on the crime of enslavement, Walcott notes the particular cruelty of denying slaves the chance to use their hands: "Men are born makers, with that primal simplicity / in every maker since Adam. This is pre-history" (*O* 150). As Breslin notes, this implies that slaves are "deprived of the bond between imagination and environment (both social and natural) their work had given them" (251), a kind of divorce from their native soil Abram argues is the very "ground of coherence" for oral cultures (178). For this reason, the enslaved have been reduced to "coals, firewood, dismembered / branches, not men" (*O* 150).

Craftsmanship becomes the chief means of making oneself native in the wake of diaspora. When hands find work to refashion the world, there is an echo of the old ways, as Walcott suggests in his description of the idle hands of slaves in the galleys crossing the sea. But what is important, ultimately, is not what the hands remember but how their motions allow the maker to begin to listen again to animate beings and to create from, rather than lament, the physical conditions of this New World. This is the moment in which craft marries itself to the lot assigned by history, does not argue with the past, and is thus able to forge a new sense of place in the wake of New World history, the moment

> when a wave rhymes with one's grave,
> a canoe with a coffin, once that parallel
> is crossed, and cancels the line of master and slave. (*O* 159)

If diaspora has led to a sense of rootlessness in a New World, rootlessness becomes its own cure because it has also created the circumstances for the emergence of a new culture, a new poetry, a new naming of things. As I continue to insist, this adamic imagination is not a naming of things for the first time but is more like a palimpsest in that what is written anew has faint echoes with names and stories that have been lost even if they cannot be ignored. Recovery of Africa, as Achille discovers, even if it were possible, would not satisfy the longing for home, "for a sound that is missing" (*O* 137). By recognizing this missing sound, New World metaphors can simultaneously acknowledge loss and begin to sound the depths of one's newfound place in the present environment, the essential work, in other words, of poetry.

The native folk knowledge of botany Ma Kilman seeks to possess eludes her just enough to keep her uncertain and deferential toward her place in the animate world around her but not enough to prevent her from intimating the source of Philoctete's cure. Although she is an obeah woman, Ma Kilman's knowledge of African deities and of the medicinal value of plants is hindered by her condition in diaspora. Even the gods have been spread across the Atlantic in advance of the seeds and people who were to come:

> She glimpsed gods in the leaves, but, their features obscured
> by the restless shade and light, those momentary
> guardians, unlike the logwood thorns of her Lord,
>
> or that gold host named for her mother, Mary,
> thronging around her knees, with some soldiery crushed
> by the weight of a different prayer, had lost their names
>
> and therefore, considerable presence. They had rushed
> across an ocean, swifter than the swift
>
> . . . .
>
> [and] swarmed in the thicket
>
> of the grove, waiting to be known by name; but she
> had never learnt them. (*O* 242)

The liminal spiritual presence Ma Kilman senses provides a tenuous, "momentary" intimacy with the natural world, one we already saw easily disrupted by the violence of the axe. Ma Kilman picks the

> stinking flower.
> . . . .
> as if her veins were [the gods'] roots,
>
> her arms ululated, uplifting the branches
> of a tree carried across the Atlantic that shoots
> fresh leaves as its dead trunk wallows on our beaches. (*O* 242–43)

The murdered trees acquiesce to their destiny as canoes, and thus human hands become gentle agents in ecological process. So too do we see here how Ma Kilman's hands are joined to the roots she pulls. This signifies how her actions in the interest of curing the inherited wound of diaspora show acceptance and faith in diaspora's very conditions. Seeking cures in a diasporic landscape represents a nativization of New World conditions that is as natural as leaves shooting forth from dead trunks. The image here recalls the 1965 poem "Verandah," in which Walcott praises the strange process by which the ruin of the plantation house, both ecologically and historically, has resulted in an ironic flourishing of new possibility. As we saw in chapter 7, he calls these "unguessed, lovely inheritors" of Caribbean history, and here they become the subjects of *Omeros*, those who have emerged from the wreckage of the Old World on Caribbean shores. Philoctete appeals to the aid of the "unknown weed" that finds "its power / rooted in bitterness" and is nurtured by a soil that "carried the smell, when it gangrened, / of Philoctete's wound" (*O* 237–38). His baptism is a bath in "one of those cauldrons from the old sugar-mill," from which he emerges

> like a boy in his bath with the first clay's
> innocent prick! So she threw Adam a towel.
> And the yard was Eden. And its light the first day's. (*O* 246, 248)

My reader will recall that Walcott had earlier written of the sea's capacity to hold the dead of New World slavery in notably more bitter terms, especially in his well-known poem "The Sea Is History" from 1974. The poem describes the absence of historical monuments in the Caribbean— its lack of evidence of "civilization" as defined by European metropolitan norms—and portrays the sea as the vault of history. The poem was not meant to express regret about history, which, as I have already argued, falls prey to the very logic of History that has left the Caribbean on the margins of the West. Rather, it is an unsentimental, clear-eyed admission that natural history is a more proper register of Caribbean history. In light of this admission Walcott's adamic duties become clear as he states in "The Bounty," "to write of light's bounty on familiar things." Poetry's task, as we saw in the previous chapter, is akin to landscape art's attempt at direct apprehension. This involves an environmental imagination so as to understand the motions of ecology that explain the sea's "self-healing coral" and why "a quiet culture / is branching from the white ribs of each ancestor"

(*O* 296). Water is the tomb but also the womb of this culture that allows poetry to turn away from the seductions of the past:

> [T]his is the true element,
> water, which commemorates nothing in its status.
>
> . . . .
>
> Its elegies had blinded me with the temporal
> lament for a smoky Troy, but where coral died
> it feeds on its death, the bones branch into more coral,
>
> and contradiction begins. It lies in the schism
> of the starfish reversing heaven; the mirror of History
> has melted and, beneath it, a patient, hybrid organism
>
> grows in his cruciform shadow. (*O* 297)

The wound of the fishermen, "loving the sea over their own country," is not only that they have loved the freedom of mobility at the cost of their homeland but that they come to love natural history more than the genealogical history implied by a love of country. A New World poetics means coming to terms with their place in a local environment that also extends beyond the limitations of geopolitical space. And while Walcott insists that this can be a self-healing wound, he also raises the specter of some attendant risks, most important of which is the very threat to the environment the New World's history of economic expansion, globalization, and restlessness continues to pose.

Unsustainable Wounds

Whitman believed that nature's "strange chemistry" that transformed evil and suffering into rebirth provided a model for New World promise. Implicit and sometimes explicit in his argument is the notion that human culture has operated on other assumptions and on another plane altogether and has yet to learn to move beyond its own unsustainable behavior. Neruda raised a similar question in his meditation at the ruins of Machu Picchu when he noted humankind's incapacity to regenerate like the flower. If dead and decaying bodies could provide rich fertilizer, a society founded on natural principles of deep aesthetic appreciation and observation of nature might bring forth a new society that similarly feeds off of the legacies of the

Old World. Neruda came to understand a deep divide between the New World modern political history and the deeper natural history in which it had taken place. Contextualizing our history in this way in his poetry teaches our interrelatedness as human communities in the New World and as such our interrelatedness as living entities in the physical world.

In their explorations of this New World poetics neither poet, however, raised the prospect that the damage done to ourselves can also signify damage done to the earth's regenerative powers. What happens when nature becomes toxic? In its own efforts to be self-healing, might it expunge the human cancer from its body? At the poem's conclusion Walcott explodes his model of a self-enclosed self-healing world with the admission that not only is the Caribbean economy dependent on the international forces of the tourist industry, but the local climate too reflects global changes beyond the control and understanding of the locals. Seven Seas witnesses strange changes in the weather that cause him to believe that " 'somewhere people interfering / with the course of nature'" (O 299). Walcott notes:

> [M]an was an endangered
>
> species now, a spectre, just like the Aruac
> or the egret, or parrots screaming in terror
> when men approached, and that once men were satisfied
>
> with destroying men they would move on to Nature.
>
> . . . .
>
> [the omens'] changing
> was beyond his strength and he was responsible
> only to himself. The wisdom was enraging.
>
> In fury, he sailed south, away from the trawlers
> who were dredging the banks the way others had mined
> the archipelago for silver. (O 300)

Seven Seas finds himself fishing farther out from the coast than he is accustomed to because of the scarcity of fish in the familiar locations, which is just one more of the many "signs / of a hidden devastation" he sees (O 300). The sea, it would appear, is no longer a counter to the land by virtue of being void of human traces, as Walcott had argued.

The degradation Seven Seas notices is, of course, a recent development, what with the effects of global warming affecting climates the world over, the growth of the oil and tourist industries in the Caribbean, and the replacement of local fishing for industrial fishing. Joy Rudder reports, for example, increasing pressures of change on the fish population and on what she calls the "artisanal fisherman": the growing threat of oil spills (St. Lucia provides harbor for oil tankers), foreign industrial fishing, satellite and sonar detectors, the use of large nets that typically catch and kill more than the targeted population, discarded nets on the ocean's floor, the use of dynamite and bleach, increased land pollution that threatens the coral reefs, and the construction of hotels and other concrete buildings that typically involve some form of sand mining and the weakening of coral reefs. Once the coral reefs begin to go, the land's capacity to resist erosion against the motion of the sea is depleted.

Like that of many Caribbean islands, St. Lucia's culture, architecture, and language have all been deeply impacted by increased alienation from nature, which is largely due to the loss of craftsmanship, such as the local fishing economy, under the pressures of a growing global economy. Walcott has repeatedly written in praise of the small fishing villages (even at the same time as he has criticized himself for appearing to love the beauty of poverty) in the inlets of St. Lucia, like Anse Le Raye, and has complained of what he called in *Another Life* the "cement phoenix" of concrete buildings, shopping malls, hotels, and office buildings that have replaced the French colonial structures that once characterized the island. In a series of poems entitled "Parang" from *The Bounty*, for example, he recalls the fishing market in downtown Castries. The place was not an Eden by any stretch. He remembers "the choked canals [that] were a part of imperial decay." Named the "Conway" after

> the port of some county
> with bright boats moored,
> . . . .
> in the nostalgia of an imperial sunset the name flared
> over the shacks and limp nets and garbage. (*Bounty* 30)

These "distinctions" emerged in the "ebb of History" and the recession, or "low tide," of empire, but now they surrender to bulldozers and "white offices." Walcott's own nostalgia forces him to admit that "to look back like the sun / is to return to the reek of canals." He does not want to glorify decay and poverty, but neither can he accept the concrete as a triumph. He instead declares his own poetry as the only adequate response to this loss: "[T]he Conway is gone, / but from its shacks and their fishnets these lines were made" (*Bounty* 30).

The current environmental situation of the Caribbean has placed the poet in a precarious position, as precarious as that of the fishermen with whom Walcott so consistently identifies. If poetry requires the close intimacy with the physical world shared by the artisanal fisherman, when that world becomes endangered, so too is poetry. As we saw in the titular poem of *The Bounty*, nature's bountiful beauty transforms poetry's elegiac tone from mourning to praise, even elation. This is the postlapsarian adamic moment in which natural regeneration provides an ironic, even bittersweet, solace for death and loss, one that simultaneously acknowledges the cruelty of loss as well as the emergent opportunities thus created for cultural renewal. That is, if awe in the ordinary once helped poetry to retain its procreative adamic power in the context of increasing destruction of the ordinary physical world, poetry can be nothing more than elegy and mourning, as the final lines of the poem above seem to indicate. Neruda and Whitman do not consider this modern question of global environmental change and degradation, the very end of nature as we know it, but Walcott's answer merely extends the logic of the adamic imagination: it cannot survive a dying world.

There is a curious paradox here, however, in that recent environmental threats to the Caribbean are an extension of a systematic degradation that began with the arrival of Columbus. Arguably, no environment has ever seen such wholesale transformation and degradation in such short order as did the Caribbean islands in the first three hundred years following that primal scene of Spanish boots on Caribbean sands and the arrival of mining and plantation economies. Its radical transformation under the plantation system, tremendous and tragic loss of hardwood forests, soil erosion, implantation of foreign flora, and the loss of native fauna have led to environmental problems of collapsing and polluted reefs and vulnerability to floods and massive mud slides. Walcott's portrayal of the Caribbean's postlapsarian state would seem to acknowledge this previous devastation to the island, but only implicitly. The swift's heavenly augur of nature's unexpected resurrections and Philoctete's healing convey Walcott's hope that despite such destruction Caribbean culture might still be able to found itself on its natural beauty. This is a confidence, however, undermined by these omens of global change. Indeed, global climate change, above all, perhaps presents a categorical shift in the pattern of degradation established with Columbus's early incarnation of Western global forces, as Bill McKibben has argued. Perhaps the environment can no longer be seen to represent a local world but is already and always portending an outcome that cannot be locally controlled. Under such circumstances, local significations of the environment are rendered ironic, impotent, and alienated, the adamic task no longer tenable.

Omeros raises the question that perhaps the resurrections of the ordinary upon which a New World poetics is based may be fatally threatened. Perhaps the fact that the Caribbean islands survived colonial trauma suggests the possibility they may do so again. The question, then, is what will happen to the humans who occupy them, since it is unlikely that the earth will die before getting rid of us. It is perhaps almost banal to admit that poetry is more fragile even than the ecosystems upon which it depends. This dilemma introduces a healthy doubt about both human invulnerability and nature's inevitable end. It may be that environmental degradation has always accompanied the various manifestations of globalized power in the local arena of the Caribbean islands, but it becomes equally unacceptable to Walcott to admit either nature's inevitable trajectory toward destruction or its limitless capacity for regeneration. The environmental effects of modern globalization may be a logical extension of colonial and plantation economies, but this would imply a telos that cannot be changed. We must admit at least the risk criticism takes in creating narratives of inevitability because by so doing it shields moral choice and poetry from answering for nature's wounds as well as the freedom to imagine and choose outcomes different from those prophesied by the past.

What is particularly powerful about Walcott's environmental critique of contemporary Caribbean culture is his awareness that the survival of Caribbean culture will depend on whatever ecological balance the post-slavery world of the region can strike in the "ebb of History" following slavery. This balance is a question of sustainable practice, which Walcott's cast of fishermen represents in the poem's opening scene. It is a matter of "using the old ways" and believing, as does Seven Seas, that "his work was prayer, / who caught only enough, since the sea had to live, / because it was life" (*O* 301). Walcott identifies here a practice of craftsmanship that brings human subjects into direct, elemental contact with the rudiments of the Caribbean environment: the sea, the trees, the beaches, the sky. Anything more than this fails to turn away from the telos of Caribbean development: "the discos, the transports, the greed, the noise" (*O* 301).

To be sure, no culture can withstand the wholesale destruction and fire sale of its natural foundations. There is, however, a sense in Walcott's work that the Caribbean is not so far removed from a past in which its culture was directly nurtured by the elements. Returning to that past, as this poem does, allows us to understand how a culture's history has become so profoundly intertwined with natural history so as to become indistinguishable from it and how, therefore, it has remaining opportunities, however increasingly more rare, for renewal.

I quote at length from a recent interview in which Walcott elaborates on his idea of sustainable craftsmanship:

> A canoe is a beautiful thing in St. Lucia, the object which is hollowed out and has great elegance and speed. So there is the emblem of a canoe going across the sea with a man on it, and it is a great image and something organic, because that tree is like wood and water. . . . So you have two elements in a way there. None of that is thought of by the fisherman apparently, but the relationship of somebody who hammers, or sculpts, a canoe, into a shape that is elegant is really, if you want to put it bluntly, creating a work of art. It is also more than a work of art: it is the thing from which he makes his living. If I put an outboard motor on that canoe, it doesn't lose its elegance and is brought up to the immediacy of the twentieth century today and is an outrigged, outfitted canoe with a powerful engine that does what it does to help the fishing industry and so on. You can even accommodate it into the design of the canoe, but a man rowing on his own sea has something a little more strange, a little more evocative, a little more baffling in terms of what he feels being on the water at sunrise, rowing with wooden oars, as opposed to starting his engine and going out. That subtlety that has been lost between the outboard motor and the oars is the area that we are talking about. One is obviously not saying "don't have an outboard motor because you are violating the symmetry of the canoe, the meaning of the canoe." On the other hand you are saying, "okay, have the outboard motor, it's good; you need it for your fishing." But if you let your outboard motor be your

equivalent of, say, a hotel, of a skyscraper, of a big building, of another something that paves the ground and pays no attention to the contours of the earth, then you have the architectural question of what you are doing to the landscape. If you magnify the argument that the outboard motor does more for the fisherman than the oars, then you have the argument of people who say, "that is progress," and therefore it is legitimate to transform every little village in the Caribbean to a mini Miami or a small functioning modern outlet. And you can look at the architecture of the Caribbean and see it change. You don't know sometimes whether you are in Puerto Rico or Miami. They are identical. And you can continue on down the archipelago. This is what tragically is going to happen. What does that do in terms of the psyche of the fisherman we are talking about and the fisherman with an outboard motor? The industry is called progress.

What has been lost between the feeling and the pace of a man rowing and an outboard motor is exactly, well not only poor countries but any country on earth now has to realize that that outboard motor distends its own sense of time. In other words, you row and get your own rhythm and then you fish and that's your industry, that's your feeling, that's your relationship to what you're doing. You get an outboard motor and it's like a third person with you—that's an engine that you use. But the ironic thing about time is that the rhythm of the human body is never satisfied with its own pace. In other words, you get in an outboard motor, and you wish you could go faster, so you build a faster boat, and you discard the canoe, and you build something made out of plastic that goes faster and faster until you get to the point that there's no more canoe; not that you can't have a relationship between sunrise and being in an outboard motor rig craft, but something has gone and what has happened recently with all of these demonstrations and riots in terms of ecology is that people are seriously, really seriously aware of the danger to the planet. This is a very large thing, but you can take a microcosmic thing like that, or like Jalousie [Hilton's recently built resort in the Pitons], or violating something that should have a certain sanctity for every tribe, once you start to do that then you start to use that argument in the name of progress. Then you are doing the historical thing. You are saying that if I get twenty-five soldiers and I go into a territory that has Indians, if I shoot the Indians and if I convert them, then I am doing it for their own good. That has always been the argument for the outboard motor. (Walcott, "Argument" 130–31)

Walcott's uneasy view of technology here recognizes the economic demands that would make such innovations necessary at the same time that he identifies its important and deleterious cultural effects. What, precisely, is the dividing line between technologies that sustain and those that destroy poetry, culture, human sensibility, and the physical environment? Walcott suggests that one important distinction is the effect of technology on one's sense of bodily pace and rhythm in relation to the "contours" of space and materials within which one works. Technologies that allow us to find rhythm, as he puts it, would be those that help us to perceive directly a relationship to what we are doing and to the places we inhabit while doing it. This concern was not raised by Whitman or Neruda in their optimistic appraisal of technological developments, which they saw as categorically enhancing democratic possibilities. Aldo Leopold, as I discussed in chapter 5, saw the axe as a form of technology more attuned to the natural history it affects. This is the implicit rhythm of the opening scene of *Omeros* in which the "axe of sunlight" reflects the "axes in [their] own eyes" and in their hands. The trees shake in response, a kind of rhythmic dance that allows the fishermen to question the necessity of the violence they are about to inflict. The implicit meaning seems to be that only after such consideration can their actions be sacralized.

Elaine Scarry's discussion in *The Body in Pain* may help to answer this question. She has insisted on the fact that its relationship to human sentience distinguishes a weapon from a tool. "The weapon," she writes, "acts directly on sentience while the tool only acts on sentience by providing it with an object" (Scarry 214). In an ethical refashioning of Marxist philosophy, she argues that power is forged on the basis of the denial of human pain and that much of a culture's artifacts can function as weapons to the extent that the bodies on which they inflict pain are objectified. For example, plantation systems derive their power by denying the pain inflicted by the machinery of the plantation on the slave body, which is valued as mere property. The slave's body is commodified and denied sentience, but this also means that the slave's labor is potentially divorced from the sentience of the world, since whatever the body can feel of its own environment is subsumed by its very instrumentation. Philoctete's wound would seem to appeal to the reader as a reminder of this physical pain that remains unassimilated. His wound is caused by his labor as a fisherman, of course, and not as a slave, but the wound was a "rusted anchor" and a symbol, as we have seen, of the Caribbean past of slavery and forgotten ancestral pain (*O* 4).

Scarry notes that the transformation of a weapon into a tool requires a transformation of the site of pain from the passive body to the active body that wields the tool:

> Sentience is no longer the passive surface on which the weapon's power of alteration inscribes itself but is instead relocated to the other, active end of the object and becomes responsible for controlling and directing that power of alteration. In this shift, weapon becomes tool, sentience becomes active, pain is replaced by the willed capacity for self-transformation and recreation, and the structure of belief or sustained imagining is modified into the realization of belief in material making. (220)

Scarry sees in the transition from the Old to the New Testaments a story of this transformation from a disembodied God who requires belief to be marked on the bodies of the believers to an embodied God who in exchange for the promise of healing of pain now requires heightened senses and "more responsible acts of perception" on the part of believers (220).

For Walcott, this transformation from weapon to tool requires a similar disavowal of power and a recovery of the senses. This is vital not only in human social relationships but also in regard to human use of natural resources. The pain of slavery was not only caused by beatings and manacles but also by the deprivation of the body's thirst for craftsmanship and how such creative activities provide the body its own rhythm in relationship to its actions. Almost as soon as Africans are captured they begin to yearn for the chance to exercise their learned crafts: "The worst crime is to leave a man's hands empty. / Men are born makers, with that primal simplicity / in every maker since Adam" (*O* 150). He notes that despite the injustice of chaining hands and feet in the belly of the slave ships, "[t]he chained wrists couldn't forget / the carver for whom antelopes leapt. . . . so out of habit / their fingers grew leaves in the foetid ground of the boat" (*O* 150). The denial of bodily pain upon which slavery depended could not stop their hands from re-creating their world. In the slave ships "now they were coals, firewood, dismembered / branches, not men," but they nevertheless could not stop

[s]cratching a board[.]

[T]hey made the signs for their fading names on the wood,
and their former shapes returned absently; each carried
the nameless freight of himself to the other world. (*O* 150)

They are borne/born in this tomb/womb of slavery, coming "up from the
darkness / past the disinterested captains, shielding their eyes" (*O* 151).

Although objectified to the point that they function as firewood, the
slaves' dehumanization has an ironic consequence. Being denied sentience
and remade into nature is only ultimately triumphant if we assume that
nature itself is without sentience. Walcott repeatedly portrays the fishermen
of his story and Achille's African ancestors as men of trees, as integral parts
of the natural environment they inhabit. Dehumanizing the African, of
course, was precisely what slavery attempted to do, but this should not
lead to the conclusion that people whose humanity is deeply embedded
in a more-than-human world are to be pitied. Walcott, of course, does
not understate slavery's violence, nor does he deny the difference being
human makes. By portraying Africans as kin of trees, however, he suggests
the advantage of a naturalized human society and that elemental forms of
craftsmanship stand to build new cultures because they rely on this close
proximity to the natural world.

Thus, as in Scarry's schema, remaking the world through craft provides
the opportunity for this overturning of the dynamics of power and pain
upon which Caribbean oppression depends. Scarry notes that a revolution
in moral consciousness occurred when ancient cultures replaced the human
sacrificial body with an animal. She notes further that when "the lamb is
moved out of that location and replaced by a block of wood under the still
looming knife . . . the object itself is now re-perceived as wholly different
object, a tool rather than a weapon, and the anticipated action of the object
is no longer an act of 'wounding' but an act of 'creating'" (Scarry 174).

It is not irrelevant, then, that for all three of these poets one of the
most powerful metaphors for poetry's capacity to make a New World is
woodworking. We saw this in Whitman's "Song of the Broad-Axe," in
Neruda's "Que despierte el leñador" [Let the Woodcutter Awaken], and
in Walcott's "Crusoe's Journal." These are representations of a shift from
violence to craftsmanship.

In *Omeros* Walcott suggests that a culture's potential depends on its direct link to the survival of the physical environment and that technology is slowly rendering "obsolete / [the] craft of the carpenter" (227). As he contemplates the loss of fishing that St. Lucia's tourist marinas represent he notes:

> My craft required the same
> crouching care, the same crabbed, natural devotion,
> of the hand that stencilled a flowered window-frame
>
> or planed an elegant canoe; its time was gone
> with the spirit in the wood, as wood grew obsolete
> and plasterers smoothed the blank page of white concrete. (*O* 227)

Even at an advanced age Walcott refuses to paint indoors from photographs or to use a computer in the production of his poetry. His preference, as Whitman once advocated for the New World writer, is to produce literature in the open air, exposed to the elements. The metaphor of the slaves' hands "growing leaves" in the belly of the ship suggests that craftsmanship of this elemental sort is itself an inherent part of a natural process. Creation of artifacts allows the human body to become liberated from its own pain and objectification at the hands of History.

This is where Walcott takes the implications of Scarry's argument one step further, however. Although mechanization of human labor might bring certain economic advantages, history is a record of how those advantages are not equitably distributed. Just as serious a concern is the way mechanization divorces human labor from being able to feel the contours of the earth and thus to feel its own force. Walcott insists that all natural resources, animal, vegetable, or mineral, have sentience and that all human labor therefore potentially acts as a weapon on the so-perceived passive or nonexistent sentience of the physical world. For this reason, only when the cedar's sentience is recognized at the poem's outset does its "murder" become a "sacrifice." The ethical evolution from human sacrifice to woodworking is only an advance if we have come close to perceiving sentience not in other human bodies alone but in all of earth's material. Wood's functionality is not because it is less sentient than an animal (one might consider Neruda's breathing hewn hardwood) but because its sentience is more observable and directly correlative to the well-being of the immediate environment. This is decidedly not true of concrete or other material that mechanization has already rendered at least once removed from the soil. Walcott repeatedly uses animism, "the spirit in the wood," to describe this sentence. We should recall that Philoctete tells that they drink rum "to give us the spirit to turn into murderers. / I lift up the axe and pray for the strength in my hands to wound the first cedar. Dew was filling my eyes" (*O* 3). The tool here is clearly a weapon, but it appears that the wielder, Achille, is himself pained by the pain he inflicts, enough so that he requires a slight numbing, which does not deny the tree's pain but enables Achille to go forward with the action. If all human labor and remaking of the world involve inflicting pain, the question is, On what grounds can we accept an assimilation of that pain?

Walcott's metaphors insist on the paradox that this pain can only be felt and recorded by nature itself. The impossibility of registering this pain is a crucial confession made by a New World poetics. Just as the depth of his pain at his mother's death is measured by a confession of betrayal, so too must poetry acknowledge what human beings cannot fully comprehend about our impact on the world. By so doing poetry enhances our respect for the sentience of the world. As cited earlier:

> Although smoke forgets the earth from which it ascends,
> and nettles guard the holes where the laurels were killed,
> an iguana hears the axes. (*O* 4)

Nature is its own mute witness to the violence done to it. What distinguishes this scene, however, from, say, a bulldozing of the forest is the fact that the technology used does not distance the actor sufficiently from the object being acted upon to deny its sentience. Indeed, Walcott's poetry seeks to record nature's witness, even if it cannot represent the full content of such testimony. He acknowledges what must be temporarily denied in order to facilitate the necessary human violence that will remake the world in a sustainable way.

Remaking, of course, is the very function of technology, always reformulating our relationship to the natural world, but, arguably, technology has become increasingly aimed at disabling our perception of those feelings. In this sense culture has become a weapon that has forged the power of human society over and against the more-than-human world. A New World culture necessitates an understanding of nature's capacity for sustainable renewal. The reason why the murdered tree's acquiescence to use is not a Whitmanesque celebration of human settlement is because of Walcott's portrayal of loss and of an action that remains in rhythmic balance with the changes it causes. Additionally, the canoe enables the fishermen to move in closer proximity to, not farther from, the rhythms of the sea.

There will be a point, as Walcott argues in the interview, at which technological innovations will prove to do just the opposite. Indeed, problems arise when the transformations caused by diaspora, globalization, and the technological innovations that both facilitate and follow in the wake of such migrations outpace natural and human capacity to adjust. Diaspora was the affect of economic and technological developments at the height of Western domination of the New World, the sugar mill being perhaps one of the most devastating. So while Walcott wishes to find reasons to accept and even find hope in the facts of the New World's transplanted history, he also recognizes the implicit problems of glorifying such radical transformations because the energy behind them fuels so much of contemporary globalization.

This is a key point for understanding the grounds for Walcott's own vision of the commonalities of New World experience across the Americas. He has often been tempted by the notion that indigenous experience throughout the Americas is cut from the same cloth and that all diasporas are perhaps created equal (this appears to be the impulse behind his extended portrayal of the late-nineteenth-century activist Catherine Weldon and North American Indian experience in the poem). However, in his contemplation of a New England fall and its own diasporic past he recognizes that the "widening mind can acquire / the hues of a foliage different from where it begins" but that we are not "simply chameleons, self-dyeing our skins / to each background" (O 207). If we can imagine a New World cultural space, we cannot travel endlessly or transhistorically across its geographies without failing to understand places for their diversity and differences. A New World community has limitations, as does the earth, which after too many seasons of movement and transition "lies barren as the dusty Dakotas" (O 207). If nature's significance for New World cultures is to be preserved, we must start with a recognition that

[m]en take their colours

as the trees do from the native soil of their birth,

and once they are moved elsewhere, entire cultures
lose the art of mimicry, and then, where the trees were,

the fir, the palm, the olive, the cedar, a desert place
widens in the heart. (*O* 207–8)

The best antidote to the desertification of the heart *and* of land is not
to flee the conditions of one's transplantation, to long to "go back" or
to go away, but to stay put and, Adam-like, begin to remake the world
from the elements of one's broken world. This is not a second-place finish,
a consolation prize for having lost the metropolitan race for belonging
among the great Western traditions. It is, as Walcott has long insisted, a gift
to be born in provincial circumstances because, as he put it in his Nobel
speech, "[b]reak a vase, and the love that reassembles the fragments is
stronger than that love which took its symmetry for granted when it was
whole" (*What the Twilight* 69). Craftsmanship, under such circumstances,
is more annealing, more congealing than anything the West might have to
offer. And this is because provincialism necessitates "making a start out of
particulars," in William Carlos Williams's words.

In "Isla Incognita," an essay he wrote in 1973, Walcott insists that we will
grow tired of the particulars of our provincial corner of the world unless we
develop the adamic capacity to pretend that "we have seen none of it before.
It will be impossible, of course, for how can we tell whether our feeling on
seeing that rock and its bay is nostalgia or revelation. Well, combine both
and the illumination made by their igniting would be discovery" (51). We do
not need to make a choice between the future or the past; the reconciliation
of both emotions that pertain here is in the experience of the elusive present.
This is discovery without possession, because, as Aldo Leopold states, "the
outstanding characteristic of perception is that it entails no consumption
and no dilution of any resource" (173). This stands in direct contradiction
to the poststructuralist argument that insists that the idea of landscape has
a history that has been anything but innocuous in relationship to land.
While not denying that history, Walcott insists that adamic discovery of the
newness of the world is still necessary, paradoxically, so as to establish a
protective but not possessive attitude toward land and a sense of belonging
in one's place. As Octavio Paz's argument correctly intuited, perception of
nature's elusive mutability and the necessity therefore of metaphor help to

balance the human in relation to the natural, without denying, on the one hand, their distinct and mutual presence or, on the other, their inevitable confluence. We can hear this tenuous balance in these beautiful concluding lines from "Isla Incognita":

> It has taken me over thirty years and my race hundreds, to feel the fibres spread from the splayed toes and grip this earth the arms knot into boles and put out leaves. When that begins this is the beginning of season, cycle time. The noise my leaves make is my language. In it is tunneled the roar of seas of a lost ocean. It is a fresh sound. Let me not be ashamed to write like this, because it supports this thesis, that our only true apprehensions are through metaphor. (57)

That is to say, metaphorical representation is the only means by which we can imagine what is most true about ourselves: that we are as natural as trees.

Conclusion

While the foundation of an environmentally and socially healthy society must begin with a deep appreciation for place, affection is not a panacea. As Wallace Stegner has warned, "we may love a place and still be dangerous to it" (55). In addition to greater affection for land we need what novelist Marilynne Robinson in her compelling book *The Death of Adam* has called "a new, chastened, self-distrusting vision of the world, an austere vision that can postpone the outdoor pleasures of cherishing exotica, . . . and the debilitating pleasures of imagining that our own impulses are reliably good" (253). Modern thought has tended to reduce the moral risks implicit in relating to the physical world by resorting to explanatory discourses that demystify human being, the mystery of which, for Robinson, is what Adam represents. Cultivation of appreciation for place is an important, if complicated, process, since how those affections are born and how they are expressed are exercises in ethical choice. Whether it has been Whitman's broad embrace that risks generalizations about the Americas, Neruda's ambition to awake an American love that becomes ideological, or Walcott's peripatetic itineraries that never seem to settle, each poet's sense of place has run certain risks based on his capacity to imagine and experience cross-cultural contact and contact with nature. Each poet, in differing degrees, has also caught glimpses of the risks his strengths have caused him to run, leading to the kind of self-distrust Robinson describes; a sense of place emerges that is cultivated by a poetic exploration of their own betrayals and prodigal returns.

In her poem "Questions of Travel" Elizabeth Bishop articulates the paradox of travel and return by which affections for nature are nurtured. Raised in North America, she also lived extensively in Brazil, and her shifting experience of the southern and northern landscapes helped her to see both with equally stunned fascination. Travel helped to expose the world's unexpected qualities and fueled the fires of her poetic imagination. For example, Brazil's "too many waterfalls" make her think that "the mountains look like the hulls of capsized ships, / slime-hung and barnacled" (Bishop 93). Out of her amazement, however, come these Dickensonian questions of travel:

> Should we have stayed at home and thought of here?
> Where should we be today?
> Is it right to be watching strangers in a play
> in this strangest of theatres?
> What childishness is it that while there's a breath of life
> in our bodies, we are determined to rush
> to see the sun the other way around? (Bishop 93)

Amazement in the face of nature raises ethical questions about the rightness of our choices, of even our most instinctual urges to praise and celebrate beauty, which may be nothing more than what Robinson means by "cherishing exotica." Instead of expressing appreciation and attachment, amazement may express self-imposed deracination from home, something self-imposed conditions of modern restlessness only make more likely.

Bishop insists for this reason on the geopolitical limitations of "*Continent, city, country, society*" that mean "*the choice is never wide and never free*" (94). Our perceptions of nature, wherever we are, are conditioned by culture, language, and history. She asks the logical question: "*Is it lack of imagination that makes us come / to imagined places, not just stay at home?*" (94). Why, in other words, is it necessary to travel elsewhere, to seek the sun "the other way around" just so we can understand where we are from and where home is? Isn't it a symptom of a restless and weak imagination to require the fleshly contact with new landscapes just so that we can then realize the outline of the inner landscapes of the mind? What difference does it make to launch literal or merely literary journeys to other regions of the hemisphere?

Pascal had written that human evil stemmed from such restlessness in one's room, but Bishop raises the possibility that he was "*not entirely right.*" The basis for this is her suspicion that what travel teaches is the comparative value of place and that if human affection is fickle, it is also adaptable. Diaspora and migration in modernity require strategies of adaptation, since "home" is itself an ambiguous category. The advantage migration affords is that by means of constant transformation the elemental human task of apprehending the world is enhanced. After a long list of what it "would have been a pity / not to have seen" as a result of her own Brazilian travels, Bishop concludes with a significantly revised and more provocative question of travel: "*Should we have stayed at home, / wherever that may be?*" (93, 94).

The poem sees the possibility that the restless conditions of modernity, especially of the economic and educational elite, while shaped by history have a more metaphysical echo. That nature amazes us is in itself a symptom of our awareness of human difference. During an interview in 2004 Robinson spoke to me of this particularly human dilemma:

> There's probably nothing stranger than the fact that we exist on a planet. Very odd. Who does not feel the oddness of this? I mean, stop and think about where we actually are in the larger sense. It seems to me as if every local landscape is a version of the cosmic mystery, that it is very strange that we're here, and that it is very strange that we are what we are. In a certain sense the mystery of the physical reality of the human being is expressed in any individual case by the mystery of a present landscape. The landscape is ours in the sense that it is the landscape that we query. So, we're created in the fact of ourselves answering to a particular sense of amazement.

If our humanity is forged in the moment of answering to this amazement, the opposite is also true. To the extent that we refuse to "query" the landscape, as she puts it, in order to probe the contours of our being, we create a culture and civilization founded on a denial of nature and consequently of our humanity. She explains:

> I think that human beings feel strange in their circumstance. One of the ways that they have of hiding from human reality is to create artificial environments. Look at people from Babylon forward; when people have power they create an artificial environment around themselves that can suggest to them that they're immune from the consequences of being mortal. And palaces, all these things, are monuments to this impulse. And as we have created a more technological civilization and one that is simply more profuse in its products, we can do more and more to artificialize our environment to the point that we have no idea where we are by looking at what surrounds us.

If we cannot learn to tolerate our human otherness and difference in the natural world, we wind up constructing a world merely of our making and thus deny both our naturalness *and* our humanity; our culture becomes a weapon that denies natural sentience and our obligations to it. Biologically speaking, we cannot be separated from the undifferentiated stuff of the physical world, but because of our capacity to contemplate ourselves in the reflections of water and of the natural world—what for Whitman, Neruda, and Walcott is the very foundation of *poiesis*, or world making through metaphor—we have a hint that we are more than mere bodies. Conscious thought alone is not sufficient to sustain or to delimit our humanity, of course, since we still face the task of learning how to incorporate, para-doxically, our biology. Our dreams of new worlds, in other words, emerge from and must extend back to the experience of our embodied being in the ancient earth. In this sense ecology and poetry face off as mirror sites of simultaneous reckoning and forgetting who we are. In this duplicitous function water, land, animal, and plant life serve to provide a rich and ambiguous sense of place. While natural landmarks serve as touchstones of a New World poetics of place, they simultaneously open us up to vis-tas of mystery and otherness that an adamic imagination can never fully assimilate. Bishop notes that her amazement leads to an awareness of the world's ultimate opacity and thus to her own experience of separation *and* delight:

To stare at some inexplicable old stonework,
inexplicable and impenetrable,
at any view,
instantly seen and always, always delightful? (93)

Although insufficient to sustain a rooted and historical sense of place, this awareness of our strange and differentiated ecological belonging to the land inspires a detached sense of awe in the face of natural regeneration. Experience of strangeness in the land paradoxically provides the transplanted subject a tentative and imagined home in a new world and a valuable ecological ethic of reverence and protection.

David Abram would have us believe that our very written language—the whole body of literary culture and its myriad metaphorical gestures—is a symptom of our profound Western alienation from nature. While lamenting Western mistakes might seem an admirable and necessary penance, we must not do so at the cost of implying that non-Western cultures do not also experience their relationship to nature self-consciously. Besides, recovering our intimacy with nature outside the bounds of Western culture does not seem likely in an age of increasingly Western globalization. I don't mean to suggest an argument here about an undifferentiated universal alienation of humanity from nature, since clearly some cultures have established and maintained intimacy better than others. My point is simply that it seems odd, at best, to ask us to put our faith in ideas, expressed in written language, that argue that written language only increases the difficulty of finding our way back home to our senses.

While Bishop's questions of travel address this experience of our self-conscious separation from the world, the poem haunts us with the odd and ambiguous possibility that metaphor is our only and "natural" home. Her metaphors of pounding rain "so much like politicians' speeches" or the trees "really exaggerated in their beauty, / . . . gesturing / like noble pantomists" communicate and even replicate our experience as strangely belonging to the earth (Bishop 93–94). Prodigals understand what to cherish, and so perhaps Walcott means to express the idea that metaphor, in holding together unlike things, as Octavio Paz argues (*Other* 149), is at its root a form of charity: "Break a vase, and the love that reassembles the fragments is stronger than the love which took its symmetry for granted when it was whole" (*What the Twilight* 69). Love of the earth is born from an awareness of natural change but also from a reckoning of human error. This is not to ontologize unethical choices but to signify the danger of assuming we can negotiate a position of existential, even Adamic, purity in some ahistorical Garden. If written language is one of the many symptoms of our natural alienation, it might also be our cure. Merely to loathe what humans have done to the earth *as* humans is only to pretend we can exist in this prelapsarian world. Our presence in the world is ineluctable, and our choices are not wide and entirely free, as Bishop reminds us. If the adamic impulse to name the world is going to avoid the deleterious effects of deluded visions of the self's innocence, it must begin with an honest reckoning of what it means to have acted humanly in *this* world. But to avoid more self-loathing, it must go one step further and accept the possibility of natural as well as human goodness. If Walcott is correct in asserting that the world-making activity of poetry is both cause and cure for our alienation, the self-healing possibilities of culture deserve our most focused attention. Though misunderstood by environmentalists less patient with working to solve this more challenging but more fundamental problem, Robinson has, for this reason, insisted that "every environmental problem is a human problem. Civilization is the ecology being lost. We can do nothing that matters if we cannot encourage its rehabilitation" (*Death* 253–54). Paz further points out that the hope for this rehabilitation in "the examination of conscience and the remorse that accompanies it, a legacy from Christianity," has been and is "the most powerful remedy against the ills of our civilization" (*Other* 150).

I suggested in my introduction that this study was an exercise in recycling. This work entails, among other things, allowing literature to rehabilitate our imaginative freedom in the face of nature's mystery and within the constraints of culture and geography. Rather than finding nature's impenetrability intolerable and thus acting to obliterate its offending difference, we can begin by embracing our uniquely human opportunities to act with conscience and accountability by imagining new worlds that allow us to explore the differences between what we dream and the experiences that history, culture, and language have thus far enabled. Bishop is right to lament that we don't have better imaginations or that we don't read widely or sensitively enough so as to be content sitting at home. As Aldo Leopold similarly argued, enhancing our sense of place has less to do with building more roads "into lovely country, but of building receptivity into the still unlovely human mind" (176). But Bishop is also right to remind us that Whitmanian travel along open roads of lovely country, even roads in other Americas, can still serve to improve our chances of understanding where we really belong. Experience with the living earth teaches us that our place of inhabitation is both more imagined *and* more geographical than we had supposed. Although inevitably delayed, in an age of increasingly degraded life on earth we can only hope that our prodigal returns home are not too late.

Introduction

1. James A. Arnold has argued that such sexual politics inform the pronounced postcolonial aims of the *créolité* movement of the French West Indies. In my conversations with Walcott he has insisted that this is not a gendered argument about literature, however. When pressed to give examples of New World Eves he has mentioned Emily Dickinson, Lorna Goodison, and Velma Pollard.

2. Victor Figueroa brilliantly articulates this breakdown, for example, in his "'Encomium of Helen': Derek Walcott's 'Ethical Twist' in *Omeros*." Walcott exposes how his own desire to see Helen as a metaphor of the island participates in the very "epistemic violence of colonialism" he seeks to undermine (Figueroa 11). Ultimately, Figueroa insists that recognizing "respect for [Helen's] opacity" allows her otherness to exist outside the claims of colonial discourse, including Walcott's own gendered and sexualized view of St. Lucian nature as woman (20).

3. See my *Postslavery Literatures in the Americas* and "Oedipus in the Americas."

1. Ecology, the New World, and the "American" Adam

1. Most historians agree that, no matter when the early inhabitants first arrived, by ten thousand years ago the Americas were widely settled. Shawn Miller's overview of indigenous land use prior to 1492 also shows a deep history of human manipulation and intervention in the environment. He writes: "If Columbus had discovered paradise, it was a humanized paradise, best described as a well tended garden. Significantly, it fell between the spontaneous, celestial Eden Columbus continued to seek and the empty, immaculate wilderness that some of us still strain to see."

2. John Elder argues that nature's temporality, evident in these dynamic changes, differentiates it from art (*Imagining* 35).

2. A New World Poetics

1. I borrow the term "negative sublime" from Dominick LaCapra, who has critiqued the emergence of the negative sublime in literature and criticism about the Holocaust.

2. My book *Postslavery Literatures in the Americas* argues that the impact of slavery's history has generated an extraordinary outpouring of parallel literary expression throughout the Americas.

3. Elder's *Reading the Mountains of Home* is based on a fascinating and convincing reading of Frost's poem "Directive," which is a work at pains to demonstrate the very traces of human history in the landscape Frost seems to ignore in "The Gift Outright."

4. See Adamson, Evans, and Stein, *The Environmental Justice Reader*, which moves beyond the "wilderness-based, white-authored nature writing, and advocates a more inclusive, class- and race-conscious ecocriticism that articulates the complex human relationships to environment expressed in culturally diverse literature" (9). Also see DeLoughrey, Gosson, and Handley, *Caribbean Literature and the Environment*, especially the introduction.

5. I am indebted to Juan Gelpí's argument about the perpetuation of paternalism in Puerto Rican literature (8).

3. Reading Whitman in the New World

1. Reynolds also notes that *Democratic Vistas* articulates in philosophical form the political views of Andrew Johnson, a former slave owner who believed that the preservation of the Union after the Civil War relied on the management of white male elites who could protect the Union against the centrifugal tendencies of a postbellum society of increased racial and social heterogeneity (468–69).

2. Walter Grünzweig responds to González de la Garza's charges by noting the important distinction between "expansionism" and "imperialism" in Whitman, the former a more naive notion of spreading influence through the hemisphere (152).

3. It should be noted that Alegría published his study well in advance of Mauricio González de la Garza's 1971 polemic against Whitman.

4. Julio Ramos explains that Martí offers the "natural man" as an autochthonous alternative to Sarmiento's view of the lettered intellectual of the metropolis, who "represents and legitimizes himself as a traveler and translator who acts as the mediator between the blank page of the desert and the plenitude of the European library" (256). Ramos suggests that he is also arguing with the positivism and social Darwinism of the Porfirian regime in Mexico (258).

5. Angel Rama explains that this was, in part, due to Martí's fascination with the philosophy of the nineteenth-century Irish physicist John Tyndall, who urged a more harmonious union between poetry and matter. He also argues that this was an early modernist fascination with the apparent capacity of science to make

apprehension of the world verifiable. As Martí wrote: "Language should be mathematical, geometric, plastic. The idea should be captured exactly by the phrase, so exactly that what you might subtract from the phrase, you would subtract from the idea" (qtd. in Rama 105).

6. Rama, however, asserts that Martí's version of this realism eschewed the obsession with ugliness in European versions (127).

7. The religious rhetoric here signifies a modernist longing for pure apprehension, which in the context of the postcolonial Americas is also a desire for independence from the mentality of Europe by means of marriage to the local environment. For Martí there had to be in this mode of apprehension some Kantian guarantee that the individual subjectivity could unite with matter in such a way as to escape the idiosyncrasies of individuality; otherwise, apprehension became mere narcissism. Rama argues that the possibility of transcendental unity "with all human beings" is precisely what made Whitman so attractive to Martí (131).

8. For more on Martí's ambivalence about race see Plummer; Ferrer.

4. Nature's Last Chemistry

1. See Boatright; Fulghum; and Zong-qi on the similarities between Hegelian dialecticism and Whitman's poetic vision. See also Reynolds 253.

2. See also Kronick's chapter "Whitman and Time" in *American Poetics of History*. Gay Allen also notes the influence of Thomas Paine's *Age of Reason*, which taught that God's revelations could be found in nature, and Chasseboeuf, comte de Volney's *Les ruines*, which gave a rationalist account of religion (175–76).

3. Erkkila argues that "[a]s the material conditions in post–Civil War America seemed to deny the theory of America and thus the validity of his life and work, Whitman turned increasingly toward the spiritual world to valorize and justify his democratic vision" (*Whitman* 273).

4. According to Piasecki, Whitman's view emerged from geological uniformitarianism, which posited that all of the universe is part of an orderly and consistent system of law. The opposing view was held by catastrophists, who posited that nature undergoes radical and abrupt shifts from one epoch to another and that in each epoch a new set of laws was instituted by a divine Providence.

5. Erkkila insists that the poem's organizational principle is Whitman's conception of the " 'triplicate process' of Hegelian evolution" by which two oppositions produce a third synthesis (*Whitman* 265).

6. Whitman suggests that the groundwork of the poet/prophet who will fulfill our understanding of New World destiny will be prepared by "the scientist, the chemist, / the geologist, ethnologist" (*PW* 279). Ethnology was particularly help-

ful because it offered a "pseudoscientific racial-extinction theory that Whitman embraced after the war," and thus Whitman's reference to interracial marriage suggests "the ethnologists' idea of so-called 'superior' races gaining dominance over others" (Reynolds 500).

7. Whitman admitted that he had "unconsciously put a sort of autobiographical dash" to the poem (qtd. in Reynolds 513). See also Stuckey-French 539.

8. Special thanks to Ed Cutler, who urged me to consider the *Calamus* poems in this light.

9. On this point see Kepner 186.

5. Natural History as Autobiography

1. Biographers have noted Neruda's problematic relationship with his father, the death of his mother at his birth, and the loss of his stepmother at an early age as reasons why Neruda may have felt such intense alienation. It is also likely this was a reason why he sought a surrogate mother/father in nature itself, since it was an early source of healing from deeply and intuitively felt adolescent pain.

2. Jack Schmitt translates "soledades" as "wilds," which is certainly a possible meaning, but it misses the way in which the word anthropomorphizes nature or communicates Neruda's human experience of the more-than-human world.

3. These critics include, among others, Federico Schopf, René de Costa, and Chris Perriam, all of whom insist on identifying this shift as a shift to postmodernism. Jorge Edwards notes that after 1956 "you have the immediate sensation that the poet, whose eyes had been set on the future, is refocusing on the things that surround him, big or small, on the immediate landscape" (86).

4. All English citations from *Estravagario* are taken from Alastair Reid's 1974 bilingual edition of the book, *Extravagario*. Pagination indicates the location of the Spanish verse; the English appears on the opposite page.

5. On Neruda's agnostic religiosity see Boero, who notes that the elements of the material world "interpellate him in such a particular way that they question his very existence," much the way notions of the divine do (54).

6. Hemispheric History as Natural History

1. This increasingly geographical and political vision led him to reject what he perceived as the overly intellectual theorizations of such poets as Vicente Huidobro, Octavio Paz, and Jorge Luis Borges, whom he considered "unfaithful to the *tierra* of Latin America" (Simon 4).

2. Nelson Osorio explains that individual subjectivity in the poem does not play off the collective: " 'Poet' and 'people' in this work are not polarized terms of

subjectivity and objectivity but a symbiosis that creates a dialectical perspective of poetic enunciation in a renewed and renewing syncretism" (183).

3. Celaya further suggests that such extension back to beginnings is an archetypical gesture for writers of the Third World: "[T]hat Third World is also of the Third Day of Creation" (24).

4. For "The Heights of Machu Picchu" I have used John Felstiner's translation in his *Translating Neruda: The Way to Machu Picchu* instead of Schmitt's.

5. The implicit natural history of human beings here, one recent Chilean critic notes, is no longer so strange to contemporary readers because indigenous history is better known and because sustainable, biocentric views of human possibility have become more common. Pedro Correa Vasquez writes: "[O]ur culture is re-assuming, little by little, its originary condition in which we are (are we?) nature. Only by being nature could we derive inspiration from a poem where the poet acts as a seer and is capable . . . of arriving at the depth where it is possible to 'kiss the secret stones'" (14).

6. Again, my emphasis on the oblivion Neruda must confront here differs from the critical consensus on the poem. Cedomil Goic describes, for example, the actions of natural forces as ultimately "caressing, nuptially loving" and that they "polish and render translucent [*no opacan*]" the affected stones (234). I insist, on the other hand, that natural erosion has had precisely the opposite effect of erasing legible traces of the past, thus increasing the enigmatic opacity of the ruins, particularly in regard to the poet's ambition to recover the past.

7. For more on the comparison between voices in Neruda and Whitman see Coleman 264.

8. I return again to Schmitt's translation.

9. For a brief analysis of these two poems see Stone.

10. Roland Barthes distinguishes between metalanguage, which would be the equivalent of language spoken about a tree, and political language, which would be the equivalent of what Leopold's woodcutter expresses about his interaction with the tree. Political language avoids becoming mythology because "the tree is not an image for [the woodcutter], it is simply the meaning of [his] action" (Barthes 146).

11. On the basis of the analysis that follows I disagree with critics such as James Nolan and Emir Rodríguez Monegal who see Neruda's "prophetic guise [*profetismo*]" without its attendant irony. Rodríguez Monegal argues that this *profetismo* emerges as a result of his "identification with mystery, with the abyss, with the stars" ("El sistema" 87). He insists that Neruda, like Whitman, "is everywhere at the same time because he is not a man anymore, nor a poet, but a voice that comes from the depth of time and sings in the present, giving voice to all the voices of the New World" (80). Similarly, Nolan asserts that "[w]ho is actually

speaking in Whitman and Neruda's poetry is an illusion peeled away in successive layers during its performance, as in a shamanic trance: not the writer, but a mask; not the mask, but a voice; not just an individual voice, but a plurality of particular voices contained within the universality of the lyric 'I'" (158). This overstatement of Neruda's poetics neglects to consider the considerable effort with which he seeks to reckon with his inability to penetrate nature's mysteries. We become aware of the larger totality of the physical universe in Neruda's poetics precisely because he ultimately refuses to pretend to speak ubiquitously and omnisciently, as these critics posit.

12. On the biblical stance of *Canto general* and its relationship to Marxism's similarly totalizing impulses see Terry DeHay.

7. The Muse of (Natural) History

1. Bruce King notes that Walcott read a copy of Selden Rodman's *South America of the Poets* (published in 1970), an anthology of major voices of Latin American literature, from Neruda to Jorge Amado to Borges. Eager to understand this literature, Walcott "began reading Borges and Neruda with more care" (King 230). Of course, he never learned to read Spanish, so this reading was limited to translations by Alastair Reid and others.

2. Edward Baugh and Colbert Nepaulsingh argue that Shelley's "In Defence of Poetry" was vitally important to Walcott's development and in particular to *Another Life*. The essay was published in a 1952 edited volume that included essays by Edmund Wilson and T. S. Eliot, both of whom were equally palpable influences on Walcott's intellectual development in his early adulthood.

3. Yvette Christiansë notes that the New World conditions of slavery and colonialism mean that, for Walcott, "language can only repeat and emphasize what is lost and, indeed, the sense of loss itself" (216).

4. In early 1966, just prior to the suicide of Harry Simmons, his mentor, the prose account of Walcott's life breaks into verse. Simmons's death in Walcott's view provided "an aesthetic completion" to the book, which raises the speculation that the poem responds to "absence, separation and loss as inexorable realities" by expressing a "renewed faith in immanence" (Ismond 198).

5. Walcott's phrase is "[a]bout the August of my fourteenth year," which echoes, with apparent intent, Wordsworth's *Prelude* where he says, "'Twas then my fourteenth summer" (Baugh and Nepaulsingh 256).

6. Although Walcott remains a believer in God, his stance on art's superiority to religion has its origins in Joyce and Arnold. As Baugh and Nepaulsingh note, Walcott has expressed a consistent "eschewal of political and other causes ill-

conceived, . . . disdain for 'fact' and reverence for ideas, and most of all . . . lifelong religious practice of art." Indeed, *Another Life* depicts art as "the birth of a New World religion" (Baugh and Nepaulsingh 178).

7. Baugh and Nepaulsingh note that "the poet knows, from Aztec human sacrifice and anthropophagy, that cruelty is not unique to the Old World" (329).

8. Baugh and Nepaulsingh report that the Indians were more likely Arawak, given recent archaeological evidence that suggests their more pervasive presence throughout the islands. Although a site in St. Lucia retains the name, Morne des Sauters, "no reliable account" of the event exists. The legend, variations of which exist on other islands, is that forty Indians were pursued by the French to the edge of a precipice, where they dove to their death rather than surrender to the French (Baugh and Nepaulsingh 280).

9. I cannot concur with Patricia Ismond's assessment that by means of his poetic portrayal of this legend "Walcott redeems the aboriginal peoples of the region from the ignominy of their traditional image as an obliterated race. This reverses, moreover, his earlier views on an amnesiac past that includes the Carib, as in the poem 'Air'" (177). It is certainly an expression of this wish, but its modesty and limitations are elsewhere evident in the poem's insistence on amnesia as a Caribbean condition.

8. Impressionism in the New World

1. Walcott's biographer, Bruce King, notes that in April 1995 Walcott participated in a conference on translation at the Tate Gallery in London, and, given the conference's theoretical and academic nature, it was a surprise that he would have participated at all: "[T]he Turners upstairs at the Tate were Walcott's main interest. . . . Seeing the paintings appeared to be his purpose for being at the conference" (586).

2. The very history of Woodford Square demonstrates the folly of such confidence, since the space demonstrates the inevitability of fading memories and markers of the past. The square was first known as "Place of Souls" by the native Indians, who lost a costly battle at the site. It was later given the French name Place des âmes in honor of this indigenous past, only to later adopt its more recent English colonial history. The course of St. Ann's river was changed to further develop the square, so even its natural history has been altered.

3. Elizabeth Bergmann Loizeaux explains that "[p]rosopopeia . . . 'overcomes' the gap between the viewer and viewed, between word and image, between subject and object. The 'I' is not countered by illustration . . . but speaks out of the body of the primary image" (94). W. J. T. Mitchell has seen in ekphrasis a corollary to

the linguistic struggle to give expression to the "other," who is conventionally understood as silent and feminized. Mitchell insists that we move beyond the binary understanding of ekphrasis as the relationship between the "speaking/seeing subject and a seen object" by positing the third presence of the "listening subject who . . . will be made to 'see' the object through the medium of the poet's voice" (4).

4. In a recent interview Walcott responded to the accusation that his paintings seemed as if they had been painted by numbers: "But if you went to the Caribbean and you looked at Caribbean light, that's what you'd say, that you have to paint it by numbers. Because you're talking about a primal kind of light; you're talking about an intensity that is incredible. There is a blue that you can't find in your palette. And if you don't have it, how are going to paint the sky? . . . It's painful to take that criticism, and they may be right. Gradation and subtlety are important, but the attitude of imperial authority says that grey is the color of a culture, of a real culture. Blatant color, brassy color, bright color is associated with underdeveloped cultures, with underdeveloped people" ("Sharing" 136).

9. Death, Regeneration, and the Prospect of Extinction

1. For more on the mutual impact of New World history on environment and culture in the Caribbean see DeLoughrey, Gosson, and Handley; Crosby; and S. Miller.

WORKS CITED

Abbreviations

CP   Walcott, *Collected Poems 1948–1984*
CPW   Whitman, *Complete Prose Works*
E   Neruda, *Extravagario,* trans. Alastair Reid
LG   Whitman, *Leaves of Grass*
O   Walcott, *Omeros*
OC   Neruda, *Obras completas*
PW   Whitman, *The Portable Whitman*
TH   Walcott, *Tiepolo's Hound*
WWA   Whitman, *Walt Whitman Archive*

Works

Abram, David. *The Spell of the Sensuous: Perception and Language in a More-than-Human World.* New York: Vintage, 1997.

Adamson, Joni, Mei Mei Evans, and Rachel Stein, eds. *The Environmental Justice Reader: Politics, Poetics, and Pedagogy.* Tucson: University of Arizona Press, 2002.

Adler, Kathleen. *Camille Pissarro: A Biography.* London: B. T. Batsford Ltd., 1978.

Alegría, Fernando. "¿Cuál Whitman?: Borges, Lorca y Neruda." *Texto Crítico* 7.22–23 (1981): 3–12.

———. *Walt Whitman en Hispanoamérica.* Mexico City, 1954.

Allen, Gay Wilson. *The New Walt Whitman Handbook.* New York: New York University Press, 1975.

Alonso, Carlos J. *The Spanish American Regional Novel: Modernity and Autochthony.* New York: Cambridge University Press, 1990.

Altman, Matthew C. "Carlyle, Thomas (1795–1881)." LeMaster and Kummings 104–5.

Arnold, James A. "The Erotics of Colonialism in Contemporary French West Indian Literary Culture." *New West Indian Guide* 68.1–2 (1994): 5–22.

Baer, William, ed. *Conversations with Derek Walcott.* Jackson: University of Mississippi Press, 1996.

Barasch, Moshe. *Theories of Art: From Impressionism to Kandinsky.* New York: Routledge, 2000.

Barthes, Roland. *Mythologies*. Trans. Annette Lavers. New York: Hill and Wang, 1972.

Bate, Jonathan. *The Song of the Earth*. Cambridge, Mass.: Harvard University Press, 2000.

Bauerlein, Mark. "'Out of the Cradle Endlessly Rocking' (1859)." LeMaster and Kummings 495–97.

Baugh, Edward. *Memory as Vision: Another Life*. London: Longman Group Ltd., 1978.

Baugh, Edward, and Colbert Nepaulsingh. "Reading *Another Life*: A Critical Essay," with "Annotations." *Another Life: Fully Annotated*. Ed. Edward Baugh and Colbert Nepaulsingh. London: Lynne Rienner Publishers, 2004. 153–336.

Becker, Christoph. *Camille Pissarro*. Ostfildern-Ruit, Germany: Hatje Cantz Verlag, 1999.

Belitt, Ben. *Adam's Dream: A Preface to Translation*. New York: Grove Press, 1978.

———. "Pablo Neruda: A Revaluation." Bloom 139–65.

Belknap, Jeffrey, and Raúl Fernández, eds. *José Martí's "Our America": From National to Hemispheric Cultural Studies*. Durham, N.C.: Duke University Press, 1998.

Berger, Mark T. *Under Northern Eyes: Latin American Studies and U.S. Hegemony in the Americas, 1898–1990*. Bloomington: Indiana University Press, 1995.

Bernabé, Jean, Patrick Chamoiseau, Raphaël Confiant, and Mahamed B. Taleb Khyar. "In Praise of Creoleness." *Callaloo* 13 (Autumn 1990): 886–909.

Berry, Wendell. *The Unsettling of America: Culture and Agriculture*. San Francisco: Sierra Club Books, 1996.

Bishop, Elizabeth. *The Complete Poems, 1927–1979*. New York: Farrar, Straus and Giroux, 1984.

Blake, William. *Collected Poems*. Ed. W. B. Yeats. New York: Routledge, 2002.

Bloom, Harold, ed. *Pablo Neruda: Modern Critical Views*. New York: Chelsea House Publishers, 1989.

Boatright, M. C. "Whitman and Hegel." *Studies in English* 9 (1929): 134–50.

Boero, Mario. "Aproximaciones a la religion." *Análisis* 30 (Jan. 1981): 54–56.

Bolton, Herbert Eugene. "The Epic of Greater America." Hanke 67–100.

Bonetti Paro, Maria Clara. "Walt Whitman in Brazil." *Walt Whitman Quarterly Review* 2.2 (1993): 57–66.

Borges, Jorge Luis. *Labyrinths: Selected Stories and Other Writings*. New York: New Directions, 1964.

———. "Note on Walt Whitman." Perlman, Folsom, and Campion 235–40.

Breslin, Paul. *Nobody's Nation: Reading Derek Walcott*. Chicago: University of Chicago Press, 2001.

Brettell, Richard R. *Pissarro and Pontoise: The Painter in a Landscape*. New Haven, Conn.: Yale University Press, 1990.

Brotherston, Gordon. "Neruda's *Canto General* and the Great Song of America." Bloom 117–30.

Buell, Lawrence. "Commentary on 'Can American Studies Develop a Method?' by Henry Nash Smith." Maddox 1–16.

——. *The Environmental Imagination: Thoreau, Nature Writing, and the Formation of American Culture*. Cambridge, Mass.: Belknap Press of Harvard University Press, 1996.

——. *Writing for an Endangered World: Literature, Culture, and Environment in the U.S. and Beyond*. Cambridge, Mass.: Belknap Press of Harvard University Press, 2001.

Burnett, Paula. *Derek Walcott: Poetics and Politics*. Orlando: University Press of Florida, 2000.

Cable, George Washington. *The Negro Question*. New York: Scribner's, 1890.

Camboni, Marina, ed. *Utopia in the Present Tense: Walt Whitman and the Language of the New World*. Rome: Calamo, 1994.

Cañizares-Esguerra, Jorge. *How to Write the History of the New World: Histories, Epistemologies, and Identities in the Eighteenth-Century Atlantic World*. Stanford, Calif.: Stanford University Press, 2001.

Carpentier, Alejo. *The Lost Steps*. Trans. Harriet de Onís. New York: Noonday Press, 1956.

Carrasco Pirard, Eduardo. "Sujeto y poesía: El segundo nacimiento de Neruda." *Revista de Filosofía* 43–44 (1994): 49–61.

Cascardi, Anthony J. "Mimesis and Modernism." *Literary Philosophers: Borges, Calvino, Eco*. Ed. Jorge J. E. Gracia, Carolyn Korsmeyer, and Rodolphe Gasché. New York: Routledge, 2002. 109–28.

Celaya, Gabriel. "Pablo Neruda: Poeta del tercer día de la creación." *Taller de Letras* 30 (May 2002): 21–24.

Certeau, Michel de. "History: Ethics, Science, and Fiction." *Social Science as Moral Inquiry*. Ed. Norma Haan, Robert Bellah, Paul Rabinow, and William Sullivan. New York: Columbia University Press, 1983. 125–52.

Cervantes Saavedra, Miguel de. *Don Quixote*. Trans. J. M. Cohen. New York: Penguin Books, 1982.

Christiansë, Yvette. " 'Monstrous Prodigy': The Apocalyptic Landscapes of Derek Walcott's Poetry." *Mapping the Sacred: Religion, Geography, and Postcolonial Literatures*. Ed. Jamie S. Scott and Paul Simpson-Housley. Amsterdam: Rodopi, 2001. 199–223.

Coleman, Alexander. "The Ghost of Whitman in Neruda and Borges." *Walt Whitman of Mickle Street*. Ed. Geoffrey M. Sill. Knoxville: University of Tennessee Press, 1994. 257–69.

Correa Vasquez, Pedro. "Ascenso a Machu Picchu." *Fundación Pablo Neruda* 18 (Spring 1993): 13–17.

Cortínez, Veronica. "*Mundo Nuevo*: Propuesta para una nueva literatura." *Revista Canadiense de Estudios Hispánicos* 19.2 (1995): 299–309.

Costa, René de. *The Poetry of Pablo Neruda*. Cambridge, Mass.: Harvard University Press, 1979.

Crosby, Alfred. *Ecological Imperialism: The Biological Expansion of Europe, 900–1900*. Cambridge: Cambridge University Press, 1986.

Cutler, Edward S. *Recovering the New: Transatlantic Roots of Modernism*. Hanover, Md.: University Press of New England, 2003.

Dante Alighieri. *Paradiso*. Trans. Allen Mandelbaum. New York: Bantam, 1994.

DeHay, Terry. "Pablo Neruda's *Canto General*: Revisioning the Apocalypse." *Literature and the Bible*. Ed. David Bevan. Amsterdam: Rodopi, 1993. 47–59.

DeLoughrey, Elizabeth M., Renée K. Gosson, and George B. Handley, eds. *Caribbean Literature and the Environment: Between Nature and Culture*. Charlottesville: University of Virginia Press, 2005.

del Río, Carmen M. "Borges's 'Pierre Menard' or Where Is the Text?" *Kentucky Romance Quarterly* (1979): 459–69.

Dillard, Annie. *Pilgrim at Tinker Creek*. New York: Harper Perennial Modern Classics, 1998.

Dixon, Melvin. *Ride out the Wilderness: Geography and Identity in Afro-American Literature*. Chicago: University of Illinois Press, 1987.

Doumont, Monique. "Notas para un estudio del 'Whitman' de José Martí." *Anuario de Filología* 8–9 (1969–70): 199–212.

Dunlap, Thomas R. *Nature and the English Diaspora: Environment and History in the United States, Canada, Australia, and New Zealand*. New York: Cambridge University Press, 1999.

Durán, Manuel. "Pablo Neruda and the Romantic-Symbolist Tradition." Bloom 179–89.

Earle, Peter. "Whitman and Neruda and Their Implicit Cultural Revolution." *Proceedings of the Xth Congress of the International Comparative Literature Association*. Ed. Anna Balakian. New York: Garland, 1985. 189–93.

Edwards, Jorge. *Adiós, poeta*. Barcelona: Tusquets, 1990.

Egerton, Judith. *Turner: The Fighting Temeraire*. London: National Gallery Publications, 1993.

Elder, John. *Imagining the Earth: Poetry and the Vision of Nature*. Athens: University of Georgia Press, 1996.

———. *Reading the Mountains of Home*. Cambridge, Mass.: Harvard University Press, 1998.

Emerson, Ralph Waldo. *Emerson's Prose and Poetry*. Ed. Joel Porte and Saundra Morris. New York: Norton, 2001.

Engels, Friedrich. *The Dialectics of Nature*. Trans. J. B. S. Haldane. New York: International Publishers, 1940.

Erkkila, Betsy. Introduction. Erkkila and Grossman 1–22.

———. *Whitman the Political Poet*. New York: Oxford University Press, 1989.

Erkkila, Betsy, and Jay Grossman, eds. *Breaking Bounds: Whitman and American Cultural Studies*. New York: Oxford University Press, 1996.

Faulkner, William. *Absalom, Absalom!* New York: Vintage, 1986.

———. "The Bear." *The Portable Faulkner*. Ed. Malcolm Cowley. New York: Penguin Books, 1977. 197–320.

Feinstein, Adam. *Pablo Neruda: A Passion for Life*. New York: Bloomsbury, 2004.

Felstiner, John. *Translating Neruda*. Stanford, Calif.: Stanford University Press, 1980.

Ferrer, Ada. "The Silence of the Patriots: Race and Nationalism in Martí's Cuba." Belknap and Fernández 228–49.

Figueroa, Victor. "'Encomium of Helen': Derek Walcott's 'Ethical Twist' in *Omeros*." Unpublished essay.

Fisher, Philip. *Still the New World: American Literature in a Culture of Creative Destruction*. Cambridge, Mass.: Harvard University Press, 1999.

Folsom, Ed. "Lucipher and Ethiopia: Whitman, Race, and Poetics before the Civil War and After." *A Historical Guide to Walt Whitman*. Ed. David S. Reynolds. New York: Oxford University Press, 2000. 45–96.

Folsom, Ed, and Kenneth M. Price, eds. "Biography." *Walt Whitman Archive*. June 1, 2006 <ftp://whitmanarchive.org/biography>.

Foltz, Bruce V. "Inhabiting and Orientation: Science beyond Disenchantment." Frodeman 25–34.

Franco, Jean. *The Modern Culture of Latin America: Society and the Artist*. New York: Frederick A. Praeger, 1967.

Frodeman, Robert, ed. *Earth Matters: The Earth Sciences, Philosophy, and the Claims of Community*. Upper Saddle River, N.J.: Prentice-Hall, 2000.

Frost, Robert. *The Poetry of Robert Frost*. New York: Holt, Rinehart and Winston, 1967.

Fuentes, Carlos. "Cervantes, or the Critique of Reading." *Myself with Others: Selected Essays*. New York: Farrar, Straus and Giroux, 1988. 49–71.

Fulghum, W. B., Jr. "Whitman's Debt to Joseph Gostwick." *American Literature* 12 (Jan. 1941): 491–96.

Gadamer, Hans-Georg. *The Relevance of the Beautiful and Other Essays.* Trans. Nicholas Walker. Cambridge: Cambridge University Press, 1986.

García, Enildo A. "José Martí and Walt Whitman: Literatura, libertad y democracia." *Círculo: Revista de Cultura* 25 (1996): 75–88.

García Canclini, Nestor. "Aesthetic Moments of Latin Americanism." Shukla and Tinsman 13–24.

García Godoy, Francisco. *Americanismo literario.* Ayacucho: Editorial-América, 1917.

Gelpí, Juan. *Literatura y paternalismo en Puerto Rico.* Río Piedras: Editorial de la Universidad de Puerto Rico, 1993.

Glissant, Édouard. *Caribbean Discourse: Selected Essays.* Trans. J. Michael Dash. Charlottesville: University Press of Virginia, 1989.

———. "Creolization in the Making of the Americas." *Race, Discourse and the Origin of the Americas: A New World View.* Ed. Vera Lawrence Hyatt and Rex Nettleford. Washington, D.C.: Smithsonian Institution Press, 1995. 268–75.

———. *Faulkner Mississippi.* Trans. Barbara Lewis and Thomas C. Spear. New York: Farrar, Straus and Giroux, 1998.

———. *Poetics of Relation.* Trans. Betsy Wing. Ann Arbor: University of Michigan Press, 1997.

Goic, Cedomil. "'Alturas de Machu Picchu': La torre y el abismo." Rodríguez Monegal and Santí 219–44.

Goldwater, Robert, and Marco Treves, eds. *Artists on Art from the Fourteenth to the Twentieth Century.* 3rd ed. New York: Random House, 1974.

González de la Garza, Mauricio. *Walt Whitman: Racista, imperialista, antimexicano.* Mexico City: Colección Málaga, SA, 1971.

González Echevarría, Roberto. Introduction. *Canto general.* By Pablo Neruda. Trans. Jack Schmitt. Berkeley: University of California Press, 1991. 1–12.

Grove, Richard. *Green Imperialism: Colonial Expansion, Tropical Island Edens and the Origins of Environmentalism, 1600–1860.* Cambridge: Cambridge University Press, 1995.

Grünzweig, Walter. "Noble Ethics and Loving Aggressiveness: The Imperialist Walt Whitman." *An American Empire: Expansionist Cultures and Policies, 1881–1917.* Ed. Serge Ricard. Aix-en-Provence: Université de Provence, 1990. 151–65.

Hamner, Robert, ed. *Critical Perspectives on Derek Walcott.* Washington, D.C.: Three Continents Press, 1993.

———. "From Winslow Homer to Marcel Duchamp and the Fortunate Flaw in

Derek Walcott's 'Omeros.'" *Ariel: A Review of International English Literature* 31.3 (2000): 75–103.

Hamner, Robert, and Paul Breslin, eds. *Derek Walcott.* Special issue of *Callaloo* 28.1 (2005).

Handley, George B. "Derek Walcott's Poetics of the Environment in *The Bounty.*" Hamner and Breslin 201–15.

————. "A New World Poetics of Oblivion." *Look Away: The U.S. South in New World Studies.* Ed. Deborah Cohn and Jonathan Smith. Durham, N.C.: Duke University Press, 2004. 25–51.

————. "Oedipus in the Americas: *Lone Star* and the Reinvention of American Studies." *Forum for Modern Language Studies* 40.2 (2004): 160–81.

————. "On Reading South in the New World: Whitman, Martí, Glissant, and the Hegelian Dialectic." *Postcolonial Theory, the U.S. South, and New World Studies.* Ed. Jon Smith, Kathryn McKee, and Scott Romine. Special issue of *Mississippi Quarterly* 46.4 (2003): 521–44.

————. "A Postcolonial Sense of Place and the Work of Derek Walcott." *Interdisciplinary Study of Literature and the Environment* 6.3 (2000): 1–22.

————. *Postslavery Literatures in the Americas: Family Portraits in Black and White.* Charlottesville: University Press of Virginia, 2000.

————. "Triangulation and the Aesthetics of Temporality in *Tiepolo's Hound.*" Hamner and Breslin 236–56.

Hanke, Lewis, ed. *Do the Americas Have a Common History? A Critique of the Bolton Theory.* New York: Alfred A. Knopf, 1964.

————. Introduction. Hanke 3–52.

Harris, Wilson. "Oedipus and the Middle Passage." *Crisis and Creativity in the New Literatures in English.* Ed. Geoffrey V. Davis and Hena Maes-Jelinek. Atlanta, Ga.: Rodopi, 1990. 9–21.

————. "A Talk on the Subjective Imagination." *New Letters: A Magazine of Fine Writing* 40 (1973): 36–48.

————. "Theater of the Arts." DeLoughrey, Gosson, and Handley 261–68.

————. *The Womb of Space: The Cross-Cultural Imagination.* Westport, Conn.: Greenwood, 1983.

Hegel, Georg Wilhelm Friedrich. *The Philosophy of History.* Trans. J. Sibree. New York: Colonial Press, 1900.

Hopenhayn, Martín. "Essential Histories, Contingent Outcomes: Latin Americanists in Search of a Discourse." Shukla and Tinsman 25–35.

Hulme, Peter. *Colonial Encounters: Europe and the Native Caribbean.* London: Methuen, 1986.

Ismond, Patricia. *Abandoning Dead Metaphors: The Caribbean Phase of Derek Walcott's Poetry*. Trinidad and Tobago: University of West Indies Press, 2001.

Kepner, Diane. "From Spears to Leaves: Walt Whitman's Theory of Nature in 'Song of Myself.'" *American Literature: A Journal of Literary History, Criticism, and Bibliography* 51.2 (1979): 179–204.

Killingsworth, M. Jimmie. *Walt Whitman and the Earth: A Study in Ecopoetics*. Iowa City: University of Iowa Press, 2004.

King, Bruce. *Derek Walcott: A Caribbean Life*. London: Oxford University Press, 2000.

Klammer, Martin. *Whitman, Slavery, and the Emergence of Leaves of Grass*. University Park: Pennsylvania State University Press, 1995.

Kolodny, Annette. *Lay of the Land: Metaphor as Experience and History in American Life and Letters*. Chapel Hill: University of North Carolina Press, 1975.

Krieger, Murray. *Ekphrasis: The Illusion of the Natural Sign*. Baltimore, Md.: Johns Hopkins University Press, 1992.

Kronick, Joseph. *American Poetics of History: From Emerson to the Moderns*. Baton Rouge: Louisiana State University Press, 1984.

———. "On the Border of History: Whitman and the American Sublime." *The American Sublime*. Ed. Mary Arensberg. Albany: State University Press of New York, 1986. 51–82.

LaCapra, Dominick. *History and Memory after Auschwitz*. Ithaca, N.Y.: Cornell University Press, 1998.

Landow, George P. *The Aesthetic and Critical Theories of John Ruskin*. Princeton, N.J.: Princeton University Press, 1971.

Legler, Gretchen. "Body Politics in American Nature Writing: 'Who may contest for what the body of nature will be?'" *Writing the Environment: Ecocriticism and Literature*. Ed. Richard Kerridge and Neil Sammells. London: Zed Books, Ltd., 1998. 71–88.

LeMaster, J. R., and Donald D. Kummings, eds. *Walt Whitman: An Encyclopedia*. New York: Garland, 1998.

Leopold, Aldo. *A Sand County Almanac and Sketches Here and There*. New York: Oxford University Press, 1989.

Lévy, Isaac Jack, and Juan Lovelock, eds. *Simposio Neruda*. Columbia: University of South Carolina Press, 1975.

Lewis, R. W. B. *The American Adam: Innocence, Tragedy, and Tradition in the Nineteenth Century*. Chicago: University of Chicago Press, 1955.

Lipschütz, Alejandro. *La ciencia en la Unión Soviética*. Santiago: Editorial Nascimiento, 1944.

Loizeaux, Elizabeth Bergmann. "Ekphrasis and Textual Consciousness." *Word and Image* 15.1 (1999): 76–96.

Loving, Jerome. *Walt Whitman: The Song of Himself.* Berkeley: University of California Press, 1999.

Loyola, Hernán. "Neruda y América Latina." *Cuadernos Americanos* año 37, 218.3 (1978): 175–97.

Mack, Stephen John. *The Pragmatic Whitman: Reimagining American Democracy.* Iowa City: University of Iowa Press, 2002.

Maddox, Lucy, ed. *Locating American Studies: The Evolution of a Discipline.* Baltimore, Md.: Johns Hopkins University Press, 1998.

Major, William. " 'Some Vital Unseen Presence': The Practice of Nature in Walt Whitman's *Specimen Days.*" *Interdisciplinary Study of Literature and the Environment* 7.1 (2000): 79–96.

Martí, José. *The America of José Martí: Selected Writings.* Trans. Juan de Onís. New York: Minerva Press, 1954.

Martínez, Renato. "Neruda y la poética de las cosas." *Revista Iberoamericana* 168–69 (July–Dec. 1994): 739–49.

Mason, John B. " 'Passage to India' (1871)." LeMaster and Kummings 507–9.

Matthews, Steven. "Jorge Luis Borges: Fiction and Reading." *Ariel* 6 (Spring 1989): 62–67.

McCook, Stuart. *States of Nature: Science, Agriculture, and Environment in the Spanish Caribbean, 1760–1940.* Austin: University of Texas Press, 2002.

McKibben, William. *The End of Nature.* New York: Anchor, 1997.

Merchant, Carolyn. "Reinventing Eden." *Uncommon Ground: Rethinking the Human Place in Nature.* Ed. William Cronon. New York: Norton, 1995. 132–59.

Mikics, David. "Derek Walcott and Alejo Carpentier: Nature, History, and the Caribbean Writer." *Magical Realism: Theory, History, Community.* Ed. Lois Parkinson Zamora and Wendy B. Faris. Durham, N.C.: Duke University Press, 1995. 371–404.

Miller, J. Hillis. *The Ethics of Reading: Kant, de Man, Eliot, Trollope, James, and Benjamin.* New York: Columbia University Press, 1987.

Miller, Shawn. *An Environmental History of Latin America.* New York: Cambridge University Press, forthcoming 2007.

Mistral, Gabriela. "Recado sobre Pablo Neruda." *Fundación Pablo Neruda* 1 (Winter 1979): 3–6.

Mitchell, W. J. T. *Ekphrasis and the Other.* May 5, 2003 <ftp://rc.umd.edu/editions/shelley/medusa/mitchell.html>, 1–10.

Molloy, Sylvia. "His America, Our America: José Martí Reads Whitman." *Modern Language Quarterly: A Journal of Literary History* 57.2 (1996): 369–79.

Morales, Andrés. "Walt Whitman en la poesía chilena del siglo XX." *Revista Chilena de Literatura* 55 (Nov. 1999): 179–88.

Morrison, Toni. *Beloved.* New York: Plume, 1988.

———. "Nobel Lecture." *Georgia Review* 49.1 (1995): 314–30.

———. *Playing in the Dark: Whiteness and the Literary Imagination.* New York: Vintage Books, 1992.

National Research Council. *Casuarinas: Nitrogen-Fixing Trees for Adverse Sites.* Report of an Ad Hoc Panel of the Advisory Committee on Technology Innovation Board on Science and Technology for International Development Office of International Affairs. Washington, D.C.: National Academy Press, 1984.

Neruda, Pablo. *Canto general.* Trans. Jack Schmitt. Berkeley: University of California Press, 2000.

———. *Extravagario.* Trans. Alastair Reid. Bilingual ed. Austin: University of Texas Press, 1974.

———. *Memoirs.* Trans. Hardie St. Martin. New York: Penguin Books, 1978.

———. *Obras completas*, vols. 1–5. Ed. Hernán Loyola with the assistance of Saúl Yurkiévich. Barcelona: Galaxia Gutenberg.

———. "We Live in a Whitmanesque Age (a Speech to P.E.N.)." Perlman, Folsom, and Campion 231–33.

Nichols, Ashton. "Colonizing Consciousness: Culture and Identity in Walcott's *Another Life* and Wordsworth's *Prelude.*" *Imagination, Emblems and Expressions: Essays on Latin American, Caribbean, and Continental Culture and Identity.* Ed. Helen Ryan-Ranson. Bowling Green, Ohio: Bowling Green State University Popular Press, 1993. 173–89.

Nolan, James. *Poet-Chief: The Native American Poetics of Walt Whitman and Pablo Neruda.* Albuquerque: University of New Mexico Press, 1994.

O'Gorman, Edmundo. "Do the Americas Have a Common History?" Hanke 103–11.

———. *The Invention of America: An Inquiry into the Historical Nature of the New World and the Meaning of Its History.* Bloomington: Indiana University Press, 1961.

Olsen, Robert. "Whitman's Leaves of Grass: Poetry and the Founding of 'New World' Culture." *University of Toronto Quarterly: A Canadian Journal of the Humanities* 64.2 (1995): 305–23.

Osorio, Nelson. "El problema del hablante poético en *Canto general.*" Lévy and Lovelock 173–87.

Outka, Paul. "(De)composing Whitman." *Interdisciplinary Study of Literature and the Environment* 12.1 (2005): 41–60.

Paquet, Sandra Pouchet. "Beyond Mimicry: The Poetics of Memory and Authenticity in Derek Walcott's *Another Life.*" *Memory and Cultural Politics: New Approaches to American Ethnic Literatures.* Ed. Amritjot Singh, Joseph T. Skerrett, Jr., and Robert E. Hogan. Boston: Northeastern University Press, 1996. 194–210.

Paz, Octavio. "Mexico and the United States." *The Labyrinth of Solitude: Life and Thought in Mexico.* Trans. Lysander Kemp, Yara Milos, and Rachel Philips Belash. New York: Grave, 1985. 357–76.

———. *The Other Voice: Essays on Modern Poetry.* Trans. Helen Lane. New York: Harcourt Brace Jovanovich, 1990.

Pedersen, Carl. "Sea Change: The Middle Passage and the Transatlantic Imagination." *The Black Columbiad: Defining Moments in African American Literature and Culture.* Ed. Werner Sollors and Maria Diedrich. Cambridge, Mass.: Harvard University Press, 1994. 42–51.

Perlman, Jim, Ed Folsom, and Dan Campion, eds. *Walt Whitman: The Measure of His Song.* Duluth, Minn.: Holy Cow! Press, 1998.

Perriam, Chris. "In Which Neruda, Approaching His Seventieth Birthday, Strays into Post-Modernism." *The Discerning Eye: Studies Presented to Robert Pring-Mill on His Seventieth Birthday.* Ed. Nigel Griffin, Clive Griffin, Eric Southworth, and Colin Thompson. Llangrannog, Wales: Dolphin Book Co., 1994. 207–16.

Philippon, Daniel J. " 'I Only Seek to Put You in Rapport': Message and Method in Walt Whitman's Specimen Days." *Reading the Earth: New Directions in the Study of Literature and the Environment.* Ed. Michael P. Branch, Rochelle Johnson, Daniel Patterson, and Scott Slovic. Moscow: University of Idaho Press, 1998. 179–93.

Piasecki, Bruce. "Conquest of the Globe: Walt Whitman's Concept of Nature." *Calamus* 23 (June 1983): 29–44.

Plummer, Brenda Gayle. "Firmin and Martí at the Intersection of Pan-Americanism and Pan-Africanism." Belknap and Fernández 210–27.

Pollard, Charles. *New World Modernisms: T. S. Eliot, Derek Walcott, and Kamau Brathwaite.* Charlottesville: University of Virginia Press, 2004.

Pupo-Walker, Enrique. "Borges, Carpentier y la lectura crítica de la historia." *Insula: Revista de Letras y Ciencias Humanas* 37 (June 1982): 11, 13.

Rama, Angel. "José Martí en el eje de la modernización poética: Whitman, Lautréamont, Rimbaud." *Nueva Revista de Filología Hispánica* 32.1 (1983): 96–135.

Ramos, Julio. *Divergent Modernities: Culture and Politics in Nineteenth-Century Latin America.* Durham, N.C.: Duke University Press, 2001.

Raviola Molina, Victor. "Presencia de Temuco en la obra nerudiana." *Stylo* 12, 1st semester (1972): 151–66.

Reynolds, David S. *Walt Whitman's America: A Cultural Biography.* New York: Knopf, 1995.

Roa-de-la-Carrera, Cristián. "El nuevo mundo como problema de conocimiento: Vespucio y el discurso geográfico." *Hispanic Review* 70.4 (2002): 557–80.

Robinson, Marilynne. *The Death of Adam: Essays on Modern Thought.* New York: Mariner Books, 1998.

————. Personal interview with George Handley. Mar. 20, 2004.

Rodman, Selden. *South America of the Poets*. New York: Hawthorne Books, 1970.

Rodríguez-Carranza, Luz. "Emir Rodríguez Monegal o la construcción de un Mundo (Nuevo) posible." *Revista Iberoamericana* 160–61 (July–Dec. 1992): 903–17.

Rodríguez F., Mario. "Expulsion de una escritura y promesa del canto: Dos instancias básicas en 'Amor Americano (1400)' de Pablo Neruda." *Estudios Filológicos* 15 (1980): 127–44.

Rodríguez Monegal, Emir. "Pablo Neruda: Las *Memorias* y las vidas del poeta." Lévy and Lovelock 189–207.

————. "El sistema del poeta." Rodríguez Monegal and Santí 63–91.

————. *El viajero inmovil: Introducción a Pablo Neruda*. Buenos Aires: Editorial Losada, 1966.

Rodríguez Monegal, Emir, and Enrico Mario Santí, eds. *Pablo Neruda*. Madrid: Taurus Ediciones, SA, 1980.

Rodríguez-Peralta, Phyllis W. *José Santos Chocano*. New York: Twayne Publishers, 1970.

Rudder, Joy. *Glimpses of the Blue Caribbean: Oceans, Coasts, and Seas and How They Shape Us*. Ed. Gillian Cambers and Alexei Suzyumov. Coastal Region and Small Island Papers 5. Paris: UNESCO, 2000.

Salska, Agnieszka. "The Growth of the Past in *Leaves of Grass*." Camboni 35–51.

Santí, Enrico Mario. "The Accidental Tourist: Walt Whitman in Latin America." *Do the Americas Have a Common Literature?* Ed. Gustavo Pérez Firmat. Durham, N.C.: Duke University Press, 1990. 156–76.

————. Introducción. *Canto general*. Ed. Enrico Mario Santí. Madrid: Ediciones Cátedra, 2000. 13–94.

————. " 'Our America,' the Gilded Age, and the Crisis of Latinamericanism." Belknap and Fernández 179–90.

————. *Pablo Neruda: Poetics of Prophecy*. Ithaca, N.Y.: Cornell University Press, 1982.

Sarewitz, Daniel. "Science and Environmental Policy: An Excess of Objectivity." Frodeman 79–98.

Scarry, Elaine. *The Body in Pain: The Making and Unmaking of the World*. Oxford: Oxford University Press, 1987.

Schopf, Federico. "Recepción y contexto en la poesía de Pablo Neruda." *Pedro Lastra, o la erudición compartida: Estudios de literatura dedicados a Pedro Lastra*. Ed. Mario A. Rojas and Roberto Hozven. Mexico City: Premia Editora, 1988. 332–72.

Shelley, Percy Bysshe. "In Defence of Poetry." *Criticism: The Major Texts*. Ed. Walter Jackson Bate. New York: Harcourt, Brace and World, 1952. 429–36.

Shukla, Sandhya, and Heidi Tinsman, eds. *Our Americas: Political and Cultural Imaginings*. Special issue of *Radical History Review* 89 (Spring 2004).

Sicard, Alain. *El pensamiento poético de Pablo Neruda*. Madrid: Editorial Gredos, 1981.

Simon, John Oliver. "A Neruda Pilgrimage." *Poetry Flash: A Poetry Review and Literary Calendar for the West* 239 (February 1993): 1–11.

Snyder, Gary. "Walt Whitman's New World, Old World." Perlman, Folsom, and Campion 452–54.

Sommer, Doris. "Martí, Author of Walt Whitman." Belknap and Fernández 77–90.

Soto, Hernán. "Neruda y el mar." *Fundación Pablo Neruda* 18 (Spring 1993): 18–22.

Stavans, Ilan, ed. *The Poetry of Pablo Neruda*. New York: Farrar, Straus and Giroux, 2003.

———. "Whitman and Darío: Un Colón, dos . . . y ninguno." *Letras Peninsulares* 5.1 (1992): 107–11.

Stegner, Wallace. *Where the Bluebird Sings to the Lemonade Springs: Living and Writing in the West*. New York: Random House, 1992.

Stone, Larry. "The Continental Voice: Whitman's Influence on Pablo Neruda." *Papers in Romance* 2.1 (1979): 1–13.

Stuckey-French, Ned C. " 'The Prayer of Columbus' (1874)." LeMaster and Kummings 539–40.

Suárez, Eulogio. "La vida mexicana de Pablo Neruda." *Fundación Pablo Neruda* (Spring 1991): 3–9.

Suárez Rivero, Eliana. "La estética esencial en una oda nerudiana." Lévy and Lovelock 82–96.

Tedeschi Lalli, Biancamaria. "Utopia in the Present Tense: Walt Whitman and the Language of the New World." Camboni 15–33.

Teitelboim, Volodia. *Neruda*. Santiago: Editorial Sudamericana Chilena, 2000.

Terada, Rei. *Derek Walcott's Poetry: American Mimicry*. Boston: Northeastern University Press, 1992.

Thomas, Brook. "Frederick Jackson Turner, José Martí, and Finding a Home on the Range." Belknap and Fernández 275–92.

Thomas, M. Wynn. "Weathering the Storm: Whitman and the Civil War." *Walt Whitman Quarterly Review* 93 (Fall 1997–Winter 1998): 87–109.

Tichi, Cecelia. *New World, New Earth: Environmental Reform in American Literature from the Puritans through Whitman*. New Haven, Conn.: Yale University Press, 1979.

Torres-Rioseco, Arturo. *New World Literature: Tradition and Revolt in Latin America*. Berkeley: University of California Press, 1949.

Walcott, Derek. "American, without America." Unpublished essay, 1974. Campus library, University of West Indies, St. Augustine.

———. "'The Argument of the Outboard Motor': An Interview with Derek Walcott." Interview with George Handley. DeLoughrey, Gosson, and Handley 127–39.

———. *The Bounty*. New York: Farrar, Straus and Giroux, 1997.

———. "Caligula's Horse." *Kunapipi* 11.1 (1989): 138–42.

———. "The Caribbean: Culture or Mimicry?" Hamner 51–57.

———. *Collected Poems 1948–1984*. New York: Farrar, Straus and Giroux, 1992.

———. "The Figure of Crusoe." Hamner 33–40.

———. "Inside the Cathedral." Unpublished essay, 1987. Campus library, University of West Indies, St. Augustine.

———. "The Insulted Landscape." Poetry Audio PR9216.W35x1980. Harvard College Library, 1980.

———. "Interview with Derek Walcott." Interview with George Handley. *Journal of Caribbean Literatures* 4.1 (2005): 95–108.

———. "An Interview with Derek Walcott." Interview with David Montenegro. Baer 135–50.

———. "An Interview with Derek Walcott." Interview with Leif Sjöberg. Baer 79–85.

———. "An Interview with Derek Walcott." Interview with J. P. White. Baer 151–74.

———. "Isla Incognita." DeLoughrey, Gosson, and Handley 51–57.

———. "The Offending Poem." *Crusader: Nobel Laureates Supplement* Jan. 22, 2000: 3.

———. *Omeros*. New York: Noonday Press, 1990.

———. "'Over Colorado' (Poem, 1976)." Perlman, Folsom, and Campion 301.

———. "Reflections before and after Carnival: An Interview with Derek Walcott." Interview with Sharon Ciccarelli. Baer 34–49.

———. "Reflections on Omeros." *The Poetics of Derek Walcott: Intertextual Perspectives.* Special issue of the *Southern Atlantic Quarterly* 96.2 (1997): 229–46.

———. "Sharing in the Exhilaration: An Interview with Derek Walcott (September 23, 2000, Salt Lake City)." Interview with Natasha Sajé and George Handley. *Ariel: A Review of International Literature in English* 32.2 (2001): 129–42.

———. *Tiepolo's Hound*. New York: Farrar, Straus and Giroux, 2000.

———. *What the Twilight Says: Essays*. New York: Farrar, Straus and Giroux, 1998.

———. "Where I Live." *Architectural Digest* 54.1 (1997): 30–36.

Warren, Jim. "Whitman Land: John Burroughs's Pastoral Criticism." *Interdisciplinary Study of Literature and the Environment* 8.1 (2001): 83–96.

West, Elliott. "Wallace Stegner's West: Wilderness and History." *Wallace Stegner and the Continental Vision*. Ed. Curt Meine. Washington, D.C.: Island Press, 1997. 85–96.

Whitman, Walt. *Complete Prose Works*. Boston: Small, Maynard and Co., 1898.

———. *Leaves of Grass*. New York: Barnes and Noble Books, 1992.

———. *The Portable Whitman*. Ed. Mark Van Doren. New York: Penguin Books, 1973.

———. *Walt Whitman Archive*. Ed. Ed Folsom and Kenneth M. Price. Oct. 10, 2005 <ftp://waltwhitmanarchive.org>.

Williams, William Carlos. *In the American Grain*. New York: New Directions Paperback, 1956.

Wise, Gene. " 'Paradigm Dramas' in American Studies: A Cultural and Institutional History of the Movement (1979)." Maddox 166–214.

Yúdice, George. "Rethinking the Theory of the Avant-Garde from the Periphery." *Modernism and Its Margins: Reinscribing Cultural Modernity from Spain and Latin America*. Ed. Anthony L. Geist and José B. Monleón. New York: Garland, 1999. 52–80.

Yurkiévich, Saúl. "El génesis oceánico." Lévy and Lovelock 385–99.

———. "Mito e historia: Dos generadores del *Canto general*." Rodríguez Monegal and Santí 198–218.

Zamora, Lois Parkinson. *The Usable Past: The Imagination of History in Recent Fiction of the Americas*. New York: Cambridge University Press, 1997.

Zamora, Margarita. "Abreast of Columbus: Gender and Discovery." *Cultural Critique* 17 (Winter 1990–91): 127–49.

Zong-qi, Cai. "Hegel's Phenomenological Dialectic and the Structure of Whitman's 'Song of Myself.' " *CLIO: A Journal of Literature, History, and the Philosophy of History* 16.4 (1987): 317–29.

INDEX

ethics, environmental. *See* environmental ethics

exceptionalism, 7, 30–33, 39, 82, 84–86, 96, 103, 294; and displacement of Native Americans, 34, 38, 120; Hispanic, 37; New World, 83

Faulkner, Mississippi (Glissant), 102, 313

Faulkner, William, 59, 102, 293, 313, 343; *Absalom, Absalom!* 60; "The Bear," 60

Feinstein, Adam, 185, 220

Felstiner, John, 236–43, 409n4

Few Days in Athens, A (Wright), 141

"Figure of Crusoe, The" (Walcott), 281, 298, 299

Fisher, Philip, 4

fósiles terciarios y cuartarios, Los (Philippi), 224

Folsom, Ed, 87, 108

Foltz, Bruce, 28, 43

Frost, Robert, 48, 283; "The Gift Outright," 50, 283, 406n3 (chap. 2)

Fuentes, Carlos, 3, 260, 281

Gadamer, Hans-Georg, 369, 375

García Canclini, Nestor, 40

García Godoy, Francisco, 33–35, 50

García Márquez, Gabríel, 3, 281; *Cien años de soledad*, 167

German Literature (Gostwick), 108

"Gift Outright, The" (Frost), 50, 283, 406n3 (chap. 2)

Gilpin, William, 120

Glissant, Édouard, 45–53 passim, 100–102 passim, 112, 126, 132, 140, 241, 325; *Caribbean Discourse*, 52, 65, 85, 327; "Creolization and the Making of the Americas," 53, 266; *Faulkner, Mississippi*, 102, 313; *Poetics of Relation*, 41, 58, 62, 204, 289, 322

Goldwater, Robert, 334

González de la Garza, Mauricio, 75, 92, 406n3 (chap. 3)

González Echevarría, Roberto, 217, 218, 229, 231, 235

Gostwick, Joseph, 123; *German Literature*, 108

Goytisolo, Juan, 99

"gran alegría, La" (Neruda), 179

"gran océano, El" (Neruda), 185, 242, 263–76

Gregorias. *See* St. Omer, Dunstan

Gros Islet, 336, 347, 350, 353

Grossman, Jay, 154

Grove, Richard, 24–25, 39

Guyot, Arnold, 112

Hamner, Robert, 340

Hanke, Lewis, 38

Harris, Wilson, 3, 59, 101–2; "A Talk on the Subjective Imagination," 63–65; "Theater of the Arts," 65

Hedge, Frederic, 108

Hegel, Georg Wilhelm Friedrich, 54–55, 82–85, 95, 100, 103. *See also* Whitman, Walt: hegelianism of

Helmholtz, Hermann von, 335

history. *See* environmental history; natural history

Hopenhayn, Martín, 40

Huidobro, Vicente, 92, 408n1 (chap. 6)

Hulme, Peter, 21

Humboldt, Alexander von, 21

Hutton, James, 112

imagination. *See* adamic imagination; environmental imagination

Impressionism, 14, 135, 319–21, 324, 333–36, 338–42, 344, 346, 350

Incan culture, 152, 234, 235, 237, 310. *See also* Machu Picchu

indigenism, Latin American, 237

"In Paths Untrodden" (Whitman), 130

"Inside the Cathedral" (Walcott), 315, 358, 359, 368

"Insulted Landscape, The" (Walcott), 323

In the American Grain (W. C. Williams), 42, 55

Isaiah, 237, 360–62, 367, 368

"Isla Incognita" (Walcott), 395–96

Isla Negra, 70, 165, 269, 270

Ismond, Patricia, 76, 281, 287, 289, 298, 307, 308, 410n4, 411n9

Jesus Christ, 241, 300, 331, 365

Jiménez, Juan Ramón, 74

John the Baptist, 330, 331, 361

Joyce, James, 3, 302–3, 313, 357–58, 410n6; *Portrait of the Artist as a Young Man*, 302

Jung, Carl, 101, 171, 274

justice. *See* ecology: and social justice; environmental justice

Keats, John, 130, 293

Kepner, Diane, 90, 408n9

Killingsworth, M. Jimmie, 108, 118, 124, 143, 146–47

King, Bruce, 76, 294, 410n1, 411n1

Klammer, Martin, 120, 142, 150

Kolodny, Annette, 22, 26

Krieger, Murray, 322, 341

Kronick, Joseph, 62, 89–90, 91, 113, 127, 135, 140, 407n2

Lamarck, Jean-Baptiste, 112, 113

Landow, George, 342–43

Latin America, 34–36; in American studies, 31; "boom" in literature of, 282; environmental history of, 23; exceptionalism of, 33–37, 86, 167; indigenism of, 237; regionalism of, 59

Latin Americanism, 33, 40, 97

Latin American studies, 12, 39–40

Laventille, 328

Legler, Gretchen, 6

Leopold, Aldo, 117, 133, 196, 259, 375, 389, 395, 402

"Lesson of the Tree, The" (Whitman), 134

Lewis, R. W. B., 30–31, 100

Liebig, Justus von, 141, 143

Lincoln, Abraham, 151, 252, 260

Lipschütz, Alejandro, 221, 222, 225

Loizeaux, Elizabeth Bergmann, 340, 411n3

"Lo que nace conmigo" (Neruda), 212

Loving, Jerome, 86, 108, 120, 134, 141

Lowell, Robert, 281, 293, 364

Loyola, Hernán, 185, 186, 188, 199, 225, 266

Machu Picchu, 206, 207, 225, 227, 286

Mack, Stephen John, 109–13 passim, 123–29 passim, 136, 139

Magellan, 247, 332

Major, William, 119, 134, 155

Manifest Destiny, in Whitman, 74–75, 107, 113, 118–19, 123, 377

Mantegna, Andrea, 330

Neruda, Pablo: and Barros Arana, 220; and Bello, 226; and Blake, 241; and Carpentier, 237; childhood experiences of, 174, 181, 220, 222, 408n1 (chap. 5); and Engels, 221; with Hegel, differences of, 186, 251, 264; and Lipschütz, 221; and Philippi, 220; and Ponce, 222; and natural science, 28; and Walcott, 69, 77–80, 104, 115, 117, 147, 151, 158, 177, 181, 194, 206, 208, 232, 240, 265, 269, 281–94 passim, 301–32 passim, 353, 358, 364, 382; and Whitman, 28, 35, 55, 69–76, 91–94, 115, 117, 122, 137, 139, 146–48, 150–53, 160, 195–97, 227–30, 249–61 passim, 281–87 passim, 319, 332, 375–76, 409n7, 409n11

Neruda, Pablo, works of: "A callarse," 193; "Al pie desde su niño," 195; "Las alturas de Machu Picchu," 14, 234, 235–45, 265, 269, 274, 409n4; "Amor americano (1400)," 230; "Aquí vivimos," 198, 199; "Aún," 180–84; "Bestiario," 204; "Botánica," 262; *Canto general*, 70, 163, 173–75, 179, 180, 185, 217–76 passim, 410n12 (*see also individual sections and poems*); "Carta para que me manden madera," 201; "El cazador en el bosque," 211; "Cierto cansancio," 194; "La condición humana," 171; "La copa de sangre," 176; "Cuánto pasa en un día," 197; "Demasiado nombres," 202; "Desconocidos en la orilla," 196; "Drimis Winterei," 262; "La espada encendida," 73; "Estación inmóvil," 197; "La estatua ciega,"

208; *Estravagario*, 185, 193–205, 207, 408n4; "La gran alegría," 179; "El gran océano," 185, 242, 263–76; "Lo que nace conmigo," 212; *Memorial de Isla Negra*, 162–72, 178, 193, 211; *Memorias*, 156, 159, 172; "Muchos somos," 198; "Nacimientos," 265; "La noche marina," 274; "No me hagan caso," 202; "Oda a la mariposa," 191; "Oda a la tranquilidad," 189; "Oda al camino," 189; "Oda al edificio," 222; "Oda al mar," 222; "Para la envidia," 213; "Pastoral," 200; "Los peces y el ahogado," 270; *Piedras de Chile*, 13, 185, 205, 207–10, 265; "Que despierte el leñador," 252–61, 391; "Sonata con algunos terrestre," 196; *Tercer libro de odas*, 156, 185, 186–93; "Tierra austral," 162, 171; "Vegetaciones," 232; "Yo soy," 173–76, 179–80, 185; "Zona eriales," 263

New Americanists, 31, 32
New World literature, 35–37, 44, 82, 95, 100, 102; in *Democratic Vistas*, 86–91
New York City, 71, 75, 280, 281
Nichols, Ashton, 168, 280, 313
"noche marina, La" (Neruda), 274
"No me hagan caso" (Neruda), 202

"Oda a la mariposa" (Neruda), 191
"Oda a la tranquilidad" (Neruda), 189
"Oda al camino" (Neruda), 189
"Oda al edificio" (Neruda), 222
"Oda al mar" (Neruda), 222
oedipal complex, 47, 59, 100, 405n3
"Of Him I Love Day and Night" (Whitman), 131

Walcott, Derek, works of (*continued*) 1–3, 10, 49–51, 77, 125, 194, 288, 296–98, 308, 312, 325, 367; *Omeros*, 117, 232, 250, 297, 306, 318, 357, 360, 368–95; "Origins," 291–92, 306; "Over Colorado," 78; "Parang," 384; "Ruins of a Great House," 292–94; "The Schooner Flight," 289–91; "The Sea is History," 145, 194, 269, 286–89, 330, 381; *Star-Apple Kingdom*, 281; *Tiepolo's Hound*, 135, 306, 315, 319–60; "Verandah," 295, 381; "What the Twilight Says," 281; "Where I Live," 289

Warren, Jim, 154

Weber, Max, 28

West, Elliott, 49–50

"What the Twilight Says" (Walcott), 281

"When Lilacs Last in the Dooryard Bloom'd" (Whitman), 151, 252

"Where I Live" (Walcott), 289

Whitman, Walt: and Carlyle, 109; and Darío, 81; with Hegel, differences of, 123, 138, 140; hegelianism of, 13, 86, 90, 103, 107–11, 114, 116, 118, 121, 125, 407n5 (*see also* Manifest Destiny, in Whitman); on Latin America, influence of, 91–101; and Liebig, 141, 143; and Lincoln, 151; and Martí, 83, 91–92, 94–101, 103; and Neruda, 28, 35, 55, 69–76, 91–94, 115, 117, 122, 137, 139, 146–48, 150–53, 160, 195–97, 227–30, 249–61 passim, 281–87 passim, 319, 332, 375–76, 409n7, 409n11; New World Bible, poet of, 7, 286; and Paley, 119; and Poe, 103; and Rilke, 137; and Swedenborg,

316; and Frederick Jackson Turner, 99; and Walcott, 12, 76–80, 122, 125, 133, 135, 145–47, 150–51, 244, 280–314 passim, 344, 364, 369

Whitman, Walt, works of: "Ashes of Soldiers," 152; "As I Ebb'd with the Ocean of Life," 146–49; "A Backward Glance," 137; "Bardic Symbols," 147; *Calamus*, 129–33, 136, 139, 145, 246, 408n8; *Democratic Vistas*, 34, 50, 76, 86–91, 121, 125, 226, 344, 406n1; *Drum Taps*, 150–53; "In Paths Untrodden," 130; "The Lesson of the Tree," 134; "Nature Notes," 134; "Of Him I Love Day and Night," 131; "Of the Terrible Doubt of Appearances," 131; "Out of the Cradle Endlessly Rocking," 143–46, 151, 284, 369; "Passage to India," 90, 125–28; "Pensive on Her Dead Gazing," 153; "Prayer of Columbus," 128–29; "Roaming in Thought," 111; "Scented Herbage of My Breast," 131; "Shirval," 141; "A Song for Occupations," 89; "Song of Myself," 70, 88–89, 124–25, 139–41, 142–43, 145–46, 149, 150, 153, 309, 314; "Song of the Broad-Axe," 114–18, 259, 391; "Song of the Exposition," 75, 121–22, 196, 286; "Song of the Open Road," 13, 123, 136; "Song of the Redwood-Tree," 75, 114, 118–20, 255; *Specimen Days*, 109, 123, 133–36, 150; "Starting from Paumanok," 111; "This Compost," 142–43, 293, 364; "When Lilacs Last in the Dooryard Bloom'd," 151, 252; "The Wound-Dresser," 150